RICH
A

Michael Feeney Callan is a screenwriter and director. He has adapted Frederick Forsyth short stories for American television and published ten books, among them the biography of Sean Connery.

MICHAEL FEENEY CALLAN

RICHARD HARRIS

A SPORTING LIFE

PAN BOOKS
in association with
SIDGWICK & JACKSON

First published 1990 by Sidgwick & Jackson Limited

This edition published 1992 by Pan Books Ltd.
a division of Pan Macmillan Publishers Limited
Cavaye Place London SW10 9PG
and Basingstoke

Associated companies throughout the world

ISBN 0 330 31721 0

1 3 5 7 9 8 6 4 2

A CIP catalogue record for this book is available from
the British Library

Typeset by Hewer Text Composition Services, Edinburgh
Printed in England by Clays Ltd, St Ives plc

For Ree

Contents

Acknowledgements

Book-writing, like living, is pleasure and pain. On this one the pendulum swung hard. I often wondered why, in a world that craves the megrims of showbiz, where star biogs rain down like confetti at a prince's wedding, no one ever embarked on a Life of Richard Harris.

And then I met Richard Harris.

Knowing him, attempting to work alongside him, calls for a Trojan spirit, a head for heights and a firm grip of the pendulum. He is a kind man who loves laughter. He is also a rebel who loves a fight.

The ride has been terrific hell. Of which I wouldn't have missed a minute.

In no particular order I wish to express my indebtedness to Rod Taylor, John Phillip Law, George Peppard, Cyril Cusack, Sandy Howard, Jimmy Webb and his assistant Laura, Peter Duffell, James Booth, John B. Keane, Frank Windsor, Don Taylor, Hazel Court, Franco Nero, Beth Voiku, Innes Lloyd, Philip Hinchcliffe, the late Ray McAnally, Ronald Fraser, Deirdre Lloyd, Karen Hodge, Caroline Dunne, Aliki Michael, Morgan O'Sullivan, Kevin Dinneen, Elizabeth Brennan, Myles McWeeney, Joe Lynch, Jim Sheridan, Kevan Barker, Godfrey Quigley, Len Dinneen, Charlie St George, Willie Allen, Dermot Foley, Manuel Di Lucia, Jim Roche, Donal Begley, Joe O'Donovan, Trevor Danker, Earl Connolly, Patrick Dromgoole, Eve Bennett, Ivan Waterman, Cathy Fitzpatrick at Home Box Office, Jim Griffiths, John Walsh, Liam Flynn, the late Gordon Jackson, John McEntee and the one and only Gerry Hannan, who taught me my Limerickese. Thanks also to Francis Feighan and Peter Vollebregt for their efficient research activities in Los

Angeles, Nassau, London and Dublin. Also to the staff of the London Academy of Music and Dramatic Art (LAMDA), the Irish Heraldic Institute, the American Academy of Motion Picture Arts and Sciences, Peter Todd and Tony Widdows at the British Film Institute, Sylvie Welib at the Theatre Royal Stratford East, the staff of the *Guardian*, the *Irish Times* (especially Deirdre), the *Irish Press*, the *News of the World*, *RTE Guide*, *Life* and *Today*.

I am grateful to the friends and fans of Richard Harris who enriched this book with their time, documents, pictures and advice. Some chose anonymity: I have honoured their wishes and, I hope, served them fairly. My primary source material, apart from my own conversations with Richard Harris and the body of interviews conducted for this book, comprise his films themselves, the transcripts of his TV and radio talk show appearances, and the literally hundreds of magazine and newspaper features to which he volunteered aspects of his multi-faceted philosophy and tales of his comings and goings. Among the main journals consulted are: *Profile*, the *Irish Press*, the *Irish Times*, *Hello*, *Life*, the *Daily Mail*, the *Daily Express*, *This Week*, *Films Illustrated*, *Woman's Own*, *TV Guide*, *US Magazine*, *London Evening News*, *The Los Angeles Times*, the *New York Times*, *Variety*, the *News of the World*, the *Sun*, the *Irish Independent*, the *Guardian*, the *Indianapolis Independent News*, the *Hollywood Reporter*. I owe special thanks to the diarists who have, with Harris's tacit blessing, charted his movements over the years. Thanks to Random House and to the many individual scribes who so generously opened their files to me. Also to Peter Doggett of the *Record Collector* for his discography.

A fond golden thank you to some special participants: to Tony Crawley, my friend and coach; to Frederick Albert Levy; to my inspirational brothers Dr Eamonn Callan and Dr Ronald Callan; to Jeannette Kearney just for being there; to my patient parents Michael Callan and Margaret Feeney; to Jeff Bricmont, executive vice-president, Home Box Office West Coast Original Programming; to my editor Susan Hill for her sensitivity and trust; to Brian Wilson and Dennis Wilson and the boys, for never giving up and for being, continually, the 'smile' in my life. And, naturally, to Ree and Corey and Paris, but for whom. . . .

Introduction: Bull

'. . . I couldn't really do an autobiography because I was far too drunk to ever recall what happened . . .'

Richard Harris in the *Daily Mail*, 16 November 1979

Jamie Harris, wired for work, offers a winning grin and says, 'My father is unpredictable.' I am on 'A' Stage at MTM Ardmore Studios in Bray, Ireland, to watch the widely predicted triumphal return of a man called Harris in *The Field*, a modern Irish theatre-classic-turned-movie. Only trouble is, the star is absent. It is week ten of a ten-week shoot, mostly on location in the stormy heartland of Connemara, and Richard Harris has collapsed on the final straight, triggering seriously creased executive brows, rejigged schedules and not a little general panic. 'He has a temperature of 100,' says Jamie, who is a modest and much-liked trainee a.d. (assistant director, third class); but around the farmyard set scurrilous technicians are quick to remind you of his chequered years of collapses and let-downs. More than twenty years before, suffering a Harris disappearance that plunged *Major Dundee* into chaos, Charlton Heston observed: 'Though he appears to be very strong, he does seem to be one of those people who enjoys ill health . . .'. 'I was', says Harris, 'simply exhausted.'

I am, personally, no stranger to Richard Harris's eccentricity. And caprices. Seven months before, after years of casual contact, I had approached him with a bold request for his authorization of and participation in this book. I had admired him for years, had cherished the memory of my best childhood discovery – not sex, not Batman, but the eye-opening realization that even a school-failing Irishman can become a Hollywood king. Richard Harris was to me a fascinating amalgam of talent, art, wildness – and childhood nostalgia. I had sworn for countless years that I would write his life story.

We met in the Berkeley Court, Dublin's elitest hotel that is co-managed by his brother-in-law (husband of his deceased sister Harriet-Mary), Jack Donnelly. Here Harris has first call on the best top-floor suites and the staff treat him like family, albeit mercurial family. Early May 1989 was a bumpy time for him. He'd seen the completion of Menahem Golan's bleary *Mack the Knife* and was distressed by it, had demanded that it be recut urgently (it was); in a fortnight he would be winging back to Britain to spend a couple of insouciant days on a TV movie (the hybrid he most hates), *King of the Wind*; in New York he had a script in development that would reanimate King Arthur, his constant lucky card; he was working on his second book of poems, announced since 1982, to be called *Fragments of a Broken Photograph*; there was so much rolling – and yet so little. Harris appeared to me a man with a double burden: too much of the wrong kind of work, and too much of the wrong kind of free time.

In 1982 he had announced the end of his acting life with the revived stage *Camelot*. He told the *Sunday Times*: 'I've had enough of acting. When *Camelot* ends next year, that's it. The only thing that might change my mind is if the Royal Shakespeare Company offered me *Hamlet*. That's unlikely, so I'm going to retire and never want to be reminded I was an actor.' Within two years of that stern pronouncement he was back on the movie set, despite the fact that, by his own estimate, he was nudging towards eight million dollars of *Camelot* profit, and considerable millions besides. He was, in the words of fellow Irish actor Joe Lynch, 'addicted to an audience at whatever cost' – an important revelation that explains much of the rage of his childhood and the roller-coaster of his life. After the stage *Camelot* he moved, aimlessly, through four rickety features, each surpassing its predecessor in clouding the memory of a high-magnitude star that shone like a beacon in the sixties. With the disappointing work came idleness. The promise of a significant revived singing career, highlighted by the extraordinary vocal drama of the album *A Tramp Shining*, was unfulfilled. The second book of poems never came. The sure thing novel *Flanny at 1.10* never materialized. The twenty short stories he bragged about vaporized, as did his second marriage, 'the perfect relationship' with much-younger Ann Turkel. On producer Kevin McClory's recommendation ('He dragged me out of the gutter . . .') he had bought a house on Paradise Island in the Bahamas and here he stayed for half of the year, watching rugby videos from England, black-and-white Hollywood classics and, occasionally, the calendar. Though advancing age didn't at all worry him, it did sometimes sadden him. 'Look,' he once commanded me, rolling up the leg of his canvas jeans and slapping the parched, loose skin of his calf. 'That was once rock-solid. I was fit to be a champion sportsman, boyo, really that fit. Now the skin shrivels and I'm sinking into old age and there's nothing I can do about it. But I had a body, begod, I had a body.'

The Richard Harris of that early May was bored and edgy but sober (in his eighth year of sobriety) and energetically covering up. He had flown from New York to participate in a fund-raiser for the ailing Abbey Theatre and after recent dental reconstruction his mouth was wired and agonized. He was, more than usually, moody. Frank Sinatra hit town the weekend Harris and I discussed the possibilities of this book. An army of musicians and gofers shepherded by Liza Minnelli and Sammy Davis Jr and apparently led by the ubiquitous Sinatra pal Jilly Rizzo avalanched upon the Berkeley Court. Liza threw up her hands, refused autographs in the hotel lobby and zoomed in on Harris, uncomfortably shifting in the deep chintz beside me. She sat by him, looped an arm round his neck and bubbled as the flashes popped. They exchanged about seven words and Harris hardly smiled. 'He's pissed off,' the reporter at my elbow dared, knowing as he did that I was Harris's guest and friend for the day. 'The photographers have been here since dawn for Sinatra and Liza. The excitement is theirs, not his. I mean, what has Dickie Harris done in twenty years?' But for a so-called brat superstar, Harris was decidedly in control. He kissed Liza, hugged Jilly Rizzo, promised Rizzo the loan of his Paradise house at the end of the Sinatra tour 'for a chance to unwind', instructed Frank Jr who he was meeting for the first time to deliver best wishes to the Chairman of the Board. 'I wanted to call up to Frank' – who by this time was ensconced in the Presidential Suite normally favoured by Harris – 'but he'll be resting. The man is a genius and a very hard worker. You have to give him space.'

The lobby crowd awaiting Sinatra eddied and swelled and Harris was increasingly mute and reflective. Watching the scavenging reporters I openly speculated on Sinatra's frame of mind: it is worldwide knowledge that a man (or woman called Kitty Kelley) with a pen is, to Sinatra, rabid vermin. 'There's a time and place for everything,' Harris mused. 'They shouldn't be here. I'll have to talk to Jackie about this. When a man wants privacy he should have privacy.'

Amid the swell of Sinatra watchers one young Richard Harris fan stayed gamely afloat. He had come, with a patient relation, all the way from Kilkee, Co. Clare, holiday home of Harris's babyhood. 'I love the man,' he told me in a quick bucolic burr. 'I have all his films on tape 'cept *Shake Hands with the Devil*. I have hundreds of photos of him. I watch him on video reading poetry every night before I turn in. He did wonderful things for Ireland, did he.' Harris greeted the fan, after a protracted, starry stand-off, with a long interrogative look and his limp, fingers-only handshake. One expected a short exchange, especially since the Kilkee farmers were noticeably under-dressed amid Sinatra's glitz; but Harris insisted to their amazement that they lunch with him in the hotel. Here, guzzling Benson and Hedges demonically, his earnest concern was his guests' diet. 'You never tried minestrone soup? You never even heard of it! Christ, you must have some now! Waitress!' Their gratitude touched him but, it seemed to me, their slack-faced admiration touched him even more. After lunch he posed endlessly for Polaroid pictures, then saw them personally to the door. They had never before been to Dublin, and had only the vaguest ideas of bus locations and train schedules, but Harris advised them knowingly. Farewells were passionate. He would, he volunteered, find a copy of *Shake Hands* and send it along.

'It'll be in the mail to you next week. Put your address there.'

'That was kind of you,' I said as we watched them depart.

'Rubbish. It's people like them make it possible for people like me and Sinatra to live like this.'

After the lunch and the fervour of the fans Harris was suddenly competitive. He watched the newsmongers awaiting Sinatra with excited eyes. Now he was less bored, less edgy. We walked to Lansdowne Road rugby stadium, where ten thousand high-price seats were being readied for two Sinatra open-air concerts. The road crew was busily orchestrating the sound equipment and security was vice-tight, but Harris's face was our price of easy admission. He walked into the middle of the internationally famous rugby pitch and pivoted to survey the stands. 'All I ever wanted was to play here for Ireland,' he whispered and his eyes were full of the distant past, lost opportunities. I drew him back to the present and asked if the ambience of the busy road crew, the violin sound checks, the whining PA affected him. He gave that mischief grin that won him Hollywood. 'Yeh, I get the buzz. I'm planning a concert tour soon. I'm going to record again. [Phil] Coulter has asked me but I turned him down. I have a new guy writing hit songs. I might record with the rock band Kiss. . . .'

Back in the hotel, without forewarning, he summoned a reporter ostensibly to complain about an inaccurate article in a rival paper concerning the education fund he had set up in his deceased brother Dermot's name. While talking to her, he announced very casually that I would be his official biographer. The reporter, Liz Ryan of the *Evening Herald*, expressed all the surprise I felt. This was the first airing of our agreement. Why, Liz Ryan asked, had Harris decided on me after years of resisting all and any offers of authorized biographies? With generosity, and not looking at me, he told her that I was the only writer he could trust. This story vied for headline space with Sinatra in the next day's *Herald*.

Some time later Harris changed his mind and withdrew his co-operation, so this book cannot be described as official. However, that evening we went to the theatre together to see his favourite Irish actor, Donal McCann, in *The Plough and the Stars*. Next day I was Harris's guest at the Sinatra concert in the stadium. After the concert and some easy, respectful conversation with Mr Sinatra (who had thoughtfully worn an Irish green handkerchief in his breast pocket and had the fastidious charm of a loved uncle) and Liza, we dined with lady friends in a happy group. He was introducing me now to acquaintances and well-wishers as his friend and biographer. And I was confident in the warmth of his friendship and the reassurance of a man who declared, apropos a dispute with producer Harry Saltzman, 'I believe in people, and I believe that when they shake hands with me they've meant what they just said.' I was secure in the fulfilment of my personal dream. The night was long and lilting, fuelled by friendship and hope. We parted at three-thirty, blood brothers, hugging a statement of intent, satisfied with the simpatico we had found.

Two weeks later I called him from Lisbon to say I was completing work on a screenplay but would be focusing on the biography in July. He was pleased. 'You can come out to Nassau,' he said. 'We must talk more.' He had previously asked me to look out for a property for him in Howth, a coastal resort in north country Dublin near my home. Now he had changed his mind. 'Forget the house in Howth. Stop looking. I want a house in Ireland again but the tax people will devour me if they hear about it. So to hell with it. My home is in the Bahamas, that's where I'll stay.'

Four weeks passed and we met again at a charity lecture held at Trinity College for the Dublin rape crisis centre. Days later I rang him with the intention of organizing my trip to Nassau, to be told, 'I can't do the book with you. It's all off. Come to lunch and I'll explain.' I came to lunch. There was an unforeseen obstacle, he told me. Fifteen years before he had signed a publishing deal for his book of poetry, *I, In the Membership of My Days*, with the American publishers Random House and a clause in the contract bound him not to co-operate with another author and to deliver his next book exclusively to them. The details were foggy, and before the lunch was over he was steering away from this cul-de-sac and promising to investigate further. We spent the rest of the lunch swapping ideas for a documentary film autobiography that I might direct and he would write. Our friendship seemed unshaken.

In June the Irish actor Ray McAnally died. A stalwart of

the Abbey Theatre and in recent years of the international star scene (he was Oscar-nominated for *The Mission*), McAnally had been the first choice of producer Noel Pearson and director Jim Sheridan for the principal role of Bull McCabe in the upcoming production of *The Field* (McAnally played the part on stage at the Olympia). Harris had been slated for a cameo as the local priest – no more than a few days of location work. Now, with McAnally's demise, Pearson boldly cast Harris in the lead. A prominent Irish producer called it 'risky casting'. He told me: 'Harris has by choice moved away from serious lead playing. All he's done for six years are TV bits and the interview circuit. His value, on the face of it anyway, is at this point just a curiosity one.'

Whichever way, Harris had the plum Irish role of the era. 'No other Irish play has the movie dimensions,' Ray McAnally had said. 'And few parts have the depth and scope of Bull McCabe.' Harris declared himself ecstatic. Not since the career breakthrough of *The Sporting Life* in 1963 had he had a chance like this. 'For me *This Sporting Life* was my *Hamlet*. And *The Field* will be my *Lear*.' His favourite superlatives, so effusively offered to promote years of less than distinguished work – 'magnificent', 'mighty', 'heroic' – were finally surpassed. *The Field*'s screenplay, by Sheridan, was 'unbelievable'.

Harris was, all of a sudden, centre stage again. The fuss wasn't Sinatra's or anyone else's. It was, in Ireland at any rate, all his. *The Field*, one of Ireland's best-loved plays by a best-loved contemporary playwright, John B. Keane, was to be primed and executed as a Hollywood high-jumper. Ireland's stuttering film industry was once more moving, Ardmore Studios were open and viable, Harris was at the helm. Jim Sheridan's previous movie (in fact his first), *My Left Foot*, won the New York Film Critics' award in December – a surefire indicator of Oscar business.[1] In its wake, industry gossip prophesied, *The Field* would be a triumph. 'Harris is going for gold this time,' said first assistant director Kevan Barker. 'He's reading and researching night and day. Because he knows this is his last big chance.'

---

[1] *My Left Foot* won two Oscars: Best Actor for Daniel Day-Lewis and Best Supporting Actress for Brenda Fricker.

Richard Harris became impossible to pin down and the friendship that had burned bright guttered low. We spoke on the phone while he was in Connemara working, and made arrangements that never panned out. 'Your book will kill my market,' he said obscurely. But added: 'Let's talk again on Sunday.'

By the time *The Field* was bumping towards completion I had come to accept the vagaries of Harris's friendship and the realities of my situation. It became clear to me that if the unbiased story of Richard Harris was to be written at all it must be written now, while the majority of the *dramatis personae* were alive and, for the most part, still 'in the biz'. It must also be written without undue focus on Harris's 'approval' or support. 'Jaysus, I could tell you some stories,' Harris promised two Limerick reporters in my company one afternoon, 'but I'll save them for the book.' He went on to give them a sample of possibilities. He told of lusting for the actress Rita Gam for many years. And he told of his long adolescent masturbation sessions over photos of Merle Oberon – and in later years having her. His yarns were detailed and purple and, most often, all but unrepeatable. They eulogized the Great Irish Hell-raiser of yore that he and Brendan Behan personified in the twentieth century. They were profane. They were reckless. They laughed at the dark past and gave no quarter in any direction. While I listened I perceived a tough man, a man of high intelligence but contained emotional depth who retained an oddly boyish fever about women. He lounged in the hotel lobby noisily appraising middle-aged women in twin-sets. This was the Harris who slugged Brando, who stole an award statuette at Cannes 'because I wanted one of the big ones', who was banned from driving 'for eternity'. This was the Harris the reporters wanted, and maybe I wanted.

But later, in his room, I saw a softer, sensitive and different man. The Irish *tanaiste* – Foreign Affairs Minister – Brian Lenihan was seriously ill in hospital, suffering liver failure. Harris did not know him but was anxious to visit and offer comfort. He phoned the hospital, ordered flowers. Later still, he showed me his own daily diet supplement of twenty-three different vitamin pills and gently advised me on the programme that would best suit my metabolism. Later again, after his Trinity lecture as I drove him back to his hotel, he agonized about how he came across. He was anguished that the MC interviewer who presented him had concentrated 'on the bullshit side of things'. 'They always want that,' he moaned. 'I didn't want to talk about getting drunk with O'Toole and how Brando hated me. But they keep steering me towards it. Every time.' Jack Donnelly reassured him: 'You were fine, Dick. You kept it moving along nicely.'

As I stood in the wings of 'A' Stage at Ardmore Studios where Harris's meteoric screen career began more than thirty years before and watched the subdued panic of the Harris-less *Field*, I recalled the myriad press reports of his turbulent nature. Here, all around me, were the echoing jokes of the technicians. And yet I was remembering the other side of the coin, the glimpses of tone and shade and light, and the franker admissions of our all too brief friendship. On *Major Dundee*, the Heston movie that incited such wrath, Harris had truly been 'simply exhausted'. In the year leading up to it he had completed four major films in four countries. He had not seen his newest-born son in seven months. And his physique was coping with an as yet undiagnosed hyperglycaemic condition that in time would almost kill him. 'Movies are bloody hard work,' he said. 'People think about the glamour and miss that.'

Richard Harris has hiked his world-touring *Camelot* beyond the box-office records of Rex Harrison's *My Fair Lady* and made almost fifty major feature films in thirty years, a colossal *oeuvre*. By comparison, actors like Peter O'Toole have had a relaxed joy-ride. He has worked, in the words of Lindsay Anderson, 'with ferocity' and has extended his craft through singing tours, poetry publication, film directing and vinyl recording. He has been no slouch. If anything, his relentless energies have denied him the serious celebrity he probably deserves – and perhaps denied him a home life and serenity that even today, at sixty, elude him. He has approached the media and the issue of celebrity with all the ferocity applied to his films. 'The singularly best media manipulator,' film writer Tony Crawley called him. 'If a distant relation breaks wind

Richard can make a story out of it.' In consequence he has become a pseudo star to some, despite his frequent fraternal references to Burton and O'Toole.

'Energy' is the sub-title of the Harris story. It is hard to watch his performance in *This Sporting Life* of 1963, or in today's *The Field*, and not be struck by the driving fortissimo motor of the man. It is harder still to share his company, no matter how briefly, and not take away a fragment of the excitement he so effortlessly generates.

This book began with a childhood admiration and took life with the spark of Richard Harris's presence and his friendship. The rocky course of its creation has enabled me to step further back than most authorized biographers might be persuaded to and view the subject in a fair objective long shot. I have tried to examine and report both sides – or rather, the many sides. 'Dick is wild,' says Jack Donnelly fondly. 'He's a narcissist,' says the actor James Booth. 'He's an angel,' says another actor, Rod Taylor. 'He's a bigot,' says Kevan Barker. 'He's a baby,' says *Tarzan* co-star John Phillip Law.

'He's a terrific actor who is often underrated' says George Peppard.

This book is about the many Richard Harrises. All of them unpredictable. And all of them, in spite of scandals, confusions and let-downs, finally, irrefutably, fun.

PART ONE

PRINCE DICK

'Keep switching the lights on and off in all the rooms until you find the one where you belong. But for God's sake shake the shackles from your feet and find your pride and dignity. The world owes no one anything and all we owe it is a death. . . .'

Richard Harris, 1968

'So much confusion to remain so pure. . . .'

Salvador Dali in *Diary of a Genius*

1

Birth of a Barnac

'Richard who?'

'Richard Harris, the actor.'

'Oh, Dickie, that *barnac*. One of our own, he is. There's a story goes: you're not a true Limerickman unless you've got a decent Dickie Harris story.'

Round the bars they gather – farm folk, factory folk, bucolic yuppies pink-nosed from the western winds – as they have done since unrecorded time, to whittle down the gossip, lay bare the heart of home truth and hail the local hero. Politics is their main staple, wry and derisive in the traditional Munster way; heroic Harris a close-runner. They remember him fondly over their Guinnesses, even those too young ever to have known him, and claims to blood-ties, or ties through marriage, are dizzyingly frequent. (Two claims to cousinhood in my very first weeks of research proved insubstantial.) By and large he is, heroically, a *barnac*, an honorary Kilkee title derived from the word 'barnacle', which celebrates his fidelity to the locality and all things Limerick-Irish (as distinct from plain Irish). He stands monumentally higher than that Johnny Carson clone Terry Wogan, a 'blow-in Limerickman' who blew out at a tender age. Harris, for so many Limerickmen, personifies a grand and winning Limerick – this regardless of the fact that just twenty-five years of his life were spent in Limerick and he has spent most of his adult life since bickering in one way or another with the city, its institutions and his friends there.

'I don't want to go back,' Harris recently told a *Limerick Tribune* journalist, Gerry Hannan. 'They hate me there.' Reassured that the absolute opposite was the case, he whacked his thigh and chirruped, 'They don't know what to make of me, that's the trouble. They never did know what to make of me.' Len Dinneen, whose father Kevin founded the Limerick College Players where Harris humbly started, tells of Harris's unending equivocality about his home town. When Harris's brother and manager, Dermot, died in 1986 Richard returned to Limerick for the first time in many years. At Old Mount St Lawrence's Churchyard on the city outskirts, home of the unkempt Harris family graves, Harris complained to Dinneen about the poor funeral turn-out. The absence of his Garryowen rugby cronies in particular irritated him.

'You're losing the run of yourself, man,' Len Dinneen told him. 'Look around. All the old faces are here. They all respect and admire you. It's you who forgets them, not the other way around.'

The confused feelings, most will tell you, owe their origins to a row twenty years ago. In 1970 he brought his directorial debut film *Bloomfield* to Limerick for a charity premiere in aid of the Limerick Handicapped Children The best charity shows then averaged £500 to £1000 takings; Harris proudly announced that *Bloomfield* took £3500. But Limerick still wasn't satisfied: 'I will never in my life ever appear in Ireland again. The local newspaper didn't cover it [or] mention a world premiere because the proprietor was not given four free seats. For charity no one gets free seats!'

Twenty years later he is a milder man, often tranquil, but still full of love-hate. He would visit more often, he told Hannan and me, and lecture there, and fund-raise there – if only anyone bothered to ask him. 'Trouble about Limerick is they don't understand Dickie Harris. They get the wrong handle on me. It's a kind of jealous prejudice.'

Understanding Richard Harris, the benevolence and the wildness, begins with a heritage exercise complicated by mixed blood, odd marriages and five generations of drifters. The Harris family is an old and originally Protestant one, Welsh-based, its name adapted from the ancient Welsh Ris, or Rhys. Harris's great-great-great-grandfather, John Harris of Llanadog, claimed ancestry from a noted peer of the realm and married Anne Stephens in November 1774 in the little chapel on the River Tywi, expanding instantly his sphere of status and influence. The Stephenses were of Norman descent, ardent followers of Vallance, Earl of Pembroke. Through intermarriage with the powerful Vallances and the Marshalls, succeeding Earls of Pembroke, they – and the Harrises after them – assumed the heraldic rights to the boar's head and the motto 'I Will Defend'. Its defiant spirit chased down the generations. The Harris clan was, according to Limerick wag, publican and diarist Charlie St George, 'hungry with ambition'.

The Irish Harris dynasty began when, at the end of the eighteenth century, John Harris moved his business interests to Waterford and brought with him his sons Richard, Tom and Henry. Richard and Henry married local Protestant sisters, but Richard's marriage was not to last. Serving in the Yeomanry, he transferred to Clonmel where he courted and wed the well-heeled Eleanor Haymon, the daughter of a prominent lawyer and granddaughter of the town's most popular mayor.

If the Harrises were possessed of a defiant spiritedness, they were also feckless drifters. One branch of the family ended up prospecting in South Africa. Richard's second son drifted to St Louis in his teens and vanished from record. Another son, Richard Jr, made for London and drowned in the Thames in 1838.

Richard Harris's tenth child, James, was born in Wexford, where the family had now settled to a life of substantial farming, in 1824. James broke from tradition by marrying a Catholic girl, Anne Meehan, and opting for a pious but industrious life – in Limerick. He built an oratory called Littleark for Anne and together they had six children, among them Richard, grandfather of the actor. It was James who established the Harris Mills business but Richard who earned celebrity as the 'aristocratic businessman' of local lore. 'It became a booming concern,' says Kevin Dinneen, a rival baker by profession, who knew Ivan, Richard's son. 'Not just a flour and meal mill but a bakery too, a huge bakery up in Henry Street. And not just a bakery. The Harrises had their Shannonside silos and a fleet of their own boats that plied the Shannon. They would dock and load at the mill, then run their cargoes down the coast. They were amongst the wealthiest people in the town, but they had a reputation for charm and warmth. They weren't snobbish. In the local lingo, they never lost the country cut.'

From the start, Harris Mills fought heavy competition. Three other major mills in the area vied for business: Russell's, Glynn's of Kilrush and Roche's. Roche's was the closest and fiercest competitor, based just a few doors away from the Harris main building where the manufacturing went on, in Williams Street. Jim Roche, grandson of the founder, recalls two generations of friendly sparring. His grandfather was on the best of terms with Richard, his father in turn with Richard's son Ivan who inherited the business. 'In the heyday Harris's was probably the biggest mill,' says Jim Roche. 'But we shared the market, which was supplying all of Clare and North Kerry. Harris's boats served the towns down to Tarbert and Kilrush. But he concentrated largely on flour and we concentrated on the meal. So there was room for both of us.'

When grandfather Richard retired at a ripe age his sons Ivan and Billy shared the inheritance, though it was perceived by most that Ivan took the bakery, the mill and the bulk of the fortune. The sum total was, according to Charlie St George, 'an exceptional booty, a prince's inheritance – and a hell of a lot of work'. Ivan put his heart into it, but by the mid-1920s the early bite of the post-war depression had taken its toll and the bakery side of the business had begun to slide. Ivan distracted himself by concentrating on outside activities – hockey and tennis were his sports – and by courting Mildred Harty, a local beauty from the wrong side of the tracks. 'In today's world it would mean nothing,' says a family friend of the Hartys, 'but in the twenties, in provincial Ireland particularly, such concerns as whether or not your family had money held sway. The Harrises were money people. The Hartys were not. It surprised many people when Ivan Harris took up with Milly.' But the surprise and disapproval were short-lived. Another Harty friend recalls: 'Old Mrs Harty came into money and spared nothing on Milly and her sister. She wanted the best for them and the Harrises were deemed the best, so there was no more conflict.'

Ivan married Milly, and their 'princely' life began in a large estate house on the North Circular Road. They had four children in quick succession but the arrival of the fifth, Richard St John, on 1 October 1930, heralded a significant downturn in fortune. That winter the bakery closed and the long, slow decline of the mill began. Throughout, Ivan retained a great calm dignity. 'He was a mild, unflappable man,' says Jim Roche, 'who always gave off a kind of air of composure.' Another mill man says, 'He wasn't a brilliant businessman and he enjoyed his pastime activities a bit too much. That was the trouble. But the mill in Williams Street and the wholesale end at Mount Kenneth, which was the Henry Street building, went on doing fair business, so he had a lot to be thankful for.' Grandfather Richard lived to see the first decline of his empire and died when Richard St John, later to be a multi-millionaire actor, was two. His grandson remembers 'being aware of wealth and luxury and all anyone could want in a home. There were maids and butlers and gardeners and big cars in the drive. And then, overnight, the world changed. One day was luxury, the next my mother was on her knees scrubbing floors and pegging out the Monday washing. I was too young to understand anything, but I knew what we lost.'

The family moved to Overdale, a six-bedroom 'return' house (two floors and a stepped-back annexe) in a terrace on the Ennis Road, a mile from the mill. This was Richard Harris's first true home, the weedy, wonderful place where his incipient creativity flowered. This was the 'green house' of his early poetry, where the vibrant fantasies of Beau Geste, Wells Fargo and Tarzan began. His recollections from the start are summery bright: 'My first memory is walking down Post Office Lane, pushing a baby in a pram. My mother said, "Whatever you do don't take your hands off that pram", and I looked in and saw Noel [his younger brother] and asked her, "Will I ever be that small again?" and she told me no.' The beauty of the moment rooted in his brain and bloomed, aged nine, in a surprisingly adult poem, 'My Young Brother', scribbled in a lined copybook that lived under his bed.

The young Harris was not, however, especially literary. Ivan read potboilers like Mickey Spillane, and lurid, gun-toting paperbacks peeped out of drawers throughout the house, but only their flashy covers inspired Dickie. An obsessive games-player, he was robust and attention-demanding – though he was usually ignored. As he tells it, Ivan barely knew him, indeed sometimes forgot his existence.

'What's his name again?' Ivan would ask Milly over his

newspaper at the end of a hard day divided between mill and hockey.

'Dick.'

'Oh yes, Dick.'

'There's a problem about being the middle son in a big family,' Harris told me. 'You're inclined to get lost amid the noise of all the others. So you make your own noise to draw attention. You have to, just to reassure yourself that you're alive and making your way. I made noise. I liked to be seen and heard.' Dermot Foley, one of the lusty 'musketeers gang' that grew around Dickie, is less wordy: 'Dickie liked a bloody racket, that's all.'

When the din failed in its purpose, Harris ran away from home and slept under the stars on the banks of the Shannon. No one ever came searching for him, he says. The drama was always anti-climactic. After a chilly night, with a shiver in his blood, he sneaked home, dodged upstairs and hid in bed.

On the better days, the days when his young identity crisis did not depress him, the apple and plum trees of the green house invited hollering Tarzan games in which – always – Harris starred. Overdale's garden was skinny and claustrophobic, but a haven as broad as the Amazon jungles existed just thirty miles down the road. Kilkee, a coastal resort, belongs to County Clare but Limerick has always called it her own. Kevin Dinneen, who has enjoyed its 'heavenly balm' off and on for eighty years, calls it 'Limerick's soul'. Traditionally Limerick's townsfolk take the waters here during the summer months. The resident population moves sideways, but it's true to say that few summer resorts anywhere in the world maintain an integrity of character so confidently. 'Write about the warmth,' Kevin Dinneen coached me as I squared up to recording Harris's childhood. 'Write about the majesty of the waves crashing in from the azure Atlantic on to the steps of the amphitheatre, carved by God. Write about the flat, blanket-white beaches and the wheeling gulls all day long . . . Write about the magic, and that will explain Dickie Harris becoming Richard Harris.' Manuel Di Lucia, who befriended Harris in Kilkee and whose father, an Italian immigrant, ran the local chip shop, agrees: 'Richard always said he should have been born in Kilkee. He would have been, says he, except for a confusion of dates. The best days of his childhood were all here.'

The Harrises, like the Roches and five thousand other comfortable Limerick families, moved *en masse* to Kilkee each June or July. Ivan sometimes stayed at the mill, but Mildred unfailingly supervised the renting of the small lodge and the children's outings. 'It was an idyllic time for him and he still dreams about it,' says Di Lucia. 'Swimming all day in the Pollock Holes [naturally formed rock pools], sandcastles on the beach, and when he was a bit older playing racquetball [squash] up at the courts.' Like most holiday families the Harrises never owned a property in Kilkee – Jim Roche has rented no fewer than twenty-two different lodges in his years of visiting the place – but Manuel Di Lucia was aware that they were, despite setbacks, a family of substance. 'The mill might not have been as sound as it once was, but they were certainly not hard up.'

For Dickie the long Kilkee idylls, sometimes rambling into early autumn, were suddenly curtailed by a head-on collision with school age. All his older brothers and sisters – Harriet-Mary (known as Harmay), Jimmy, Audrey and Ivan – were attending St Philomena's Jesuit junior school on the South Circular Road, but Dickie, just four, didn't see himself as a candidate. 'Frankly he had no interest in school,' says Dermot Foley. 'That class in primary school was a disaster. I believe myself he slept through it all. He certainly slept through the Crescent.' In a painful but unrecorded transition the Limerick Crescent College, a notably successful Jesuit stronghold, inherited the fast-growing Dickie Harris for secondary education. 'Before he was ten,' says a Crescent colleague, 'he had shoulders on him like the bridge of a battleship and a look about him that had nothing to do with academic life. He was, as we say, a messer. He dozed through class, farted for attention, knew nothing. The teachers, God bless them, despaired. There was corporal punishment and he was regularly thumped, but he didn't give a damn. He was in school for the fun – that was all.'

But he did not fail to win admirers. Among the Crescent boys a wayward but bright, tight group gathered round him, attracted by his wit – and a certain sense of danger. Dermot

Foley, Paddy Lloyd, Gerry Murphy, his cousin Niall Quaid and Teddy Curtain were among his gang. All of them shared an interest in sport, and rugby in particular. 'Father Guinane was Dickie's saviour,' says Dermot Foley. 'He was the rugby coach and at heart a saint. He saw to it that Dickie stayed in the Crescent basically because Dickie was a good second row and the main concern of the College was turning out a good junior team.' Harris's attraction to rugby as a study-substitute is easy to understand. All the family were sporty. Apart from hockey, Ivan was a dab hand at golf and enjoyed spectator sports of all kinds. The Harris family had founded the Limerick County Tennis Club, and both Ivan and Mildred played (Mildred, like her sister, was also an ace card player). Jimmy and Ivan, and Noel later, were sound rugby players, all earning their stripes with the Crescent junior sides. 'It was a wonder to pass the Harris house and see the rows of blue-and-whites [jerseys] billowing in the wind,' says Willie Allen, a favourite of Harris's on the rugby field. 'The whole family was physically active and the lads were built for rugby.'

Harris himself blithely accepts that he was a dunce at school, and that rugby was his anchor and his focus of self-esteem. In 1973 in *Profile* magazine he summed up his schooldays by recounting the tale of an American journalist who trekked to Limerick in the sixties to research his life story. She knocked on the door of the Crescent and asked the principal if Dickie Harris had gone to school there. 'I'd prefer you didn't mention his name in relation to this school,' was the reply. In the article Harris says the school simply didn't want him, 'so they invented a class for eleven difficult boys.' Dermot Foley concurs: 'It wasn't just Dickie who was bad – there was an entire special class of troublemakers, with Dickie at the centre of them. I'll tell you how bad he was: four lines of poetry was too much for him. When he became famous I read about all these two-hour one-man shows, with him reciting poems and singing. Judging by his Crescent days, I just don't know how he did it.' Harris himself says, 'When I remember schooldays I remember the rugby, that's all.'

In contrast to the hearty hysteria of the school playing field, classroom life faded to a faint monotone. A popular joke, oft repeated, had Dickie yet again dozing during maths:

Pupil: Sir, Dickie is asleep!
Jesuit teacher: For God's sake don't waken him.

The yarn, more than one friend claims, is true. True too is the story that has Father Durnen SJ, the Irish teacher, secretly passing the forthcoming term exam papers to Dickie in order to help him through. With time to investigate the specific exam answers, no pupil could fail the test. Dickie failed – 'nobly' in his own assessment.

Harris's love for rugby was further ignited in 1940 when, aged ten, he followed Garryowen, one of Limerick's proudest teams, to Cork and witnessed their spectacular win against the rival Dolphin. Crescent was a junior team, rampant with the demands of tribal loyalty, but Harris was objective – and ambitious – enough to admit non-partisan admiration. 'It was', he still remembers breathlessly, 'one of the Light Blues' greatest days.' Willie Allen is quick to defend any possible charge of betrayal: 'There were great relationships between various teams, for example between my own team, Young Munster, and Old Crescent. We'd often go over to their ground and help them scrummage the pack. And remember these were junior teams, and Garryowen was a notch above that. So it was natural for an ambitious player to want to play with the toughest and the best, to graduate to a higher league.' In 1944 Harris was still following Garryowen's fortunes avidly, sometimes with his Crescent gang, sometimes solo. When they wiped the senior Young Munster team in Limerick that year he followed them to Cork for the final, once more against Dolphin. Harris was screaming for Garryowen but Dolphin, despite the loss of star player O'Loughlin in the first twelve minutes, still took the honours. Harris and his brother Jimmy, another wild Garryowen supporter, were deflated – but inspired.

The game corresponded with the start of Harris's serious endeavours on the Crescent pitch. 'He was a great player,' says Willie Allen. 'A whole-hearted player, and a great man to get the ball in the line-outs.' Donal Begley, an opponent from the rival St Munchin's, is less flattering: 'He was a great warm-up man, full of vigour in practice but all show. He *looked* dangerous and useful, but when it came to the game he was not up to much. I've always reckoned I witnessed the start of Dickie Harris's acting career there and then, in those mid-forties' warm-ups. He *acted* the job of being a player.' Trainer Guinane, at any rate, had faith in Dickie – as did Jimmy, Ivan and Noel and the gang. Paddy Lloyd was the least serious gang player, but he was in no doubt that Dickie was good. Maybe not as good as Noel, who developed into the finest Harris player; but still top-quality. Quality enough, it seemed, to be chosen for Paddy Berkery's 1947 Cup-winning team and later the 1949 Grand Slam side that swept the boards in the Munster Schools Rugby.

The day after he won his second Schools medal Dickie Harris left the Jesuits, never having sat a public exam. The thrill of the medal, and the final farewell to academe, was seriously dampened by events at home. Two years before, Audrey, his second sister, had fallen ill with a stomach complaint that was finally diagnosed as intestinal cancer. After repeated operations and intensive therapy, she died, at home, in February 1946. Deirdre Lloyd, Paddy's sister, knew her as 'a beautiful and gentle girl who never had a chance to live'. At the time of her death she had recently become engaged to Donogh O'Malley, later to be a flamboyant and controversial Cabinet Minister. She was just twenty-one.

'Jimmy was closest to Audrey, but Dickie took the blow hard too,' says Deirdre Lloyd. 'He was a sensitive fellow, though the bluster of his personality covered it. He was the kind of fellow you *heard* coming down the street before you saw him. Wild, but lovely. And Audrey's death stopped him in his tracks. It was a charmed, happy household, you see, and Audrey's death was the first really serious setback.'

Jimmy and Ivan, the elder brothers, had now left the Crescent and joined their father in Williams Street, working hard to save the mill. A girlfriend of Dickie's remembers: 'Dickie told me things were not looking good. Ivan's brother [Harris's uncle] had spent a lot of money purchasing special equipment from Germany. It turned out to be a bad investment. The equipment failed, and Ivan and the mill were in the stew. It was on the cards for Dickie to join his brothers running the mill, but Dickie knew he wasn't cut out for it.'

According to Harris, his father urged him to 'go into business' – and then placed him without any apology in charge of hunting the mice that invaded the Henry Street wholesale stores. 'To be honest, not one of the brothers had a great head for the milling trade,' says a mill worker. 'Jimmy was at the helm but he didn't really grasp the complexities of the business and it was only a question of time before they ran out of steam.' Dickie was certainly no asset. Jim Roche remembers: 'He was in charge of the Henry Street place for a while, you might say he was serving his apprenticeship there. But he had no great interest. I recall him standing at the door, out in the sunshine, semaphoring all day to one of his cronies who was up the street working in another store. It was the crack he was interested in, not the work. The best way of describing him then is harum-scarum.'

The camaraderie of Paddy Lloyd, Dermot Foley and the others – and the fixation on rugby – remained the central focus of his life. His father might have been concerned, but the sporting progress of his sons was as important to him as their 'business' lives. Ivan actively encouraged Dickie's pursuit of Old Crescent and was rewarded by rapid, mature progress. In four years Harris won three caps, succeeding best with scrapes against Young Munsters. 'But we were all good mates,' says Harris. 'We had all those heroic matches at Thomond Park. They'd kick the shit out of us and we'd kick the shit out of them . . . but then we went out at night and got drunk together.'

Curiously, Dickie Harris was known as a light drinker at that time. 'He would get drunk on the notorious away weekends,' says Betty Brennan, soon to be his lover and confidante, 'but he was not a heavy drinker. In fact, against the typical pub scene of today he would rate almost as a non-drinker. He was not, then anyway, a pub person.'

Harris's own accounts contradict the Limerick version. British actor Ronald Fraser, who became a lifelong friend, remembers: 'From what he told me he was pissed from the time he was out of short trousers. I'll give you an example. He was about seventeen and his father despatched him to Dublin in a tall truck to collect provisions. Harris told me he made immediately for the Bailey [a well-known pub]. His father had warned him to be home at seven-thirty *on the dot*, or he would be in the shit! But Harris overstayed it and got well oiled and said, "Doesn't matter, I'll make it back to Limerick on the back roads, no trouble." So he set out, pissed as a proverbial, going hell for leather with this fourteen-foot truck. And suddenly, straight ahead, he sees a bridge with a sign saying: "Clearance 12 foot". So he says to himself, "If I buck up I can make it. And he wallops into the bridge. At the other side there's a Garda, checking out of the local pub, and himself well tanked. He flags down Richard, who tells him, "Sorry, officer. You see, I'm just delivering this bridge to Limerick and it fell off the back of the truck." The Garda had a few glasses up, so he agreed to repair to the pub to discuss the problem over a bottle of porter.'

During one of these irregular Dublin trips Harris lost his driving licence. Driving a borrowed family car he veered blindly into Abbey Street – 'I was a bit short-sighted' – and knocked over a double-decker bus. The magistrate who heard the case commended Harris on a near-historic feat. Surprisingly, Harris's state of inebriation was unrecorded.

In the winter of 1947 Richard Harris was rugby-capped for Munster Schools and Colleges, sipping Guinness, mouse-catching in his father's mill – and mentally idle. He was in love with Grace Lloyd, Paddy's older sister, in a desultory, adolescent way and still romping, whenever the mood took him, in Kilkee. He continued to rove with the gang, but sometimes even they bored him, and his mind – and his feet – started to wander. It was then that the 'other Dickie', the Dickie whom Betty Brennan got to know, drifted in the direction of the Playhouse Theatre that Kevin Dinneen had built with his own hands.

2

Playing House

No purpose-built live theatre existed in Limerick in the 1940s. Since the city's development from a Viking settlement nine hundred years before, theatre-going had never been a key part of the social scene. Visiting groups did come, usually to play in ill-equipped converted halls or, in the thirties and forties, the Savoy Cinema. Dublin's Abbey Theatre Company, one of the world's most celebrated, played the Savoy several times, but conditions were regarded as theatrically primitive. Over the pre-war years Limerick aficionados had the joy of seeing such notable stage performers as Cyril Cusack, Anew MacMasters, Michael MacLiammoir and Hilton Edwards tread the carpeted Savoy boards, but famine rather than feast was the order of the day. Out of such paucity grew Kevin Dinneen's vision of the Playhouse and the College Players.

A bakery manager by trade, Dinneen was in his middle thirties when, with some friends, he took a lease on a spacious section of building behind the Transport Union headquarters in O'Connell Street, not far from the Harris Mills. Len Dinneen remembers 'playing under the raised stage as my father was hammering it together single-handed'. The finished theatre seated 250 and was, according to Kevin, 'modest but true'. In 1942 Kevin had founded the College Players, the part-time actors' group that would enact the Playhouse programme. 'They were drawn from far and wide,' he says. 'Some of them actors in their blood, others – well – non-stop triers.' Apart from Richard Harris, two or three College Players went on to successful, if low-key, stage careers in Canada and America. The process of selection was rigid and fussy. An interview/audition session before two or three of the group

directors was followed, if successful, by a one-year apprenticeship with the Society of Dramatic Art, the Players' litmus
test. Richard Harris passed the interview/audition and joined
the SDA, but never made it as far as the College Players.

'Dickie was the all-physical action man,' says Joe O'Donovan,
one of the Crescent's few non-rugby men. 'You have to see
him in that light. He was never easy. All the family were
active, but he was hyper-active. He was good at the rugby,
good at Kilkee racquetball, not bad at tennis – and he was a
very fine water polo player. When school was over and the
rugby wasn't in season he wasn't happy to sit on his arse.
He joined the Limerick Swimming Club with me, training at
Corbally Baths three nights a week. He was madly competitive
– that was always an interesting facet of his personality. But
he was a fine team man too. While he was with us he won a
Munster Junior Medal to add to his rugby collection. He was
a power-house of energy and just plain restless.'

It was restlessness – and the desire for attention – that
drove Harris to the College Players. 'He did love theatre and
films,' says Deirdre Lloyd, 'because he was an inquisitive sort
of fellow who liked to be distracted and entertained. He liked
company, and he liked to go with the gang to the pictures,
or to whatever big show was in town. He went for a good
time. That was his way of seeing the world: let's have a good
time.'

When Harris approached the Playhouse late in 1947 Kevin
Dinneen already knew him and had a fair idea of his theatrical
potential: 'I remembered him as a lad in Kilkee, aged about
twelve. I was walking along the beach by the racquet courts
where the wall is very high, higher than a two-storey house.
One of the great childhood games of daring is to walk across
the top of the wall, ignoring the deadly drop. I saw a lad doing
it, with a crowd gathered in silent admiration. I looked again
and was dumbfounded to see that the boy was walking *on his
hands*. The boy was Dickie Harris.'

Harris started with the SDA 'like a hundred other lads,
interested but not particularly with any strong direction'.
The hope and expectation of the Players was a week-to-week
hands-on involvement from all young members, but Harris
was not, from the start, entirely committed. The son of a

member recalls: 'He wasn't disciplined enough to fit strictly
into the College Players programme. He was an exhibitionist
who liked to be centre stage all the time and wasn't bothered
about serving his time or proving himself. He loved the Ink
Spots and their music and he always wanted to be on stage
strumming a guitar and singing Ink Spots songs. No, his voice
wasn't exceptional – Noel, who sang with St Cecilian's choir,
was the family singer – but Dickie liked the glamour of being
Bing Crosby.' Kevin Dinneen endorses this view: 'You couldn't
say he demonstrated significant acting ability in the SDA. He
simply wasn't tested enough. But he had a flair for the variety
end of things. It seemed to me he might one day be a star of
the variety theatre more than anything. He was not a charmer,
but he was a *charming fellow* and he had such energy!' Harris
appeared in one Players' production, Strindberg's *Easter*, in
which he played the not-too-demanding part of Sebastian.
'His younger brother Dermot was a much better actor,' says
Kevin Dinneen. 'He could command the stage. I remember
him in a small part in one of our major productions. He swept
silently across the stage and his grace and confidence won the
audience. I always thought Dermot Harris might be the one to
win theatrical success. But, ironically, he ended up as Dickie's
manager.'

Throughout 1948 and 1949 Harris maintained a fitful interest
in the Players, and in the touring theatre groups that came to
Limerick. When Anew MacMasters visited for a Shakespeare
Week Harris, among many, offered himself for walk-on and
'stand about' parts. Those who saw him admired his gusto
and wit – not so much as an actor but, inimitably, as Dickie.
'All that stage stuff was a great lark,' says Dermot Foley. 'But
Dickie wouldn't *sit still* long enough to qualify for the College
Players or anyone else. Most of the time he thought they were
boring old wankers. All these play scripts! Too much paper,
he thought! Let's get some action!'

His greatest performances in those days were, unquestionably, in Kilkee. The summer madness that lingered, in
the Irish way, from May till November centred increasingly
on the amphitheatre, a natural saucer of rock with stepped
walls perfectly suited to play-making. Amateur groups used
the amphitheatre regularly (though the College Players didn't),

and it was here that unscripted Harris shone – in his own adlibbed productions. Manuel Di Lucia says, 'He was always looking for new angles for fun in Kilkee, always trying to turn a new trick.' He was also gregarious and interested in other people, in their lifestyles and problems. In the west end of Kilkee a summer hotel housed the Clarelleagh organization, a Presbyterian and Methodist group of locals. Harris, staunchly Catholic and screamingly proud of it, wasn't perturbed by gossip when he arranged an open air entertainment for them at the amphitheatre. 'It was astounding,' says Jim Roche. 'He was a great organizer *and* performer. He commanded the scene, doing take-offs of American actors and Shakespeare. He was an eccentric, a humanitarian and a very likeable lad.'

The cinema in Kilkee, like the cinemas in his home town, found Harris less likeable. By his own admission he was banned from every one of them in a very short time. He liked the movies – though mostly when there was nothing better to do, in the opinion of a very close girlfriend – and had an annoying fondness for standing on the seats and reciting the dialogue along with the screen characters. Manuel Di Lucia remembers him 'clattering about from seat to seat, laughing and catcalling and making fun of everything . . . but you couldn't go against him any more than you could go against a clown at the circus'. The Savoy banning order seemed particularly amusing when, more than twenty years later, Harris brought the premiere of *Bloomfield* there. Some of the staff, he noted, were the same people who had enforced the ban. It was, he likes to claim, 'touch and go' as to whether the *Bloomfield* star would be allowed past the door.

At the Carlton Cinema, long gone, Harris embarked on his first Hollywood crush, falling head over heels in love with Merle Oberon playing Cathy in Sam Goldwyn's classic *Wuthering Heights* (1939). He found her 'mesmerizing' and she became his Ideal Woman, the personification of a perfect femininity beyond Milly and Harmay and Audrey. He kept her photo, along with his secret poetry collection, in the recesses of his bedroom. The impact of Merle Oberon's beauty spelt more than just a sexual awakening. *Wuthering Heights* fixed itself in his imagination, and his admiration for the story – a hybrid of Gothic and quality drama – hints at his attitude of approach to his early career. *Wuthering Heights*, secretly, was the sun and stars. After his eventual main success, *This Sporting Life*, he and director Lindsay Anderson parlayed everything on a remake of *Wuthering Heights*, with Harris as Heathcliff. The project was, sadly for all, stillborn.

Despite the temporary interruptions of the Playhouse, Kilkee and the movies, Harris's main occupation was still rugby. After his mid-teens and the discovery of Merle Oberon the scales were balanced by a lusty interest in the opposite sex. 'I always was a horny bastard,' Harris later said. But to Gracie and Deirdre Lloyd, Mary Kennedy and other available bob-curled Limerick colleens, he was simply the personification of 'niceness'. The obsession with Gracie Lloyd thrived, but her affections went elsewhere. Deirdre Lloyd says, 'He had plenty of dates, so I wouldn't say it broke his heart. He was never short of admirers among us girls. All the Harris boys had different facial bone structures. Dickie's was like his mother's, very square and handsome. As far as we were concerned he was a right good catch.'

Harris dallied with a few compliant local girls, but his first serious relationship – and the model for all his earnest friendships with women throughout his life – was with an out-of-towner, Elizabeth Brennan; maybe not a Merle Oberon duplicate, but certainly a fair ringer for Audrey Hepburn. Wexford-born 'Betty' Brennan was nineteen when she arrived in Limerick from Waterford on transfer from the Munster and Leinster Bank. Her mother had died when she was three and her guiding influence, remote but firm, was her father. Chocolate-eyed, light-limbed and graceful as a *Vogue* mannequin, Betty had a sense of adventure that was unusually well developed. In an Ireland of rigid sexist restriction, where women wore a uniform 'decent' attire and never went alone into bars, Betty was a trendsetter. 'I was always a free bird,' she says today. 'Always out for a laugh.' The buoyant vivacity hides a rock-solid, courageous character. Betty wryly recalls the wagging tongues when she first wore trousers into an all-male preserve. 'It was all so different then,' she reminds you. 'Ireland has changed colossally in forty years. Today, it might be commonplace. But the kind of relationship I shared with Dickie was outrageous in 1951.'

It was just after Harris's twenty-first birthday – a grand party attended by all the family and numerous friends – that Betty first encountered him. In her early Limerick days she flirted with his older brother Ivan who was, to all intents, managing the mill. But her heart was quickly won by Dickie. 'The social scene was very innocent,' says Betty. 'We didn't really go into pubs. My favourite places were the ballroom at Cruise's Hotel and the Stella ballroom. There was also the tennis club, and a few other sports venues.' It was in Cruise's Hotel at a Saturday night dance that Betty Brennan fell for Harris. He asked her to dance, walked her home to her nearby digs – and a burning romance began. 'He was strikingly handsome and terribly *kind*,' she remembers. 'He looked like Danny Kaye, with his orangey-coloured hair and bright eyes. He was great fun – that memory lingers above all – and was a great, endless talker.' Harris was no longer a virgin, but Betty was. Their relationship was consummated – 'perfectly,' she says – in a summerhouse in the grounds of a nunnery on a spring day.

'It was a happy affair full of activity,' says Betty. 'Dickie's energy combined with mine was a potent mixture. We went everywhere together, did everything. Occasionally he drifted away for rugby weekends with Paddy Lloyd and Gerry Murphy and the others, but mostly, whenever we could, we shared our time . . . and our money.' Harris was still idly kicking his heels at Mount Kenneth, sponsored by his father. Contrary to popular mythology, he was often short of a bob or two. 'We spent our money liberally,' says Betty. 'My wages saw us through the first half of the week, his wages paid for the weekend.' Weekends were spent at Cruise's, which was managed by Dickie's brother-in-law Jack Donnely, married to Harmay. 'Dickie and Jack were more like brothers, actually. And Dickie was very well behaved.' A gang friend fills in the background: 'Yes, at Cruise's Dick was on good behaviour. But then he'd go down to one of the pubs, to Charlie St George's or somewhere, and let go with the lads. Down in Charlie St George's the company was a bit rowdier – rebel songs and talk about the Brits and the suppression of the Irish, and all that. By my understanding Dickie got his real education there, in the pubs. What he did with his women, I don't know. You see, he could be quite private about himself. I don't really think he liked sharing himself with people.'

Movie-going did not play a major part in the shared life with Betty. If anything the theatre, and the Playhouse in particular, was the magnet. 'He admired people like Anew MacMasters and liked to take me to the Playhouse productions,' she recalls, 'but you certainly wouldn't call it a craze – for either of us. My clearest memory is of attending a Playhouse production and being amused by a character who repeatedly came on stage and started blurting a line, only to be interrupted. When finally he got his line across Dickie was roaring the words with him. Dickie had a magpie mind with a real interest in books, but that side of him was subdued, almost hidden.' Harris has gone on record more than once admitting a duality of character. In 1974 he told David Lewin, vis-à-vis his private side: 'I have always played a double game.' Though he was unquestionably candid and intimate with Betty Brennan, there was, it seemed, also a private inner dialogue. 'Maybe the suppression factor was Limerick itself,' says a local writer who knows him. 'Like so many provincial self-contained towns, it has a lingo and a way of its own. It is quirky, dictated by the notorious Curse of St Munchin that decrees that the locals shall perish while the foreigner shall prosper. Limerick doesn't like people jumping beyond their station. The Harrises were millers, doing a fair trade, and that was that. Other people were actors, other people were writers. And, on top of that, Dickie's crowd – the chaps he hung around with – weren't the long-haired poet types. They were all knock-down rugby men, all lads out for the crack. Dickie was strong, sure, but whatever artistic feelings he had he kept inside himself. He kept it in because he didn't want it knocked out of him.'

With Betty Brennan or alone, Harris trekked back to the Playhouse. On a rugby trip to Dublin with the lads Harris skipped a boozing sortie and took in the Gate Theatre production of Pirandello's *Henry IV* instead. He was slack-jawed in admiration. The story of simple man hiding behind the mask of madness fascinated him. 'I was *staggered* by the play,' he told me in 1989. 'I swore that one day, somewhere, I would act it.' These heartfelt arty promises were not shared with Betty. What she saw was a happy rugby fanatic – though with his eyes open to future possibilities. 'We didn't really talk about *our* future, or whether we would stay in Limerick, or stick each other out. We lived from day to day. But there was a feeling of restlessness in everything Dickie did, a feeling of excitement about his future. I dare say he thought more about it than I did.'

Dermot Foley remembers Betty as 'a right wild one. She was a match for Dickie in a lot of ways. In fact, as I think about it, they were *perfectly* suited.' But Milly Harris – 'Mildew' to Dickie – didn't agree. Before the affair was a year old Milly had expressed her disapproval in an assortment of indirect ways. 'The Ennis Road house was off-limits for me,' says Betty. 'Again, you must remember the time and the place and the attitude to such close relationships. Dickie and I were as close as people get. He didn't stay in my digs, but let's say he spent more than a little time there. The old woman who owned the place – a ratty old bag – didn't at all like what she saw. To this day I believe she wrote to Milly Harris and complained, and Milly, who positively disliked me, contacted my father. As a result my bank suddenly decided to transfer me back to Waterford. It wasn't a shock because I smelled it coming. But it was a big strain on my relationship with Dickie.'

Harris did not, apparently, contest the parental decision. Instead, in his cavalier way he enjoyed the circulating gag that beautiful Betty had been 'harrised' out of town. Borrowing Jimmy's rattlebag Citroën car he quietly pursued the affair with Betty at weekends. 'We were so close emotionally,' she says, 'that the separation hardly mattered at first. It was an inconvenience, no more.'

After a few months Betty was again transferred, this time to Dublin. 'By then our relationship was changing,' she says. 'We were simply apart too much. And I had decided exactly what I wanted to do with my life. I wanted to work hard, earn as much money as I could and go travelling in Europe. It wasn't that I didn't adore Dickie as much as ever. It was just that circumstances were what they were and there was no use crying over spilt milk.' At first Harris was reluctant to let go – as was Betty. The four-hour drive to Dublin didn't deter him and he continued to borrow Jimmy's car or Ivan's.

His visits were short but, as Betty describes them, full of the madcap laughter that was the glue in their affair. In his first visits to Dublin Harris stayed at the Avoca Hotel in Harcourt Street, a long walking distance from Betty's flat in the south of the city. But his days, and substantial portions of the nights, were spent with Betty. 'After our experience with that first dreadful landlady Dickie was extra-sensitive to the problems facing us,' says Betty. 'One morning he decided to make an open gesture of appeasement to my landlady by bringing her an early breakfast on a silver tray. He brought it from the kitchens of the Avoca and marched through the morning rush-hour traffic with this fully laid-out hotel breakfast. My new landlady was enchanted.'

Harris's rakish humour went on winning unlikely friends. Betty's brother, a seminary student who was also called Dickie, became one of his most loyal admirers. Though Dermot Foley and other gang pals found Harris to be 'basically a danger man' in his antics, Dickie Brennan wallowed in his warmth. A Sunday foursome drive with Betty and a girlfriend inspired the future priest to write a long celebratory poem which is fondly recited by the Brennans today:

> . . . From Tallaght then to Templeogue we sped most merrily
> The driver now a female, oh, how skilful she could be
> As she passed out other motors by the thickness of a flea
> While behind her sat the brethren turning every shade of green . . .
> Arrived at last on the mountain top, it was wonderful to see
> Those glens and hills of Dublin which don't flow into the sea
> And I think our joy and rapture were well voiced by glad Dickie
> As he muttered in his rapture, 'This caps it all for me.'
>   (Or if you would prefer it so, 'What glorious ecstasy!') . . .

The epic continues by extolling the virtues of the scenery and the company, then conforms to a uniquely Irish lyricism:

> Oh 'twas at the Hotel Leinster in that day in fifty-three
> That we four to mirth inclined were and to jollity
> Oh, how we quaffed the nectar there, supplied so thoughtfully,
> By that wonderful young chappie, Dick – the busy bee!

Betty Brennan remembers no final break-up blow. 'Whenever we were together it was like the old times: fun and activity and few if any rows. But Limerick was my past then, and I had only the vaguest ideas of what was going on, apart from the letters Dickie sent me every couple of weeks.' Betty was vaguely aware of his continued success with rugby, which appeared to be a shrinking compartment in his life. 'He never lost his devotion to rugby,' says Len Dinneen, who went on to captain the London Irish rugby teams in the sixties. 'But while he had tremendous potential, it wasn't clear that his talents would take him to the National side.' The evidence of Harris's pitch performances, however, continued to show promise. With the full encouragement of his father he joined the Garryowen seniors in 1952 and went on to contribute to several hard-fought victories. In his first senior cup match against Dolphin in Cork, captain Kevin Quilligan and prop forward Sean McNamara coached him to excellence. His field work was, by his account and others', the best of his rugby life.

Harris's lovelorn letters to Betty kept coming. In them he spoke mostly of his affections, occasionally for rugby, more often for rival girlfriends. He was cheerful and cheeky, but sometimes he broke her heart. With a smile of forgiveness Betty recalls lamely threatening to kill herself when Harris forwarded photographs of the new girl in his life, an air hostess. 'It was the heat of youth,' she says. 'A blaze of emotion that never affected our friendship.' Despite this, it was obvious the finale of their relationship was at hand. Probably both of them wished it, tacitly acknowledging the roving spirit growing in the other; but the declarations of love went on till the end. Among the endless photographs mailed from Limerick was a studio portrait of Dickie grinning with a self-possession that already hinted at Hollywood. On the reverse he wrote:

> Am I a mystic? What mental strife
> Plays thoughts upon my mind;
> What genie's philosophy of life
> Inside this brain you'll find.
>
> Is it so strange – to lose the sun
> The winter breeze and rain,
> The stars at night, the moon so bright
> And life of gay, not pain?

O God from my life my dream you stole
And left me in this world alone
How can I live without my life?
How can I die without my soul?

As Betty drifted away, a frustrating gap opened in Harris's life. It wasn't just the absence of a like-minded female friend with whom he could communicate, nor the focus for fresh devilment. Betty's departure underscored his need for poetic expression. With her he had relaxed and grown enough to reveal some of the extraordinary roundedness of his developing personality – specifically a feminine side every bit as lively as his rugby scrum persona. 'The Limerick Dickie set out to conquer was the hard man's Limerick,' says a local acquaintance. 'It was boxing orchards [scrumping], carousing at the Hydro Hotel, getting off with the dames, cocking a snook at your elders. But there was another side to him. He had a knack of getting on with all the ould fellas, as well as the young dames. People tend to stick to their peer groups here, but Dickie moved around. He had a great friendship with a middle-aged insurance man, Alf Kirby, for instance. And he had unusually easy friendships with many women. He was a hard man and a loud-mouth – but don't confuse that with bully. Really he was as gentle as a dove. And often a bit depressed, a bit of a broody thinker.'

The perks that Limerick offered – be it the Crescent wide boys, wise Alf Kirby or the pageant of the Playhouse – no longer absorbed Harris. Nor did the strained, phoney working life in Henry Street. If anything, Alf Kirby was a father substitute, and it was an open secret that, apart from sports interests, father and son had little time for each other. 'The mill was a mess,' says a local businessman. 'The management arrangements were awful and Ivan wasn't progressing things at all. Dickie wasn't cut out for it and made no pretence otherwise. He just went there when he was bored, or when he was trying to please his father.' Betty recalls that Harris's greatest interest in the mill was a secret trysting spot, where they romped among the flour sacks. Beyond that his professional involvement, she says, was 'just going through the motions'.

In Harris's own version, his friendship with the mill ended when he organized a protest walk-out in a labour dispute. His father was disgusted, but hardly surprised. He had come to accept the rebellious, unstable nature of his middle son. Richard was summarily fired.

Gradually the indulgent gaiety of cartwheeling youth died. The Crescent gang members started marrying and drifting away. Rugby cronies sworn to lifelong friendships moved to Cork, or Dublin, or London. A few went to the brave new world across the Atlantic. Harris talked a little about his life to Kevin Dinneen at the Playhouse – but never a lot. 'I knew he would move on. He wasn't the kind of personality that queues up to wait his turn. You only had to look in his eyes – if ever they stayed still for a minute – to see how busily he was planning his future.'

Missing Betty and sick of Limerick and home, Harris conspired to emigrate. With his cousin Niall Quaid he applied for a Canadian visa. But the application called for a medical and Harris knew he was in trouble. A few years earlier, at nineteen, he had been diagnosed as having a tubercular spot on his lung, but had taken medication and ignored the risk. During the 1952 Munster Senior Cup campaign he felt ill, but a chemist pal gave him benzedrine to keep him going. At six feet three inches, he was losing weight throughout 1952, and was down to twelve stone before the Cork cup match. Now, in mid-1953, his GP, Dr Corboy, confirmed that he had tuberculosis and must be confined to bed. Treatment and recuperation might take up to three years.

Harris was shattered. His Canadian escape was gone, his rugby life over: 'I never played again. And I have often thought that it was rather ridiculous getting a Munster Cup medal and TB all at the same time.' His life went into crash-reverse. He had been strategically loosening the bonds to Overdale; now he was housebound. The night life ended: there would be no more women at Cruise's, no more treason talk at Charlie St George's, no more Kilkee play-acting, no more movies. He took to his bed, at first in anger and fear, finally prostrate with boredom. Looking back, he later reflected, his confinement had been inevitable. After the first diagnosis he should have rested for a few months. Instead: 'I got up when I should have been lying down and to break the monotony I began to drink. First to forget. Then to remember.'

Milly was a sound though sometimes cranky nurse, and Noel and Dermot particularly were good company – but Harris was inconsolable. So often the soul of the party, he had only the house pet – a dog of Harmay's – to entertain. 'Time became of great importance to me. Whenever I asked the doctors when I would be cured and begin doing something with my life they would reply, "In six months." It was always six months. Never any more, never any less. And like two dots on a circle, the two dates never drew any nearer. . . . I was dribbling away my youth, identified with nothing, achieving nothing.'

Harris remained housebound for nearly two years, for six months of which he lay inert in bed, staring at the damp Irish walls that, he reckons, caused his TB in the first place. It was this period of silence and reflection that forged the direction of his career. At last he was sitting still long enough to unscramble the threads of his life and make decisions. 'From the beginning Dickie lived life at the gallop,' said Dermot Foley. Now the running was over. 'In illness you are a great burden to your friends,' said Harris. 'In the first week they all come and say you'll be up in a month, you'll be up in a week. After a couple of months you have fifteen friends, and a couple of months later you have six. And then you've got three, and then you have one, and then you are on your own. They come only at Christmas and birthdays, either looking for or giving presents. So I was put on my own, and I invented people out of light bulbs. I had conversations with people in light bulbs, and I invented hundreds of people coming to talk to me. I was King of England, or I was the Pope. That is how my acting career started.'

Throughout Harris's life the variety of story-telling in his interviews is dizzying. 'Story-telling is a Limerick speciality,' says local writer Gerry Hannan. 'You don't call the inconsistent interview subject a liar – you call him colourful.' Harris's imagination was, even so, exceptional. During his confined period he wrote copiously, filling copybooks with surreal notes that were the first lucid indications of artistic potential.

Though he was never successful at art (his constant doodles are basic matchstick men with balloon heads), his mature writing, removed from self-pitying love hymns, was often remarkable, boomeranging from Nietzschean *vers libre* to elegiac Dylan Thomas and back. It was all the more remarkable because he was not widely read, and had often experienced difficulty reading. Only now did he seek out books to while away the time, showing a preference for buccaneering adventure yarns and, obsessively, the letters of Vincent Van Gogh to his brother. But still he kept his dreamer side to himself. Almost none of the jottings of his bedridden years remain, and just one nineteen-line piece was published in his eventual book of poems. It is called 'My Blood Reflects Nothing of Me' and speaks about the double life of a hard-drinking hard man, and the Catholic suppression of passion.

'During this period of incarceration,' Harris told a women's magazine in 1965, 'I lived my life at second-hand through the adventures of others, in books. And I decided that, when I was cured, I would like to direct my own scenarios, to bring to life the whole world of my creation, to look at my life through the telescope of truth. I wanted to bring a little shock, a little disease into middle-class drawing rooms, to lift up the carpets and shake up the dust a bit.' This bold calculation wasn't evident in the sternly run Overdale, nor beyond. The local pubs that knew his business were only vaguely aware that he was seriously ill. 'He just disappeared,' says Charlie St George. 'It was a time when a few of us wondered if we'd seen the last of him.'

Dickie Harris was well familiar with the Limerick expression 'alickadoo'. It describes the rugby man who knows all, but stands forever on the wings. The world of Crescent and Garryowen was full of alickadoos. He knew many of them personally, but disliked them. Always a man of movement, and one who liked to see things through, he had no sympathies with back-scratchers and idlers. In the autumn of 1955, as his condition improved, he dodged out of the house seeking only one nourishment – the ether of the theatre. His mind was made up: he wanted no future in the family business, even if Ivan forgave him and dragged him back. Instead he would go abroad and study theatre. Mildred was shocked, Ivan silently annoyed. Harris later said, 'My parents couldn't understand what drew me to the make-believe world of acting. I didn't know myself.' He had not consulted Dermot Foley, nor Betty, nor Kevin Dinneen. He had made his enquiries in secrecy and sent applications to two London drama schools. Ivan, he knew, would not support him. But he had a small shares inheritance from an aunt who had recently passed away: it was enough money for the Holyhead mailboat and survival for a few months in the Smoke.

Milly, Ivan and his brothers didn't debate the issue too long. Dickie had been in prison for countless months. His strength was back and he had living to catch up on. He loved action, laughter, daring – and all his old sparring cronies had flown. It was, in the end, inevitable that he would bolt. But he would be back to Overdale and the mill, they knew, in a week or a month or a year.

3

Honeymoon on Sixpence

Richard Harris arrived in London at a time that was arguably the lowest ebb of British theatrical and film endeavour. The greatest stage performances of Olivier, Richardson and Gielgud were in the past. And in film as in theatre a post-war 'norm' had been established that refined Victorian melodrama and offended no one. The jolly-good-fellow charm of Kenneth More and Dirk Bogarde dominated, and cheery-spirited Ealing Studios thrived. This apparent intertia masked a society ripe for change. The Conservatives had been in comfortable power since 1951, a fairytale queen was enthroned, rationing had ended the previous year, council housing was booming . . . and TV was spreading across the land like bushfire, reporting the alternatives. Britain was, as Churchill promised, a people set free, and in their freedom – and with the spur of an improved quality of life – the mood was afoot for major change.

While British movies dozed, Hollywood was cracking. Brando had just finished *On the Waterfront*, James Dean had wrapped *Giant* and Marilyn Monroe's latest was the seminal comedy *The Seven Year Itch*. Harried by the success of television, Hollywood was energetically pushing out its best contenders, but British movie moguls had yet to recognize the need to fight. Before the decade was out Ealing Studios would be finished, and an anti-Establishment movement begun in literature and fanned by the neo-realist film successes of Italy would utterly change the face of British cinema. Richard Harris, needing to express a duality of character that ill fitted Limerick, would find a perfect home here, at the forefront of a blind, bursting movement to change the world. It was perfect timing.

But Harris's arrival in London didn't feel like good timing. He stepped off the boat train wide-eyed, unsure of his own emotions in the capital of the colonial empire he had been taught, in romantic principle anyway, to despise. But his heart was full of wonder, not hate. He was alone, but utterly at peace in his own company, having learned the benefits of isolation. His own internal universe, he later said, was always fuller than other people's lives. His first urge was not the pursuit of food and shelter, rather a desire to see the historical sights. Speakers Corner was his first port of call and he stood, entranced he says, for hours, his few belongings crammed in a grip at his feet. It reminded him of the Kilkee amphitheatre, where unrestricted art thrived. But it was different in an important way. Limerick is a tight-woven community of seventy thousand people of one race; London was a mishmash and the voice it aired at Speakers Corner was polyglot. Harris delighted in the many tones and hues of the Park – and missed his check-in time at the YMCA, where he had hoped to spend the first few weeks. Instead he hailed a black cab and tipped the driver to find him 'the cheapest decent lodgings'. The cabbie obliged and Harris later laughed at the irony of searching for a doss-house in a cab. 'This weird poise between penury and prosperity was symbolic of my future life.'

He had applied in writing to the Central School of Speech and Drama and to the London Academy of Music and Dramatic Art. Central was the plum hope and he went there for his audition call on his second day in London. Before he crossed the threshold he was aware that the stakes were against him. He was twenty-five; the average Central student was seventeen or eighteen. Even today Harris relishes the story of his rejection. 'It was the day of the pretty boy,' he says, 'and fellows like me were not in vogue. I walked in, with all these aristocratic-looking ladies and gentlemen sitting looking back at me, saying, "What are you going to do for us, young man?" So I said, "Shakespeare." I did my piece, my audition, and they said, "What right do you think you have to enter our profession?" So I looked up and said, "The same right as you have judging me. . . ." Then a bell rang and a little man came in and they put me out.' Harris has frequently broadcast various accounts of this story, venting his anti-institution feelings colourfully. Whichever way, he was turned down. 'His Irish accent wasn't particularly noticeable,' says fellow Irish actor Joe Lynch who was successfully carving a film career in London at the time. 'But he had the Irish way about him. He swaggered. He talked loud and brash. He made no apologies for himself. You got the impression of a fellow who was happy with himself and was waiting for the world to discover his greatness.'

After an interview his second choice, LAMDA, accepted him and he was enrolled as a day student. He took a bed-sit in a house in the Earl's Court Road and sat down immediately to budget his two-year course. The booty from his aunt's shares allowed him £3 10s a week for food, rent and fees and he wrote home expressing victory. It was just a matter of time now before theatrical success and fortune found him. If Milly viewed this deduction with scepticism she was probably mollified by assurances that Dickie would not be an actor, but more sensibly a director. Acting was show-off stuff; 'director' at least smacked of respectable industry. But not everyone at home was pleased by Dickie's optimism. According to family friends Ivan viewed the unfolding events with a shortening fuse. 'It's just as well Dick was well out of his reach,' says one of them. 'If it had been acting school in Limerick or Dublin he would have changed Dickie's mind.' Harris himself later said in surly regret: 'I never got to know my parents, and they never got to know me.' Communication with Limerick came in staccato bursts, dictated by the new nomadic world of Harris's London liberty. Sexual adventures kept him busy when LAMDA didn't and he shifted from flat to flat as love affairs dictated, straining his £3 10s a week budget in no time.

LAMDA holds no record of Harris's labours, but the actors who knew him then talk of unusual energy and impact. Frank Windsor who encountered him later voices the general impression: 'The moment you met him you thought one word: *dynamism*.' After six months at LAMDA Harris was bored with the non-progress. James Booth, who grew to know him well, observed: 'He had an aptitude based on supreme confidence. I think some people are just born with it in that degree. He was loud and sure of himself and made London his own. His friends weren't only fellow actors. They were musicians and hobos. That was something you noticed about him: a need to keep in touch with the average Joe, which some academy trainees weren't so much inclined to do.'

Len Dinneen, too, points out that back in Limerick Harris had a 'fixation with the colourful underdog'. Toasty McKnight, an unctuous, crooning tramp on the pub scene, was one of Harris's cherished pals. 'Almost everyone tried to avoid Toasty,' says Dinneen, 'but Dickie clung to his every word. And mimicked him. It was a study-and-copy routine.' Manuel Di Lucia in Kilkee saw a similar study technique: 'My father was broadly Italian and Harris worked on it till he got the accent to a "t". The family chip shop sometimes attracted a local yob or two. Once, one of these yobs was pressing his luck at the counter. Richard crept up behind him and, in classic half-Italian, warned the fellow to back off. It was a scurrilous take-off but very, very effective.'

Actor Ronald Fraser, who 'knew Harris from the start, old boy!' found him 'deliciously naughty but you had to be cloth-eared to hold it against him'. Not everybody at LAMDA agreed, and the upstart qualities that offset the boredom made him many enemies. 'He could be the most awful dose of hot air,' says one actor.

But Harris wasn't all hot air. Unlike most, he had the courage to do something about the slow stodginess of the training. Unprompted – indeed strongly warned off the notion – he decided to pool his finances and mount his own production. 'You have to hand to him,' says Booth. 'He was half-trained – and that's being kind to him – and bereft of financial support, like us all. He was studying method acting and was besotted to death by Brando and Clift and the so-called rebels. But let's be honest, sticking his neck out to mount a West End play took some balls. He really didn't know what he was doing.'

Harris chose the now defunct Irving Theatre off Leicester Square, which was in financial difficulties and thus affordable (it later became a striptease joint). The play he opted for – which he would direct and not star in – was Clifford Odet's *The Country Girl*, at the time a movie hit starring Grace Kelly and Bing Crosby. On Broadway the play won a Tony for actress Uta

Hagen; Hollywood stayed faithful to it, and it went on to earn an Oscar for Grace Kelly. Harris watched the movie, examined the Bill Perlberg script – and decided on a total revamping. His production became *Winter Journey*, something altogether new. Georgie Elgin, the suffering heroine defending her alcoholic actor husband, underwent dramatic metamorphosis, but the girl's role remained important. No one in Harris's LAMDA class matched the part, so he sank more cash into an advertisement in *The Stage*. Two hundred hopefuls responded, but Harris still wasn't satisfied with what was on offer.

The girl he eventually found – by the purest fluke – fitted the role and then some. Elizabeth Rees-Williams was a RADA student and daughter of the tearaway Liberal peer Lord Ogmore. She found out about the play from lead actor Peter Prowse, an acquaintance of Harris's, whom she encountered while hitching a lift across London. Prowse, being of the immediate opinion that she would suit the show, brought her to meet Harris. Elizabeth's sky-blue eyes and the Nordic looks that belied her Welsh background enthralled Harris from the moment they met – though Liz recalls he treated her brusquely. In James Booth's words, Harris's interest was 'not all professional'. Booth was in Liz's RADA class and reckoned her a poor actress: 'She was outdated, she talked too plummy and it was known that RADA would drop her. She auditioned for Richard just before the RADA executioners came in.'

To be fair to Liz, her instincts counterbalanced her ambitions: she loved the theatre world, but knew she was no great shakes as an actress. To be fair to Harris, patently half-trained, he can only have judged her RADA background, her beauty and her relaxed confidence. Fancying her can only have hastened his decision.

Rehearsals began in the cellar of the Troubadour Café in Old Brompton Road, Harris's regular breakfast-and-supper joint run by Michael and Sheila van Bloeman, patrons of out-of-work young actors. Elizabeth was nineteen, the rest of the cast all under twenty-five, and Harris's seniority in years was an advantage he used unashamedly.

Revealingly, Harris didn't make much of this hugely ambitious venture in his home correspondence. Dermot Foley 'didn't know what the hell he was up to over there', and the friends of the College Players were not kept apprised of goings-on. As it turned out, the play opened and closed inside ten days. Audience and critical interest were minimal, and in one fell swoop all Harris's legacy was gone.

What followed was a rambling period of 'life in the gutter' that Harris has variously described as heaven and hell. At first he scrambled the 2s 6d-a-night rent for doss-house accommodation, then the van Bloemans gave him the marble counter of the Troubadour on which to lay his head. When the bitter spring weather chased him 'out of the freezer' he slept under piles of coats on the Embankment. Later he camped in doorways in Earl's Court, close to LAMDA where he was still studying, if haltingly. When he collapsed from hunger at the academy actor-singer Robert Young, another Troubadour hangout, offered him accommodation at his small flat in Nevern Place.

The compensation that kept him upright was the blooming of a love affair to end all love affairs. Within weeks of his meeting Elizabeth, she and Harris had become unofficially engaged. The attraction was obvious to all who knew him: not just Liz's beauty and intelligence, but the 'forbidden' air that hung about her – being, as an actor friend suggests, 'next door to royalty'. The friend remembers: 'Their friendship was unusually passionate. Dickie was always grand and demanding in his gestures, but she was also a strong, demanding woman. They should really have fought a lot more than they did – in fact, they shouldn't have survived one another – but like the best love stories, it just magically worked.'

Elizabeth Rees-Williams did not call on her father for support. Like Harris she was energetic and independent – if more doubtful of her future in theatre. She continued to audition widely and take what work she could get, all the time keeping half an eye on Harris's fortunes. 'From the beginning I think she adored him,' says theatre actor Godfrey Quigley, later a Harris co-star. 'Her career ambitions came second. *He* was the talent, and the personality, and the future.' Liz recalls the limbo period at the end of LAMDA without regret. The days of scurrying through dingy rooms, making whatever time they could together, were also days of 'making love, playing Stan Kenton records, and always reading. Sometimes Richard

worked on his poems. . . .' He also took time to introduce her
to Joyce and Yeats and the literary discoveries of his TB years.
Dylan Thomas was 'an obsession' and he read aloud to her
from *Under Milk Wood* and the poetry notebooks.

What Harris calls his 'starvation period' drew to a close
when Joan Littlewood and her Theatre Workshop Company
came into his life. What initially appeared like a chance one-off
job as a small-part actor in one of her productions was destined
to grow into a long educational relationship that would outstrip
LAMDA in every way. 'It was all down to luck,' Harris said.
'One lunchtime a friend had bought me a cider in a bar when I
heard two people talking in the cubicle behind us. They were
obviously theatricals, and one mentioned that Joan Littlewood
had not yet filled parts in a production. . . . That was enough
for me. I borrowed 4d for the telephone call and rang her.
She was out, but I spoke to the company's general manager,
Gerry Raffles.' Raffles said sorry, the part available was for a
fifty-year-old. But Harris wasn't so easily deterred. 'I *look* fifty,'
he swore – and Raffles smiled at the blarney and summoned
him to the Theatre Royal, Stratford East, where the Workshop
was based. Bertholt Brecht had trusted Littlewood with the first
production of his *Mother Courage* the year before at Barnstaple,
and its success had encouraged the rising Irish writer Brendan
Behan to give her *The Quare Fellow* which had already been
staged in Dublin. Littlewood cut the play considerably and the
result, a hard-hitting social commentary, had been a summer
hit at Stratford East. It was now transferring to the Comedy
Theatre for a bigger staging and Eric Ogle, playing Mickser,
had fallen out. Littlewood met Harris and cast him before he
auditioned. It wasn't just his Irishness, but his face had a
brazen cheek that *was* Mickser. And he had charm. The fee
was £15 a week.

The Quare Fellow is a strident, painful play abut the injustice
of capital punishment, and its power – and the notoriety it
sparked – called attention to all the principals at the Comedy
Theatre. Harris's part wasn't big – no more than fifty lines
in the middle of three verbose acts – but his enthusiasm
won Littlewood's admiration. 'His way with scripts makes
him special,' director Jim Sheridan says today. 'The way he
learns everyone's lines and intellectualizes it all. That energy is

always impressive.' Littlewood saw this energy and promised him work with the Theatre Royal group, which was actively acquiring new talent (at above Equity rates!) for the coming season.

By Christmas 1956 Harris had around him the framework of career and domestic bliss. He had the hopes of the Theatre Workshop and the £6 a week it might yield, the hint of professional acceptance – and a beautiful and sophisticated fiancée. But it wasn't plain sailing. He had to tackle his parents and, much trickier, the Ogmores for their marriage blessing. At Christmas he took Elizabeth home to Ireland for the first time. Milly approved of her breeding, while disdaining her Protestant upbringing. In her memoir *Love, Honour and Dismay* (London, 1976) Elizabeth records nothing of the marriage discussions beyond the general remark that neither Richard's family nor his friends cared at all about his London hopes.

Back in London Harris finally tackled the Ogmores, a formal rite of proposal he had been dreading. He borrowed a suit, a clean shirt, a tie and a pair of shoes. But, in his version, he could find no one to lend him socks. The ensuing meeting with Lord and Lady Ogmore was memorable for Harris's attempts to keep his trouser legs tugged hard down, lest the true extent of his poverty be revealed. Lady Ogmore gave 'a sort of wail of despair' when the springtime marriage plan was announced, and Lord Ogmore made it clear that Harris could not marry his daughter until he could afford to keep her. The option of calling on Limerick for help was really no option; Harris didn't even try. Instead he bragged about his imminent breakthrough and kept smiling. His legendary charm, and his gusto, swayed the Ogmores and it probably helped that he was cast again, by Peter Brook and playwright Arthur Miller no less, in the background of *A View from the Bridge*.

In spite of religious bickering, the wedding went ahead as scheduled on 7 February 1957 at the Church of Notre Dame in Leicester Square. There was a reasonable Harris family turn-out but Ivan didn't come, sending instead £25 as a honeymoon gift. The reception ranks – there were three hundred people in all – were ably filled out by the Ogmores and their friends, and the House of Lords venue emphasized the financial ironies of Harris's life. The Ennis Road neighbours who had seen the couple at Christmas saw not a struggling, nervous actor and his bride, but rather two Hollywoodites. Helen Fahy, who lived in a flat that overlooked the Harris's house, recalls: 'Elizabeth had the clothes of a starlet and silken blonde hair, and Dickie strutted like the world belonged to him. They were a fairytale couple in our eyes, a dream come true.'

In truth, wedded life was every bit as hard as what had gone before. Conjuring money from thin air, they rented a bed-sitter in Paddington which was shared with an out-of-work Irish actor, Donal Donnelly. When Liz found rep work in Blackpool they abandoned the flat and Harris temporarily moved in with the Ogmores in Queen's Gate. At the lowest ebb Liz came into a small inheritance which she immediately invested in a short lease on an Earl's Court maisonette above an underwear shop. It was draughty but roomy, and cost £6 10s a week. Harris knew they could never continue to pay the rent unless he found regular work, so he knocked on Littlewood's door until she took him, as promised, at £6 per week. Still, their outgoings were in excess of £8 and now, to complicate matters, Liz was pregnant. Harris never stopped smiling. 'It was', according to Joe Lynch, 'achievement delirium'. Even today, Harris's close acquaintances will tell you, small encouragements and victories can inspire him to near-hysterical optimism, just as marginal negativity can plunge him into despair. 'Harris's happiness is particularly infectious,' says Lynch. 'You don't really have a choice with him. When he's on top the whole world shares it. You just have to give in to him when he's on a run.' Harris's 'run' was winning Elizabeth, the conquest of London and now, vitally, Littlewood.

Joan Littlewood's Workshop group was the perfect garden for Harris's career to take root in. Littlewood herself was a sizeable rebel, London-educated, Manchester-grown, banned from the BBC and ENSA, the armed forces entertainments branch, for her leftist political opinions. She had started in street theatre, then developed the Workshop with her life-long partner, Gerry Raffles, in 1945. In 1953 the Workshop had taken over the Theatre Royal in the unfashionable East End and Littlewood moved to the classics, in some of which she starred as well as directed. Two years later international acknowledgement of her achievement in establishing a quality 'off Broadway' London theatre came with an invitation to the Theatre of Nations festival in Paris. Over the next ten years three of her shows won the coveted Best Production Award. Her style, and the dictates of the Workshop, were specific. The spectrum was broad, and not favouring the Establishment. She liked innovation, Brecht, music hall, social commitment, song and dance. It was a potent blend, instantly palatable to Dickie Harris. Here he could flex that duality of character, the masculine/feminine seesaw that he had first exercised with Betty Brennan. Here he could laugh aloud and chant his Ink Spot songs – and get paid for it. Here he could be himself.

Once over the hurdle of getting into the Workshop group, Harris stopped dead. 'Joan Littlewood was marvellous,' he later said. 'She taught me everything there is to know about acting. But it was frustrating convincing her to give me the big parts. For a long time I was lost in the wings somewhere. And that wasn't me. I didn't like hanging around.' In September Littlewood cast Harris in her radical modern dress version of *Macbeth*, booked for a tour of Zurich and Moscow. Harris wrote gaily home to Limerick describing a major career breakthrough. Milly, Harmay and the brothers were electrified to hear that Dickie was already doing Shakespeare on the London stage. Quite possibly they had visions of him in neon lights, playing Macbeth or Macduff. Harris later told *Profile* magazine: 'I thought: Shakespeare, this is it! This is really it. So I wrote to all my friends in Ireland: You must come. . . . Come, come, I said. Everybody come. Mother, father, brothers, aunts, the rats from the firm. Be up there in the front! . . .'

Harris had a handful of lines as Ross, appearing briefly in four scenes. The dishonour, as he described it to *Profile*, was unbearable. In his Limerick-coloured version the Thane of Ross had not four scenes but four lines: 'I had to walk down, say these four lines, wave my arm, go off stage right. So Harris is standing at the back, all dressed up in uniform and sword. Suddenly my cue comes and I pick up the sword . . . but I can't remember a line. And I can hear my mother in the front say, "Isn't he marvellous!"'

After the try-out *Macbeth*[1] left for Zurich where, in Gerry Raffles's account, it was met 'with cheers and boos'. Moscow proved better but the general response was hostile and, for a first-time touring actor, disconcerting. When they came home Littlewood cheered up Harris by casting him immediately in *You Won't Always Be on Top*, an early Angry Young Man effort by a Hastings builder's labourer, Henry Chapman. The play was a raunchy, adlibbed diatribe that seemed innocuous at the time but was to have after-shock consequences the next year. It was about this time that James Booth joined Littlewood on a regular basis. He recalls seeing Harris in *You Won't Always Be on Top* and being impressed by 'an unquestionable presence'. Booth was so taken by him that he brought his friend, the ICM (International Creative Management) agent John McMichael, to see Harris. Although McMichael admired the show, no immediate relationship was formed; years later, however, McMichael became Harris's manager and a superb career navigator.

Harris was busy, earning much more than a freelance small-part actor, but as Christmas approached he and Elizabeth were all but starving. They hocked their wedding presents to pay for food, but Harris rejected the gentle suggestions of his new London friends to give up. He had heard that the American producer-actor Lee Strasberg had seen *The Quare Fellow* and called his performance 'The sharpest impact I have received from an English [*sic*] actor during my stay.' This was encouragement galore to keep his momentum. Immersed in Stanislavsky, he was pushing all the time to impress Littlewood and Gerry Raffles and, as ever, losing patience. 'He really could be a bastard,' says Booth unapologetically. 'He had a chip on his shoulder that told you *he* was the future star. He was contentious. I think it went back to his childhood. If he was a school dunce – and this was probably the dyslexia he later learned about – he was probably sick and tired of being bashed for it and covering up. When you fail and fail and get admonished for things you develop great insecurities. I believe this was the core of Harris's aggravation attitude at that time.

[1] Sean Connery was among those offered major roles with the touring *Macbeth*. He turned it down, preferring to concentrate on his film opportunities.

It was more than unhappiness with his lot. It was a childhood problem rearing its head.' Another friend believes, 'It was the frustrations of a suppressed Irish home life that made him crazy at times. He didn't talk about his father, but I had the feeling there was a tension there that sprouted wings.'

If Harris fought with his peers, he also bit the hand that fed him at Stratford East. He was deeply respectful of Littlewood and Raffles, but he wasn't beyond arguing with them. In one incident, warmly recalled by all, Harris ended up dumping a sack of cement on Littlewood's head. 'But mostly he was well behaved with her,' says Booth. 'He had to be, because she held the keys to his future.' Finally Littlewood got the message: Mickser, as he was now known, had had enough of spear-carrying. She granted him a lead role in a forthcoming trial piece.

Harris was horrified, 'I thought to myself, Christ, anything but this! This was a terribly *Britishy* piece of casting, not at all me. I could do accents, sure. But this one was drawing-room *Eeenglish*. I sweated and worried and I didn't think I could pull it off. I went to Joan and said, "I cannot do this." And she heard me out very impassively and said, "Come to the theatre on Monday, alone."'

When Harris arrived as bidden Littlewood, seated in the stalls, told him to strip naked on stage. He did as instructed. She then told him to 'clothe yourself in the character'. As Peter Hay records in his *Theatrical Anecdotes* (London 1989), Littlewood's genius was that of director as psychologist: 'If she thinks an actor needs putting down she'll put him down. But she won't come the boss-director on you. She is always saying, Don't let yourself be *produced*!'

Harris found the experience of performing naked 'liberating'. Apart from artistic release he had always been, in an un-Irish way, comfortable with his nudity. Manuel Di Lucia recalls Kilkee skinny-dipping. Actor John Phillip Law, who co-starred in the Sri Lankan jungle with Harris on Bo Derek's *Tarzan, the Ape Man*, speaks of Harris's 'brazen resistance to trousers and underpants. It was quite amazing: all of us in our Brooks Brothers jungle wear and Richard appearing for lunch with his business hanging out all over the place . . . and him constantly drawing attention to it, saying, "Excuse my balls, it's just such a lovely day . . .!"' During the Littlewood exercise, says Harris, he experienced 'a turning point, a feeling of getting in touch with the heart of being an actor'.

The rite of passage led to his major casting in Edgar de Rocha Miranda's *And the Wind Blew* – 'a crease-browed, costumey thing that was quite dull,' says James Booth. In Gerry Raffles's diary of the era it was 'a magnificent theme . . . but failed to bring us an audience and nearly closed us down'. After it, by way of compensation, Littlewood put Harris in the romantic lead in the Pirandello classic *Man, Beast and Virtue*. This, in real terms, was to be the turning point. An actor friend recalls: 'You have to understand that many if not most of the Workshop people, like acting groups everywhere, failed in terms of "star" status. That's not to say they didn't want to achieve it. I believe ninety per cent of the people who join groups like Joan's *want* celebrity. They have dreams of going to the top, up to join Olivier . . . and Marilyn Monroe. So they mostly fail. But Harris didn't. He broke through fast. Partly because his timing was good. It was good to be Irish in London then, with Behan and all that happening. As well as that, he had an urban working-class toughness that was coming into fashion. His great fortune was getting noticed so quickly by TV. That's what led to the movie break.' James Booth feels: 'It was inevitable that he'd make the next step into TV and a wider audience. He was so bloody-minded and ferocious about it. He wanted it. And he was not without talent, let's remember. His talent was, in my opinion, that blend of two things: that thug-with-a-steel-bender's face combined with a great Irish intellectual soul. You saw Harris outside the Railway pub and you thought, "What a heavy!" You had a quiet drink with him and heard all his romantic talk and you thought, "This guy has a lot of depth."'

Harris was appearing in Pirandello at the Lyric Theatre, Hammersmith, at Christmas when his TV chance came. It was, he told *Woman's Own* in 1965, a depressing time, despite all the momentary successes with Littlewood. He had come to London, he said, 'determined to find my crown', but the poverty was destroying him. It can't have helped that the word from Limerick in Milly's letters was equally grim: the mill was rapidly failing. Rank had been 'ghost-labelling' Harris flour for years and now Rank, smelling imminent collapse, was attempting a takeover. Neither Jimmy nor Ivan had managed to divert the prospect of a total disaster, though they were working at the mill from dawn till dusk. Clearly there was no going back for Dickie Harris . . . but how bounteous was the future? The question had added urgency because of Liz's pregnancy and the prospect of a new mouth to feed.

'My favourite flower is the rose,' said Harris. 'Because to pluck it you risk bleeding. When I was cast in *Man, Beast and Virtue* . . . out of the torment of my private worries I poured my whole soul into the part.' Harris was Paulino, the first real casting that gave him scope and opportunity. He played it, Booth recalls, 'over the top'. Clifford Owen, the London-born director who had had TV successes with *Guinea Pig* and *Johnny Belinda* and who was destined to go on to movie celebrity as a feature director with Morecambe and Wise and *Steptoe*, was in the first-night audience. He was struck by Harris's booming passion and his Irishness. Owen had been commissioned to direct the first play of Irish-based actor-author Joseph O'Conor, called *The Iron Harp*, for Granada TV. It was a talkative, sub-Behan piece about the IRA, set during the 'Troubles'. Owen had already contracted a number of leading Irish players in London, among them Donal Donnelly and Maureen Connell, but he had yet to cast the blind IRA 'hero' Michael O'Riordan. Instantly, from the stalls of the Lyric, he knew he had found his man. He visited Harris's dressing room and invited him to an interview at the Warwick Street offices of Granada TV next day.

Harris broke into the gas meter at home for the bus fares across London. He was kept waiting an hour, and was pent-up and edgy when Owen finally faced him. 'I don't know why it is that so many producers and directors treat actors like Hogarthian puppets,' Harris ranted in the director's face. Owen liked the aggression. He smiled through the meeting, gave Harris the script of *The Iron Harp* to read and made an offer on the spot: it would be the standard top actor TV drama fee – 55 guineas, plus 22 guineas to cover rehearsals. Of a cast of fifteen, only three performers, all far more widely experienced, received higher fees (Robert Urquhart, the star, was paid 150 guineas, plus 24 guineas rehearsal). Harris pretended to ignore the money and addressed the script instead. 'Cliff told me afterwards that I came into his room as though I was weighed down by all the crosses and cares of the world,' Harris said to *Woman's Own*. 'And certainly that day I felt as if I were [but] my mood changed when I read the script. . . . This was something I could believe in.' Harris was signed; so, with his recommendation, was James Booth – though Booth's part was way down the cast list, with just one good scene opposite Harris.

Rehearsals for *The Iron Harp* were conducted at the Mahatma Gandhi Hall off Fitzroy Square on Sunday, 16 March 1957; then the group took a train to Manchester for further rehearsals on the Monday. On Tuesday a full-dress camera rehearsal took place, and Harris's performance – amid the technical maze of TV for the first time – was, according to Booth, 'relaxed and totally at home'. Booth elaborates: 'Mickser liked to preen and pose. He was the one actor who spent half the day performing for himself in the mirror. His big take-off was Brando: he was always doing Brando in the mirror, directing himself like a movie director. When it came to doing TV he was ready. The camera merely became the mirror, and he did his performance for himself. Like posing for photographs, Mickser had a great love affair with himself, and that's a good starting point for TV stars.'

On Wednesday the play was transmitted live at prime time from Studio 6 of the Manchester TV Centre, and Richard Harris's face was flashed across the nation. His part was weighty, but Cliff Owen's gamble paid off. The crew clapped when the tapes stopped rolling.

It was the *Daily Mirror* that first paid due attention to an emerging international star. For columnist Richard Shear, the play was 'an intensely moving document of human beings caught up in war'. The central relationship between an English prisoner and his blind IRA guard who, against all the odds, become friends transfixed Shear. And Richard Harris was the reason why. 'His was a first-class performance, rich with the tenderness of O'Conor's words.' In another column the *Mirror* advised its readers to watch out for Richard Harris. 'He is regarded by Granada as a real find – and they have given him the chance to jump from obscurity to stardom.'

Harris read the notices with relish and took Elizabeth out to celebrate when he got back to London. For five days' work he had earned £80 – more than ten times the Workshop rate. That was wonderful and inspirational, as were the looks of recognition and admiration from strangers in the street.

4

Heaven and Hell-raising

The overflowing legend of Hell-raiser Harris, so efficiently broadcast by Richard Harris himself for thirty years, had its origins in his childhood. It was not, as many have suggested, a PR creation of false but marketable Errol Flynnery. Rather he was, as Dermot Foley and his school chums insist, 'born to be wild'. In his early teens his nickname 'Prince Dick' owed as much to his attention-grabbing antics as to the supposed wealth of the Harris clan. 'He was', says Foley, 'incorrigible. If there was trouble to be found, Harris found it.' The Ringroses, Limerick neighbours and friends, recall the horror of the turkey that disappeared on Christmas Eve. And Harris himself admits to stealing the West of Ireland Tennis Championship cup on the eve of the final. When his father found it behind a chair in the parlour he exploded in rage and told his son to give it back. Harris planted it in the loo at Cruise's Hotel and rang Williams Street police station anonymously. This kind of mischief won him attention, but regularly misfired. 'Dickie sailed close to the wind,' says a friend. 'And all he was really scared of was making Ivan angry. The family tolerated his larking around – but there were limits. Once he was arrested for being drunk and disorderly in town and was taken to Williams Street police station. After a caution he was released, but the local press carried the story of "Harris Mills son arrested". This was despite his pleas to them not to run it. Ivan read the story and went mad. Dickie never forgave the newspaper for what happened. I don't know if Ivan ever forgave Dickie for the public embarrassment.'

But Harris couldn't help himself. 'He liked the fun,' says Charlie St George. 'And he took the risks that went with it.' He also spoofed the fun when fun was absent. At the start of the fifties his adoration of Merle Oberon extended to embrace numerous, usually dark-haired, visions of Hollywood pulchritude. Among them was Rita Gam, a gorgeous stage actress who had just broken through in Hollywood, acting opposite Ray Milland in *The Thief*. Gam's screen presence was unsubtle but dynamic and Harris was instantly smitten. She was glamour with a raunchy edge, the combination he adored. Limerick's connections with Hollywood were non-existent and Harris can never have hoped actually to *meet* any of his heroines there. But when the one-in-a-billion chance happened he capitalized on it.

Rita Gam was returning to New York from a European promotional tour when her plane was diverted to Shannon with engine failure. Gam decided to spend a day shopping and Harris found her – by the sheerest fluke – ambling up O'Connell Street. Bold as brass, he immediately asked her to join him for coffee at Cruise's.

Jack Donnelly was bewildered, but he knew his pal Dickie well enough not to bother challenging the request to 'Lay it all on: food, cakes, drinks, whatever it takes.' Gam was bowled over by the munificence of this apparently out-of-work Limerick lad. But Harris had an ulterior motive. 'I excused myself and slipped away and rang a pal [Dermot Foley] and asked him to get down there with a camera.'

Dermot obliged and 'bumped into' his pal taking tea with the Hollywood star. Next day the *Limerick Leader* had a visit from Harris. Earl Connolly, a journalist there, recalls: 'Dickie came in and plonked these pictures on the desk. Here, says he, is a Hollywood exclusive: Rita Gam and her Limerick companion.'

Later, in Charlie St George's, Harris observed with fascination how the gossip grew . . . 'And every so often I threw in a new angle myself just to keep the interest alive'. Harris's ace angle was the hint that he had, in fact, slept with Gam. 'The whole of Limerick soon knew about my sex frolics with this big star,' he says. But the gag backfired. 'Here was I spoofing all the glorious details. And then Dermot Foley confronts me and says, Harris you're a liar. You're telling the world you slept with her on such-and-such a day and you didn't, couldn't have. Because at that time she was in [Foley's] chemist shop buying sanitary towels!'

In London in the immediate aftermath of *The Iron Harp* Harris encountered a new and alluring perspective on trouble-making. The October production of *You Won't Always Be on Top* had attracted good audiences, but it also attracted the interest of the Lord Chamberlain's office – the Government censor. In the course of preparing this down-to-earth play about brickies, Littlewood had despatched the cast to real building sites, urging them to beef up on the proper lingo. Harris loved the task and had given what many rated as his finest stage performance to date as Mick, a dirty-faced navvy. The Lord Chamberlain's office allowed no script 'additions' once a play had been cleared for production and the adlibs were, in effect, unpreviewed extras. On 31 October and 1 November a representative from the department attended showings of the play and, as a result, Harris, Joan Littlewood, Gerry Raffles and theatre licensee John Bury were visited by detectives in January 1958 and statements were taken. It all seemed like a preposterous joke to Harris, who was used to an uncensored (Ivan and Milly apart) existence. But Littlewood knew what was coming. Establishment values were so far unshaken by rebel British theatre: the spiralling success of the Workshop was a red rag to the Lord Chamberlain's office.

On Wednesday 16 April, just days after his TV screen hit, Harris, along with Littlewood, writer Henry Chapman, Bury and Raffles, was charged at West Ham Magistrates Court with a breach of the peace. The charge read that they had: 'Unlawfully for hire presented parts of a new stage play . . . before such parts had been allowed by the Lord Chamberlain contrary to Section 15, Theatres Act 1843'. The maximum penalty was £500 for each of the two performances seen and charged against, plus closure of the theatre. Harris's amusement turned to fury. Defiantly, along with the others, he spoke of his proud 'guilt', declaring a commitment to support Littlewood in changing the antiquated rules of modern theatre. A Defence Fund was launched by Raffles and an open letter appeared in *The Stage*, signed by the group's champions, Frith Banbury, Richard Findlater, Peter Hall, the Earl of Harewood, Wolf Mankowitz, Kenneth Tynan and Henry Sherek. West

End actors flooded to the court building to offer support, and Harris, ignited with the tumult of encouragement, quietly waved his fists at the Establishment.

In court, to a packed gallery, Ian Smith for the prosecution told how the plot itself had been altered from the text submitted to the Lord Chamberlain's Office; the third and final act was, in effect, new. The London *Times* reported Smith isolating 'a scene outside a building bearing the word "Gentlemen" in which a character called Mick made a speech in which he appeared to be opening the building. During this speech he altered his voice and the accent was taken as being an imitation of what Sir Winston Churchill would have said if he had been called upon to open a public lavatory.' Mr Smith concluded that this interpretation was 'vulgar and not in good taste'. For the defence Gerald Gardiner QC and Harold Lever MP, who both appeared without fees, explained that, 'In this play they tried to build up a realistic scene. . . . These five persons have no money. The actors receive only £2 to £8 a week and the Company, which is limited to non-profit making, is overdrawn in the bank.' There was no implied apology in the guilty pleas, Mr Gardiner indicated. The only reason his clients admitted guilt was that they acknowledged the law of England that prohibited theatrical free speech.

Joan Littlewood appeared as the sole defence witness. She stated that: 'The plot was weak but the thing that won us to it was that for the first time in England I saw written down without taste or discrimination the simple expression of working men on a building site on a wet Monday morning. For the first time I heard the speech of the English people put down with such beauty and simplicity as I've never heard it before.' This beauty and simplicity was not sampled by the magistrate, but he accepted the guilty pleas unceremoniously and translated them into modest fines. Raffles and Bury were each fined £5, with £2 9s 11d costs against Raffles. Littlewood was fined £1 with costs, and Chapman and Harris given conditional discharges on payment of 11s 6d costs each. At the 'victory' celebration in the bar of the Theatre Royal in Angel Lane afterwards there was standing room only. By its brazen action the Lord Chamberlain's office had resoundingly tilted public opinion in favour of Littlewood and the rebellious stance of the Theatre Workshop. Never before had the Workshop attracted such press and public attention, nor found so many friends from one humble production. More than £150 was raised by the Defence Fund and its treasurer, Wayland Young, offered to return the surplus; but the wheel had started to turn, so the cash went into the formation of the Censorship Reform Committee which met for the first time, within days, at the Royal Court.

In the Angel Lane bar Harris accepted the congratulations with a mixture of gratitude and intrigue. Sipping beer, he told journalist Peter Kinsley, 'It was an underhand way they did it. The remarks were just asides, at the back of the stage. The audience loved it. I think it is just a question of evil in the eye of the beholder.' The play's author, Henry Chapman, disagreed, believing the adlibbing should not have happened. But Harris stood his ground and chatted easily with the journalists, befriending them as he had befriended Earl Connolly on the *Limerick Leader*, and as he would do with many journalists throughout his life.

The row gave Harris his first national news coverage and his photograph appeared, smiling gamely between Littlewood and Chapman, all over the press. The controversy, and the gossip that followed, was extremely beneficial, serving as it did to circulate the Harris breakthrough further. In a matter of weeks he was, by dint of one TV play and a minor controversy, known and discussed throughout the land. Still flat broke (*The Iron Harp* didn't clear his debts), he was at least being asked for his autograph. And Fleet Street had pencilled in his home phone number and the hacks called in the evenings, asking about Liz and the baby and the future.

Harris was too busy to realize exactly how lucky he was. As the court case ran he was appearing as George Bernard Shaw in Littlewood's weak production of *Love and Lectures*. The Theatre Royal was busier than it had ever been, the audiences more receptive – and big offers were coming in. In May the Bristol Old Vic took him for a short spell playing Tommy Ledou alongside Peter O'Toole in James Forsyth's *The Pier*, a production remarkable only for the beginning of a lifelong friendship with O'Toole . . . and the alcoholic binges the Irishmen shared. Harris has described this period as 'golden days. We kept each other up half the time. It was days of chat and yarn-spinning and great boozing.' At one point Harris and O'Toole had refined their drinking schedule with a precision that allowed them to leave the theatre for a 'booze intermission down at the local'. Harris tells of being interrupted by a breathless stage-hand who dashed into the pub to remind them they were running late. He and O'Toole leapt up. O'Toole out-ran him to the theatre, sped through the backstage door, past the nail-biting crew, on to the stage . . . and fell face-first into the audience. A woman in the front row sniffed his toxic breath and whinged, 'My God, he's drunk!'

O'Toole leered: 'Wait till you see the other fella.'

Drinking was by now Harris's main pastime. 'But no more than many scrounging actors,' says James Booth. 'Harris had a good capacity for booze – but I wasn't far behind. I think he liked the way drink loosened his and other people's inhibitions. And there was the Irish tradition thing too, all the late-night get-togethers for tales from home. That's probably what he shared with O'Toole, who was born in Connemara.' Harris told writer Tony Crawley: 'I never touch a drop when I'm happy.' But he added, 'It's a well-known fact that Irishmen are never happy.'

Booth eloquently describes life in Angel Lane, aflow with louts and literati attempting to make their way. The railway station next door maintained the non-stop pulse of reality and those who were out of work congregated to cadge fruit from the market stall-holders outside. Faustian deals were made and forgotten, borrowed clothes disappeared with the borrower, songs were sung, girls made pregnant, careers billowed and folded.

Suddenly Harris was beyond all this. Elizabeth was due to give birth in August, and Harris's paternal concern sent him scouting for a film agent to pump up his cash flow. By freak chance he was sitting in hotshot Jimmy Fraser's office, stating his case with Stanislavskian sincerity, when Bob Lennard, casting director for Associated British Pictures – the British equivalent of, say, MGM – called. Lennard had spoken to Harris after the transmission of The Iron Harp and predicted good offers in movies. Now he was testing the grapevine, sounding the views of quality agents like Fraser. Fraser saw his moment and told Lennard *he* was representing Harris. Lennard immediately suggested a seven-year contract, at £30 a week. Harris hesitated, but Fraser set up further meetings and talked turkey with his new find. ABPC was more than a fat meal ticket. At that time Maggie Smith, Tony Hancock, Sylvia Syms, Millicent Martin and Richard Todd were on its contact books. To top it all, an offer was being made of a featured role in *Alive and Kicking*, a wholesome slice of Ealing-type confectionery that would be sampled worldwide. According to pal Ronald Fraser, Harris hated the notion of a long-term contract that might anchor him in movie mediocrity; but the money was too good to refuse. Liz comes straight to the point on his major reasons for signing with ABPC: 'We realized that we'd have to start thinking of a life insurance policy for Damian's education, so Richard took the contract.'

Harris applied himself to his first movie-making challenge with more emphasis on the studio-posed publicity that attempted to 'soften' him to decent middle-market acceptability than on character acting. Which was fair enough, since his role as the lover (opposite blonde Olive MacFarland) was incidental and required just a day or two's work at Associated British Studios and on Scottish location. *Alive and Kicking* was an 'old people' twist on the same Studios' *It's Great to Be Young*; essentially *It's Great to Be Old*, with old-timers Sybil Thorndike, Estelle Winwood and Kathleen Harrison playing mischievous residents of a retirement home who break out, hop on a boat to a remote island and set up an internationally successful knitting industry. Conservatively mounted by producer Victor Skutezky and director Cyril Frankel, the fizz of the comedy is low-key with Estelle Winwood alone stepping beyond smug granny-playing to provide a second-layer wit. Harris hardly registers, apart from giving a broadly attractive macho presence to one or two short scenes, and none of the reviews mentioned him. *Films and Filming* noted that the movie was over-sentimental but went on: 'The movie is as fresh as *Genevieve* in its day, and we wish it the same international box-office and prestige success.'

Such a success would hardly have helped Harris, who knew the casting was wrong, albeit half-hearted. Politely but firmly he let Lennard and the executives at ABPC know his feelings:

he had studied Stanislavsky and was expert at improvisation; he was reading Shakespeare and studying the classics; he was born to play rebellious key parts.

By Harris's own admission and the frank confessions of Elizabeth's writings and interviews, Harris's flamboyant nature, fuelled in equal measure by success and frustration, now became pronounced. The relative wealth of the ABPC contract changed their Earl's Court lifestyle. Where once they had lived on 'a stew made of Oxo cubes and carrots', in rooms that boasted only a solitary king-size bed as furniture, now there was money for minor luxuries. In a matter of weeks Harris paid off many of his debts, decorated their flat – and extended his 'entertaining circle'. The hangers-on syndrome, noticeable since LAMDA, went out of all proportion to his wealth, influence or achievement. People 'crashed in' to the family flat weekly and – baby or not – the living room vied with the Angel Lane bar for business. In drink he liked to brawl, and the nose broken first on the Young Munster rugby pitch was now broken and reset with unusual regularity. 'Curiously enough,' says a journalist, 'he liked the company of journalists best. Maybe they're the best boozers, I don't know. But he always seemed to have some old hack drinking with him. And then, at the end of the night, they'd be slugging it out in the gutter over a dispute about Joyce, or the IRA, or the future of theatre. . . .'

Harris found the routine of drawing money for nothing from ABPC undignified and emasculating. Never lazy (when I asked him once what he most abhorred he almost spat: 'Laziness!'), he was irritated by the dullness of domestic life and the lack of taxing intellectual endeavour. He continued to go to the theatre and the movies but he was not (and isn't today) a relaxed fifty-row-from-the-rear audience. He wanted action, and scary challenge.

A brief vogue for IRA-sympathetic movies reanimated him. His agent Jimmy Fraser came up with a cracking loan-out offer, shooting for a United Artists picture in Ireland from September to November. The movie was *Shake Hands with the Devil*, sub-*Odd Man Out*, but equally ambitious. Harris's would be a minor role, tenth billing, but above stalwarts Ray McAnally and Noel Purcell. The real attraction was the calibre

of the script, and the lead casting. James Cagney, toughie
pin-up of the Savoy and the Lyric, was to star, along with
Don Murray and a beautiful newcomer, Dana Wynter. The
director was Michael Anderson, then internationally hot with
a string of hits like *The Dam Busters* (1954) and *Around the World
in Eighty Days* (1956).

Disengaged from the Theatre Royal but keeping in touch
with the goings-on in bi-weekly booze-ups, Harris was relieved
to be busy again. With Liz and Damian he flew to Dublin and
joined the heavyweight cast at Ardmore Studios, Ireland's
ambitious new Hollywood-oriented venture. *Shake Hands* was
Anderson's baby (his own production company, Troy Films,
had developed the script from Rearden Conner's novel), and
from the start everyone was made aware of special high
hopes. Only once in recent history had an American international movie been staged in Ireland, and that movie, John
Ford's *The Quiet Man* (1953), had not had the advantage of
studio-basing and was, in fact, serviced and post-produced
outside Britain. *Shake Hands* would be the flagship that tested
Ardmore's viability and, hopefully, open the way to a string
of cost-effective American-Irish movies. The subject Anderson
chose to tickle American fancy was obvious, but not easy.

Born within earshot of Bow Bells, Anderson had served
his time with the Royal Corps of Signals and learned his Irish
history the English way. Despite that, *Shake Hands*, while being
mainly anti-violence in its message, had distinct moments of
pro-IRA sentiment. James Cagney, at that time fifty-four and
in semi-retirement on his New England ranch, had accepted
the movie because of its heart, and its finale, where love
conquers violence and politics. 'Brutality for its own sake
no longer interests me,' he told *Picturegoer* magazine. 'I turn
down about forty gangster roles a year . . . but this part is
different. It proves the uselessness of violence.' Despite the
message, even *Picturegoer* anticipated an anti-IRA backlash,
or an anti-movie backlash from the restless IRA. When questioned about these possibilities, Anderson would only sidestep
to the useful movieland exercises taught him by his recently
deceased mentor Mike Todd, producer of *Around the World
in Eighty Days*. The razzamatazz of publicity, good, bad or
suspenseful, was a positive plus. 'The main thing I learned

from Todd is *when* to blow your trumpet. Ballyhoo publicity
is important, but only if you've got something to shout about.'
And was the movie something to shout about? Anderson
seemed to think so. He had 'an embarrassment of talent.
The Irish Players from the Abbey Theatre are so good I don't
know how I'm going to stop them from pinching the picture.'
With Anderson's guidance *Picturegoer* went on to select the
best of the young talent, singling out Marianne Benet, John
Cairney, Harry Corbett and Ray McAnally. Harris was not
mentioned, though his part as IRA runner Terence O'Brien
was of reasonable importance.

Harris used his time at Ardmore to study the interaction
of departments on a big American-style movie – and to study
at close hand the ways of the stars. Cagney he found 'very
encouraging and free with advice. He moved like a butterfly,
which wasn't surprising of course because he had done all
those athletic musicals. But I was new and I needed advice
and he was a very generous man.' Cyril Cusack, Ireland's
most celebrated character actor, befriended Cagney easily too
and observed Harris attempting to cut his teeth. 'Harris was
immensely vibrant and active,' says Cusack, 'but I don't think
much was thought of him then, or indeed I don't think
he thought much of himself. He was quite loud and called
attention to himself by his manner, which was a habit of
bumping into people and things.' Cusack was charmed by the
Harris blarney, too. 'He told me a story which was very sweet,
but might well be apocryphal. Years before I was touring my
own company's production of *The Playboy of the Western World*.
It had never been seen in the provinces [of Ireland] and I was
very gratified to be bringing it. We played Limerick and Harris
told me that he was abed with TB but he crept out of bed,
against doctor's orders, and saw the play not once, but several
times. He said that that precipitated him into our profession.'
Cusack's eyes twinkle as he goes on: 'That was his story to
me at the time. He may well have omitted it since.'

Despite the IRA sympathies of the movie and the obsequi-
ous local press the paramilitaries were reported to have voiced
a certain antagonism by the unequivocal act of blowing up a
statue of the Lord Lieutenant of Ireland outside the Shelbourne
Hotel, temporary home of many of the movie's brass. Though

the report appeared in *Picturegoer* and in other papers, Cyril Cusack denies it vehemently. 'I'm not surprised it was alleged, but as far as I know nothing of the sort happened. I kept away from the business and the hype side of the movie – it never interested me. But, yes, the IRA characters depicted were of the heroic poet mould, which befitted the times and the type of the plot. That possibly did not find favour in certain communities. Mickey Anderson approached the film for its film story value and worked it well. That was my point of reference throughout.' Anderson, for his part, kept his head down for the duration of the nine-week shoot, avoiding press interviews.

Shake Hands with the Devil had been budgeted at £600,000, with a schedule that involved shooting in the Wicklow Hills and at St Michael's Lane in Dublin dockland as well as Ardmore. A total of 742 set-ups were required, and a complicated system of running relays to London for film processing and 'rushes' added to the problems of the film-makers. Nevertheless, Anderson brought his movie in on time and under budget, scoring the phase one business success that the Ardmore bosses, part-sponsored by the Irish government, had hoped for.

For Harris a hit was not make-or-break, but it was certainly desirable in terms of nudging ABPC and Lennard. As it turned out, the film was successful (though Cusack calls it 'not a first-rater'), and once again Harris sat back to observe the value of controversy. After a gala Dublin premiere attended by President Sean T. O'Kelly and, representing the Pennebaker production company, Mr and Mrs Marlon Brando Snr., the Northern Ireland authorities baulked at an uncensored screening in Ulster. The *Irish Independent* attended the Dublin opening and praised 'an exciting and dramatic movie' where 'the Irish case is presented with sympathy and understanding'. But the Belfast Corporation Police Committee called for a preview screening and recorded 'cheering' from a Unionist member when the plot synopsis detailing the execution of an IRA man was read out. On 18 June 1959 the Police Committee formally recommended the banning of *Shake Hands* in Ulster, just as it had recently forced the withdrawal of *Nudist Paradise* and the fleshy *Isles of Levant*. The effect emphatically increased interest in the film, and in a short time a censored version was on release and widely attended. Few write-ups about the movie did not hint at controversy, and Harris cannot have missed the further lessons of publicity. In truth, the straightforward thriller plot of a medical student (Don Murray) who becomes embroiled in IRA activities when his friend is killed in a skirmish is nothing other than light melodrama, played against a gritty uprising backdrop. The story might work just as well in any civil war setting and the philosophical messages, if any, are very gently delivered. The *Monthly Film Bulletin* found it ambitious, but ultimately 'the film has all too little to say'. *Films and Filming*, on the other hand, drew similarities with Ford's classic *The Informer* and hailed 'a notable achievement'. Both discussed the controversial background.

Harris' work on the film wasn't singled out, but he was impressively relaxed and Anderson liked him. Within months Anderson offered him another movie, this one with the kind of lead casting all young thespians dreamt about: opposite Charlton Heston and Gary Cooper in MGM's planned sea epic *The Wreck of the Mary Deare*.

First, though, came yet another clutch of stage opportunities. 'His loyalties weren't rigidly in favour of the Workshop,' says James Booth. 'He was too ambitious for that. No, call it arrogance. But he had this attraction to the basic *intelligence* of good stage-playing. His first go at movies was a rocky start. Many of us started with rocky movie beginnings, then went nowhere. So, on top of everything, he went back to the stage as a kind of security blanket.' Littlewood cast him in Frank Norman and Lionel Bart's Soho musical *Fings Ain't Wot They Used T'Be* in March 1959, playing a double role. His part was down the billing and considerably smaller than James Booth's, but the show sold to packed houses and was eventually transferred to the West End. 'He sang briefly on one of the numbers,' Booth remembers, 'but I wouldn't say his voice was great. He could sing, sure, but he wasn't a *singer*. What I remember more than anything about that time – apart from the boozing, that is – is his tendency for hypochondria. He was without doubt the worst hypochondriac I had ever met. It wasn't unusual for him to collapse on the floor screaming the house down, shouting, "It's a brain haemorrhage, for

Chrissake! I'm fucked! Get a doctor! Get an ambulance!"
Maybe it was a symptom of the drinking, I don't know. But
it also got him plenty of notice.'

After the musical Harris went straight into the revival of
John Marston's *The Dutch Courtesan* and, Booth observed, his
confidence as a performer was noticeably better than ever. 'If
the movie experience, and the cash, did anything, it urged him
to take more risks in his projection. I would say he became a
more commanding performer after his first film experience.'
He hesitates. 'It also made him a mighty pain in the arse.'
The Dutch Courtesan met mixed reviews ('When the cast have
looked at the script more carefully this play richly deserves a
transfer,' said *Plays and Players*) but was significant in Harris's
first appearance alongside Rachel Roberts, an inspired piece
of 'outside' casting.

The part in *The Wreck of the Mary Deare* was a supporting
lead, and a chance that Harris grabbed with both hands. Based
on the best-seller by Hammond Innes, it was very much a
three-man show, the story being a dispute about the salvage
of a cargo ship between Cooper and Harris, with Heston as the
hero in the middle. Eric Ambler adapted the book with Michael
Anderson, and the result is a powerfully faithful rendering
of the yarn with little concession to three-act movie-making.
Heston, later to be one of the Great Harris Antagonists in
Hollywood, started the movie at MGM Studios in California on
9 April, favouring the script but disliking Ambler's dialogue.
Cuts and rewrites ensued, and Cooper came aboard to enjoy
a good working partnership that lasted until the movie's
completion in June. In his notebooks Heston admits to a
competitive spirit, glumly recording serious misgivings when
he realized that 'This is Cooper's film.' Once that fact was
accepted, a long-lasting friendship was launched.

This warmth was not extended to Harris. As the proverbial greenhorn he was outside the top table invitations and
largely ignored by studio diplomats. In consequence, his long-
haul trip to Los Angeles and friendless arrival was slightly
depressing. Minimizing expense, the route chosen for the
Harrises' Hollywood debut (Liz accompanied him) was a hop-
and-skip turbo-prop jaunt that lasted forty-eight hours. They
arrived exhausted and uptight, to be greeted by an MGM

reception committee that was anything but sympathetic. As Liz tells it, she and Harris spent their days shuffling aimlessly around LA, trying to find their feet and establish the geography. The Studio had booked them into a motel that seemed reasonably plush and appropriate. But after a couple of re-orienting days it became clear that the motel was in the wrong part of town. The message from on high was clear: Richard Harris was an unknown quantity and part of no Hollywood tribe. He was an out-of-towner worthy only of minimal attention. The chance to shine was the only luxury being afforded to him.

Hollywood at the best of times is a steamy kitchen. Harris was used to the heat of battle and appeared to settle quite quickly. But Liz didn't. Rows began – aimless rows that articulated their separate tensions – and then Liz decided to go home. Harris kept his mind on the movie and sank his own fury in the aggravations of Cooper's regular bouts of illness which slowed down the production from time to time. The nightlife of Hollywood made little impression on him at this time; in Liz's absence, though, he was tempted to explore a little more.

Liz went home aboard the *Queen Elizabeth* where, according to her memoirs, she met and befriended 'a charming RAF officer'. She remained fauthful to her husband but, in her account, the threads of marriage now began to unravel. In the four-day voyage home she suddenly became aware of the weakness of their relationship. She had been living in the shadow of an aggressively ambitious man, voicing no opinions of her own, abandoning all her old friends, even her old, cherished habits. She no longer felt at ease with Harris, she said. Those who knew his destructive potential might have said she was scared of him. But, she wrote, it wasn't fear, just a certain wariness. Hollywood showed her their future; it gave her no reassurance.

Early in June *Mary Deare* moved to Elstree Studios in England and Heston and Cooper continued their closed-ranks friendship with dinners at the Guinea and the Piggy in Bruton Place and city sight-seeing. Harris continued to give his everything and, when the end result was observed, his efforts paid off. Given the disparity of experience, alongside Cooper's and

Heston's his work is remarkably assured. For their various reasons Heston and Harris liked the finished picture, but the popular verdict was unsure. None of the leading reviews mentioned Harris, although his part as Cooper's nemesis is eye-catching. The *Monthly Film Bulletin* limited praise to the movie's first half, while *Films Illustrated* reduced the whole thing to 'simply adventure for the masses'.

Associated British was pleased with Harris, but already he was aggressively voicing his restlessness with the seven-year deal. Payment of the weekly £30 was suspended whenever he worked in theatre, but he worked anyway, choosing to go to Paris in May with Littlewood's production of Behan's *The Hostage*, despite the fact that his part, according to James Booth, was 'next to nothing'. Says another actor, 'It was go-go-go for him and we were quite envious. But we knew his marriage was coming apart because of the pressures, so there was a downside to all this glamour.' Booth elaborates: 'The problem about Richard was that he picked on people. And when he started to get the big parts he picked on more people than ever and used more savage tactics. He was badly behaved at this time – to Liz more than anyone. I was kind of surprised the marriage was surviving at all.'

Without a rest Harris jetted back to Dublin – alone this time – for another IRA movie, *A Terrible Beauty*. Tay Garnett's film was an altogether lesser piece than Anderson's *Shake Hands*, though Harris's role was more visible and he had become, in Cyril Cusack's words, 'hard to miss'. Largely a two-fisted potboiler for Robert Mitchum, *A Terrible Beauty* was set during World War II and had an acutely pro-IRA plot that enraged many reviewers. *Films and Filming* attacked it fiercely, giving short shrift to Robert Mitchum and his co-star Dan O'Herlihy, and again ignoring Harris. 'The producers have miscalculated British audience reactions and in many halls their film will be received with a stony hostility camouflaged as a bored indifference.' Cyril Cusack, again playing the peace-loving man in the middle, remembers the production as 'altogether less structured than *Shake Hands*. We were on location more and the working relationships were less serene. It was a messy kind of picture that leaves a messy memory.' Friction between star Anne Heywood and her producer husband

Raymond Stross and, initially, between Harris and Mitchum made the production uncomfortable for many involved. Harris disliked Mitchum at first, but when the Hollywood star came to his rescue in a pub brawl they became best friends. 'Our relationship changed and we had a great time from then on.' Harris wasn't so sure of the end result, though, Cusack says, 'The title was appropriate. Very terrible, and not much of a beauty at all.' Harris told journalist Tony Crawley he viewed it as a complete dud. 'But actors have to learn some way, and you can learn from your mistakes.'

During the movie Liz attempted to revive their flagging relationship by paying a surprise visit to the location at Bray in Co. Wicklow. She was apprehensive and unsure of herself, undecided if she wanted to continue their marriage. By the time she arrived in Bray, Harris's friendship with Mitchum was thriving and his mood had eased. Instead of the rows she expected, there were comfortable days in the company of Bob and Dorothy Mitchum, dining, laughing and sharing Hollywood tales. Harris's relaxation wasn't surprising: in Mitchum he had at last found a Hollywood bigshot who treated him with the respect he felt he deserved.

By the end of 1959 Harris had four features to his credit and was up in the top-five billing, a considerable feat for a moody late-starter. He could boast Hollywood friendships and full pages in fan magazines, and the predictions of Big Success that had begun with a whisper in the Mirror were now an unstoppable welter. In Limerick, those of the Crescent gang who remained read about his progress in the tabloids with awe. Dermot Foley couldn't believe it: from street spoofing to movie-headlining alongside Bob Mitchum was too much to digest. Foley went to London to see with his own eyes. The friends met in Harris's new flat in Allen House, an upmarket block in Kensington. 'He was doing bloody all right,' says Foley, not concealing his surprise. 'My family were in the chemist's business so I sold him a few cameras. He was his usual devil-may-care self. His first producer was there and Harris was saying he wondered how long this was going to last. He said it might be three or four more pictures. But the producer reckoned he was lucky to pull off the first one!'

Sauntering through central London on a summer's afternoon, Harris bumped into Betty Brennan. They greeted each other with the unembarrassed ease of old, true friends. Betty was absorbed in her promised European Grand Tour, and loving it. Harris, she found, was the fun-seeking, confident Dickie of old. The difficulties of his home life that were already leaking into the press were unknown to her. 'He was just as out-going and optimistic. We had a chat just like old times, and a kiss, and said goodbye. He was doing well and I felt delighted for him.'

Others saw the flipside of the coin. Godfrey Quigley, the Irish actor-producer who championed Dublin's Globe Theatre group, the Abbey's main competitor, enjoyed a companionable afternoon's drinking with Harris but was surprised by what followed. 'I drank hard myself in those days and I suppose we were both the worse for wear. We went back to the flat in Allen House and Liz was there being the good and kindly wife but obviously uncomfortable, to say the least, by our state on arrival. She made some cynical remark, justifiably I'd say, and Dickie lifted up a wardrobe . . . *and threw it at her*! He was – and remains – a great character, a greatly generous character. But he had a temper you wanted to avoid.'

Indecision racked Harris. In the opinion of those close to him, that duality of character so often commented on was rearing its head again: the home-loving poet wanted Liz and the steady, unchallenging life of a wage-earning dad; the talent-possessed hard man wanted far horizons. As ABPC offered endless routine B pictures Harris became querulously evasive, turning everything down. There were those who believed his manner would estrange the mainstream movie moguls and his career would be ruined. Instead, at the watershed, he found a stage play that set London on fire and won the eye of a brilliant emerging film director, Lindsay Anderson.

5

Gingerly on the Bounty

The Ginger Man was a battering-ram of the new wave theatre movement that resoundingly won the case for Harris's
lead-playing talent and also brought him to the verge of a
nervous breakdown. Harris actively hunted the part, sensing
an Irish play to outstrip Behan. Set designer Tony Walton,
then married to Julie Andrews, mounted the production with
director Philip Wiseman, and both felt Harris was right for the
secondary part of O'Keefe, but not the lead. The final decision
was not theirs, but author J. P. Donleavy's. As actor Ronald
Fraser tells it, Donleavy 'was a fussy bugger who wanted
every comma, every full stop perfectly rendered'. Donleavy
was unsure of Harris, but Harris screamed in his face: '*I am
the Ginger Man! You cannot cast anyone else.*' Irish-educated
and offbeat in all his views, Donleavy finally agreed to the
casting. Years later Harris was still proclaiming his right to
the part: so much of the Ginger Man's life and plight was
his own . . . right down to the strains of a mixed-religion
marriage to an upper-crust girl. Ronald Fraser was also cast
by Donleavy and started rehearsals optimistically, looking
forward keenly to a projected six-month run. 'But it was
difficult right from the start. There were these awful rows.
Richard was trying to manhandle himself into the part, taking
it very, very seriously, and then he would explode and say,
"I can't do it! I can't do it!" – and storm out. I was sent to
retrieve him from the pub, since I was the one they knew
he'd listen to.' Fraser chuckles: 'It had its advantages. Dear
old Dick introduced me to my drink then – vodka, lime and
soda!' An actor adds: 'Philip Wiseman was a lovely man, but
he couldn't for the life of him *direct*. It was hard on Richard,

it was hard on everyone, but perhaps the adversity brought the best out.'

In *The Ginger Man* Harris was for the first time fully immersed in a part, and the consequences shattered his home life. Before the play opened at the Fortune Theatre in September Liz broke the tension of his domestic indecision by making the choice herself: she left Allen House, taking Damian, and moved back to her father's home.

The *Daily Express*, among many, cheered the ground-breaking *Ginger Man*. The play was of the mould of Osborne's recent hit *Look Back in Anger*, but less restrained. Sebastian Dangerfield, the Trinity student hero amok, was a verbal bastard, at war with himself and all civilization. The *Express* wasn't coy: 'Three years ago this play about the facts of low life in Dublin could never have been shown because of the censor and because the West End was becoming a cemetery . . . Olivier, Gielgud, Coward and Rattigan brilliantly dominated. The Big Successes came from America, or from history. Now look what's happening . . . plays deep in living. Tough, uncompromising, promising and unpredictable.' Donleavy chipped in: 'I expect a couple of rows will walk out each night. But I'm sure for every two that walk out four more will be encouraged to come in.' Harris's opening reviews were excellent, which didn't surprise Liz because she had observed him *become* the central character, an emotional thug awash in his personal confusions.

Godfrey Quigley's Globe Theatre in Dublin had a reputation for staging oddball classics and Quigley knew Donleavy – indeed, 'I knew the Ginger Man of the story. I socialized with him in Dublin. Reckless days!' Quigley went to London and attended a performance. 'I thought it was a remarkable play and I knew it would do well in Dublin, so I went straight backstage and proposed it to Philip Wiseman.' Quigley liked Harris's energy, though, in the words of an actor centrally involved, 'His performance was really quite light on its feet. It hadn't the depth that Dangerfield should have. It was a jittery, slight characterization.' Nevertheless Quigley made his deal to transfer the production to Dublin once the London run ended. Harris was ecstatic. Liz wrote in her memoirs that he hungered for a triumphant Irish theatrical return.

The return came sooner than anyone expected. After six weeks audiences dropped, so the play was shifted to Dublin. Once again everyone breathed deep in anticipation of a long, money-spinning run. 'I had my shirt on it,' says Quigley. 'I loved this show, and I trusted the Irish theatregoer, and Dickie was just the energy Dublin needed then.' The leading British casting of Wendy Craig, Ronald Fraser (playing O'Keefe, the part Harris had first been offered) and Isabel Dean was replaced by Genevieve Lyons (Quigley's then wife), Godfrey Quigley and Rosalie Westwater. Wiseman was again directing. The production was housed at the Gaiety Theatre and overseen by owner-entrepreneur Louis Elliman, Dublin's 'Mr Showbiz'. The first night saw a packed house, with Dubliners flocking to see the new Hollywood star, Richard Harris, on stage in the capital. Quigley was delighted as he came off-stage, but Louis Elliman confronted him and asked abruptly for two cuts in the text. Quigley was surprised, but not alarmed. Harris sauntered past them, bound for 'a jar or two in the Green Room', unaware of the crisis looming. Quigley says: 'Louis said he wanted a profane reference to Dangerfield getting absolution from some church on the quays removed. He also wanted the song "Down in Dingle Where the Girls Are Single" cut. This, I must say, absolutely baffled me. It was harmless, I couldn't see the sense of it.'

Philip Wiseman was chatting to stage-hands ten yards away and Quigley naively called him over to hear Elliman's 'suggestions'. 'I think I might have made the drastic mistake of not formally introducing them. I just said, "Philip, come and hear what Louis is suggesting for cuts." Wiseman flared up instantly, saying he would not cut a single line for any reason. Elliman, never coy, exploded back: "If you don't cut this I'll close the show and, what's more, I'll see that you never work again . . . particularly in Hollywood!"' Godfrey Quigley laughs today at the memory of Elliman's rage and the baseless threats. But at the time it was anything but funny. A slanging match started, with Wiseman inviting Elliman to shut the play down. 'It'll help me publicity-wise,' Wiseman declared. 'Especially when I take the play to New York in a few weeks. Go on, try it!'

Within a half-hour the word was circulating: the show

was in censorship trouble. Harris caught wind, and loved it. Quigley recalls: 'He took up residence in the Bailey pub across the street and started giving interviews to the world press. His play was under fire from the Papacy! This was magnificent! Joycean! I remember being dragged into the street to pose with him for a posse of photographers.'

What the *Sunday Times* had described as 'an uproariously funny' production was now, simply, uproarious. The *Irish Independent* reacted with all the hostility Elliman showed: 'The current production . . . is one of the most nauseating plays ever to appear on a Dublin stage and it is a matter of some concern that its presentation should ever have been considered. It is an insult to religion and an outrage to normal feelings of decency. . . . The best course open to all concerned is to withdraw it with the greatest possible speed.'

When Quigley, Harris and the cast arrived for the second night's performance they found the Gaiety in darkness, with surging crowds blocking South King Street. Inside, Elliman was discussing the proposed cuts with a priest-administrator from Archbishop MacQuaid's office, the Dublin equivalent of the Lord Chamberlain's man. Quigley recalls 'a priest from MacQuaid's representing the fascist inquisition-style values of MacQuaid and his era. A storm brewed up in that meeting and Elliman told me flat that the play must come off if changes were refused. Well, we refused. Elliman allowed us to play that night, but the next day we were off.'

Harris held court in the Bailey, recounting every murmur from Elliman's office. When the show went on for what was to be its final performance he milked every ounce of pathos from it, adding special emphasis to the concluding farewell scene where the Ginger Man bids adieu on this, his final night in Dun Laoghaire. Quigley observes: 'I never knock an actor for his egomania. And Dickie's leanings in that direction were, shall we say, well developed. He liked playing chess with the newspapers too – in fact, he liked playing chess with everyone – so he saw ample mileage for fun.' Once again Harris summoned the journalists, now to announce his letter to Archbishop MacQuaid in which he humbly asked for divine guidance in his awkward situation: what could the archbishop suggest by way of assistance? The letter was sent by courier motorbike and the Bailey awaited a reply with well-filled glasses. 'MacQuaid outmanoeuvred him,' Quigley says. 'He sent a note back saying Mr Harris would be advised to contact his personal spiritual adviser if he had a conscience difficulty with continuing this play. Beautiful chess-playing!'

Wiseman, like Harris, used the counter-publicity tactic. In a telegram to the *Irish Independent*, the publicly perceived leaders of the lynch mob, Wiseman stated: 'Your article concerning the play . . . we consider a deliberate attempt to incite a breach of the peace. We are therefore giving you notice of our intention to protect our interests . . . and hold you directly responsible for any damages arising from such a breach.' Threats and counter-threats flew, and Quigley paid off his cast and crew and got out of town. 'It cost me £800 or more. My great pal Brendan Smith came for me and put me in his car and took me to a hotel in Dundalk where we drank a lot of soup over the next few days.'

Harris's soup was hard alcohol. Liz spoke of his particular vulnerability to brandy. His tolerance of beer and other spirits was high, but brandy drew the worst from him. Now, to the newspapermen, he was suddenly on the verge of collapse. At his last-night performance the *Evening Press* had commended his fine, though edge-of-the-seat acting: 'He prances and postures like a marionette on the verge of collapse. . . .' He told reporters: 'This play has ruined me and it has ruined my marriage. I rehearsed it for ten weeks before it opened, and because of it my wife can't stand me any longer.' Godfrey Quigley had not observed a man in trouble: 'He courted the press with incredible vigour, that's all I saw.' Curiously, the acolytes and hangers-on that crowded the Bailey saw the bluster, not the pain. 'He was a bag of laughs,' says an elderly Bailey barfly who remembers the Gaiety excitement. 'And generous with the drink.'

Harris entered a Cornish nursing home when *The Ginger Man* folded. He and Liz appeared to accept the inevitability of divorce, but the pain of his failure flattened him. The boisterous, heartless boyo depicted so often through the years – even by Harris – did not fit this picture. Here was a gibbering, exhausted man who could not eat or sleep, rich with acquaintances but lost for friends, achingly lamenting what might have been. When I once asked Harris about *The Ginger Man* row and its effect on him he waved it aside indifferently. I then mentioned his escape to the nursing home and he winced at the memory: 'That was my marriage failing and all the agony, that wasn't anything to do with professional failure.'

To add to his personal agony, Harris received news from Limerick that Milly was dying of cancer. Devastated, he called Liz and together they returned to the Ennis Road, politely concealing the split. Liz stayed with Harmay and Jack Donnelly, while Harris tended his mother with a comfort that no one else in the family could quite find. In Liz's account of Milly's final illness she speaks of the mother's request to her son to assume responsibility for the family troubles. In Dickie as in no one else Milly saw a courage and energy that might save family face. It wasn't surprising. Dickie was the long-odds outsider who had been galvanized by adversity to win the world. He *was* winning. He might yet save the day for the mill and Ivan.

Liz returned to London as Harris kept up his bedside vigil in Limerick. Within hours he was on the phone to her with the news that Milly was dead. She flew back to Dublin and took a train to Limerick. At the funeral and afterwards, the depths of his tiredness touched her. She knew he needed the comfort of a real escape and encouraged him to take the first offer that came along, a TV play of *The Hasty Heart* in New York. He flew out alone directly after Milly's burial in the family plot at St Lawrence's in Bengal Terrace on 14 December. Two weeks later, revived and inspired by good work, he winged back to Europe to romance his marriage back to life. He met Liz in Paris and dined with her at Maxim's, a long-time fantasy of hers. They lingered in a suite at the Ritz, rewriting the terms of a relationship which would confront all the old problems of his work obsession and their non-communication. As Liz describes it, they settled on a plan for 'a series of beautiful affairs' with each other, as opposed to basic domestic routine.

Whenever they were separated, they would meet anew in hotel rooms; she would wear lilac, his favourite colour, and they would behave like lovers on an assignation. Liz was happy to be back with him but still wary. Within a very short time the brash and attention-addicted aspects of his personality had depressed her again. After Milly's passing, death preoccupied him and he fixed on the notion that the world would end in 1965. It was a serious conviction. To Liz's utter dismay he formed the 65 Club, with Edna O'Brien and Donal Donnelly among its members. Stationery was printed and profound philosophical debates encouraged. On top of that came the reawakening of self-advertising. A popular topic for interviews was his new-found political opinions, many of them launched mischievously against Liberal, even Labour, values. Lord Ogmore was indirectly, Liz knew, the nub of the joke. 'The House of Lords is just a rich man's labour exchange where the old boys sign for their £3 a day,' Harris was reported as saying. Liz tried to persuade him to be more subtle, but knew it was a waste of time. More than anything her husband loved to do precisely what he was told not to do.

Associated British at last cast him with star billing in one of their productions, a movie adaptation, shot at Elstree, of Willis Hall's theatrical hit *The Long and the Short and the Tall*. Peter O'Toole had led the stage cast (but wasn't in the movie) and Harris, who looked up to O'Toole, was impressed by this and by the toughness of the screenplay (by Wolf Mankowitz). Pal Ronnie Fraser, another member of the stage cast, was also aboard. Harris took second billing to Laurence Harvey, unseating fifties' favourite Richard Todd to third billing. The bitching one-upmanship of the movie game reared its head again during this production and taught Harris a thing or two. Considerably shorter in stature than Harvey and Harris, Richard Todd took pains to even the score. As cast and crew sweated in a mock-up Malaysian jungle Todd discreetly built gentle mounds of dirt on which to stand in his scenes with his co-stars. Harvey spotted the trick and, with Harris's and Fraser's delighted co-operation, out-foxed every Todd move by sneaking in little mounds of their own. Nowhere in the movie is Todd eyeball-to-eyeball with Harvey or Harris. 'The old prat was dumbfounded,' says Fraser.

A grey parable about the differing effects of war on a group of jungle soldiers, *The Long and the Short and the Tall* was entered, along with its contemporary twin *Saturday Night and Sunday Morning*, in the Festival of Mar del Plata in Argentina as being representative of 'the spearhead of the new wave of British cinema'. Though the film failed to expand beyond the claustrophic confines of its stage conception critics, if not audiences, liked it. C. A. Lejeune declared it was 'not the type of film I like myself, but I have a profound regard for it as first-class work. . . . It has dignity, humanity and, under the rough exterior, a very tender heart.' The *Monthly Film Bulletin* was less impressed and spoke of its two-dimensional playing and self-conscious candour. Cast as the bully Corporal Johnstone, Harris presented just 'a tabloid verisimilitude'. In Argentina, as in Britain, general audiences preferred *Saturday Night and Sunday Morning*, perhaps because of its easier identification with life at the dawning of the sixties.

At home in Allen House Liz played the game of the redrafted marriage, increasingly aware that the Ginger Man – not the play but the character – had not left her life. Harris *was*, as he had told Donleavy, the Ginger Man. All the whim-and-fury mania of the Ginger Man was his, and all the vainglorious indulgence. Home life centred round him, and held its breath while he made up his mind. A drop-in acquaintance says, 'Sex, death and the movies absorbed him. He was the least likely husband and father.' Others saw Harris struggle to come to terms with his strengths – gregarious charm, physical stamina and sound arty instincts; and with his weaknesses – apparent dyslexia (it was formally diagnosed only in 1971), occasional melancholy and outbursts of violence. More than anything, close friends observed Harris silently positioning himself for stardom in the most coolly calculated way. He sensed a need to project his rebellious nature at a time when the restless post-war generation was coming of age and, after years monopolized by conservatism, youth politics was in the ascendancy. Home life had its undeniable pleasures – he never stopped telling people how much he adored Lil, as he sometimes called her, and the baby – but now more than ever he must not compromise.

The half-success of Les Norman's *The Long and the Short and the Tall* led to producer Carl Foreman giving Harris a role in *The Guns of Navarone*, based on the Alastair Maclean best-seller. Harris played a heroic flyer, well down the billing from Gregory Peck and David Niven. But the cash was fine and Foreman's track record of commercial success, combined with director J. Lee Thompson's audience-bashing all-action approach, gave Harris exactly the Hollywood nudge he openly sought. Within weeks of completing the film – which was destined for excellent box-office – a fresh flow of American scripts landed on agent Jimmy Fraser's desk. Among the phone calls was one from Carol Reed, currently preparing the MGM remake of *Mutiny on the Bounty*, earmarked to star prince-of-rebels Marlon Brando. Reed, and producer Aaron Rosenberg, were keen to sign Harris for a part somewhere in their movie on the strength of his meagre first films. Harris knew instantly the critical value of this casting. Here, finally, was upper case Hollywood.

Mutiny on the Bounty had had a scrappy start. Rosenberg had engaged Reed early on but Brando refused the project, just as he had refused *Lawrence of Arabia*. His reasoning for the *Lawrence* rejection was straightforward: 'I'll be damned if I spend two years of my life on a fucking camel.' In the case of *Mutiny* he saw no point in Rosenberg's initial intention simply to redo the 1935 Gable–Laughton classic. After endless negotiations Brando finally signed on, winning script approval and casting consultation. Eric Ambler was assigned to write the screenplay, but Brando disliked his approach and asked for redrafts, with more emphasis on the aftermath of the mutiny and the mutineers' lives on Pitcairn Island. In fact, during those early planning days at MGM Studios in Culver City Rosenberg was very aware that Brando was constantly diverting discussions towards a movie version of the story of Caryl Chessman, a convicted rapist. Reed was exhausted by Brando's demands but proceeded with the British end of the production, booking his old pal Trevor Howard, along with superior character actors Hugh Griffith, Gordon Jackson and Noel Purcell.

Harris was thrilled with Reed's offer of a chance to star with his idol. But when the script arrived in Dublin, where he was boozing with Gaiety friends, he was disappointed. The part was animated background with an Irish accent. Harris wouldn't have it. As Liz points out, he was getting wise to the games of filmdom. James Booth rounds off, 'He had plenty of practice at being a bollocks in his private life, so he was ready to use it when called on professionally.'

Harris turned down *Mutiny*, saying the role was insultingly small – though it was hardly smaller than his part in *Navarone*. Reed and Rosenberg reconsidered, and offered a bigger role, this time as principal mutineer (after Brando's Christian) John Mills. Harris instructed his agent to accept, provided he got equal billing with Brando. This demand was patently absurd: Brando was peaking with recent victories like *The Young Lions* (1958) and *One-Eyed Jacks* (1961) and was regarded as Hollywood's best property. Rosenberg cabled an immediate 'No', and repeated his offer in very favourable cash terms. But Harris wasn't manoeuvring for money. As Liz tells it, money *per se* was of no interest to Harris. When he had it he was extravagant, throwing away handfuls on unnecessary antique tables and first-class air fares. Already he was turning down big British movies with dud scripts, regardless of the cash involved. Jimmy Fraser and close friends reminded Harris of all the reasons why he should be jumping at this major casting, but Harris kept his cool and took his time making his mind up.

Finally he telephoned a compromise: he would do the film if he could have equal billing with Trevor Howard, who would play Captain Bligh. Again Rosenberg refused, stating that Howard was better known than Harris. Harris quickly returned this lob: *he* was presently as well known as Howard had been at thirty.

Liz and Harris waited tensely as the scheduled production date, 15 October, drew nearer and Rosenberg declined to respond. Harris now all but accepted the fact that he had blown his chance. Respite from absolute dejection came when Liz was cast in a small role in a Manchester play, but she departed gloomily, feeling every ounce of Harris's misery. Liz was labouring in Manchester the day before Harris's proposed flight to Tahiti when the call came through: Rosenberg had reconsidered. Said Harris: 'Yes, they'd agreed my terms . . . but for God's sake be on that plane! . . . I rushed out and bought what I thought I might need, added the usual two hundred records and twenty-seven books that make up my luggage . . . and I was on my way.' In her book Liz recalls that Harris's main item of luggage was a bottle of bourbon.

It was a nerve-racking start to what promised from the

outset to be a nail-biting production. When Harris arrived in Tahiti to join Brando, Howard and the crew, no script was ready and no good ship *Bounty* was to be seen. Brando was still disputing Ambler's work and more writers had been summoned. Currently Charles Lederer was reworking it, but no end was in sight. The replica *Bounty*, hand-crafted at a cost of $750,000 in Nova Scotia, *was* ready, but had run into storms *en route* and might not be expected for some time. Harris found himself stranded with a company of a hundred in the sultry jungle of Tahiti, watching $50,000 a day of production funds go down the drain.

Rosenberg's patience went and on 4 December the movie finally started shooting on the shores of Matavi Bay, with the actors given their lines by word of mouth. Trevor Howard immediately fell foul of Brando, by virtue of accurately delivering his lines. Brando fluffed – and fluffed again – and Carol Reed hauled patiently, ultra-careful lest his friendship with Howard and the British contingent offend the star. Harris watched and worked with respectful interest, gently building a fair relationship with his idol. But then the December rains came, lashing the production to a standstill.

On Christmas Eve Liz arrived with Damian and a nanny, eager to announce her own news. After Manchester, she had decided, she would pursue acting no longer. And she was again pregnant. Brimming with the news and fighting jet-and-baby-lag, Liz was dismayed not to find Harris at the airport to greet her. Damian had been ill on the journey and the nanny was jaded, but an odyssey lay ahead. Nobody in Papeete, the shanty capital, knew where Harris or the production might be found. Liz had cabled ahead via Culver City, but in fact Harris had received the wrong information. After a search lasting hours Liz found the jungle hut hotel where Harris was based and collapsed into his bed with Damian, to be awoken later by a loving embrace – and tears of celebration. Harris loved children, and longed for a daughter. He had told the press more than once that he planned to have a *huge* family.

Life in Tahiti staggered on, bedevilled by scorpions, land crabs, rats and Brando. The Harrises fought gamely to keep up their spirits, throwing open their 'hut home' to convivial

company. Hugh Griffith, Gordon Jackson, Eddie Byrne and
Noel Purcell came by regularly to sup and fan the fun –
though Byrne's dislike of Purcell soon necessitated a revised
guest list.

After Christmas Rosenberg pulled the production back to
Hollywood for sound stage interiors – and fired director Carol
Reed. The cause of dismissal was not, as widely reported, a rift
with Brando. Rather, Reed argued with Rosenberg about the
portrayal of Captain Bligh. Rosenberg wanted a direct copy
of Laughton's Bligh; Reed wanted something fresh. Most of
the cast, led by Harris and Howard, demanded a meeting
with Sol Siegal, MGM's chief. But before they could beg
Reed's reinstatement Siegal told them: 'Gentlemen, before
you say anything I want you to understand one thing: the only
expendable commodity in a great movie is a good actor.'

Lewis Milestone, veteran director of *All Quiet on the Western
Front* (1930), took Reed's place. A meticulous craftsman, he
approached his job lustily – until the reality of a Brando-driven
epic dawned on him. His task was not to direct; Rosenberg,
Lederer and Brando had grouped to do that; instead he was
a kind of technical foreman, knowledgeable but (and this is
why they engaged him) amenable. He backed off, much to
the horror of most of the experienced actors.

During February Harris spent much of his time extend-
ing his trade friendships in the Retake Room, a Hollywood
restaurant favoured solely by the Brits. Brando stuck with
Tarita Teripaim, the Tahitian discovery who became his new
girlfriend (and who later bore him a son and daughter, though
they never married). Their lives ran on separate tracks – except
for the shared studio days, and the rare occasions when Liz
brought Damian to play on Brando's lawns. But Harris's
regard for the rebel idol had, understandably, changed. The
rows with Reed, and now with Milestone, and the frequent
no-show days wore him down as they wore down Howard
and the others. Never criticized for keeping his opinions to
himself, Harris suddenly flared up: he was shooting a key
confrontation scene with Brando and Brando, internalizing
maddeningly, was hardly reacting. In the scene Brando is
obliged to strike Harris, laying him out. The blow when it came
was a limp-fisted tap. Harris was outraged. 'It wasn't enough

to knock down a butterfly,' Harris later said. 'I demanded it to be shot again.' When Brando persisted in lightly slapping him, Harris kissed him on the cheek and hugged him roguishly. 'Shall we dance?' Harris suggested with a leery grin. Brando stormed off the set.

After that, Harris and Brando refused to appear on set together. In consequence Brando played his Harris scenes opposite a stand-in, and Harris stooped to further insult: 'He used a stand-in, I used a box. I got a little green box and I drew his face on it and performed to it.' Milestone didn't bother to enter into the dispute. Days later Harris wrapped his final Brando scenes, only to be summoned back to the set by the great rebel himself. Brando asked him, 'Would you mind giving me your lines?'

Harris shook his head and presented Brando with the green box. 'This was you before lunch, and it is me after lunch. And you can look at that little box to your heart's content and perform, and you'll probably get as much out of that box as I got out of you.' Harris didn't speak to Brando again for more than twenty-five years.

Back to Tahiti in March, Harris settled down to a final four months on what seemed like an interminable production. Liz and Damian had returned to London, where Liz wanted her baby born, and Harris missed her 'at home' organizational flair. Relief from the tedium came when British director Lindsay Anderson flew twelve thousand miles to discuss a fledgling art-house movie called *This Sporting Life*. Anderson was thirty-eight, untried in feature work but with a clutch of substantial creative credits behind him, among them an Oscar for co-scripting and co-directing the short *Thursday's Children* with Guy Brenton (1955). Anderson's feature debut was to be an adaptation of David Storey's rugby novel, which he had hungered to direct since reading a review of it in the *Sunday Times*. The previous year he had seen Harris at the Fortune in *The Ginger Man* and there and then privately cast the film. From day one Harris was his lead, and he set out to get him with unwavering resolve.

'Anderson wasn't *interested* in Harris as an actor,' says a co-star. 'He was fascinated. He would have done anything to sign him.'

Weeks before, Anderson had mailed a copy of the novel to Harris and received a densely packed, handwritten critique from him. Harris adored the book and saw in it multi-layered reflections of his own life experience. The story revolves around Frank Machin, a star-of-the-hour rugby player, whose success is sponsored by team owner Weaver, a kind of surrogate father who wants to clean up Machin's gutter life. Machin follows the dictates of Weaver and spiralling fame but fails to win the battle he is keenest to win – the hand and heart of Mrs Hammond, the widowed landlady who resists the deception of fame.

While Harris loved the novel, he despised the first draft script that Anderson followed up with. 'He hated it so much,' Anderson later said, 'that he didn't even bother to write back about it.' Anderson was on shaky ground but, thus far, *This Sporting Life* had been a charmed project for him and he wasn't about to let go. When he had first tried to acquire the rights, with the hope of Woodfall Productions backing him, he was outbid by Independent Artists, the comedy-making company of Julian Wyntle and Leslie Parkyn. Independent Artists offered the film to Karel Reisz, brilliant director of *Saturday Night and Sunday Morning*. Reisz was keen, but wanted experience in production. He nominated his friend Lindsay Anderson to take over directing, while he produced. Anderson never believed that Independent Artists would accept him but, in the spirit of the times, after youthful genius had produced hits like *Saturday Night and Sunday Morning*, they did. With Reisz's blessing Anderson commissioned the novel's author, David Storey, to develop a screenplay built around Ginger Man Harris.

The cultural and political youth revolution manifest in the daily headlines told Independent Artists that the time was ripe for daring films. Comedian Leslie Phillips, mainstay of the Independent comedy school, saw 'the tidal wave' coming. 'I knew we had turned a corner in movie-making in Britain,' he says. 'I recall working at Beaconsfield on comedies like *Crooks Anonymous* with Julie Christie, who was just starting. To tell you the truth, we all wanted to be next door making gritty stuff like *Sporting Life*. We knew the soft-shoe era was over – Ealing, the posh toff movies, all those things.' What had crucially changed, it seemed, was the arrival of a sense of commitment beyond commerce in movie-makers. There was suddenly social comment, a peace movement, real freedom of expression. Henceforth movies would expand in depth, demanding the talent of radical actors to find and expose the new truth.

But Harris was saying no. Anderson spoke to him long-distance to Tahiti, then opted for a personal visit. The trip to the South Seas took more than twenty-four hours' flying time, and Anderson's best memory of it is his 5 a.m. arrival at the airport where, despite the rigours of filming, Harris met him 'with his eighteenth-century seaman's hair down on his shoulders, bursting to tell me what he thought of the script'. Few niceties were observed: 'Within minutes we were at it, and though neither of us had slept much the night before, we talked and argued right through the day.' Harris's intellectual clarity delighted Anderson and told him instantly that the journey was worthwhile. In its simplest terms, Harris told the new director, Storey's first draft was wrong because he had departed from his own novel. The novel was the power. All of them must readdress it and start afresh.

Mutiny on the Bounty neared completion in ever-worsening disputes. Brando had taken to wearing ear-plugs and ignored Milestone half the time. Extras mutinied for better money. The rains returned. Nevertheless, for Gordon Jackson as for Harris, the genius of Brando still shone: 'He didn't speak about acting, he didn't analyse. It was all a child's game for him . . . but he *was* brilliant.'

By the time Anderson winged back to London with a sketchpad outline of a new script, Harris could see the light at the end of the thirteen-month *Bounty* tunnel: already the picture was $10 million over budget and the production time allotted had been doubled. Whether or not Brando was happy with the results, the curtains were drawing. Before the movie wrapped, the *Saturday Evening Post* ran a feature entitled 'The Mutiny of Marlon Brando', brazenly accusing the star of hindering the production. MGM stayed silent, but Brando replied with a hefty lawsuit. He told *Variety*: 'If you send a multimillion dollar production to a place when, according to the precipitation records, it is the worst time of year, and when you send it without a script, it seems there is some kind of primitive mistake. The reason for all the big failures is the same – no script. Then the actors become the obvious target of executives trying to cover their own tracks.'

MGM did not moan, as Lewis Milestone did not moan, when Brando insisted on reshooting the final scene in which Fletcher Christian dies. Rosenberg was too exhausted to argue, and Brando directed himself in an elaborate retake of the last sequence.

For Harris, free at last in October, the movie had been 'nightmarish'. He told journalist Peter Evans, 'Mutiny on the Bounty almost made me a drunk and a tramp. It was disgusting. But I survived. I survived and made myself a promise. I promised myself that however poor I got I would never again do anything I didn't really believe in.' For some, the much-reported grumbles seemed churlish. Others saw Harris perfecting the art of the hype: he had clawed his way into the limelight and wasn't about to give all the post-production column inches to Brando of all people. It took real ingenuity to keep the press keen, but Harris had the wit and the stamina. Nine months later he still had chins wagging as he passed up the London premiere in favour of a Beethoven concert at the Festival Hall in the company of his new-found guru Lindsay Anderson.

Mutiny on the Bounty was not the outright failure everyone had foretold. Though it differed dramatically from the superb Gable–Laughton version, it maintained a credible tension between Bligh and Christian and gave a fuller evocation of the attractions of island escape for the mutineers exhausted by Bligh's sadism. Harris was smoulderingly effective as second mutineer Mills, but many of his best scenes were cut and his interaction with Brando's Christian – blowing hot and ultimately cold – presented frequent moments of apparent discontinuity. Still, by any yardstick, it was three coherent hours of epic entertainment that looked lavishly epic. And expensive.

In order to show clear profit the movie had to gross $27 million. Even MGM doubted the likelihood, but in a short time the gross passed $30 million, with sales to television yet to be taken into account. Reviews were, predictably, fire and ice. Reviewing the fanfare opening at Loew's State Theater in New York, Bosley Crowther in the *New York Times* exalted 'the sheer magnitude of this enactment' and 'the energy that passionate performances impart to it'. The *Los Angeles Times* was no less supportive, encouraging viewers to 'settle back in your chair to enjoy first-class escapist entertainment' (reviewer Philip Scheuer's one reservation was the death scene of Brando, 'whose mumblings left me unmoved'). The *Hollywood Reporter* lavished praise on Milestone's control – 'except perhaps in the noted inconsistencies of Brando's playing'. But the British *Monthly Film Bulletin* lamented an overblown production where 'character is deployed not for purposes of human drama or historical accuracy or social conscience, but for showmanship and showmanship alone'. Harris's reviews were, at last, highly visible. For the *LA Times* he merited special attention; the *Hollywood Reporter* thought him 'fine as the seaman who first sights in Brando's Fletcher Christian decency beneath the fop'. Elsewhere he was 'good', 'impressive' and 'interesting'.

Before *Mutiny* was completed Liz gave birth in London to a second son, Jared. Harris had to make do with envelopes of photographs in the mail, but when he returned to Los Angeles Liz flew out to meet him, bringing Damian. They rented Boris Karloff's old house, and again the reunion was full of promise. The Ginger Man bogey seemed deflated, even absent, and Liz held hopes for a new peace. Richard Harris's name had finally found a niche amidst the Hollywood hierarchy. Along with Brando and Trevor Howard his credit was *above* the *Mutiny* title, the highest of all Hollywood accolades. Robert and Dorothy Mitchum and Laurence Harvey were their trusted LA friends, introducing them to all the swishest clubs and reflecting the glory of the moment. 'Everybody is suddenly asking who the fuck is Richard Harris?' Mitchum liked to tease, applauding a new star's emergence, goading onwards and upwards.

The Karloff house was, appropriately, dark and Gothically gloomy, but it began to feel like home. Jared was in London, being cared for by the Ogmores. But Liz was already toying with the idea of bringing him out to LA and building a fresh, settled family life away from the London of boozers and hangers-on. Then, just as the Spanish mansion began to feel like a new beginning, the owners reclaimed it. Harris and Liz moved into the Bel Air Hotel but, plush as it was, it could never be a home. Liz reconciled herself to the situation. *Mutiny* was on everyone's lips. Her husband was accepted in the Hollywood fraternity. There was much talk about this new rugby picture that Harris swore would be 'an earthshaker'. . . . There was fire in her husband's face and suddenly she knew this could never be the time for peace.

The Harrises packed again and returned to Ireland, stopping off in London to collect the new baby. Dickie was at his best with the British reporters, bursting with triumphant plans. The *Ginger Man* fiasco was pushed aside. Irish censorship hadn't cowed him. He was, he said, considering an offer to take the play to Broadway. His next movie project would be *This Sporting Life*, a new classic, but he had formed his own company which would be producing Liam O'Flaherty's *Insurrection*, about the 1916 Easter Rising, at Ardmore within the year. His friendship with Carol Reed was untarnished by *Mutiny*. Reed would direct *Savort*, starring Harris, about an island community repressed for many years but reanimated by twelve characters who preach the doctrine of humanitarianism. With his first foothold on the ladder of Hollywood power Harris was showing himself to be just as much the strongly opinionated pacemaker as Brando. He had a social conscience, a personal theory of acting, a theory of script. The declaration of independence made to Peter Evans was, it seemed, abidingly true: he wanted quality, and significant work. 'Savort will really represent the struggles of oppressed people all over the world, and the preaching of the twelve people will be a sort of conscience for governments.'[1]

The opening of Radio Telefis Eireann, Irish national TV, delighted Harris and he followed its first broadcasts with enthusiasm, speculating openly on its benefits in educating and entertaining the country, and on the work he might some day do with it. His pride in broadening Irish horizons was obvious to everyone, but he travelled back to Limerick with some trepidation, knowing that home pastures would remind

---

[1] *Savort* was abandoned.

him of Milly and bring him face to face with a vanquished Ivan and the inevitable passing of Harris Mills, in which Rank Flour Mills had now acquired a majority shareholding.

Ivan and his hopes and unexpressed expectations he had never come to terms with. In Milly's absence, more than ever, he wanted Ivan's approval. But he knew it was a pipedream. Ivan had never accepted his son's Hollywood visions. With the last-ditch problems of the mill he had less time than ever for Dickie and the strange world he dwelt in. Their only exchange, shortly after Harris's Hollywood debut, had discouraged Harris from further efforts. Richard had been proudly telling the family of his LA buddies, of Bob Mitchum and Gary Cooper and all the others. Ivan hardly raised his head from his newspaper. 'Did you meet Betty Grabble?'

'You mean Betty Grable?'

'Um.'

'No, Dad, I didn't.'

Ivan clucked and returned to his paper. He knew it all along. His son was just puffing hot air. He was making no headway at all.

6

Try!

According to Liz and the businessmen who knew him, Ivan Harris remained blissfully unaware of the true devastating extent of his mill's failure. Ironically, the son he least believed in saved him from a final indignity. And, doubly ironically, the movie Richard Harris was warming up to, *This Sporting Life*, was to be financed for distribution by Rank Films. So Dickie Harris found himself in the absurd position of taking money from Rank to pay Rank to withhold closure of Harris Mills. In a quiet deal, Harris's £25,000 fee acquired the Henry Street property and ensured that the mill remained – shakily – in business. It was, of course, only temporarily effective, but it spared Ivan's honour. Ivan's health declined quickly after Milly's death and he too would shortly die, never witnessing the mill's closure, never reconciled to his saviour son. Harris told Gerry Hannan: 'When I bought the building I swore I would keep it, come hell or high water, until time wore away the Harris name from over the door. It was a monument to my father and brothers and my forebears and the work they did. And by God I did keep it!'[1]

After the briefest of Limerick holidays – in which he took time too to renew his acquaintanceship with Manuel Di Lucia and Kilkee and speculate about purchasing a house there – Harris hurried back to Lindsay Anderson's side. Progress on *This Sporting Life* was fast once the distribution deal was in place, and Liz sighed resignation as the midnight routines of

[1] The 'James Harris & Sons' sign faded in the 1980s. Harris sold the building to Limerick Corporation for £150,000 in 1989. It will be developed as a car park.

'prep' meetings began, once again bringing domestic life at Allen House to a standstill. Anderson had now replaced Donal Donnelly and the Dublin drop-ins in monopolizing Harris's time and devotion. Liz liked him – and welcomed his calm intervention in the latest round of husband–wife dissension – but she resented his condescending attitude to her which she interpreted as intellectual snobbery. More than anything Liz saw Anderson's overt rebelliousness, which found its perfect twin in Harris. Together they laughed and conspired against all sorts of visible and invisible enemies – most of all the old institutions of Church, State and Hollywood. As a peer's daughter Liz was fair game, so she took the jibes with good humour (or the best she could muster) and contented herself with tending the babies.

For his part Harris was starting that slow metamorphosis that would drain his generosity and congeniality and produce instead the shell that could be filled with his fictional character. He was tunnel-visioned, and in his own quirky way, spectacularly disciplined. He stopped talking to the press. One of his last pronouncements was razor-sharp: 'I want to take responsibility for all I do. I don't want to be handed someone else's baby and be told to bring him up. I want my own.' The kinship with Anderson made *Sporting Life* his own. Wary of losing his power over the script in progress he doggedly refused to meet David Storey: 'David was another thing, something separate. I felt if I got to know him I'd like him. If that happened, then in the debates and arguments with the chap I might have given in. So Lindsay and I would go away to the coast at Rottingdean and sweat it out together. Then Lindsay would go back to David with our notes. When finally I met David, I *did* like him. But by then the script was ready for shooting.'

In the middle of pre-production Harris was offered his biggest cheque yet, to star in producer Samuel Bronston's history epic *The Fall of the Roman Empire*, slotted for shooting in Spain that autumn with Anthony Mann directing. The proposed part was that of Commodus, mad son of the Emperor Marcus Aurelius whose dissipation led to the sacking of Rome by the Barbarians. It was the finest role in what started as a fine script, and Harris jumped at it. As his agent worked out the deal,

Harris enthusiastically took riding lessons to prepare himself for ancient Rome. The fee was to be an incredible $200,000 – almost $5 million in today's terms. Liz started house-hunting. Then the redrafted script (by Ben Barzman and Philip Yordan) arrived and Harris exploded. After the cutting of his scenes in *Mutiny* he had insisted on a no-cut clause in his contract. But already Commodus was changing, his character assuming a celluloid lightness that Harris abhorred. Producer and writers dithered, happy enough with their invention. But Harris gave Bronston a simple ultimatum: shoot the first script or forget it: 'If they go back to the first script I will play it gladly. . . . Now it's up to Mr Bronston.' Bronston stood his ground and Harris was replaced by Stephen Boyd. Liz's disappointment at the loss of almost a quarter of a million dollars is unrecorded, but the bank manager let Harris know how he felt. When he read about the row in the newspapers he rang up, complaining that Harris's account was overdrawn. The house-hunting was progressing steadily, and in the circumstances, he advised Harris, he would have been wise to take Bronston's offer. Harris was unapologetic: 'I told him, "I don't tell you how to run your bank. So don't you tell me how to run my life."'

Harris focused on Anderson again. The principal revision in *This Sporting Life* arising from the Tahiti discussions was a shifting of emphasis from melodrama. Though Harris's initial attraction to the subject was the lure of the rugby field, neither he nor Anderson saw it as a film about sport. Anderson told *Films and Filming*: 'I suppose that the film is primarily a study of temperament. It is a film about a man. A man of extraordinary power and aggressiveness, both temperamental and physical, but at the same time with a great innate sensitiveness and a need for love of which he is at first hardly aware.' That summary might easily have described Harris's own character, though neither alluded to it. For Harris the misconception had been 'removing the poetry' from the story. Anderson did his utmost to restore it, hanging on Harris's every word. Harris said, 'He has a genius for listening to other people. With him I have a feeling about getting to the truth of a part that I've not had with other directors.'

In preparation for the physical trials of a story centred on the rugby field Harris went back to training – not, as might be expected, with his old friends at the London Irish grounds at Deerpark (where Len Dinneen would soon be captain) but at Richmond. 'I could have gone to the London Irish,' said Harris. 'But that would have turned it into something of a giggle. I knew I would not become involved with the Richmond people. They are kind of snobs – bank clerks and lawyers. I knew they would ignore me. They never even asked my name.' Spectator rugby remained a full-time passion, but the realities of the scrum pack after ten years of absence were horrifying: 'Physically I thought I was big enough, but I wasn't as big as most rugby players really are. I used to hang about the dressing rooms making mental notes on how they behaved. I worked at preparing my body – training runs every morning, muscle-building with weights, clenching rubber balls to build up the hands and wrists.' David Storey too was helpful in a practical way when they eventually met. Three years younger than Harris and a former coalminer, Storey had decided to study art and signed on with Leeds Rugby League Club to pay his way. For four seasons he played with the club's 'A' team, earning an encyclopaedic knowledge of the game. He coached Harris keenly, and Harris did his bit to build on the empathy by dyeing his hair black like Storey's. Anderson was further fascinated by this imaginative discipline which belied Harris's press. One of Harris's sixties' co-stars offers a typical contemporary view: 'I'll sum it up this way: he couldn't have had a career in theatre. He was too light. The theatrical fame he eventually got in *Camelot* was exactly right for him. It suited someone who wanted all the limelight.' James Booth counters: 'There were moments of great maturity, and great generosity to actors and directors. You cannot survive without your fellow artists. And Richard was a survivor above all.'

Surviving was the name of the game in the dank low life sets of Independent's Beaconsfield Studios when shooting finally began. The grotty claustrophobia was far removed from Tahiti, but Harris relished it. Here were the smelly Crescent changing rooms, the Kilkee pubs, the front rooms of old cronies. The late Rachel Roberts, an acquaintance if not a pal since *The Dutch Courtesan* at Stratford East, was cast as Mrs Hammond, the unattainable object of Frank Machin's desires. Born in Llanelly, Wales and a prize-winner at RADA, Roberts had all the qualifications Harris liked in leading ladies. She had vast experience – from the Old Vic to comedy revue – and a manner that was both warm and blunt. In the words of a co-star, 'She was a non-bullshitter' whose only visible weakness was a tendency to gloom. The fifties had not been rewarding for her in star terms; to many she became known mainly as Rex Harrison's fourth wife. But a popular breakthrough came in her casting as Albert Finney's married mistress in *Saturday Night and Sunday Morning*. Reisz and Anderson had huge admiration for her talents and felt the co-lead opposite Harris was 'made for her'. The rapport between Roberts and Harris enthralled everyone who visited the set. Roberts's technique was clenched and intense; for Harris this was inspirational, not oppressive. He looked up to her: 'She is Welsh, a Celt, sensitive. She knows it all. She's so good you don't have to act with her.' Anderson echoed this. For Mrs Hammond he had sought 'an actress of exceptional interior quality, with real wildness within, as well as a capacity for iron restraint'. Roberts was all these things.

All the other main parts knitted seamlessly too and the film, boasted Anderson, 'evolved miraculously'. Frank Windsor, one of the few cast members still alive, played the pivotal role of the dentist to whom Machin is brought at the start of the movie and whose knockout injection stimulates the waves of memory that make the story. Windsor was high-flying in a TV career, playing Inspector Watt in the seminal cop series *Z Cars*, when Anderson approached him for the role. 'Lindsay had been promising for years that we would work together, but I had been very absorbed in television and the times and dates of his projects never fitted. Finally this came along and it fitted between bouts of *Z Cars*.' Windsor was deeply impressed by Anderson's radical film-making and the rapport he created: 'The way Lindsay worked was quite insidious. For example, the dentist scene, which was only a few days' work, was of hardly any importance in the script I got. It was quite simply that up-and-coming Machin got his teeth knocked out and is taken to visit me, to get them fixed. But it became much more. It became a motif that Lindsay kept cutting back to – the spine of the film, if you will – and said its own piece about man's inhumanity and all that. That's how Lindsay succeeded: by taking every tiny scrap of the script and shuffling it for the best possible effect. The actors loved him for the care he took.'

Karel Reisz kept a benign eye on the production and was excited by what he saw of Harris's double nature: 'These complementary qualities – a huge, commanding presence and a beautifully subtle sensitivity – make Richard an actor in the big, heroic tradition. Above all, he possesses a rare courage that allows him to explore the heights and depths.'

What Reisz was observing was a coming of age – not just for Harris but for the new wave cinema that had grown from the 'kitchen sink' stage successes of the late fifties, and to which his personal contribution had been colossal. Five years before, the ball had started rolling when young entertainers like Cliff Richard and Tommy Steele spurned the 'trad' glamour image in favour of tee-shirts and jeans. Writers like Alan Sillitoe and Stan Barstow took the baton, telling tales of the working and lower middle classes. Simultaneously John Osborne launched his 'angry young man' concept at the Royal Court and Arnold Wesker took it on to West End audiences. After that, the U-turn in movies was inevitable.

The spirit of relaxation and social awareness was all-pervasive. British imperialism had taken a knock with the Suez fiasco; marchers flocked to Trafalgar Square to demand the removal of British troops from Egypt; the anti-nuclear Aldermaston rallies began; values and attitudes were up-ended. John Braine's *Room at the Top* in 1959 signalled the start of the exhilarating movie changeover. Reisz's *We Are the Lambeth Boys* in the same year gave notice of his joining the movement. Woodfall Films – representing the combined talents of Tony Richardson and John Osborne – established the pace. They made *Look Back in Anger* with Richard Burton and – the decisive winner – *Saturday Night and Sunday Morning*. Despite the obvious new trends Woodfall had difficulty financing a movie about a factory worker's life crises, but the success of this film – beating all other British box office records – finally proved that artistic endeavour, the working classes and commercial ambition were not mutually exclusive. Once the old formula was deflated, everything altered. Full studio-based film-making ceased; instead, gritty location shooting was pursued whenever possible; the star system sponsored by Rank, ABPC and the others went up in smoke. In its place came the open season that gave room for tough, close-to-life performers like Harris.

Off the set Harris's relationship with Anderson deepened, though it would never achieve the serene balance that would ensure its lifelong survival – in terms of movie-making, at any rate. The two men had more in common than anyone imagined. *Wuthering Heights*, the fantasy fixation of Harris's teenage years, was also a favourite of Anderson's. Both men were on the crest of their separate careers, attracting public interest and industry support; consequently, the timing for long-term partnership seemed perfect. A new company was formed with themselves as directors, and a portfolio of projects was planned. After *This Sporting Life* they would embark on a piece of prestige theatre work, then a movie of *Wuthering Heights*. Evenings were filled with rosy speculations about future casting. Cathy was a critically difficult role. In his dreams Harris would opt for Merle Oberon any time but, more practically, Julie Christie seemed appropriate: 'I can rattle off the names of six brilliant actors in England – no, seven. But there is only one girl who has any merit at all. And that is Julie Christie.' Harris fought for Christie as his Cathy, but Anderson was not so sure. Anderson had his own female favourite (Harris refused to divulge her name), so casting was never finally agreed.

This Sporting Life was finally wrapped, inside time and budget, and to everyone's satisfaction. Anderson, Harris and Roberts felt sure they had a new wave hit to outstrip even *Saturday Night and Sunday Morning*. Even Karel Reisz said so. But Anderson was wary of rooting for the new wave per se. His film was, he believed, an original. The realism movements of French and Italian cinema were worthy, but self-limiting; audiences and film-makers should think twice. 'These British films have loosened up in style in a very healthy way, but with quite a different emphasis from the French. Here the first achievement has been the opening up of new territories, both of subjects and of the social backgrounds in which they are set. This has been a great development – in fact an indispensable one. But it could also be restrictive. It certainly will be restrictive if we make films for too long with an eye on

what is representative – films about "working-class people"
... Throughout *This Sporting Life* we were very aware that we
were not making a film about anything representative; we were
making a film about something unique. We were not making
a film about a "worker", but also about an extraordinary
(and therefore more deeply significant) man, and about an
extraordinary relationship [with Roberts]. We were not, in a
word, making sociology.'

The British critics overwhelmingly approved, greeting
excellent entertainment with brand new undercurrents. Cecil
Wilson in the *Daily Mail* wrote: 'By now the oafish unhero with a
gratuitous grudge against society is a stock figure of British films
but in this one Richard Harris begins where the others left off ...
the actor comes tremendously into his own as the new British
answer to Brando.' That review more than any gratified Richard
Harris: unbiased, even comparison with his idol based not on
media-hustling but on hard work. The *Daily Mirror*, Harris's
original champion, tripped over the plaudits: '. . . powerful,
smouldering and superbly gripping performance. . . . I would
lay odds that this virile piece of acting will not be bettered this
year . . . first league stuff.' In due course the American release
(17 July 1963 at the 34th Street East Theater, then nationwide)
elicited reviews of no lesser excitement. 'A smashing victory,'
A. H. Weiller of the *New York Times* sang, echoing the *Mail*'s
Brando comparison: 'Credit . . . must go to Richard Harris's
portrait of the ravaged Frank Machin. He is a realistically
rugged rugby player. The prognathous jaw, the overhanging
brow, the dented Roman nose, piercing eyes and massively
muscled torso are reminiscent of the early Marlon Brando.
But, more importantly, this comparative newcomer projects in
artistic, fumbling nuances and in rough, gentle and explosive
terms. . . .'

At the British premiere in February Harris accompanied Liz
ebulliently, unable to conceal his sense of triumph. Harris wore
an astrakhan-collared coat 'that seemed straight from Richard
Burton's wardrobe', according to one tabloid, while Liz wore
a flowing vampire cape. In the black-tie crush of the foyer at
the Odeon, Leicester Square, Limerickmen were conspicuous
in their presence. 'The atmosphere throbbed with adulation,'
wrote Irish columnist Des Hickey. 'Other young stars of the

new wave school like Albert Finney and Tom Courtenay were shaking his [Harris's] hand. "Richard, you were enormous," said Courtenay. . . . Outside the crowds waited hopefully in the rain. . . . They were astonished when the star stood bare-headed on the pavement . . . calling greetings to friends and relatives from Limerick.'

Harris shied away from a caviar supper at the Savoy to cut a celebratory cake – in the shape of a tiered rugby field – with Michael and Sheila van Bloeman, old supporters at the Troubadour. The gesture was, he told everyone who would listen, the poetic fulfilment of a promise. The van Bloemans were the first to believe in him when all he had to show was a grand imagination and a sharp line of blarney. Six years and one special movie had proved them right: in the classy press, evident all around him, he was at last a star. Karel Reisz, Lindsay Anderson, David Storey, Betsy Blair and J. P. Donleavy were Harris's headline guests – along with key pressmen and 'half a dozen good Limerickmen'. Reisz and Anderson professed themselves too shy for speech-making, but the heady mood told them to be ready for it: this movie would win awards. Harris, never shy, took the podium: 'Thank you for coming, my friends. I hope you go back to see *Sporting Life* again and pay for your seats. Remember that I get five per cent of the profits.'

The classical future career that Harris and Anderson mapped out was destined to evaporate, though Harris was even then probably aware of it. He told Hickey at the Troubadour party: 'The word has gone around among the film men about *Sporting Life*. I suppose it's inevitable that I will make another Hollywood picture. But I'll agree to no picture unless the part is right.' More than twenty years later Harris looked back on the era and on the script choices he made. Anderson, Reisz, Donleavy were pulling him in one direction; reality in another. He told *Hot Press* : 'I had children and we were living in a tiny flat in London, sleeping together, all of us, in two rooms. And though there was no pressure from Elizabeth I sat down and said, "I've got a choice here. I can do *The Luck of Ginger Coffey* [a quality Irish novel by Brian Moore] – it's a fantastic piece but it will only pay what I got for *Sporting Life* – or I can get a fortune to do *Major Dundee* in Hollywood." And the latter is the choice I made. That choice was the right choice. I still believe.' This apparent contradiction was not the paradox it seems. Script quality *did* matter; *Major Dundee* was a decent, if Hollywood-glazed, scenario. Throughout subsequent years Harris's choices were often tempered by money concerns; but they remained, resolutely, *his* choices, *his* films, *his* essays in the art.

After the discipline of his toughest movie came the release of pent-up social energies surpassing all that had gone before. Joe Lynch recalls: 'Mad days with a madman. Harris loved the noise and glitter. I remember being in the flat and suddenly he wanted to sing some song for me. It wasn't good enough just to sing it, he wanted the piano accompaniment as well. So he says, "There's a piano upstairs" – and goes trundling off up the stairs and bangs down some poor sod's door and demands the use of his piano. The fellow was shocked but he knew who he was dealing with so he let us in. Harris jumps at the piano and there we are carolling away into the night. . . . I think it was hard on the nine-to-five neighbours, to be honest.' The residents of Allen House finally lost patience with the all-night-long celebrations of success. A petition was signed by all the residents except one, requesting the removal of the Harrises. The non-contributor was Peter Jeffreys, a printer from Penge, biased because he was Harris's principal drinking partner at the Britannia, the current favourite pub. By the rules of residency *all* the neighbours had to agree to the eviction of an offender, so the Harrises had a reprieve. Joe Lynch says, 'Harris decided they were a snooty bunch of killjoys and he wanted to get his own back. So he paid a friend, an out-of-work actor, to march up and down outside the block with a sandwich board on which was written "Love Thy Neighbour – Signed Harris". I think it inflamed the situation.'

The neighbours didn't have to suffer for long. Liz was pregnant again and now, without doubt, the apartment was too small. Another spate of house-hunting began.

After moving temporarily to a furnished flat round the corner from Allen House, a proper home, purchased with a loan guaranteed by Lord Ogmore, was finally found in Bedford Gardens. It was anything but perfect – upright, sombre, prettified only by two cherry trees, one in the back garden, one in the front – but at least it had kicking space for the kids and lent the Harrises a patina of family permanence. For her third baby Liz booked into a private nursing home, a well-earned luxury. The night before, Harris boozily serenaded her from the pavement – not perhaps the exemplary dad-to-be, but fair to form. On the actual day of delivery he was caught short. He had come to the nursing home for a last polite check-in before the big event and was sitting by the bed, chatting casually, when suddenly Liz went into the final contractions. Jamie, yet another red-headed boy, presented himself there and then.

The idealism of the Harris–Anderson partnership flourished. In March, just weeks after the *Sporting Life* premiere, actor and director presented their next – and last – shared work: in the theatre. It was Gogol's *Diary of a Madman*, and it was to mark Harris's withdrawal from serious theatre for twenty-seven years. For a finale it was auspicious – and tragic; tragic because it showed yet again the capacity of the teamwork. The play, a one-man piece about a poor government clerk who comes to believe he is King Ferdinand VIII of Spain, was restyled radically by Harris and Anderson and had similarities with Patrick Magee's recent rendition of Samuel Beckett's monodrama *Krapp's Last Tape*. But it was an all-original Harris, reprising the theme of the lowly man in love beyond his station, and the torture of intellect.

The play opened before Princess Margaret at the Royal Court, in a disastrous state of tension. The narcissism and confidence of Stratford East were nowhere in evidence, and by Harris's own admission he was, at first, 'awful'. Backstage he shook in his boots: 'I stood in the wings gripped with the sudden horror of the ordeal before me. Two hours and twenty minutes on an empty stage without a cue . . .!' Herbert Kretzmer of the *Daily Express* found it 'the most tedious evening's entertainment in the theatre'. Harris and Anderson hurried into conference, sparred, fought back. Within days the celebrated Clive Exton was suddenly applauding: 'The greatest thing I have seen in the theatre.'

As it evolved it became Essential Theatrical Harris – a brilliant, deeply personal duologue that spun from paranoia to self-aggrandizing, with voices whispering from the TB isolation bed, and from the peak of the Bel Air harem. Harris's

Askenti Ivanovitch's duologues were Harris v. Harris. Their well-practised fluidity impressed the *Times*: 'In these scenes Mr Harris's playing is superb. He acts like a piece of mobile sculpture. Every gesture is composed as a deliberate displacement of space and the line of his movement precisely reflects the line of his thought. Besides ensuring unbroken contact with the audience, this gives dignity and meaning to a part which might easily have evaporated in self-intoxicated egoism.' Overnight Harris became a new wave synonym, overshadowing Finney, Stamp and O'Toole.

There was more. As anticipated, *This Sporting Life* began collecting award nominations. In the late spring the announcement of the *Palme d'Or* was made and later, triumphantly, an American Academy Award nomination. Harris was ecstatic about his personal Best Actor Oscar nomination.[1] He told Peter Evans: 'For the first time in my life I have come close to some sort of fulfilment. Until now I've been kicked around, trodden on, beaten down. No more, boyo. No more.'

Before flying to Cannes with Anderson, Harris was optimistic of his chances for the *Palme d'Or* Best Actor. He was childishly excited as the trophies were handed over. Visconti's *The Leopard* – about the fall of a Sicilian prince in Garibaldi's time – won Best Film. French star Marina Vlady took Best Actress. . . . As Harris describes it, his glee turned to dismay while he watched the *big* palm-shaped statues disappear one by one. 'There were two big ones,' says Harris, 'and eleven or twelve little ones.' The big ones went to Visconti and Vlady – but Harris resigned himself to taking a little one. Then MC Jeanne Moreau called out his name and he ran on to the stage expectantly. There were plenty of small palm statuettes left, but to his horror Moreau walked past them and took up a small box which she proferred.

'Richard Harris – Best Actor!' Moreau cheered.

'What's this?' Harris demanded.

'Cuff links.' She saw his annoyance, so explained: 'It's a tradition with the Best Actor.'

---

[1] Harris did not win the Oscar. He was up against Albert Finney, Paul Newman, Sidney Poitier and Rex Harrison. Poitier won for *Lilies of the Field*.

Harris would have none of it. He recalls: 'I already *had* cuff links. I'd borrowed a pair from Lord Ogmore. I didn't need cuff links!'

Harris turned his back on Moreau and grabbed one of the gold palms. 'Two gendarmes grabbed me. So I gave one of them a little shove. And I gave the other a little shove. And they kinda fell over. I think they were out-of-work actors . . . so I kept the statue.' The *Palme d'Or* Committee later demanded the statuette back. Harris had snatched the Best Animation Film award, already inscribed, and the winners had gone home empty-handed. In time he relented, and the cuff links were mailed to him. 'I have them still today,' he told Michael Parkinson proudly.

Harris's most frequent talk show yarn, not all Limerickese, related to that time in Cannes and demonstrates an identity dilemma that was to aggravate – and richly inspire – him in the seventies and eighties. During his stay he indulged in a bar room brawl of modest proportion. In the following day's British tabloid press the headline read: 'Irish Actor in Pub Brawl'. Once the *Palme d'Or* victory was announced, the headline had shifted to: 'British Actor Wins Award'. 'Ironic,' says Harris. 'And really quite stupid.'

To those who knew him, Harris's pride in his Irishness had never been compromised. Ronald Fraser calls him, 'Fabulously Irish!' Though he abandoned plans to film O'Flaherty's *Insurrection* he was already wet-nursing another native classic – this time a Joyce short story to be adapted as a musical. Music played a bigger and bigger part in his life. When he was happy – and he was happy mostly these days – he sang. Fervent Irish ballads. Friends at the Britannia nudged him and egged him towards recording. 'Jaysus, Dick, you haven't been discovered at all! Give us another "Mountains of Mourne"!'

Harris laughed and back-slapped and promised, 'You haven't seen the half of it. Nor heard the half of it. Wait till you see my Irish musical! I've got projects the Brits are afraid of, stories and movies they wouldn't even touch!'

He was a *barnac*, for sure. But he was also now a film star, a commercial commodity. As such, he was no longer master of his own destiny.

Try Again

In terms of cinema quality the early sixties belonged to the Italians. While audiences in America, Britain and France faltered, shifting their interest to TV, Italy's cinema attendance figures remained constant, reflecting the high quality of output since the start of the decade. In the late fifties Italian film-making slumped, but in 1961 some 223 features emerged from the sixty sound stages available and the international award records show clearly a thrust of varied intellectual ambition. Only Japan competed for the quantity score (547 features in 1961), but American and British endeavours paled in comparison.

America particularly had hit a slide. The studio system responsible for forty years of movie-making was coming apart and 'runaway productions', with formerly resident directors and producers chasing the four corners of the globe for independent deals, had become the order of the day. According to studio bosses the stars, not the drifting audiences, were the main cause of American decline. Major players like Brando and Paul Newman could command $400,000 per picture. To justify that upfront outlay the studios calculated they needed a box office gross of $10 million, an impractically high target. The odds were huge, so fewer risks were being taken.

In Britain the rallying of kitchen-sink drama that launched Albert Finney, Tom Courtenay, Alan Bates and Richard Harris gave hope. The Ealing era of parochial, inert smugness was over and a spirit of confidence was manifest in the opening of new cinemas. The Odeon in London's Haymarket and Rank and ABC cinemas in Woking, Catford, Sheffield and Southall spoke optimistically for widening audiences. But it was a confidence founded on soft sand. As Lindsay Anderson had foreseen, the working-class-rebel cinema had its limitations and the sweetening, upwardly mobile sixties urgently wanted to know: where next?

For Richard Harris personally the answer was simple: the best pictures were coming out of Italy and Michelangelo Antonioni, Italy's most daring director, was writing fan letters and courting him on the long-distance telephone. Antonioni loved *This Sporting Life* and begged Harris to 'Come walk the backstreets of Roma, and find the inspiration.' Antonioni's next film would be *Deserto Rosso*, his first in colour, to star Monica Vitti who three years before had shared the laurels of Antonioni's first international success, *L'Avventura*. The film would be a deep exploration of a woman's mental breakdown, told in the naturalistic style of the day – but with the magical *auteur*'s touch. Antonioni's friends and crew talked of *Deserto Rosso* being the crown to top his existential hat-trick of *L'Aventura*, *La Notte* and *L'Eclisse*, all resoundingly successful films.

Harris took Antonioni's invitation and flew to Rome at a time when many thought he would pursue a slate of production with Anderson. Others prophesied an inevitable split. There were whispers of artistic divergence and personality clash with Anderson, summed up simply by James Booth who says, 'How quickly love can turn to hate.' For the moment the friendship remained, the plans remained – but a shared future went 'on hold'.

As he had done when first addressing himself to Anderson, Harris did his homework on Antonioni – and Italians in general. He had been told that the fifty-year-old director was introverted and spoke no English. Neither proved to be true. But Antonioni was a man of many contradictions. Fellow traveller with the anti-fascists of the Centro Sperimentale, he was film-critic-turned-documentary-maker who rejected commercial considerations but craved a wide audience. *Le Amiche*, which won the Venice Silver Lion for him, was still regarded as his masterpiece, but he was out to beat it, and the others, with a definitive film.

Harris arrived in Rome keen and trusting. But his trust was naive in an industry of egomania and dodgy creativity at the best of times. To begin with, there was no conclusive screenplay. A similar half-cocked pre-production had almost run *Mutiny on the Bounty* aground. But Harris liked the pages Antonioni gave him and got ready to give his character Corrado Zeller – the lover-catalyst in the life of Vitti's Giuliana, an engineer's wife on the verge of breakdown – all he had to give.

The movie started in confident mood, but Harris swiftly fell foul of Antonioni who seemed to enjoy 'composing' his film impulsively. Harris tried to readjust and get his balance. He was nothing if not a willing learner and adept at many techniques. But Antonioni was suddenly aloof and evasive. Though the director assured Harris he was improvising as the script developed, interviews with Vitti in a Rome magazine suggested otherwise. After the collaboration with Lindsay Anderson, Harris had expected more of the same. He showed his anger: ' I believed at the beginning that he would give me this participation, because he is a great artist. I assumed he had great respect for my talent because he picked me. When I got to Italy I felt quite the opposite. I felt that Antonioni, after about five weeks I think, probably through his own insecurity, found a new formula for making the picture. I think Antonioni's pictures have their own style . . . but he sort of panicked.' For Harris, good films arose from 'an absolutely fifty-fifty compromise' between actor and director. Furthermore, despite his former blockbusters he was not an action star and would not be moulded as such. Antonioni did not seem to understand this. But, says Harris, 'I certainly would not suggest that he's not a great director. He's a marvellous director. He understands Monica Vitti well, and Monica needs to be sort of wound up like a doll, and then let loose. Then she goes through all the emotions of acting, what she is told to do.'

Another problem was Antonioni's fascination with the man in the street – a fascination that clashed with Harris' similar interest since it showed itself in a fondness for casting amateur actors in main roles. In its lengthy and damning review of *Deserto Rosso* the *Monthly Film Bulletin* singled out Carlo Chionetti, the amateur who played Vitti's husband Ugo, as the film's best performer.

By Christmas the strain of incompatibility had caused the production to sink into chaos. *Deserto Rosso* was behind schedule and Harris was constantly bickering about unrehearsed lines and confusing direction. It didn't help that Antonioni avoided using English and insisted on communication by semaphore. When Liz visited, it was obvious that the disenchantment had blown the fuses on the film: Harris still called the Italian a genius, but he wanted out. Hollywood, the burden and challenge that was always at the fringe, was all of a sudden a welcome intrusion. Producer Jerry Bresler and emerging director Sam Peckinpah flew to Rome in December to woo him into *Major Dundee*, a western of the type he had played a thousand times in the green garden of his childhood. Anthony Quinn and Steve McQueen had been first choices (both turned it down) but then Charlton Heston saw Harris in *This Sporting Life* and was swayed. Heston barely remembered his co-star 'in a small part' in *The Wreck of the Mary Deare*. In his diary he details his initial hesitation: the part on offer was that of Confederate Captain Ben Tyreen who, against form, rides with Union Major Dundee and his men to catch a renegade Apache group; the story depicted North–South prejudices and Heston had hoped for distinctly American players. When Peckinpah saw Anderson's film he was elated and persuaded Heston – hence the trip to Rome. Regardless of the throes of Antonioni anguish, Harris hesitated – and hiked up his asking price. The gesture was a clever one that revealed his grasp of the game rules. In *Dundee* he was selling out – but at a price. Bresler backed off, telling agent Fraser that Harris was too expensive. On 12 December Anthony Quinn was declared available and Harris seemed to have lost his moment. But he didn't lose his nerve nor drop his fee. On 18 December, against everyone's predictions, Bresler agreed the fee – reputedly $300,000 – and Harris signed on.

By New Year 1964 Harris was itching to leave the freezing, fogbound location of Ravenna, near Milan, but he was still putting all he had into it. A friend says, 'He was giving it 110 per cent till the end. When he committed himself, he committed himself.' Antonioni's schedule was upside down, but for *Major Dundee* Columbia had an immovable start date of 5 February in Durango, Mexico. Antonioni resisted. He cabled

Columbia, requesting more time. Columbia refused. Harris toiled on, but a week later, with *Deserto Rosso* seemingly no nearer to completion, he walked off the film and booked a direct flight to Los Angeles. Harris says: 'I just walked out. It came to a point where enough was enough. I wasn't being treated fairly and so I left them with the problems of their own creation. They had to shoot the remainder of the picture without me. Consequently it's not me you see in some of those long shots. They found someone who looked like me and slotted him in.' In the version issued in late 1964 Harris's dubbed Italian voice is unflattering and unconvincing, though his presence has the solid impact of an accomplished, in-control actor. In Italy the film succeeded, fulfilling expectations. In France it was popular. Elsewhere it was hardly seen. Jean-Luc Godard called it 'the conscious or unconscious summit' of Antonioni's recent films and in an open letter told the director: 'Your art has reached a new place; *Deserto Rosso* . . . is for you a fulfilment and completion.' Godard itemized the ingenuity: Antonioni's 'psycho-physiology of colour' was impressive and the stylized effect of telephoto lenses to flatten the depth of field, infrequent close-ups and slow fades, reduced the realism and created a suitably unnerving mood. *Films and Filming* found it stylish, but without compassion – a view apparently supported by Harris, who even today reviews the movie with extreme ambivalence.

Harris's own account of his departure from Italy reads like the diary of a nervous breakdown. Throughout January he had been working around the clock to catch up on tangled schedules. By the middle of the month he wasn't even getting to bed; instead he slept under a quilt on a shakedown near the set, to be awoken at five each day with strong black coffee laced with brandy – the tipple he most loved, but which guaranteed his worst hangovers. On the final night he worked till five in the morning non-stop – then threw in the towel. He grabbed a unit car and dashed across the fogbound, icy hills towards Milan airport. He missed his direct flight and patched together a series of jet hops – to London, New York, St Louis – rushing to catch the rehearsal date on *Major Dundee*. In London he waited six hours for his connection and drank hard to stay awake. When finally he made LA he was in a limbo of semi-consciusness and several hours late for the arrangements he had made. Bresler had wardrobe fittings, riding lessons and a rehearsal talk-through set up.

Harris recalls being on Stage 29 of Columbia Studios, bleary and detached after weeks of tension with Antonioni and his amateurs, daydreaming about the heroes of his youth who had worked here before him: *It Happened One Night* was shot here; and *The Caine Mutiny*, and *The Bridge on the River Kwai*. At that time he never wore a watch, since its hastening face constantly reminded him of the next whistle-stop. He recalls shouting to Sam Peckinpah across the set, asking the time . . . and then *blackout*.

'The rise and fall of the siren wail; tyres squealing on a greasy road; rubber-soled shoes squeaking on vinyl floors. A monk in a dark habit is painted on a white wall. No, he's not. He's moving. Speaking. Latin. Schooldays. *Veni, vidi, vici. Amo, amas, amat.* But he's not talking schoolboy Latin. He's speaking the Latin of the Catholic church. He's giving somebody the last rites before dying. . . . I open my eyes. It is not a dream. It is real. And that someone is me. "Am I going to die, Father?" I asked him. The priest ignored my question but went on with his prayers. . . .'

In the shock of collapse Harris was hysterical, briefly fearing that he had suffered a heart attack. Heston, who was putting him through his horsemanship paces at the time, was unmoved. In his published diary he wrote: 'Dick was . . . stricken is the only word that leaps to mind. I can understand it, I guess. He's been working damn hard with Antonioni and now must feel some pressure on this part because of the riding and the southern accent. . . .' Jerry Bresler phoned Liz in London, informing her that her husband had collapsed with nervous exhaustion and was sleeping under sedation. Bresler was calmly reassuring but minutes later Harris himself was on the line, railing at her for not being by his side. The accusation was, of course, unreasonable: Liz had her hands more than full with the pressures of a new, half-furnished home and three lively children. She made her case, but Harris was in no mood to listen. He was convinced of a real and lingering illness. After his first collapse at LAMDA, when malnutrition had been diagnosed, he was always wary, always ready for the next.

To be safe, the best available heart surgeon was summoned to perform electrocardiogram and other tests. The results were comforting, though in hindsight probably misleading: it would be fifteen years and many more collapses before a blood sugar irregularity that was indeed life-threatening would be revealed.

Heston's relative indifference to Harris's health is understandable. A staunchly 'proper' family man, Heston had a reputation for discipline that was as legendary as Harris's brawling braggart notoriety. It can hardly have escaped Heston's notice that *all* Harris's Hollywood welcome notices were spiced with tales of daring, even dangerous, abandon. In Italy he had experimented with LSD, preceding the Beatles by two years. The experiment almost killed him. He told writer John Kobal: 'I felt my mind leave my body. I was in that room but not of it . . . and I knew that I didn't want to be the success I was with all the chains that it brings to a man. . . .' He had tried to jump out of a window, but was restrained by film crew friends. Since the Ginger Man had come into his life he was, he admitted, 'basically a destructive personality'. This cannot have impressed fussy, fatherly Heston who addressed himself to film-making, according to Harris at a film lecture in Dublin in 1989, 'as one might, say, run a bank'. On *Major Dundee* Heston wore the mantle of almost-producer, endlessly ploughing the back fields of bit-part casting, choice of horses used and characters' deep histories. He had *Ben-Hur* to live up to, and wasn't about to allow an unrestrained greenhorn Irishman ruin his show. Harris redeemed himself quickly, pursuing earnest conferences with Peckinpah once the worst of his exhaustion was over and worrying away at the discrepancies in Captain Ben Tyreen, just as he had honed Frank Machin. After days of talk he had found Tyreen – 'a displaced man without roots, and basically I find that easy to understand. My family left Wales in 1747 [*sic*] and arrived in Ireland and then generations of the family were Irish . . . and then my father was very pro-British. But I am very Irish in temperament. And then I left Ireland and my family died off [*sic*]. When you finally land in a foreign country and you stare into strange faces and pass shops that don't mean anything to you, these things make a deep impression on your mind, and you store them. They're like stickybacks. They stick to my back and I can't get rid of them . . . and I attempted to bring a part of that to Tyreen.'

With a nervous insurance cover of $4 million riding on him, Harris left hospital and flew to Mexico City to start filming. The unit doctor was put on all-day alert to watch over him and provide vitamin injections when required.

Apart from Harris's own state of health, after the unbearable strain of Italy's cold he now had to face the unbearable strain of Mexico's heat.

The first day's shoot, he recalls, involved – appropriately – a fist fight with Heston. It was a sampler of the unfolding relationship. 'Chuckles', as Harris knew him, was still sceptical and generally frowned on his latest co-star; this hauteur sickened Harris, who did not conceal his reciprocal dislike.

'He was a pain in the ass,' Harris said. 'He was so damn square you wouldn't believe it. I had been ill. I was tired. I had barely seen my children, my new son, in months. I came to this scorching location and here was this superstar laying it on hard for me. I was late once or twice for the early morning call and he started making a ridiculous deal about it. He got a stopwatch and sat there each day in his trailer waiting for me to clock in. It was like some stupid factory. I soon got pretty pissed off. So I got a load of alarm clocks and set them all around his make-up trailer. And I showed up before the call time and had them all set up to go off *on the dot* of the call time. So Heston came in – and suddenly all these alarms went off, a huge explosion of noise. He jumped out of his skin with the shock. I told him it was just me clocking in. But he wasn't amused at all. He had no sense of humour, not a bit. So it made an already difficult production very tiresome.'

On 17 April Heston was describing Harris as 'something of a fuck-up, no question', but he later generously wrote that this was unfair: 'I seem to have been unloading all my frustrations over the [scorchingly hot] location on poor Dick Harris. . . . Dick wasn't used to working with either horses or guns. If he was a fuck-up, I was a hard-nosed son of a bitch.'

Peckinpah was no great delight either. On his first major studio film he was 'going European', and 'shooting the sky'. Heston respected Peckinpah's nerve in departing from the precise script to 'find a mood', but Harris had had enough false poetry with Antonioni. There were open rows, spreading beyond the principals. At one point Peckinpah left the unit and drove off alone into the desert at night, declaring, 'I'd rather sleep with the snakes than with actors.' Harris saw in Peckinpah a fundamental inadequacy, and an attitude towards collaboration that fell short of total honesty. Harris says: 'I think making a picture is a very serious business. And I think that if you commit yourself you must do so in a serious way. I didn't like [Peckinpah] very much. He didn't prepare enough for me. I prepare very strongly but I found him lacking in application . . . and consequently he was not getting the best out of his subject, or out of me and Heston.'

Early in April Columbia executives made an attempt to replace Peckinpah who was seriously over his budget and costing more money than anyone imagined. Already the movie was a quarter of a million dollars over budget, with no chance of catching up. Fearing the worse evil of changing horses in midstream, Heston voiced objection to Mike Frankovitch, head of Columbia, and offered his six-figure salary by way of compensation. Frankovitch was mollified. 'Oh no, Chuck, we wouldn't dream of taking your salary! It's a nice gesture, and we appreciate it, but we'll just go ahead as we are.' Heston's agent didn't for a minute believe it, and chastised his client for offering the salary. In the event, Frankovitch *did* withhold Heston's cheque, but Peckinpah stayed on the movie.

After the Rio Mescala location, the faltering unit repaired to Estudios in Churabusco for the last sequences. Peckinpah held his nerve and continued to shoot what he wanted, and Heston had to admire 'this facet of Sam's method: keeping the structure of a scene loose enough to inject adlibbed lines'. On 27 April particularly, the trick worked supremely, overcoming the difficulties of a bedroom scene with a small-time actress who spoke no English. It all smacked of autocratic Antonioni and his amateurs and his one-man way of making a movie, and Harris once again wished himself out of it and on his way.

After his collapse and the angry phone call Liz flew to Mexico to be by her husband's side. She kept close company with him, encouraging his relaxed friendship with actor James Coburn and their outings to clubs and bull rings. But Harris's tiredness was clearly in evidence. At the Plaza de Toros in Mexico City Liz and Coburn watched in horror as Harris physically attacked a Mexican spectator who knocked down Harris's bag of candy in response to a matador's poor showing in the ring. This summary violence was unnerving to Liz – as was the preoccupation with disease and death, in Mexico more noticeable than ever before. When Lindsay Anderson flew out to join them for a short holiday the suggestion of a spot of recreational 8mm film-making was made. Each would contribute a brief film essay about Mexico. Anderson shot the landscape; Liz shot the peasants; Harris, to universal dismay, shot a child's funeral. 'He could be morbid,' says a friend. 'Especially when he was tired. At that time he was utterly fagged out.'

Liz's concern about their sliding marriage hardly reached Harris. Instead he was eager to chat with Anderson and Coburn and the few sympathetic friends about the obstacle course of stardom that lay ahead. He was idealistic, but he wasn't stupid. A streetwise instinct told him to prepare for possible problems by mustering his forces. Jimmy Fraser was a supreme agent, and internationally respected, but Harris had – and still has – an innate wariness of all ten-per-cent agents. In 1989 he told me: 'I had an American agent, one of the best. He rang me and said, "I haven't *seen* you in six months. We *never* meet. We must have dinner!" And I said, "I don't want dinner. You are my agent, not my friend. Your job is to look out for the business, period." . . . But all these agents want more.' As he tiptoed through the Hollywood minefield at this shakiest of times, the perfect alternative suggested itself: Dermot, the young brother whom Kevin Dinneen had tipped for stardom, was on the phone expressing his desire to study the movie business. Harris embraced the opportunity. Back in London they would set up shop. Dermot would get busy hunting new projects and learning the accountancy ropes.

But first there was an invitation that was too good to pass up. Ironically the call was again to Rome, from director John Huston, widely regarded as Hollywood's most intelligent innovator, with classics like *Moby Dick* (1956) and *The Misfits* (1960) to his credit. Huston was another Frank Machin fan, and he was lavish with praise. He wanted Harris to play Cain in the

Italian-financed production of *The Bible . . . In the Beginning*. As outlined on the phone, the part was no more than a cameo in a complex movie of cameo essays, but Huston's Irishness, his immediate intellect and his willingness to listen and exchange made Harris keen to accept.

Major Dundee finished on 1 May, hugely over time and budget, and Harris flew to Rome, stopping over briefly in London to see newest son Jamie. His spirits were now restored and he was sanguine about his western – with good cause. Bresler, Heston and Peckinpah continued to slug it out through post-production but the end result, premiered at Chicago's Roosevelt Theater on 2 April 1965, was a hit at the box office and gave the world its first look at Harris the Hollywood Hero. Eugene Archer in the *New York Times* noted 'an interesting cast, unexpected bits of character revelation and a choppy continuity'. And Philip Scheuer in the *Los Angeles Times* begrudgingly admitted 'no reason to complain about the performances'. Later, in London, the film was praised for its 'realistic, almost Continental approach' (*Films and Filming*) and at last the Brando comparisons (still offered in several reviews), seemed contrived and inappropriate. Viewed today, with the perspective of Harris's and Peckinpah's later work, *Major Dundee* is an intelligent parable of paranoia in American life; furthermore, it boasts a daring that actor and director later surrendered in favour of parody. It is not among Harris's first-league work, but it trails not far behind.

In Rome Harris was back on the front pages in no time. Mauro Bolognini was among a group of leading directors setting up a portmanteau movie to launch society beauty Princess Soraya, former wife of the Shah of Iran, to international stardom. The film was being sponsored by entrepreneur Dino De Laurentiis and was, in theory at any rate, a no-expenses-spared enterprise. Bolognini courted Harris and fixed a dinner date with Soraya for Harris's arrival in Rome. But Harris stood the princess up. The media hollered in delight. 'The facts of the matter were very simple,' Harris later said. 'I didn't want to meet Soraya socially until I had first met the director [they had only spoken on the telephone]. For if I didn't get on with him, and I did not think much of his earlier pictures, I had no intention of making this particular film. Now, if I met Soraya before I had made my mind up about working with her and finally decided not to go ahead, people would say that it was because we did not hit it off together.' The accusations of rows with Soraya, groundless as they were, made the headlines anyway. Harris wasn't bothered. He knew the strategy of pressmen, had studied it and manipulated it himself, and when it went against him it did not – mostly – offend him.

The stirrings in the British press had ceased to alarm Liz. Since *Sporting Life* she had watched it all in a curiously detached way, aware but immune. The Richard Harris of the press was a barn-storming, horny acrobat, balancing two non-complementary, improbable lives, drinking beyond human endurance, philandering beyond belief. That the stories were exaggerated she was in no doubt; but the smoke contained corrosive fire. Liz clung to her Bedford Gardens family routine as the era of Harris-mania began.

8

On thin Ice

After his collapse on *Major Dundee* Harris made a serious attempt to control his boozing. On doctor's advice he cut out spirits and confined himself to beer and champagne. He was proud of his courage and the ensuing change of temperament, and spoke widely about it. A year ago, he told British journalist Roderick Mann, he had been drinking with a lunatic abandon. During the American promotional junket for *This Sporting Life* he had grown tired of the non-stop kiss-ass interviews and crept away from the five-star New York hotels to drink 'awful rot-gut with the winos' of the Bowery. He told Mann: 'I spent four days there while the studio [*sic*] was going crazy . . . but it was wonderful.' Afterwards he was 'sick as a dog'. That was all in the past. Now he was reformed, getting fitter, and he could sensibly enjoy the taste of alcohol – which he loved – without pushing himself to the edge. Those who welcomed the declaration as a recipe for an improved, more relaxed marriage ill understood Richard Harris: it wasn't his drinking that fractured the relationship, rather the stress of his chosen career. In other circumstances, all his friends agree, the made-in-heaven marriage could have thrived. But now there was stardom and a hastening schedule and wider temptations. Very quickly the animal energy that had first attracted Liz became predatory and unacceptably aggressive, and a love that had slid to apathy turned, in her words, to hate.

The actor Franco Nero met Harris in Itri, near Sperlonga, their location for *The Bible*, and found him 'serene, but bursting with a boy's energy'. Their relationship grew into warm friendship, but Harris did not share with Nero any of his personal worries nor revelations of his family life. Instead his young

co-star – billed as 'John Huston's Great Discovery' – was a
bachelor to share bachelor fun with, and lend encouragement
to. 'I was quite shy really,' says Nero. 'This film was my Big
Deal. I had started at sixteen in Parma, playing with a singing
group called the Hurricanes. We sang Pat Boone and Frank
Sinatra songs and made a little money. But I couldn't speak
English, so I just made up these English-American-sounding
words to go with the songs.' The removal of his tonsils when
he was twenty-one put paid to Nero's singing dreams. 'They
made some kind of mistake and damaged my vocal cords. But
it didn't matter, really. I was interested by then in documentary
film-making. With Vittorio Storaro [the cinematographer who
later shot *Apocalypse Now* and *Reds*] I went to Rome with a
story outline I'd written, looking for a producer to finance me.
I thought I might become a director. But this producer saw me
and said, "You are young, you have a pretty face. You are crazy
to go *behind* the cameras. I have a film for you."' The producer
cast Nero – whose real name was Francesco Sparanero – in
a cheapie, *The Third Eye*, for Italian release. Nero is in no
doubt that Huston's casting of him as Abel opposite Harris's
Cain, and the press excitement that followed, launched his
real career. He had been a moviegoer since childhood, and
knew Harris's name, but the excesses of Harris's publicity
had not reached him. Members of the crew pointed out that
Harris had rowed with Mitchum, Brando, Heston, Antonioni
– that no movie of his passed without a fracas – but Nero
approached him with frank admiration and was rewarded by
'a brotherly friendship that has withstood the years'. Nero is
stoutly defensive: 'I learned he is a private man and I learned he
is the most loyal of men. There was no hot-and-cold. Richard
was totally consistent with me and very good – except once.
The once was when we were filming the death scene, where
Cain attacks Abel. Richard had to hit me with the bone of an
animal, a pretty big bone. Well, he did it realistically and hit
my eye, and I had some trouble with it for days afterwards.
But that was accidental, believe me. If he had a reputation for
fighting, I did not see it. On *The Bible* he was helpful, and I
was an amateur.'

Harris loved Huston and *The Bible*, even though his scenes
lasted just six minutes in an epic that ran for 175 minutes. In a

Above: Teenage rugby with Old Crescent. His front row pals are Teddy Curtin and Niall Quaid. (courtesy Elizabeth Brennan)

An actor apparent: ...n drag for a Christmas ...imerick, circa 1953. ...sy Willie Allen)

Above: With Betty, shortly before she was 'harrised' out of town (courtesy Elizabeth Brennan)

Centre: The Harris family home on the Ennis Road, Limerick. (Newgarden Photographic)

...e: Richard Harris used his earnings from *This Sporting Life* to buy the failing Harris Mills. He swore ...would not sell the building until time wore away the Harris sign. By 1988 the sign was faded. Today ...the building has been acquired by the local corporation. It will be a pay car park. (Newgarden Photographic)

Top left: With Elizabeth and baby Damian in London, 1959. (author's collection) *Top right:* First TV work – in Manchester. Harris in Joseph O'Connor's *The Iron Harp*, for Granada, March 1958. (Granada T.V.) *Bottom right:* In *Mutiny on the Bounty*. (Tony Crawley Collection) *Bottom left:* Indulging his great passion in *This Sporting Life*, the breakthrough movie, 1963. Harris is on the ball. (National Film Archive)

Top left: Major Dundee in 1964, his first Hollywood leading role. Co-star Charlton Heston and Harris fought off-screen, too. (Youngblood Production) *Top right:* Harris as Cromwell; controversial casting, but, he declared, 'It's not necessary for the actor to believe in the character . . .'. (Tony Crawley) *Left:* King Richard! Harris on the Hollywood set of *Camelot*. 'It was a happy movie set,' said co-star Franco Nero. 'They were making us stars!' (Camera Press) *Below:* Back home in Kilkee, Ireland, for time out on his beloved racquet courts. Manuel Di Lucia makes up the foursome. (courtesy Manuel Di Lucia)

Above: The unshakeable attraction of rugby. Harris and Sean Connery with crew team mates impro ,during filming of *The Molly Maguires*. (Rex Features)

Above: Richard Harris, pop star. Songwriter Jimmy Webb gave him 'MacArthur Park', which had been turned down by the Association group. It went to Number Two in the American charts. (Universal Pictorial Press)

Above: With Linda Hayden on vacation in Ireland, 1970. (Tom McElroy)

Above: A major hit in *A Man Called Horse*, 1970. The historical accuracy of the film was widely pra (Tony Crawley Collection)

Above: In *The Heroes of Telemark*, 1965. The row this time was with Kirk Douglas, but it was short-lived. (Kobal)

Above: Harris, 1987. (Irish Press Archive)

Above: Richard Harris, poet. At the London launch of *I, In the Membership of My Days*, collected jottings from 1939-1973. (Universal Pictorial Press)

Above: On the *Gulliver's Travels* set at Pinewood Studios, 1975. (Youngblood Production)

Above: Portraying an unusual Maigret – in a whisper. Audiences and critics were divided, 1988. (HTV West)

Above: Reconciled – as best pals at least with first wife, Elizabeth. 'I would kill for my two wives,' he said. (Irish Press Archive)

Above: With Doris Day during *Caprice*. Hollywood, 1960. (Kobal)

Above: Harris with second wife, Ann, and brother-in-law, Jack Donnelly (who was married to Harris's sister, Harmay). (Irish Press Archive)

Left and below left: King Arthur returns! On the Apollo Victoria Theatre stage, 1982. (Universal Pictorial Press)

Above: Harris as Bull McCabe in *The Field*, 1990. The Connemara locations were difficult in the November gales. (Robert Doyle) *Left:* HTV's *King of the Wind*, 1990. 'I'm doing this for the money.' Here with Glenda Jackson. (HTV West)

Above: Richard Harris at fifty-nine. In the west of Ireland. November 1989. (Tom McElroy)

1966 interview he said: 'I think it's the best thing I've ever done. I really do. I found it a fantastic experience, quite remarkable. John Huston is certainly one of the two most exciting men I've ever worked with, a great artist and a great story-teller; so understanding with the actor and so helpful. John is an actor at heart and he let me go, let me get into the part and do it, then he moulded it.' Franco Nero, whose expectations of a director were somewhat different given his newness, admired Huston every bit as much. 'He was a loving director', Nero says, 'who believed in pushing you on to your best.'

They weren't the only ones satisfied with Huston. Despite the logistical complexity of *The Bible* – Christopher Fry's ponderous script covered the Creation (with Huston as the voice of God), Eden and the Expulsion, Cain and Abel, Noah's Ark, the Tower of Babel, Abraham, Sodom and Gomorrah, Lot's wife *et al* – Huston kept the budget reins tight and impressed Darryl F. Zanuck, head of 20th Century-Fox, who was considering investment in the production. One year after the completion of the Harris–Nero sequence at Itri, Nero was surprised to be called back to Rome by producer Dino De Laurentiis for yet another shot. 'It was astounding, and shows how big that project was,' says Nero. 'Huston had his work cut out keeping it all together.' In June 1965 Zanuck called a mammoth press conference in Hollywood, attended by more than 130 reporters. Flanked by a very tired Huston, producer De Laurentiis and his own executive vice-president Seymour Poe, Zanuck announced Fox's biggest-ever distribution deal, reflecting his admiration for *The Bible*-in-progress.

The deal, in association with Seven Arts and involving the highest minimum guarantee ever given to a movie, gave Fox world exploitation rights – apart from Italy, Israel, Switzerland and Austria, which De Laurentiis had already sold when pre-financing the movie. Zanuck told the world: 'On 25 July I will have served three years as President of Fox. Many significant events have occurred in the rebirth of this corporation. I consider no single event more significant than the acquisition of the release rights of this monumental production. As one of the privileged few who has seen *The Bible* in its unfinished form, I would like to record to show that in my estimation *The Bible* is the greatest example of motion picture-making that I have seen. It is my considered estimation that it will outgross in the theatres of the world any motion picture that has ever been made.' That was a hard act to deliver, even with the hand of God involved. But the actors felt that Zanuck's faith was appropriate, and that the movie would break world records.

The prophecies – unlike those enshrined in the movie itself – were not realized. When it was finally released in November 1966, *The Bible* staggered. Not a turkey perhaps, but it fared no better in reviews and in box office than many quarter-as-cheap Italian 'toga movies'. Filmed in 65mm by the brilliant Giuseppe Rotunno and decorated throughout with sparkling cameos – George C. Scott, Michael Parks, Ava Gardner, Peter O'Toole, Stephen Boyd – *The Bible* failed mainly because of its hype. It had initially been announced (in Italy) as a movie directed in segments by Luchino Visconti, Orson Welles, Federico Fellini and Robert Bresson, but the surfeit of promise choked it. Most reviewers criticized great expectations and the publicists who fanned them. But Rex Reed delivered judgement on the creative whole, not sparing anyone: 'At a time when religion needs all the help it can get, John Huston may have set its cause back a couple of thousand years.'

This disappointment was a year away when Harris debated whether to return to London for career discussions with Anderson or to stay in Rome for the Soraya movie, *Three Faces of a Woman*. When finally he met the zesty young director Mauro Bolognini, the decision was easily made. Reconciled with the Italian persona by the good grace of Nero and the natives among Huston's crew, Harris took to Bolognini instantly. The involvement of British writer Clive Exton – whose review of *Diary of a Madman* Harris liked to quote – helped the issue, as did his instincts on meeting Soraya. Whatever preconceptions he had about the former Empress of Iran disappeared the moment they met. Soraya was not the brittle, imperious princess the media often reported, rather a gentle woman of thirty, wounded by fate but fighting back.

In 1951, aged just eighteen, Soraya Esfandiari, of mixed German–Bakhtiaria parentage, had married the Shah in a true love match that won the Islamic world's heart. Their life was blissful – until it became clear that Soraya could not bear children for the Shah. The best doctors were consulted and Soraya made no bones about her distress. The problem of her infertility was openly discussed. She and the Shah tried 'four times a night and twice in the afternoons,' she said, to no avail. When foreign gynaecological experts were imported she told them: 'I'll keep making the omelettes and you figure how to crack the eggs.' After seven fruitless years the Shah was forced, by the demands of the throne, to divorce her. In a radio speech to the nation reminiscent of Edward VIII's, the Shah spoke of 'sacrificing our love for the sake of the country'. Soraya was pensioned off to live in Europe, where she became a leading socialite and jet-setter. Her friendship with the Shah remained and, in the eyes of many, her film star ambitions arose from a desire to impress him and demonstrate her independent worth.

Soraya is reputed to have contributed to the financing of *Three Faces of a Woman*, and certainly her personal stamp was all over the production from the outset. Initially Bolognini informed Harris that the princess wanted full artistic control. But when Harris met Soraya the atmosphere changed and she politely deferred to his higher status and experience. Remembering her today, Harris sighs warm-heartedly. It is evident that he liked her, and that he encountered the movie with enthusiasm. Soraya celebrated their initial good chemistry by sending Harris a half bottle of champagne . . . day after day throughout the production.

Chastened by the contrasting experiences of the last two years and by the continued disarray of his life, Harris had devised a shorthand analysis approach to his movies which gave a semblance of tactical order. This film was commerce, not art – so he would give it all his action-man, press-bashing gusto. The trick was no secret. He told Tony Crawley: '*Sporting Life*, *Deserto Rosso* and *The Bible* are artistic pictures. I balance those against *Major Dundee* and this one. . . .' Crawley saw a big personality, bigger than his physical frame or any single existing artistic achievement, wrestling for expression but somewhat at sea.

Bolognini's half-hour film (there were three mini-pictures in one, by three different directors) moved along pleasantly, if not enrichingly. Harris tried to turn a blind eye, but once again the problems of Italian film-making gave cause for alarm:

'I like Bolognini immensely as a man. I think he's immensely talented, very sensitive, and I like his views. But the Italians have no regard for acting at all. They shoot without any regard for the actor. We are puppets to them. They don't regard acting as a craft, or an art form. They think it's totally dispensable in motion pictures. The theory is they let two or three cameras follow you round a room . . . rather like documentary shooting. But if they want that, why don't they get someone off the street? There is an art of acting, where everything must be geared to a single camera lens. It is a studied technique. But they – Antonioni especially – have no regard for that.'

Princess Soraya – a classic example of the Italian preference for non-actors – presented additional difficulties. On the set he called her 'Soya', like the sauce, which vexed her entourage. When it was requested that he call her 'Your Highness', Harris retorted by demanding that Liz's brother Morgan, visiting with Liz, be referred to as 'The Honourable Morgan'. This absurdity brought everybody down to earth and reinstated the good-natured atmosphere of the start. When his segment was in the can, Harris expressed satisfaction with the work. Despite his avoidance of all her extravagant parties, Soraya liked him a lot. 'If my first film is a success,' she told the press, 'I shall owe it partly to Richard Harris's kindness and understanding.'

Harris avoided any further encounter with Antonioni, whose segment was shot directly after Bolognini's. When grilled about it he would only repeat his admiration for Antonioni's talent – 'but the romance only lasted five weeks'. He would not work with Antonioni again, no matter what. It was, as graciously as could be expected, goodbye to Italy and the rickety School of Realism.

The magnet of Hollywood, and Hollywood bucks, yanked at him instantly. Surveying opportunities in London, Harris was dazed by the offers. A possible Broadway show, *Baker Street*, was the singing chance he longed for; grapevine word said it would top *My Fair Lady*. A major anti-hero spy spoof to challenge the monopoly of James Bond was on offer from director Jack Cardiff; it was called *The Liquidator* and might place Harris up in the box office top ten drawing names. . . . Advice was coming from all quarters, but Harris stalled. He

disliked the idea of yet another commercial venture intensely
– and anyway *The Liquidator*'s script was bad towards the end.
He had great visions inside his head, great movies to be made
with Anderson, or with Karel Reisz, or with Sidney Pollack,
an undiscovered American TV director. *Hamlet* occupied much
of his spare-time reading – he was reworking it, minutely
examining the various published texts and finding 'a new
play' in the gaps.

Then came the Hollywood bid. This time it was a block-
buster with Kirk Douglas, a war yarn called *The Heroes of
Telemark*. Harris baulked, but then 'The fee got so high it
seemed immoral to say no.' He accepted, on condition that he
got a ten-day holiday over Christmas to spend with the family.
The production was reshaped, Harris was accommodated, and
Anderson and the art world watched the Golden Hope drift a
little further from view.

The Richard Harris who returned to Limerick at Christmas
1964 was in effect a pop star. Surrounded by adoring family
and back-slapping friends-who-told-you-so, he was everyone's idea of a monumental success. The fans rolled up,
haunting the corridors of the Old Ground Hotel in Ennis –
Jack Donnelly's new management responsibility – where the
family was ensconced, begging autographs and hugs. The
reporter fans of the Ginger Man from the Bailey were also
present. At his press conference Harris sat between Harmay
and brother Dermot (who would be his assistant on *The
Heroes of Telemark*) and spoke of his contentment. He would
be buying Creghan's Castle in the Burren, an area of Brontëan
moorland, he said. The locale would be perfect for shooting
Wuthering Heights and he must soon bring Lindsay Anderson
to visit. Great career leaps were coming and, yes, he was
taking control of show business as opposed to vice versa.
Dermot would henceforth work alongside him as producer
and guardian. He was hand-picking projects, regardless of
financiers. Harris would do a short fim based on his new poem
'Guns and Drums', crossbred from *Wuthering Heights* and *The
Ginger Man*: 'I suppose you could classify it as nostalgic. It
is based on the theme of a man against the world and I'll
film it in the Burren country in the coming year. It will be
a half-hour. . . .' There was also *Mavourneen*, a satire written

by Frank Tarloff and Peter Stone, co-authors of Cary Grant's finest sixties' film, *Father Goose*. (None of these projects was realized.)

Absolute contentment? Maybe not. There was the gripe of the $100,000 promised for *Three Faces of a Woman* and as yet unpaid: 'They'll pay me interest on that, count on it.' And acting had its limitations: 'I'm going to chuck it in as an actor in three years' time, and take more interest in directing and producing. It's good to have ambitions and dreams. And this way I can test my own abilities.'

On 30 December at Ennis Pro-Cathedral family business came back to the fore. Jamie, twenty-one-months old, was finally christened by the Reverend Kenny, with Jack Donnelly and Mrs Billy Lloyd (sister-in-law of pal Paddy Lloyd) as sponsors. The luncheon that followed, with the biggest gathering of Harrises since Milly's funeral, gave back optimism to the family members who worried about the future of Dickie and Liz. Their love seemed secure. They had a bonny family and were gathering substantial wealth. What else could they want?

After New Year celebrations the Harrises flew back to Oslo in Norway and Richard began work again on Kirk Douglas's western on skis. Harris had rented a luxurious chalet on the 'Bel Air slopes' of Rjukan, the location 120 miles west of Oslo. Here, promptly, the entire family went down with a dose of chicken-pox – except Harris, who remained upright fortified by a largely non-alcohol diet. This 'diet' was just as well, since Rjukan village had no liquor licence and the few dowdy nightspots made do with tropical mineral drinks. When the now inevitable fan-journalists braved the climate to pay homage, Harris kept his no-booze pledge. Philip Oakes visited and wrote: 'Given a bottle of whisky he pulled the stopper and sniffed the contents with the rapt expression of a woman anaesthetized with Chanel.' Still, the journalists wanted Hell-raiser Harris, so they got him, albeit half-heartedly.

At the start he and Kirk Douglas had not got on. This was, historically, Douglas's picture. Anthony Mann, who was directing, had been fired from Douglas's earlier epic *Spartacus* (1956) in a dispute arising from artistic differences. But Douglas liked him and promised: 'The next time you want me for a picture, just call me.' The previous summer Mann had called, proferring a screenplay based on the Norwegian wartime underground movement and their efforts against the Nazi heavy water installations that were the nursery for the German atom bomb. Douglas didn't even ask to see the script. He had made a promise to Mann and had every intention of discharging it. He would support Mann and carry the movie as far as he could.

Harris had equal billing, above Michael Redgrave. From the moment production started, Harris said, he was aware of Douglas brashly asserting his authority: 'At first it was tricky. I knew his reputation for aggression, you see . . . Richard Brooks, the director, once said, "The trouble with Kirk Douglas is that he thinks he's Kirk Douglas." And it's true. He's been impressed by himself far too long. I knew I couldn't knuckle under to him or I'd be finished. So we had this big clash right at the start. And I can roar as loud as anyone. I told him, "You're too old to start anything. Twenty years ago you could have handled me – maybe – but not now. So don't press your luck."' The journalists lapped it up. Douglas had been bragging about his latest lady friend, a local beauty who had been Miss Norway. Harris allegedly chided: 'Oh yeh? What year?'

But by January the waters were calm, and Douglas and Harris enjoyed a trouble-free shoot under the strict, professional control of Mann, a religious adherent of the old Hollywood tradition of the story-driven movie. Mann was passionate about the film, which he saw as a notch above the usual syrupy war flick. He had been given the book *Skis Against the Atom* by Knut Havglund and had immediately flown to Norway to walk the landscape: 'I saw the visual possibilities [of Rjukan]. . . . You keep elaborating and collaborating and eventually the place brings ideas.' The movie would have the orchestrated story tightness of his previous films like *The Glenn Miller Story* (1954). 'I don't believe in talk in films. That's for theatre. Here, you *see* the story.' This rigid concept excluded collaborative negotiations with Richard Harris or anyone else. Harris didn't moan, but he was quick to announce his reduced involvement – with a kick: 'When I work as an actor I usually *live* the part I play. Well, this is one of the very few times I'm just playing the part. I'm not going into any deep psychological motivation. Why? The characters aren't important. Here it's the story that's important, almost like a documentary.' Beyond that, there were no arguments.

For recreation Harris practised the skiing he had half-learned for the movie. His stand-in Frank Harper was his closest friend on the location, though Liz joined him regularly on the slopes. In the evenings there were get-togethers in the bar of the solitary hotel and his talk, when not that of a reluctant hell-raiser, was all about death. He told Philip Oakes: 'If I die tomorrow, everything is taken care off.' The Bedford Gardens house he hated, but Liz liked it, so . . . so be it. It didn't sound like a thirty-five-year-old, newly arrived millionaire with fans in the woodwork and the world at his feet. His dreams, too, were often about death: 'In one dream I was back home and the streets were full of people streaming in the same direction. I saw my mother crying and I tried to comfort her but she couldn't hear me. There was a funeral going on and I asked whose it was. Finally someone said, "Richard Harris." And I shouted out, "No! No! I'm alive!" – but no one took any notice.' Another dream was about death in a plane crash.

Anthony Mann, ironically, had directed *The Fall of the Roman Empire*, the movie over which Harris fell out with producer Samuel Bronston. During the Rjukan location shooting the film's Norwegian premiere in Oslo occurred. Mann proudly organized a trip for his leading players, with the option of travelling overland – a four-hour car journey – or flying in a light plane for half an hour. Harris couldn't afford the driving time and considered not going at all. But he would not insult Mann. When he boarded the plane with Frank Harper he was shaking from head to foot, certain that this was the flight of his nightmares. But it all passed without incident and the premiere was a pleasant night on the town . . . with beer to hand.

When Liz and the children returned to London, Harris had only industry talk to amuse him. *Three Faces of a Woman* opened in Rome but in vain he tried to rustle a print, chasing Bolognini and De Laurentiis. He, Dermot and Harper searched for reviews, but all they could find were 'these social-type write-ups'. In fact, the movie was barely seen and never succeeded in finding an international distributor despite decent reviews for its special American screenings. *Variety* found Harris 'fine as the lover [and Soraya] performs ably and exudes undeniable fascination'. But there were no takers, and the movie – and Princess Soraya's acting career – vaporized.

The snowy isolation of Norway had its advantages, giving the Harris brothers the ideal opportunity to reacquaint themselves with each other and plan for the future. A new management arrangement was decided, with ICM whiz-kid John McMichael – 'the sharpest, nicest agent in the business,' according to James Booth – finally taking the helm. When finances and time allowed, the group would set up offices in London and navigate new waters.

The money seemed crucial. In theory (and in the press) a millionaire, Harris had a backlog of debts and suffered from a heavy-handed generosity. Dermot had witnessed the decline of the mill and the fatal poison of no cash flow; a similar fate on Richard's part must at all costs be avoided. Fortunately the big Hollywood scripts were still spilling in – so Harris shuffled the best, choosing James Michener's *Hawaii*, a complex, challenging soap opera in a warmer climate.

Back in London the project-building with Lindsay Anderson had all but ended. 'It wasn't so mysterious,' says an actor friend. 'Lindsay and Richard were two *very* different people. In the end Richard turned away from Lindsay and the relationship fizzled – it's that simple.'

Harris started packing for his busman's holiday in the sun. A reporter called Weston Taylor dropped by and revelled in the Limerickese yarns of 'the hottest property around'. What was the recipe for so perfect a marriage? Taylor asked.

'I get tremendous fun with my wife. The other Saturday lunchtime I went out with a pal to a match. "When will I see you?" she asked. "Tuesday," I said. "And it might be in the police courts."'

He was, he said, lucky to have such a blissful domestic arrangement. It was clear that he, and he alone, ruled the roost – right down to ordering the children's lives: 'I don't send them to school. They have private tutors. The eldest has been going to the Tate Gallery every morning with his tutor, or the National Gallery, or the Tower of London. . . .'

And he was no longer (despite the inherent contradiction) a hell-raiser: 'Can you imagine a hell-raiser making arrangements to ship out to Hawaii an entourage including a wife, three sons, a brother, a niece, a secretary and a nanny?'

The laughter rang out. He was still off the hard stuff. His life was an idyll. But in Hawaii would come the fall off the wagon and, in its tracks, the tantrums and self-indulgence that would deliver the kiss of death to his marriage.

PART TWO

KING RICHARD

'Take me out of my turbulent waters and you extinguish my flame. . . .'

F. Scott Fitzgerald

'An actor acts, that's all there is to it.'

Richard Harris to the author, 1989

9

Caprice and Consequences

It is hard to overstate the rosy bonuses achieved by Harris in ten years' acting: the Rolls Royces, the vases of roses whimsically dyed his favourite lilac, the servants, the gifts, the girls. But it is also hard to overstate the grilling intensity of the limelight, the freedom and privacy that he and others who make the first league surrender. Today Harris is squarely objective about it all: no actor is worth the $7 or $8 million paid to superstars like Dustin Hoffman or Warren Beatty. 'The money should be on the screen,' says Harris now, 'not in their pockets.' But then, in the mid-sixties when hedonism was booming, riding the wave was the name of the game. Harris had a natural vigour that ensured he exploited his situation better than most. By the time he departed for LA and Hawaii again Harris was firmly enthroned as king of the West End trendies, friendly with Princess Margaret (he purchased her Rolls Phantom V and cherished it) and never short of the company of theatrical groupies. He ate in the best restaurants, travelled first-class, lived to the full.

In Hawaii, despite the arduous production, he did not apply the brakes. If anything he pumped the accelerator, throttling up a lifestyle that kissed his limited-booze diet goodbye. The weather was heavenly after Rjukan and London, the native women interesting and exquisite and just as he always liked them – plumpish and not too coiffed. He discovered Miatie, a powerful local speciality that had the hot burn of brandy and he devoured it, paying no heed to the renewed withdrawal symptoms. With Liz, Dermot and the entourage he rented a huge house with a pool on Diamond Head Road, but he was rarely there, spending twleve-hour days on the set instead and vanishing mysteriously into the seductive tropical night. Liz withstood his moonlight whims but the horrors of Miatie frightened her, and she wrote in her memoirs about fearsome outbursts when Harris dashed into fast-moving traffic and mindlessly attacked passing cars with his bare fists.

Harris's infidelities were widely known, but in an era of young promiscuity and masculine chauvinism there was nothing too surprising about them. He has described himself as sexually hyper-active, and in the LA sorties of this period he revelled in his reputation − more like a kid in a sweet shop than a husband with any malicious intentions of being unfaithful. The A-list cocktail circuit was at last open to him and he went to the same parties as Frank Sinatra (with whom he became quite friendly), Cary Grant ('Just said Hello to him'), Liz Taylor, Richard Burton . . . and Merle Oberon.

As Harris tells it, the real-life encounter with Oberon, after nearly twenty years of dreamy lust, was the stuff of men's magazine fantasies: 'They wanted me at every party. I was the *new* thing, the flavour of the month. So Merle Oberon summoned me to one of her lavish parties. I remember this fabulous mansion, with these spectacularly landscaped gardens. I remember thinking, "Boyo, you've come a long way from Limerick." It was like something from the Roman Empire. It was magical.'

At first Oberon took no notice of him and mingled with her guests. But 'I had taken a couple of drinks so I walked up to the woman, sat beside her, looked into her eyes and said, "Merle, I have slept with you many times, dreamed of you, fantasized about you, touched every part of you, kissed every part of you, kissed your breasts and your belly . . . and made love to you in every position that man has conceived . . ."' The actress appeared shocked and walked away. Harris was undaunted: 'I knew in my heart that I would have her that night.'

The party swung, and died. But Harris lingered on. With a purpose. 'Sure enough, I finally got into conversation with her again. The final guests drifted away and we were alone.' Oberon's eyes gazed inquisitively into his. Maybe she was amused by his cheek, maybe enchanted by his childlike openness, so alien to Hollywood.

'These fantasies of yours,' she said at last. 'Would you like to make them come true?'

Harris followed her up to the master bedroom where he stripped and lay – in a trance of disbelief – on the bed. Oberon disappeared into the bathroom.

'I waited breathlessly,' says Harris, 'my whole life since Limerick passing before my eyes. Was this really happening to me?'

Oberon came back into the bedroom 'wearing a see-through pink nightgown with a slit in the side going all the way up to her waist. She had nothing on underneath.' She embraced Harris on the bed and leaned over to turn out the bedside lamp. Harris jumped up and flicked the light back on. 'I have made love to you so many times in the dark,' he told her. 'Now I want to see you, to touch and experience *everything*. Just to be sure it's all real.' The love-making that ensued, says Harris, was 'fabulous'.

On location in Hawaii, meanwhile, Harris applied himself strenuously to a project that had been honed from a thousand-page novel and expressed no misgivings – apart from a loathing for his co-star, Julie Andrews. He had, he said, 'rarely if ever experienced such hatred for a person. Her ambition was so ugly to behold.' Otherwise the film was a monster undertaking with the highest of hopes. The project had started with screenwriter Daniel Taradash and director Fred Zinnemann (*From Here to Eternity* and *High Noon*) attempting to tell the entire history of Hawaii, from the Middle Ages to modern times, in one mammoth screenplay. Originally the movie was planned to be shot and screened in two parts – each separate movie playing in side-by-side cinemas across the world. Zinnemann was enthusiastic about this imaginative concept but the realities didn't pan out. Mirisch Brothers, the production company, had paid $600,000 for the rights to Michener's best-seller and they wanted surefire box office returns, not a long-odds risk. They had alotted $8 million to the movie but writer Taradash, widely experienced and respected in Hollywood, overruled his own work: 'I felt that it was impossible for Fred Zinnemann, brilliant director that he is, to do what he had anticipated – which was to shoot two pictures without a pause. In other words, he might have been shooting for *two hundred and fifty days* – I just couldn't believe that an artist could stay on top form at the end of that period.' Taradash, supported by the Mirisch Brothers, opted to cut and rework the script. Instead of Michener's entirety he would concentrate on the establishing of the first Christian church in Hawaii in the 1820s. Initially no one at Mirisch or United Artists, the major investors/distributors, liked Taradash's device, but it eventually 'clicked' and the film was reshuffled. Rock Hudson and Audrey Hepburn were the proposed stars – but they were superseded by hotshot Harris and equally hot Andrews. Fred Zinnemann withdrew, exhausted, and George Roy Hill, fresh from the popular *World of Henry Orient*, joined as director. The final screenplay based on Taradash's various efforts, was drafted by Dalton Trumbo, who had written *Spartacus*.

Hawaii was the earnest – almost deadweight – Hollywood movie Harris needed to gain the cachet of *serious* star, up there with Newman, Lancaster *et al*. Widely reviewed as 'an exceptional film', it did badly at the box office but was immaculately timed from Harris's point of view since he suddenly had a new American career target in sight. Normally Hollywood mostly bored him, but now the town was alight with casting gossip that set his pulse racing. *Camelot*, the smash Broadway musical of the early sixties, was to be made into a movie. Two actors he was friendly with – indeed sometimes in awe of – had played the leading role of King Arthur on stage: Richard Burton in the New York version and Laurence Harvey in the London Drury Lane transfer. Jack Warner would produce, and it was known that he and scenarist/lyricist Alan Jay Lerner wanted Burton to reprise his stage role, though Burton was kicking his heels and expressing doubts.

Camelot was everything Harris wanted in a film, the sublime blend of art, action, glamour and pedigree. What's more, it was, at last, his chance *to sing* – not his beloved Irish paeans, but gloriously melodic ditties well within his limited (though ambitious) range. On top of that – supremely – his casting as a king would appropriately symbolize his meteoric rise from the Kilkee amphitheatre . . . to this.

Alan Jay Lerner, Jack Warner and director Joshua Logan courted Burton relentlessly throughout 1965, but finally Burton upped his price beyond reach and Warner announced that the film would be cast afresh. In Harris's much-published account of his winning the casting race, he 'chased Logan and Warner around the world' in order to persuade them. Egged on by astrologer Patric Walker, who had read the stars and predicted that he would get the role of King Arthur, Harris sent endless notes and telegrams to Logan, who was in London scouting. The telegrams read: ONLY HARRIS FOR ARTHUR and HARRIS BETTER THAN BURTON.

When Logan ignored the missives he altered his tactics and flew to London to tackle Logan personally. When Logan refused to see him he sneaked into a private party thrown by the director at the Dorchester and borrowed a waiter's uniform for a tenner. Camouflaged, he invaded the party and delivered a note to Logan on a silver salver that once again begged 'Harris for King Arthur!' In a variation of the Harris version, his offer to pay Jack Warner for a screen test won the day. He tested, proved his flair and was duly cast.

Franco Nero offers another account: 'I'll tell you how I got *Camelot* and how Richard got *Camelot*. John Huston recommended us to Jack Warner and to Josh Logan on the strength of *The Bible*. It was his recommendation that settled it, I'm certain of that.' In Nero's case the casting interview took place in London. An appointment was made to see Logan, but when Nero arrived the director was distressed to find that the handsome hero could speak almost no English. 'This is crazy,' Logan said. 'I need a Lancelot that can speak English. This won't do!'

'I can do Shakespeare in English,' Nero said brightly. And went on to deliver with precision the part he had learned, on Huston's recommendation, from *Romeo and Juliet* – by sound. Nero laughs when he recalls that he only half-understood what he was saying. But it didn't matter. The passion worked. And Logan told him there and then that the part was his.

In the London hiatus between *Hawaii* and *Camelot* Harris and Liz avoided each other, both anxious to delay the inevitable. During this time Liz indulged in a brief affair with nightclub pianist Robin Douglas-Home, nephew of the former Tory Prime Minister, which she confessed to her husband. Harris exploded, but the companionship and succour of Patric

Walker defused the situation. A good-hearted and talkative man, Walker foresaw a career improvement for Harris – so his words assumed a mystical ring. Like the Beatles' soon-to-be 'spiritual leader' the Maharishi Mahesh Yogi, Walker was elected man-in-the-middle and travelling counsel. When the call came to return to Hollywood, Harris deemed it 'a new beginning' and booked passages on the *Queen Mary* for himself, Liz and Walker. The journey was fraught, with Harris throwing tantrums nightly, but once in Hollywood a light-heartedness – albeit stimulated by tinseltown fantasy living – improved the situation. On his first night Harris threw a party for 350 guests, most of whom hardly knew him. Rex Harrison and his wife Rachel Roberts came, and the Harrises reopened a chummy friendship that long preceded the eventual romance and marriage of Liz and Harrison. The exclusive Bel Air villa they rented, the Villa Vesco, cost an arm and a leg so Harris quickly decided to squeeze in an extra movie on offer, the Frank Tashlin-Doris Day comedy thriller *Caprice*. More unlikely co-star casting is hard to imagine, but Day too had fallen for the hunky hit of *This Sporting Life* and reckoned him an interesting sub-Sean Connery macho Celt. What her research failed to reveal was that Harris's swarthy Celtic looks owed much to dyed hair and the black-and-whiteness of *This Sporting Life*.

Harris recalled Doris Day's horror on their first meeting – and his surprise. He told *Profile* magazine: 'She told her husband [producer-manager Martin Melcher], "You must get him for me." And I said, "All right", and I'd arrived and come for a make-up test with Doris . . . Now, she expected this six-foot-four man with dark, sunken eyes to walk in. So Doris is sitting down, right? – and suddenly they say Richard is here and the door opens and in comes Harris, barely six feet [*sic*: his official ABPC studio bio has him as 6ft 3ins], pale, red eyes, balding. And Doris was sitting there and she goes . . . [he makes a gesture, aghast]. And I look at her, and she's dressed like a nineteen-year-old . . . I said, "Don't look at me surprised, you're surprising me too."'

High on the prospect of *Camelot*, Harris worked fast and well on *Caprice* at 20th Century-Fox studios, and on location in downtown LA at the Bradbury Building at Broadway and

3rd Street, a Paris Exposition 1900-style mansion that doubled for the cosmetics headquarters round which the movie turned. Swiss sequences were shot at Mammoth Mountain in the High Sierras, not many miles away. Those who predicted turbulence between the egotistical stars were in for a let-down, though the publicists clung to their hopes. Harris respected Day – 'I liked her, she was a ball' – and described kissing her on screen as 'the most dangerous piece of acting I've ever done!' When Day collapsed with back strain late in the production the tabloids were quick to speculate inanely: 'All-American Dream Girl Day and contentious Mr Harris are Beauty and the Beast'; and Miss Day's back pains were caused 'it was rumoured by the fiery acting of Mr Harris in the love scenes . . .'

In reality, burly director-writer Frank Tashlin crafted a painless, professional production that took its place alongside his earlier ironic classics *Artists and Models* (for the Lewis–Martin comedy duo) and *Will Success Spoil Rock Hunter* (with Jayne Mansfield and Tony Randall). A writer first and foremost, Tashlin developed *Caprice* as an industrial espionage satire – though the script was upended when Doris Day insisted on taking the male-written role, leaving Harris with the 'female' part. Tashlin fashioned it, like his earlier satires, as an attack on conformity: 'The nonsense of what we call civilization, leisure, push-button living.' In the movie Day plays Patricia Foster (written as the male Patrick) trying to avenge the murder of her father, an Interpol agent. Ostensibly she is probing the world of cosmetics formulas, but the cosmetics concern is in fact a front for a narcotics operation. Harris plays camp Christopher (originally Christine), a mysterious agent who shadows Patricia and saves her from a murder plot. The film skips along from one colourful incident to the next, dextrously weaving through consumer-heaven in full designer rig – but by and large the critics missed the point. The point was Bondian irony, a comedic magnifying glass on a time of life and film culture when liberal lunacy, not logical story, was the order of the day (and, it must be said, *fond* magnifying glass: Tashlin welcomed the new era of California gaiety; he declared that all his films were aimed 'against all the forces that will reduce variety in the world, limit sensations and experiences and impose in their place a sort of unified mass-produced existence'). For the critics the movie was confusing and incomplete. The *Hollywood Reporter* complained that it 'flits and flutters', while Harris 'does an imitation of Richard Burton which increases one's respect for the original'. Bosley Crowther in the *New York Times* reported Harris affecting 'the arts and airs of a very sissy gentleman, even to wearing eye shadow'. Interestingly, as far as Crowther was concerned Doris Day acted 'with masculine muscularity', indicating that her script reversal notion didn't pay off. Crowther also spotted the Bond association, suggesting that Harris's role was the equivalent of Ursula Andress's in *Dr No*. In Britain the *Monthly Film Bulletin* found the movie 'incomprehensible', while 'Richard Harris seems understandably ill-at-ease'.

Harris's unease was real enough. In the run up to *Camelot* Liz suddenly decided she had had enough of the faking life. Harris was drinking recklessly again, and paying the price. On the soundstage at Fox he collapsed, stalling the production. He told writer Henri Gris he had been boozing with Jason Robards Jr, then Lauren Bacall's husband. It had been a particularly long and hazy session which Harris remembered mostly for that one last jar: it was 'a large vodka diluted with water from my swimming pool. Full of chlorine, bees, ants and spit.' Harris had a huge capacity, but Robards could match him. According to Gris, Harris could 'down two quart bottles in a day and remain beautiful'. But this session delivered more than the usual hangover. Harris was again rushed to hospital. The symptoms this time were terrifying: chest and arm pain. At the Cedars of Lebanon Hospital Dr Rex Kennamer checked Harris thoroughly. 'I'm losing my mind,' Harris told Kennamer. 'Something is the matter. I'm drinking because [of the fear] of it. Find out, once and for all.'

Kennamer told him: 'Take it easy. We won't let you out of here till we find out what's wrong.'

After days of tests Kennamer diagnosed a scarred oesophagus, deducing 'inflammation caused by emotional tension'. Kennamer's prescription was the usual one: ease off, cut out the booze. Harris told Gris that he had; he had purchased a food mixer and was making his own carrot health drinks; he would never drink alcohol again – *ever*!

But it was too late to stop Liz filing for divorce. She flew alone back to London and called her lawyer, David Jacob. As Harris tells it, he remained at the Villa Vesco unaware, being looked after by Lupe and Edgardo, the cook and housekeeper. On 23 July 1966 the *Daily Mirror* carried the headline: *'Star's Wife Says: I Am Scared of Him'*. It outlined Liz's application for two injunctions: to stop Harris molesting her, and to restrict his removal of the children. 'I am frightened of him,' Liz wrote in a sworn statement. 'I seek the protection of the court from him.' Her counsel, Joseph Jackson, told Mr Justice Park that this was a matter of great urgency. While acknowledging that Harris was a man of 'considerable talent and exceptional success', Jackson went on, 'Unfortunately his wife alleges he drinks regularly to excess and when he is drunk he goes berserk with whoever is in sight. As his wife is the person most often in sight, she is the victim.' Mr Justice Park agreed to both injunctions ex-parte until October on the understanding that Richard Harris, not represented, could apply to have them discharged.

Harris was shattered, and verbally more expressive of his love for her than ever. He told journalist Gerard Garrett in Hollywood: 'On the very Friday that my wife saw her lawyers to arrange for the divorce, almost to the hour, I was suddenly certain that our difficult times were over. In fact I booked an airplane on the spot to go over and bring Elizabeth and the children here for the weekend. When I flew to London on the Friday I swore the airline to secrecy . . . I was planning to go to my local at the top of Camden Hill and phone, pretending I was still in Hollywood, and tell her to come out of the house in a few minutes. She would have come out expecting flowers or a brass band – she'd know that with me either would be possible – and I would have come out of the trees to surprise her.' Harris did go unknowingly to London, only to be met by a press brigade at Heathrow Airport. Later he expressed his hurt to columnist Trevor Danker: it was Liz, he said, who informed the press of the impending split, while he was in the air flying there. 'But she was encouraged, or misadvised I think, that it would make a big splash . . . It made a tremendous story – on her behalf. There were the most fantastic allegations made against me. Totally untrue. Dreadful things . . .'

It was, for once, excruciatingly bad timing. Here he was, on the eve of his mega-musical, the perfect poetic synthesis of art and commerce and ambition, his popular knighthood – and now he was faced with Liz's desertion and the attendant bad publicity. But it was not callousness on Liz's part; she had overstretched herself coping with the children and with this overgrown child in the play world of tinseltown. She didn't leave Harris. She left Hollywood, and returned to her family.

Franco Nero recalls Harris starting work on *Camelot* 'outwardly serene', but he was, more than ever, a very private man, a man who preferred his own company in spite of what people thought of him. 'He had a deep love for the part of King Arthur. I think he related to the character in some profound way. This hero who overcomes his own flaws to show goodness to the world.'

When Henri Gris talked to Harris in his Bel Air house, he admitted to serious unhappiness.

'Richard, do you miss your children?'

'Yes.'

'Do you miss your wife?'

'Yes.'

'Would you like to make up with her?'

'Yes.'

'Do you miss your things? Your books, your clothes, your mementos?'

'No . . . only my cherry blossom tree. Actually trees. Plural. I have two.' He continued: 'I won't be back in London for ages. If I try to see my wife and children in London now, I'll end up in jail. I mustn't go near them. Lawyers' orders.'

Villa Vesco had once belonged to Alan Chase. It was a rambling, leafy estate glowing with the grandeur of ancient Hollywood, with swimming pool and tennis courts and ballroom and seventeenth-century ceilings carted at unutterable expense from Rome. It was several times the size of the Bedford Gardens house, bigger than the previous year's place in Hawaii, bigger than the terracotta extravaganza in the Roman campagna before that. It was bigger and better than any castle King Richard had yet built – but it was also empty. When the servants were out the only sounds that disturbed the lonely stillness were the latest Brit-invasion hits playing on the living room turntable.

'I thought I had it made,' Harris brooded. 'The combination of *Camelot* and Doris Day had really made me famous at last . . . But I thought there would be more of us living here . . .'

10

Didn't We

Camelot, a major milestone for Warner Brothers, Jack Warner personally and Richard Harris, had a jinxed history. Born on Broadway in 1960, it followed the hardest of all acts for the same composing team, *My Fair Lady*. Lerner and Loewe painstakingly fine-tuned it for two years but its stage run was, says Lerner, 'plagued by enough misfortune to send everyone connected with it into the desert for forty years'. Set designer Adrian died during its preparation, director Moss Hart suffered a heart attack, Lerner himself fell ill and Fritz Loewe, exhausted by it, decided to retire. The opening night was a flop but the original cast – Burton, Julie Andrews as Guinevere, Robert Goulet as Lancelot and Roddy McDowell as Mordred – clung together and force-fed a hit. *Camelot* limped through two years on Broadway before hitting the jackpot in world tours.

Jack Warner's decision to acquire the movie rights was spurred by the gigantic success of the movie version of Lerner and Loewe's *Gigi* (1959), which won more Oscars than any movie up till then. Warner planned *Camelot* as a big promotional push for the studios, but by the time the artillery of movie-making was assembled – $10 million budget, bankable director (Josh Logan, who had directed *South Pacific*), glove-fit casting – Warner Brothers was on its knees. The movie started in Spain in September 1966 in a relaxed, well-serviced mood . . . and wrapped up nearly a year later in a thunder-rush of money panic.

'It was amazing,' says Franco Nero. 'In our first two months in Spain we shot wonderful stuff, none of which ever reached the screen. In our last *one week* in Burbank we shot almost *one hour* of used screen time.'

The trouble was the shifting sands of modern Hollywood. Jack Warner was the last of the great autocrats who answered to no conglomerate. But the one-man-show days were over. In November, just eight weeks into shooting, Jack sold Warner Brothers to Seven Arts for $32 million and essentially handed over the reins. Though he kept an office on the lot and saw *Camelot* through to the end, his passion faded and its absence gravely reduced the movie.

The perky optimism of Josh Logan as *Camelot* began kept Harris away from domestic autopsies. The first scenes to be shot were those of Lancelot's campaign fights – the 'C'est Moi' scenes – and King Arthur's knighting him. The unit flew to Madrid where Nero relished 'lovely weeks among the most beautiful scenery I had ever seen'. Warner and Logan had spared no expense in ground-laying. Months of location checks had identified the best castles and the most picturesque medieval sites. Nero had been voice-coached daily by UCLA professor Daniel Bandregenen. Back in Burbank a hundred craftsmen toiled under the direction of designer John Truscott, assigned to 'reinvent' the story. 'I came into it thinking of it as ultra-romantic in the adult sense,' said Truscott, 'but the director didn't want the picture made that way so I had to lose all my pre-conceived ideas very fast.' The chocolate-box glamour of traditional Hollywood mythology was abandoned for sets hewn from natural stone 'and beds which look as if they might provide a decent night's sleep'. A fortune was spent creating new, realistic costumes – $12,000 alone went on Guinevere's wedding dress – and a work-of-art Round Table, 38ft in diameter, 119ft in circumference and weighing 3000 lb, was chiselled by the best available carpenters. 'The feeling one had was of every attention to the smallest detail,' says Nero. 'It was unlike anything I had done before.'

Harris had only a few days' filming in Spain but, like Nero and the knights, he enjoyed the splendour of Granada and the Castle of Coca in Old Castile. For his part, Logan was uptight: 'I used to lay awake at night and worry about the complexities. But as the production got underway I began to feel happier . . . Every day I viewed things with increasing confidence. Basically we have tried to be original the whole way, without recreating anything that has been done before.'

Logan was delighted with Harris, whom he found to be very methodical and involved, and especially Vanessa Redgrave, his chosen Guinevere. He had known Vanessa, and the Redgrave family, for many years but had not considered her for a moment for King Arthur's bride. Then his young son Tom saw her in *Morgan, A Suitable Case for Treatment* in New York. 'Dad,' he told Logan, 'I've seen your Guinevere!' Logan saw the movie and arranged a print for screening for Jack Warner. Warner agreed, provided Redgrave could sing. Logan flew to London, summoned her and listened to her one recording venture, a ballad on the album of *The Tempest*. He hollered with delight: 'She was gorgeous *and* she had a beautiful voice!'

In late October the unit returned to Burbank and Harris moved from the Villa Vesco to a rented house on the beach at Malibu among the surfer/hippie community. Nero took an apartment at the Sunset Marquee not far away. 'We were the *big* production in town,' says Nero. 'All the superstars came to look us over. Steve McQueen came by, Warren Beatty – everyone you could imagine.' Nero was wide-eyed but still fretting to meet one star – his co-lead Vanessa Redgrave. 'I still hadn't met her, though Joshua Logan kept saying, "You'll love her."'

Harris hunted the company of musicians. His appetite was as eclectic as ever – from Sinatra to 'Danny Boy' – but the youngsters he mostly hung out with were attuned to Dylan, the Byrds and the early psychedelic scene. It suited Harris fine. Disdainful of the early youth groundswell – 'I hate the Beach Boys, they're so *American*' – he felt cosy among the socially-conscious protesters. Kathy Green he particularly enjoyed. She had long hippie hair, slim hips, bare feet – and a wildness in her silky songs. Harris spent time with her, advised her, argued with her and promised some day soon to record her work.

The Malibu set, and the $25,000 a week of *Camelot*, restored his confidence. After a wound-licking retreat he was back on the happy party circuit, the oldest hippie in town but with the energy of a whippet. He danced, boozed, sang the nights away – but always made it, bright-eyed, for the set call next day.

Nero joined him on the party circuit – 'but I always said bye-bye at ten or eleven'. The Italian witnessed the hard drinking – 'but Richard was very disciplined, no matter what'. *Life* magazine observed the heroic boozing too. Reporter Jon Borgzinner followed Harris on a weekend off to New York, where 'the royal' held court at fellow Irishman Malachy McCourt's pub, Himself. Borgzinner wrote: 'Though he postures, swaggers, swills, he fulfills the demands placed on him as an actor with painstaking discipline. At Warners technicians do not stint in their praise of Harris as one of the most careful craftsmen whom they have ever met.' Logan told Borgzinner: 'I felt that I began life again working with Harris.'

After a week or two at Burbank, Nero finally met the queen he was to steal from King Richard: 'I was walking in a corridor with Logan and this girl in jeans had her back to us. Logan said, "This is Vanessa" and I said, "Hello" . . . but when she was gone I said to Logan, "Are you crazy! She's so ugly!" Logan laughed and said, "Just you wait and see her with make-up and her hair done and all that."' When Nero returned to his dressing room a note in Italian from Redgrave invited him to dinner at her Pacific Pallisades house. His Italian girlfriend was in town, but he accepted the invitation anyway and drove his rented car up the coast. He found the house, 'with a pretty woman cooking in the kitchen. I rang the bell and asked for Miss Redgrave and she said, "I *am* Miss Redgrave!" She was very lovely, and I understood what Joshua meant.'

Nero was endlessly popular with the women of *Camelot* – he was particularly friendly with Logan's wife – but a deep, long-lasting relationship with Redgrave developed within a few months. 'My girlfriend got tired of LA and flew home, so I was alone,' he says. 'Then Vanessa asked me to drive a professor friend of hers to the airport. We all drove out and when we were alone, when he had gone, she said, "Are you working tomorrow?" I said, "No, and you?" She said she wasn't and suggested we do something together. So we caught a plane and went to San Francisco and got to know each other properly.' After the movie Redgrave became pregnant and the couple had a son, though they never married. They remain, says Nero, 'close like a family.'

The affair with Redgrave arguably deflated Nero's international career. 'After *Camelot* Jack Warner took me aside and said, "I have all these pictures lined up for you. They will make you a great star. A picture with Natalie Wood, lots of big stars." But I said, "No." Vanessa was doing *Isadora* in Europe and I wanted to go with her. I said to Mr Warner, "Thank you, but maybe in a couple of years I can come back . . ."' Nero never significantly 'came back', though he has no regrets about his choice. 'I love Europe. I adore Italy, especially round Parma, where I was born.' When I spoke with him he was on location in Denver, Colorado, for *Die Hard 2*. 'I am sitting in a freezing hotel room in this godforsaken place asking myself, "Why do I need to do this? I should be back in my beloved country, making the little budget pictures I still make, enjoying myself. I love to play football and I take care of a village of orphan children. Those are the things I love. Not American movies. . . .'

Harris remained officially unattached, though never short of companions. The Daisy was his favourite disco hangout and *Life* traipsed there obediently. Borgzinner wrote: 'Never happy without women at his feet, an impression he hardly bothers to destroy. But, in truth, Harris's lust is for life.'

As Harris squared up to the musical recordings – he had five major songs in the film – his enthusiasm grew. He wanted to give his best in the studio, under the direction of musical producer Alfred Newman, but he also wanted to render the songs 'live' during the filming. Such a complicated, risky endeavour appalled Logan, who frantically discouraged him. Harris wasn't to be out-foxed. He had discussed the optimum way of delivering songs on film with his friend Rex Harrison, Professor Higgins in *My Fair Lady*, and was impressed when Harrison informed him that he had delivered all his songs live. Harris decided to sidestep Logan and make straight for Jack Warner, immersed in his own woes.

'So I jumped on my bicycle – I cycled everywhere around the lots – and pedalled across to Jack Warner's office. I ran up to him and grabbed his hand and shook it and said, "Thank you, Mr Warner. Thank you from the bottom of my heart for letting me sing my songs in *Camelot* live. I don't care what everybody is saying about you. As far as I am concerned you are a gentleman!"'

Warner gazed at Harris, dumbstruck, his brain running the gauntlet of whoever 'they' might be and what they might be saying about him. 'Sure, kid, sure,' Warner told Harris. 'You do your songs your way, don't listen to anybody.'

As *Camelot* speeded up, inside budget but behind schedule, so Harris's concentration intensified. Alan Jay Lerner hadn't particularly wanted him as King Arthur and now he was in dispute with Logan about the revision in the movie script that depicted the consummation of the illicit love affair between Lancelot and Guinevere – the affair that brought disgrace to the King's court and ended the Round Table. 'I was always against the showing of the consummation,' said Harris, 'because it creates wrong-doers. It showed the *sin*. The love triangle should have been retained, where each loves the other equally but keeps their dignity. The movie alteration was a bad idea.' In the event, Harris was this time over-ruled and the explicit love-making was shot. 'It was ridiculous,' Harris said, 'to see them cavorting, with Vanessa's breasts dangling in his face.' But work relationships remained good.

When the production ran out of time and was quickly finished Harris and the others turned their attention to the looping (post-dubbing) and musical tweaking. Once again fussy perfectionism reared its head, contradicting the Malibu dropout aura that sometimes hung around him. 'You can change your whole performance in looping,' he said. 'I did 228 loops on *Hawaii*.' Borgzinner sat with him as he indefatigably dubbed new voices on the projected clips. He records Harris spending a full hour dubbing one word, 'Camelot', demanding seventy-two loop runs to find the exact intonation for the three golden syllables. In the final tearful scene where the King meets young Tom of Warwick, played by Gary Marsh, and warns him away from war with the famous exhilarating 'Run, boy, Run-n-n-n-n-n!' Harris called for twelve replays, roaring like a lion till his throat was raw. Logan loved the twelfth take and swore, 'That's good, Dick. Good.'

Harris told him, 'Good isn't enough. It has to be great.' They went again.

When *Camelot* finished he waved goodbye to the lot – taking keepsakes, as he always did. On *Caprice* he had 'stolen' the yellow and black pop-art socks that defined his character. He repaid in kind, however. Now he bought expensive Tiffany's trinkets for almost every member of the *Camelot* crew, in return for the Warners bicycle and the King's gold crown. He told Borgzinner: 'I'm only going to play kings from now on.'

The violent jolts in his fortunes – the 'up' of *Camelot* and the 'down' of his marriage break-up happening on top of each other – undeniably unbalanced Harris. He later described his frame of mind at this time as 'utterly distraught' – though for *Life* and the other fans he made a brave show of it. Without plumbing his depths, *Life* observed that 'The Ginger Man dies hard' and noted that just three hours after wrapping *Camelot* he had *once again* broken his nose, this time roughhousing with his masseur. Harris didn't object when the papers fixed on the upward signs. This time it wasn't professional strategizing; this time it was a frantic bid for optimism.

In truth, there was much to cheer him. After the good word of *Camelot*, Columbia Records had taken an option for a singing album and the A&R men were already suggesting ballads. 'It was more than he deserved,' says a co-actor, undeniably envious. 'He wasn't the world's greatest singer – in fact he was sometimes as hoarse and off-key as a dog – but at nearly forty they were relaunching him as a tag act for the Beatles. Nice work if you can get it.'

Harris might easily have slipped on to vinyl ineffectually with the bland, cash-in directives of Columbia, but a chance encounter at an LA benefit saved him. Black actor Frank Silvera, who ran the integrated American Theatre of Being, a non-profitmaking experimental group, became friendly with him during *Camelot* and listened to his poetry at Malibu. Silvera was impressed and asked Harris to organize a poetry recital to raise funds for the theatre, then fatally in debt. Harris complied, not just lending his poetry, but actively canvassing leading stars to contribute to a gala night of classic performances. Harris won Edward G. Robinson, Walter Pidgeon, Jean Simmons, Yvette Mimieux and Mia Farrow to the cause – and Johnny Rivers, the leading vocal artist/producer, who would contribute the music.

Rivers offered the piano accompaniment services of one of his 'finds', a nineteen-year-old songwriter from Oklahoma whom he had on a $100-a-week contract. Preacher's son

Jimmy Webb recalls: 'Apart from the $100 I had a car, which is what I loved best about the deal. I was to turn out songs for his artistes, among them the Versatiles, who later became the Fifth Dimension group.' Webb remembers the first meetings and the impact that Harris had on him: 'He had that love for music that all Irishmen seem to possess. We would be sitting backstage during rehearsals and he'd come up to me and say, in his velvet brogue, "Jimmy Webb, play this song", or "Play that song." And of course I would, and he would chirp along. He was like a big brother. I felt safe with him. He was so wise and experienced, and I was a kid.' The formal communication, never Harris's forte, wasn't especially memorable. Instead Harris performed the role of friend beautifully. Webb says: 'He took me wherever he went. It was great. No matter where we went, even the rowdiest bar in LA, I knew I'd be looked after.'

Shortly afterwards Webb let his contract with Rivers lapse and signed with Jay Lasker at ABC Dunhill. In the space of a few busy months he had two of his songs hit the national charts: 'Up, Up and Away' performed by the Fifth Dimension and 'By the Time I Get to Phoenix" sung by Glen Campbell. He was still the impressionable teenager who ill understood the workings of the biz, but by then he was 'doin' more than OK'. But, 'Richard kinda drifted out of my sights for a while.'

In fact, Harris drifted back to London in the hope of making up with Liz. 'He was drawn to her and the children,' a friend says. 'You can't have lived the hard years they shared without some deep, immovable bond. She may have hated him then, but she never stopped being in love with him. Nor he with her. It sounds a cliché, but it was true.'

Harris rented a flat at 37 Chesham Place, Belgravia, and decorated it with his *Camelot* crown and impulse-bought antiques. It was the semblance of a permanent home designed, friends say, more to lure Liz than anything else. But after luckless negotiations, within a few weeks Harris resigned himself to a bachelor's fate. Columnist Roderick Mann called and found him philosophical and tame. 'Maybe I have changed a bit. All that fighting. I was really just fighting myself. Frustration, I suppose. Now I've learned it's a sign of great weakness to take the discord of your own life and attempt to pass it on. Now I put my melancholy down on paper. You shouldn't regret one moment of sadness: just let others feel it through poetry, music.' It might almost have been conciliatory King Arthur speaking, he who said 'Might's not right! Might *for* right!' He had, he confessed, abandoned his Catholicism and replaced it to some degree by astrology. He praised his astrologer for guiding his decisions and accepted that his marriage was all but over: 'You can't go back. Only fools go back. The thing is to grow, and be happy with the way you are growing. All of us look up at the sky when we're born and plan one day to reach it. But most give up. They content themselves with standing higher than their neighbour's roof. They forget about the sky they once so desperately wanted to touch. Me, I never want to forget.'

With John McMichael's coaching Harris had signed for two forthcoming pictures, *Nobody Loves a Drunken Indian* (finally made as *Flap*, with Anthony Quinn, in 1970) and Lerner and Loewe's *On A Clear Day You Can See Forever*. But both productions were controversially delayed. *Indian* had investment troubles and the Lerner and Loewe project, based on their Broadway play, was, said Harris, 'just a terrible script'. A further cause for dispute was Lerner's removal of key male songs from the *Clear Day* screenplay. 'I signed on condition that I could do those songs,' said Harris, 'and then they cut them. It became Streisand's movie, and I had no intention of playing second fiddle to her. At this stage in my career I don't have to sit around and watch someone act, or sing.'

Harris caroused with his brother Dermot and the Irish journalists who flocked to his door – then abruptly U-turned from alcoholic idleness. Jimmy Webb, grafting for Lasker in LA, received a cable from out of the blue: COME TO LONDON STOP LET'S MAKE A RECORD STOP LOVE RICHARD. After the initial amused surprise, Webb reflected that it might not be such a bad idea. Harris was more widely in demand after *Camelot* and, anyway, Webb had never travelled outside the United States. 'I hadn't been *anywhere*,' says Webb. 'So I took up the offer and packed a briefcase full of songs I'd written and took the polar flight to London.' Webb arrived exhausted and straightaway took a taxi to Chesham Place: 'I remember this rambling big elegant house with open fires. I was jaded and I recall sinking into a huge bath – I recall the smell of the English soap, and the crisp white sheets.' When he had slept off his flight Harris was ready and eager: he wanted to hear Webb's new music. 'He was very self-assured and in control,' says Webb. 'He was a man who knew precisely what he wanted.'

Webb sat at the grand piano in the living room, surrounded by the trappings of a king. The *Camelot* crown hung jauntily from a great gilt mirror over an antique Irish refectory table. Turkish odalisque cushions littered the chairs. There was a seventeenth-century Venetian bishop's throne, porcelain ornaments, silk fringes. In Webb's eyes Harris had changed little; he was still 'Just lovely, a confident, positive-minded man who was great to be with'. But to the Warners' publicists and many besides he had *become* King Arthur. Later Harris said, 'There probably was a time then when I did get caught up in the part.'

Webb banged out 'thirty or forty songs' and Harris sat, paced, shouted, whooped. 'It was, "I like this one. I'll take that one. No, pass on that one!"' says Webb. Then the songwriter aired one of his own favourites, a complicated, 'rather cumbersome tune' he had written for a group (the Association). 'Harris instantly lit on it. He said, "That's the one. That's the song I want to record now." He was absolutely assertive about it. His decision alone.'

'MacArthur Park', Webb's serpentine symphony, was the least likely choice for a single record follow-up to *Camelot*. Laced with neo-classical female harmonies, studded with time changes, it seemed more a show number, best conveyed with lights, dancers and a live audience. Held against the chart hits of the day – the songs of Jimi Hendrix, the Beatles, the Lovin' Spoonful, the Beach Boys – it was a startling oddity, at seven minutes-plus almost guaranteed to lose out on pop radio airtime. 'But he was *so certain* of it,' says Webb, 'it was uncanny.'

Dermot Harris took over the business arrangements, working with Webb and his agents. Columbia, with whom Harris had his outline deal, baulked at the idea of spending the proposed $85,000 on 'MacArthur Park' and the nine-song album. 'If it had been just me and a guitar,' Harris said, 'they would have agreed. But this was a big production number, with orchestra and all the rest.' Columbia bowed out, Webb's ABC Dunhill stepped in, and Webb flew back to LA to start musical scoring at Sound Recorders, sometime studio home of Phil Spector and the Beach Boys' Brian Wilson.

Harris was glad to be working again. The brief idleness at the end of the summer had yielded nothing other than a petty libel case, in which producer David Newman sued Harris for libel damages arising from remarks made on the Eamonn Andrews TV show. The jury found for Harris, but the publicity served only to revive the hell-raising image that Harris was trying to escape. He told the *Daily Mail*: 'It's boredom, frustration, not drink that makes me aggressive. I haven't been in a fight since 19 May . . . I felt so ashamed afterwards. I swore it would be the last time. The worst thing I do is . . . *nothing*. There's always got to be a new challenge.'

During the winter Harris brought Webb to Ireland, first to Kilkee, where he had purchased a three-storey lodge near the Pollock Holes, then to Dublin. Webb said, 'He took me everywhere, to all the old places of his childhood. In Kilkee he showed me the amphitheatre, with the wild Atlantic crashing all around it, and said, "Down there is where I gave my first performances." Then he took me to Dublin, with his sister Harmay. They had a big rented house and he said, "Jimmy Webb, I want you to sleep in the bed where I was conceived." And I did . . .!'

Vocal recording for 'MacArthur Park' and the album *A Tramp Shining* began at the tiny Lansdowne Road Studios in the middle of Dublin. 'I had already finished the tracks in LA with a full orchestra,' says Jimmy Webb, 'which might have caused some problems since the tracks were I think a little high for him – though that added to the emotional intensity of the album. Then I put my sixteen-track recorder under my arm and flew back to join him in Ireland.'

Harris had shipped his Rolls to Ireland and enjoyed parading in style. 'Every day we left the house in the Phantom V,' says Webb, 'always with a big pitcher of Pimm's close to hand. Then we went into this little studio and Richard took his place at the mike, with a tall stool to his left and the Pimm's on the stool. Then we started recording, for maybe three or four hours, or however long it took till the Pimm's was gone. Afterwards we reloaded the Rolls and went back to the house. It was a very pleasant experience.'

Harris was never sloppy. 'He could never have gotten through that music in a drunken state,' says Webb. 'He did like to lubricate his vocal cords, but that was as far as it went.'

Of the songs on the highly innovative album Harris especially related to 'MacArthur Park' and 'Didn't We', which he interpreted as an intimate account of the break-up with Liz. The lyric is direct and dizzy with regret:

> This time we almost made it to the moon
> Didn't we, girl?
> This time we almost sang our song in tune
> Oh didn't we, girl?
>
> This time I had the answer right here in my hand
> But I touched it and it had turned to sand . . .

But Webb hadn't tailored it for the Harrises' breakdown. 'That one was in my bag for quite a few years. But I think Richard heard something deeply personal in it, and he served it with incredible vocal sensitivity.' Before the record's release Harris played the tracks for Liz, announcing them as personal statements. He told journalist Victor Davis, '[Didn't We] tells of our parting and our three or four attempts to come together again.' Liz liked them, and had no objection to their content or his interpretation.

Larry Newton, president of ABC Dunhill, objected to the single record release of 'MacArthur Park', considering the airplay problem insurmountable. 'It could ruin the record business,' Newton said. 'A record as long as this takes away potential air time from three other records.' Such crass commercialism didn't deter Harris or Webb, who both insisted on the single release and got their way.

Their judgement was spot on. Released in April 1968, 'MacArthur Park' and A Tramp Shining both made the charts immediately. In four weeks the single had jumped to No. 2 on the Billboard listings, with sales of more than 600,000 copies. In Britain it reached No.4. It has been claimed that its impact influenced the Beatles whose 'Hey Jude', all seven minutes eleven seconds of it, made worldwide No. 1 in August 1968. The success merited a second single release ('Didn't We' in September), a six-records-in-three-years deal and the formation of a new division of Harris's company Limbridge, aimed at record-making and promotion.[1] 'I don't know if any of us expected the scale of "MacArthur's" success,' says Webb, 'but I *had* laid a bet with Richard that that song would chart.'

This wager, dealt from the heart by both participants, would later cause a hiccup in their friendship that lasted nearly ten years. During the recording at Lansdowne, Harris had volunteered: 'If this album goes top ten I'll give you my Phantom V.' Webb is at pains to say, 'I *loved* Richard, so I *loved* the idea of having his Rolls. I didn't *need* a Rolls. I had money, fame, all that. But I adored Richard, I looked up to him. So I wanted *Richard's Rolls!*' The fact that the car was of royal descent – 'literally had the Royal Household medallion on the grill' – wasn't of special interest to Webb. He just wanted his friend's car. When the album did break internationally – 'all over the bloody, fucking world!' Webb reminds you – Harris gulped, and offered Webb *a* Rolls but not *the* Rolls. Limbridge mailed catalogues to Webb's New York office showing all the latest available models. He could pick the car he wanted, no expense spared.

But Webb wanted the Royal Phantom, and never got it.

The year 1968 was one of varied discord amidst the music. *Nobody Loves a Drunken Indian*, the project that Harris was most looking forward to, was finally cancelled. Harris took the news badly, collapsing and staying in bed for two weeks. 'It was a marvellous part,' he told Roderick Mann. 'I banked everything on it and now some fat shareholder in New York has sat on the basket and it's off . . . I foresee a disastrous year for me.'

But, bouncing back, he accepted the co-lead with Michael Caine – an actor whom he describes as 'OK' – in James Bond producer Harry Saltzman's *Written on the Sand*, later renamed *Play Dirty*. Saltzman told Harris that rewrites of the offered

---

[1] Limbridge was christened by Harris. The name is a blend of his and Liz's birthplaces, Limerick and Bridgend.

script were in the works, but Harris only agreed to sign
provided a clause was inserted stating that 'the substance and
nature of the part would not change to any appreciable degree'.
Harris flew to Spain before the release of *A Tramp Shining*, to
be met with thirty redrafted pages from the rewriter. He was
upset. Four of his main scenes had been removed, considerably
weakening his character. Supported by director René Clément
he attempted a protest to Saltzman, but Saltzman refused to
negotiate. For four days Harris turned up each morning for
his set call, all the time insisting on the reinstatement of the
agreed script. No discussions were offered so he left the
movie, flew back to London and threatened legal action.
Days later Clément also left, to be replaced as director by
executive producer André de Toth.

Harris's lost fee was £150,000, but more damaging was the
negative media reflex. Harris was hurt, but blustered anyway.
In the absence of anything more solid he was forced to discuss
unconfirmed projects. Kevin McClory, the fellow Irishman
who had sued for and won rights to make the James Bond film
Thunderball (in partnership with Saltzman-Broccoli, the Bond
'owners'), had a film in preparation about Michael Collins, the
controversial Irish patriot. Harris would do that, and he would
do his long-promised *Hamlet*, to be directed by buddy Frank
Silvera with $500,000 backing from Paramount. Faye Dunaway
would play Ophelia and Jimmy Webb would write the score.
The movie would be a radical reworking of Shakespeare that
would turn the theatrical world upside down.

In keeping with the fate of most of his recent artistic
idealism, neither movie happened. Instead *Camelot* had its
much-hyped release and he went alone to the premiere,
while Liz was accompanied by her new boyfriend, Canadian
actor Christopher Plummer. The reviews were the pick-up he
needed. 'Stunningly beautiful,' said the *Hollywood Reporter*,
under a banner headline that screamed: 'Redgrave, Harris,
Nero now among the Great Stars.'

Harris basked temporarily in the musical afterglow, drifting
to Mexico for a working vacation with Webb to choose songs
for the next album, to be called *The Yard Went On Forever*. Says
Jimmy Webb: 'We dug deep in the satchel [of his earlier songs]
for that one, which might have been a mistake. I think I should

have worked up more new material.' The title track, a loosely veiled anti-Vietnam war song, started with the lyric:

> *Is everybody safe?*
> *Does everybody have a place to hide?*

The lyric was adapted from Senator Robert Kennedy's last words, and once again industry bosses voiced reservations, declaring the song too political. Once again, Webb and Harris held out and the track was released as a single – though it failed to ignite the pop charts as 'MacArthur Park' had. 'But the album was probably better,' says Webb. 'The real aficionados will tell you that that one is their favourite. The songs had a wider range.'

According to press statements, Harris was advanced £250,000 for *The Yard Went On Forever*. Much of the money was channelled into Limbridge's new office suite in a palatial block on the Victoria Embankment, where Dermot and John McMichael ruled the roost. Much, too, went into promoting new talent. Consistent to his promise Harris imported Kathy Green, the Malibu songstress friend, and got her ready for recording. 'There's a lot of bread in this game,' said Harris. 'You've got to have guts. When I made my first record my agent, my manager and all my advisers said I was mad, the pop scene is only for kids . . .'

Liz was again by his side – but only for professional reasons. Blossoming in her new independence, she had started a business: 'I've been bursting for something to do so I've started interior designing. I've got several commissions already . . .' Among them, as a peaceable demonstration of their continuing friendship, was the decoration of Harris's new offices.

Cyril Cusack and other Irish colleagues were invited to dinner at Chesham Place. One describes Harris then as 'a man in mid-air, like a trapeze artist between swings.' He was certainly not static, though the vagaries of success frequently had him disoriented. Some said his marriage would mend, others dismissed the notion. Harris gave the last word: 'I tried to fix it, but now I don't want to fix it.' With Kathy Green he had co-written a song that might launch her career. It was called 'I Won't Go Back'.

11

Battle Cries!

Elizabeth Harris was granted a decree nisi in London on
25 July 1969. Harris offered no defence to her allegation of
adultery with an unnamed actress on a number of occasions
in October 1967. The *Times* sombrely noted: 'Discretion was
exercised in respect of Mrs Harris's own admitted adultery.'
A private financial settlement was agreed and joint custody
of the children was granted. Mr Justice Latey observed that
both participants had made a number of efforts to save their
marriage, the latest as recently as June of that year, but the
situation was clearly irretrievable. Years later Harris told Joe
Jackson of *Hot Press*: 'Elizabeth and I would have been divorced
three or four years previous to the time we were if I'd conceded
to her demands for custody of the children. I said, "No, I want
joint custody. I don't want to have to ask you, 'Can I see what's
mine?'" Luckily Elizabeth wanted to marry Rex Harrison, so
she finally said, "This is the only way I'll get my divorce, so
I'll concede to that." And now she says, "Thanks be to God
you fought for it because that's what the children needed."'

Liz's love affair with Harrison was in fact a slow-burner that
didn't make the headlines until long after the divorce. For the
time being her friendship was with Christopher Plummer, but
Harris turned a blind eye. When Roderick Mann asked him
about it he said only, 'It must be hard for the fellow she's
going round with now. Because I know she still thinks about
me a lot. At a party the other night she said, "This is a dull
bore. What it needs is Harris to liven things up." That can't
be easy for a man now, can it?'

Ronald Fraser, close friend to both, says: 'They never
stopped loving each other. There were bumps. But they had

a deep private communication that never stopped, divorce or not.'

The bonds of association, work apart, remained. After the divorce Liz rented a house in Wiltshire with Susy, wife of actor Keir Dullea, and took the children for the remainder of the summer. When she returned to London she continued to visit Harris's flat and for a time befriended Kathy Green. Kathy moved into Bedford Gardens to continue preparatory work on her Limbridge album and Liz fondly recalled the dismay of the neighbours who, celebrating what they thought would be the departure once and for all of the rumbustious Irishman, now had to contend with the shrill outpourings of an American hippie folk singer at all hours.

Harris hauled anchor. After *Camelot* solid movie offers were coming in again, so he went for the best he could get. Tried-and-true director Marty Ritt had the prime proposal, a movie called *The Molly Maguires*, deftly scripted by Walter Bernstein. What attracted Harris was not the story but the subtle morality and political undertones of dissent among the impoverished workers in a nineteenth-century Pennsylvania mining town. A friend of Harris's says, 'After the divorce he suddenly became very political. It was as if some home responsibilities had been shorn and he wanted to express himself as a responsible, mature man and not some rake-about-town. It had something to do with the influence of good King Arthur, we all believed.' The evidence of Harris's interviews of the period lends weight to this. For a while quickfire politics occupied him. He was bluntly against the Vietnam War, but refused to believe anti-war films served any purpose. 'I think one of the things that might ease world tension is a better understanding of people. With air travel increasing, people have greater opportunities to communicate with each other and perhaps this will decrease the possibility of war.' The naivety of his politics was astounding to behold, and yet the journals that unfailingly fell to him – most of them middle-market – carried the comments with faithful gravity.

Controversy, inevitably, was the base ingredient. He did not, emphatically, support Ronald Reagan's popular governorship of California. 'I cannot accept him. I believe in being politically groomed.' Lord Ogmore, finally distanced, was no longer a bone of contention. 'You must have due regard for such men as Asquith, Churchill, Macmillan, who by training and heritage were natural to politics. Or, as in the Labour movement, where people started as miners, became trade union officials and then went on to politics in a logical way.'

The Molly Maguires of the film were a secret group of first-generation Irish 'slaves' who fought the injustices of the mining system in the 1870s, courting violence and anarchy. Though the movie wasn't overtly political, Ritt's crusading reputation coloured it (he had been blacklisted during the McCarthy era but gamely manoeuvred himself back) and hinted at parallels with the Black Panther activists in sixties America. Neither Bernstein nor Ritt said much to counter this suggested metaphor.

Harris played opposite Sean Connery, then the world's number one box office star. Connery's reputation merited chief billing, but Harris demanded – and got – first name above the title. 'For the kind of money they're paying me,' said the Scotsman with more than a touch of irony, 'they can put a mule ahead of me.'

The movie was shot through the first part of 1969 on uncharacteristically scorching location at Lancaster and Eckley, mining ghost towns in southern Pennsylvania. Paramount rebuilt Eckley in all its anthracite glory for a modest $250,000 and the entire production was budgeted at $5 million, the American equivalent of Lindsay Anderson's art-house endeavour. Harris brought his New York sociable pal Malachy McCourt aboard to play, appropriately, the inn-keeper. Jimmy Webb was also invited to drop by and he watched in admiration as Harris gave one of his most understated yet vigorous performances, playing the undercover Irish detective who betrays the dissidents. Connery was the main enemy.

Temperatures soared as spring became summer. Connery collapsed from dehydration and exhaustion but Harris kept going, greatly inspired by the high regard in which the crew held him and by the whispers of a possible second Oscar nomination. A visiting reporter wrote: 'This time he'll get one. Harris himself says that it is the best part he's played since he won critical acclaim in the Rugby League story.'

The Molly Maguires should have succeeded hugely, but it

didn't. Photographed by ace James Wong Howe, scored by Henry Mancini, it was a sweetly baked confection with a valuably strong aftertaste that implied continuing injustice and the plight of the down-at-heel immigrant. Ritt himself confessed that 'It didn't do any business at all and, though I wasn't completely without employment after it, employment wasn't as accessible to me as it had been.'

Harris didn't get any award nominations, but his reborn movie energies remained. London offered no solace so he stayed in Hollywood and agreed to do Sandy Howard's alternative western, *A Man Called Horse*. Howard admits that Harris was not his first, but his *fifth* choice as star. 'It had a tortured start,' says Howard, a clear-thinking and prolific independent producer almost universally admired in the business. 'It started when I was *en route* from India – where I had drunk the water, unfortunately. I was flying to Japan and I thought I was going to die I felt so bad. In Japan I called a doctor and I was lying there, dying, thinking I'll get a Japanese doc who doesn't understand I'm dying, but this nice Jewish doctor, Dr Birnbaum, from the Bronx, arrived. He said, "You've got three days in bed to get over this, so do some reading." So I gathered all the English books I could and one of them was a western compilation with a story by Dorothy Johnson called "A Man Called Horse". It had been done as a *Wagon Train* episode [on US television] but I saw it as a potential hit movie. I acquired the rights as soon as I got well again – for $250. And then I set up a production deal, hopefully to star Robert Redford. Redford went and did something else, so we looked around. Richard I always admired, but he was the fifth choice and the first who said yes.'

Dorothy Johnson had already written a movie hit in *The Man Who Shot Liberty Vallance* but Howard went for experienced screenwriter Jack De Witt, then in his mid-sixties, to script the film. Elliot Silverstein, director of *Cat Ballou* which won an Oscar for Lee Marvin, was assigned the hot seat. 'But that was a disastrous choice,' says Howard. 'Richard was allright to manage, but Silverstein and he just didn't get on. I'll explain the working atmosphere in Mexico like this: Richard fought with Silverstein; I would have killed him. He was a rat, and a bad director. He turned in a movie that had such great potential, but it was a dud. We previewed in Oakland and everyone hated it. Richard had worked his ass off in the desert, portraying this English gentleman who is captured by the Sioux and takes to their ways – in the book, by the way, he was Bostonian – but when he saw what we had he wanted nothing to do with it.' Howard saw his precious western slipping away, so he elbowed Silverstein aside and, with the help of Cinemacenter manager Jerry Henshaw, a shrewd and determined friend, he recut the whole thing. 'We salvaged it from the brink,' says Howard, 'and presented something we all liked, and which did good business.' The miscalculation of Silverstein had, however, added $2 million to the budget – 'and put nearly an extra year on to the production'.

What Howard and Henshaw finally delivered was powerful, and unusual. Its significance rested in the fact that it made no concessions to standard Western concepts and depicted the universe of the Indian in sympathetic, even poignant terms. *A Man Called Horse* was a noble polemic in defence of the humiliated Indian, two years before Brando's eloquent boycotting of the Oscars (he won for *The Godfather*, but refused to accept the award as a protest against the persecution of settlement Indians) and forerunner of a host of lesser efforts in the same vein.

Harris shone as Lord John Morgan, the aristocrat who becomes a Sioux warrior. The graphic Sun Vow initiation ritual, in which the white man is hung from a high tepee scaffold by claw-hooks in his pectorals, drew huge audiences and gave Harris his biggest box office takings in years. 'Anthropological Grand Guignol,' wrote the critic Gordon Gow, but that sounded like intellectual sour grapes against the audience consensus. 'It is a story the public has been waiting for,' Harris said on its release. 'This is why it has been successful. Not just in the United States but . . . in Italy, Norway, Sweden, Denmark. Everyone is fascinated because the Indian was a rugged individualist – which all of us hope we are, try to be and most of us, unfortunately, fail at. The public has never seen the American Indian as he was before the white man.' Portugal alone rejected the movie, deeming it racist, and some native Indians claimed exploitation. Harris leaped into the debate, emphasizing the many months of unremitting research. Everyone involved had studied the background minutely, including himself. It was understood that the Sun Vow had latterly been replaced by a more humane Sun Dance ceremony, but the ritual was precise and accurate in context. There was no gratuitous licence. Sandy Howard told *Photoplay*: 'We go so far back in the ethnological background that the Indians have no colour blue. That came afterwards, with the white man. Too many [modern-day] Indians have not been educated in their heritage.'

Harris's eventual pleasure with the movie, combined with Howard's scrupulous honesty and hard graft, made for a business partnership that would deliver a *Horse* sequel and other movies. 'We were similar in our strong-mindedness and our style of straight-talk dealing,' says Howard. 'I treated him fairly, he treated me fairly. That's how Hollywood should be, but sometimes isn't.'

Harris had faith, heart and purpose again. Creatively he was on a high. More importantly, he seemed suddenly to isolate his special suitability for strong, alienated-loner parts. The role he went for next was potentially his most challenging – and most controversial. *Cromwell* was a screenplay that had been hanging in the wings for five years. Written 'with hope if not sense' by director Ken Hughes, it had the ingredients of a mega-movie – right down to its essential king-size budget of around $8 million. Harris had read the script years earlier and pledged himself to it, despite his seeming unsuitability for the title role. The promise had amused many prospective backers who saw the paradox of a confirmed Irish republican portraying Oliver Cromwell, the *bête noire* of the Irish. But Harris would not let go of the notion which now, more than ever, felt right. 'Until I did *Camelot*,' he said, 'they would not positively trust me to play Cromwell. But I always wanted it. It's not necessary for an actor to *believe* in the character he is playing. With Cromwell I admire the rigorous self-discipline of the man. I admire his aim: to take the country out of aristocratic hands.'

Hughes traipsed the studios with his script for years. The sprawling nature of the film, packed with battle sequences, dissuaded investors. But Hughes proposed big star leads (Alec Guinness playing King Charles I opposite Harris) and cost-efficient location shooting in northern Spain. It was while directing the children's classic *Chitty Chitty Bang Bang* that Hughes met producer Irving Allen (a friend of *Chitty* producer Cubby Broccoli), and at last the cash structure to mount the English Civil War epic was found.

Allen, like Hughes, was confident that the battle of titans between King Charles I and Cromwell would make thrilling cinema and he persuaded Columbia to invest. Harris's fee was allegedly close to $500,000, but his real motivation was political. Cromwell he saw as a symbol of integrity, anxious to reform society in the same spirit of King Arthur but forced to arms. 'He was a quiet, peace-loving chap who was put in the unfortunate position of either inciting an uprising against the King, or abandoning his ideals. He chose to fight and, surprisingly, became an excellent tactician and strategist.' Cromwell's call was for education for the masses and an end to the licentious behaviour of the ruling aristocrats.

On one count, anyway, Harris's active politics concurred. In a break before filming he visited Limerick to support the city's University Project Committee. Unlike most major Irish cities Limerick had no university, and a well-manned action group headed by Cecil Murray was campaigning for government funding. Harris told the gathering of students and teachers: 'I have travelled all over the world and I can see the necessity for education. In every country – Russia, America, even Mexico – the emphasis is totally on education.' If any Crescent Jesuits were in the audience they kept silent and settled for polite applause. But Harris had no axe to grind with them. Educated in the University of Life, he nonetheless greatly admired the Jesuit system. 'It breeds great individuality,' he told me. In future years his educational crusading would become even livelier, and vigorously supportive of the Jesuit system.

Before flying to Spain for location work on *Cromwell* Harris made the law courts – and the tabloids – again. During a supper cabaret featuring Sammy Davis Jr at the Talk of the Town he became involved in a fist fight. Davis he knew and liked from Sinatra's Hollywood parties, and Harris rose to his defence when someone in the audience chanted anti-Jewish remarks while Davis sang the theme from *Exodus*. Harris told Bow Street magistrates court: 'I found the remarks offensive and distasteful. Sammy Davis is a great friend of mine and

I know he is sensitive about remarks that he is Jewish and coloured . . . I twice warned the man to shut up but he kept on. So I went over and hit him.' Harris also hit Detective Constable Andrew Davanna and Detective Constable George Napier, who tried to detain him outside the restaurant. He was fined £12, with £12 costs. Sammy Davis, oblivious to the kerfuffle, commented from his Park Lane penthouse: 'What more can a man ask of a friend than that he should come to his defence while he is performing on stage? I didn't really know what was happening . . .'

Only weeks later Harris was in court again, this time for assault on a traffic warden. Marion McClean, the warden involved, claimed that Harris had obstructed while she was trying to place a parking ticket on the car of a friend of his. Harris danced an Irish jig and embraced her: 'It was as if he folded his arms very tightly in front of him – and I was squashed in between.' This time the sentence was six months' conditional discharge. The magistrate, Kenneth Barraclough – obviously a fan – noted, 'I think it was misplaced friendliness', but cautioned Harris: 'You must not think that everyone enjoys being hugged and jigged around by a film star.'

During his time in London Harris indulged in 'the biggest gift I've ever given myself' – Tower House, a veritable Arthurian red-brick castle in Melbury Road, Kensington. The house stood out against its dowdy neighbours, almost Gothic in its imposing, fussy façade, missing only the gargoyles and pantiles. A journalist who knew him says, 'It was a great extravagance, a bit of King Arthur bravura. No one would seriously want to live there. But that's what he wanted, that's why he pursued *Cromwell* and all these regal trappings: he believed himself to be the King of Kensington.' The irony of socially conscious Cromwell going home to a 'fantasy palace' Harris ignored.

Built between 1876 and 1881 for his own occupation by the eminent Victorian William Burges, architect of Cardiff Castle and Cork Cathedral, Tower House had exerted its fascination on Harris ever since he first arrived in Kensington. In the late fifties it was derelict; and he had, he claimed, often slept rough in its overgrown garden. He always coveted the house, and always *knew* it would be his one day. 'I just loved the strange, doomed, Gothic place. I'd tell myself: one day I'll buy this house.'

Danny La Rue, who visited the house with Liberace, the competing prospective purchaser, described it as 'spooky, with a sense of evil in it'. Neither Liberace nor Richard Harris appeared bothered. As Harris tells it, he found out late in the day that the house, at last refurbished, was for sale. His source of information was the *Evening Standard*. 'Next morning at a quarter past nine the estate agent had my cheque – for £75,000. It was £5,000 more than Liberace had been willing to pay. He hadn't got his deposit down, so the house was mine.'

Harris devoted himself to the house with an obsessive fervour. What the previous owner had sidestepped he keenly addressed. A major overhaul was needed to bring the twenty-five rooms up to scratch; Burges's original design drawings were unearthed in the Victoria and Albert Museum and the stone and plasterwork reconstructed to match them. The architect had planned the house as 'a model residence of the fifteenth century', and legend had it that it was intended as a shrine to Chaucer. Harris returned to the motif lovingly, even going as far as booking the same firm that had undertaken the decoration work a century before.

Once again over-taxed and over-tired, Harris returned to Spain in the autumn to complete the long-running *Cromwell*. The nature of the movie – heavily populated, clanging with battles, dotted with intense character scenes opposite Alec Guinness – burned away his already depleted energy. The Spanish army loaned out four hundred trained soldiers to recreate credible hand-to-hand battlefield action, but the constant complex retakes in the broiling heat exhausted even the hardiest crewmen.

Towards the end it was obvious that Harris was near to breakdown. When the time came to shoot the execution of Charles I, he flipped. He described the breakdown – a combination of intemperate drinking and overlong stress periods – as 'a terrifying experience'. He awoke in his hotel at dawn in a cold shivering sweat: 'I actually thought we were about to cut off Charles I's head. I was shouting down the telephone: "We must give him another chance! We must think twice about this!" I was convinced we were doing it for real.'

The production nurse was summoned, and a psychiatrist was found. Harris was hysterical and no one could get through to him by talking calmly. The doctor prescribed plenty of urgent rest. Harris was given a jab that knocked him out for eighteen hours.

He was prime material for professional counselling and analysis – but, he insists, he rejected it. He later told *Hot Press* magazine: 'I studied psycho-therapy in America for years. I became part of a school. And I found that the most fantastically damaging thing about modern thinking is: Let us discover why, why, why . . . [Analysis] can be good for people who are damaged, seriously mentally damaged. It can be a useful medicine therapy. But in America it's a rage, a fad.' Harris's self-analysis in Spain was simple. He had once again overdone it. The remedy was: Take it easy.

But his success revved him up. *The Molly Maguires*, *A Man Called Horse* and *Cromwell* were in their ways all winners and all indisputably *his* movies. The records were selling like hot cakes and Grammy nominations had just been announced (for Best Contemporary Singer and Best Album)[1] – though Jimmy Webb was smarting and no longer so accessible on the telephone. No matter, there was plenty of interest elsewhere. A number of songwriters were flooding Dermot with material, and a publisher was expressing ardent interest in a book of Richard Harris poems. Leslie Bricusse, musical brains behind *Dr Dolittle*, had written *Scrooge* as a possible showcase musical for Harris. And the Las Vegas International Hotel was offering – crazily, thought Harris – £150,000 for a cabaret show centred round 'MacArthur Park' and the *Camelot* songs. The music continued to represent a refreshing counterpoint to the movies – 'But no more, I am an actor, not a singer' – and Harris thought he would probably agree to a cabaret act, opening at a smaller Las Vegas venue like Caesar's Palace or the Sands, then doing a world tour.

Tantalizingly, the *Hamlet* project seemed to be on. This more than anything kept Harris from the Greek islands holiday he constantly promised himself. All of a sudden, all the

---

[1] *A Tramp Shining* took just one Grammy: Best Orchestration, for Jimmy Webb.

ingredients were slotting together. The industry trusted him again. He could do what he wished. Mia Farrow was slated for Ophelia, Peter Ustinov for Polonius, George C. Scott for Claudius. Writer Gavin Lambert helped Harris find the right modern voice for his two-and-a-half-hour script, while backer Arthur Lewis, and Paramount, agreed on Harris himself as director, even though he had never directed film before. Harris found it hard to conceal his enthusiasm. He had talked about the project for so long, come so close, but never this close. He was forty and now, he knew, was his last credible chance. Locations were scouted on Holy Island, off the coast of Northumberland; it was *that* close. Harris told *Today's Cinema*: 'If I had to choose between working another twenty years as an actor or doing *Hamlet* and ending my career, I'd take *Hamlet*. I feel that strongly about it.' But that pronouncement, like the constant threats of retirement, was more an expression of tiredness than a real intention. Like *Wuthering Heights*, *Hamlet* was destined to die, a victim of the moguls' boardroom. Its demise, on top of his exhaustion, left Harris especially vulnerable.

John Kobal was among the journalists who regularly met Harris and warmly recorded his progress. He talked to him in America, Norway and England and found him, as he approached middle age, battle-worn but full of vim. In his notebook Kobal wrote: 'He speaks rapidly, punctuating his sentences with facial commas and periods. There is a shrug about him, an air of dogged optimism, self-assurance, a touch of smugness. He is part idealist, part romantic . . . There is about him a feeling of size, of large-scale bonhomie, and of the sincerity of what he believes in. What he believes in is himself. He looks his age, but has an adolescent intensity which makes him look youthful. He moves like a dancer, delicate, introspective – but can also "turn it on" when observed and encouraged. He knows himself so well as to use his real self for his public self. His bouts of drinking and brawling were played up in the press – for sales. Which he understands. What he doesn't understand, or says he doesn't, is the betrayal of people he trusted with himself, with his "private" self . . . as when he told Roderick Mann something re his wife, off the cuff, and Mann printed it. He no longer talks to Mann because of it. In a grown man there are traces of gawky boy . . .'

Weston Taylor of the *News of the World* was another whom Harris felt had betrayed him at a low ebb. An Irish journalist friend of Taylor's recalls: 'During that period Dickie was drinking heavily – not as heavily as his brother Dermot, who could really down them – but still overdoing it. Both of them, Dickie and Dermot, were great romancers, with women all over the place. Weston Taylor wanted to do a piece and he came to the Savoy, where I had been drinking with Harris. By the time he got up to the suite to see Harris, Harris was well jarred and spluttering all over the place. He would drink for days without even eating and be quite ill. When Taylor talked to him I don't think he was fully aware of what was going on. So he blabbed and blabbed about Elizabeth and her blossoming romance with Rex Harrison and the kids.'

Taylor later wrote a double-page spread outlining his talk with Harris and making spiky references about Liz and her new life. Harris instructed Wright & Webb, his lawyers, to sue, but the case was settled with a High Court apology. The transcripts of Weston Taylor's notebooks and tape make revealing reading about Harris – not in their mouthy invective, but in the confessional candour that showed a gentle and regretful man, and a man obsessed by his craft to the detriment of all else. References to Liz are overshadowed by his concerns for the children and by his interest in the movie world. His comments on David Lean and his Irish venture, *Ryan's Daughter*, fill pages of text. Harris considers *Ryan's Daughter* a mighty work, and would have given his right arm to play the Robert Mitchum role. Beyond that, his comments about his fellow countrymen suggest a deep and ongoing self-analysis: 'There is an image of the Irish projected . . . They have qualities which are admirable to me and most exciting. What happens is that when they move out of Ireland to New York they have a great fear of being absorbed into the nation they have moved to. And by doing that [*sic*] they are inclined to project their individuality too strongly and therefore become professional Irishmen.' The footnote comments were contradictory but provocative: 'I find the Irish people live from Friday to Friday. There's no ambition. They amble through life. They freewheel through life with great abandonment. They're not ambitious because there's nothing to be ambitious about.'

Despite his protectiveness towards his and Liz's privacy, the lingering discord resounded publicly. In October he departed for Israel to shoot his next movie, *Bloomfield*, under the direction of Uri Zohar. Within days Zohar was removed from the film and Harris was announced as new director. The film was finished in February, and Harris returned to London with the eager intention of seeing his sons. But when he telephoned Bedford Gardens he was informed that Liz had taken Jamie on a cruise with Rex Harrison. Harrison had just instructed his solicitors to issue a statement announcing his separation from Rachel Roberts, and Harris understood the implications. He immediately went to court, demanding Liz's return of Jamie in keeping with the terms of their divorce settlement. He told Mrs Justice Lane in the High Court: 'The boy needs continuity of school. I am afraid that even if Jamie returns shortly my ex-wife will take him away again.'

The judge took Harris's side: 'She should come back and be made to understand that this kind of thing won't do.' An order was issued for the former Mrs Harris to return Jamie within forty-eight hours. Harris's lawyer, Stephen Tumin, left the court saying Harris was 'overwhelmed with concern' about Jamie. Liz returned in due course, but in March Harris applied for her committal to prison for contempt of court. She had failed to file a general undertaking not to take the children out of the country which, Harris asserted, was contrary to the divorce agreement. Liz's solicitors apologized and offered to give the undertaking; by mutual consent, the application for imprisonment was dropped.

Harris returned his attention to post-production on *Bloomfield* and the restoration work on Tower House as Liz made arrangements to become the fifth Mrs Rex Harrison. The marriage took place shortly afterwards, at Alan Jay Lerner's Georgian mansion on Long Island. Richard Harris was not among the guests.

12

Blooming Poetry and Dying Blooms

Bloomfield arguably marked the end of Richard Harris's serious artistic striving for almost twenty years. After it he made two careful films – *Man in the Wilderness* and for TV *The Snow Goose* – but then began a cycle of staccato, half-intellectualized work that only rarely threw up a movie worth watching. Half of the problem was weariness – his was the most productive and varied of all sixties' star careers – and half was disillusionment. When the Israeli director Zohar foundered, Harris jumped for his directorial chance as a substitute for the *Hamlet*-that-would-never-be.

The movie had been made possible by Limbridge's input and Harris's investment of his own fees in the production. Producer John Heyman and Limbridge set up a 'co-op picture' scheme in which ten individual investors and a number of leading banks – among them the House of Rothschild, Fund of Funds and Henry Ansbacher & Co. – pooled resources. The budget was tiny for a film of its type – just $2 million – but it was all Harris needed to fulfil the ambition of his TB bed: '. . . to direct my own scenarios, to bring to life the whole world of my creation, to look at my life through the telescope of truth'.

Wolf Mankowitz's outline script was as far removed as possible from the radical *Hamlet*. And yet it is easy to see why Harris perceived it as a blueprint for a personal essay. Mankowitz had written the schmaltzy *A Kid for Two Farthings* (1955), about a Petticoat Lane boy whose pet goat appears to have the magical powers of a unicorn. *Bloomfield* used the same scenario of authentic, if sentimental, childhood and focused on a boy's dreamy adulation for a tired football star. It wasn't rugby, but it wasn't far off. And it did provide a forum for dissecting idealism, disillusionment and middle-age inertia. Mankowitz's was a script of fertile opportunities, and Harris gave it his all.

Always the willing scribbler, Harris now took the screen-play apart and redrafted it frantically, working against the clock. Not since *This Sporting Life* had he contributed so much to the building of a script. With producer Heyman he scoured Tel Aviv and Jaffa for locations, resolutely avoiding the heavy costs of sound stages and settling for apartments, front gardens and hotel rooms. Even his own suite at the Dan Hotel in Tel Aviv was used.

In the movie Harris portrays Eitan, Israel's greatest football star, approaching his last game at the age of forty. Nimrod (Kim Burfield) is the child who treks to Tel Aviv's Bloomfield stadium to see his idol's last great game and befriend him. Nimrod discovers a disgruntled, bored man under pressure to 'throw' his final game in order to secure a decent coaching contract for his retirement. Nimrod reawakens the star's fighter spirit but the movie concludes tearfully when, despite Eitan's sincere efforts, age and tiredness lose the game for him.

Harris milked the metaphor and laboured hard with Israeli trainer Josef Merrimovitch to get the football right. But it was an uphill, breathless battle. Zohar's sudden departure gave no one adequate revision time. The schedule was hopelessly upended and trade gossip suggested that half the time half the technicians were at sea as to the style and intention of the movie.

On 2 February 1970 *Bloomfield* was finished and Harris flew to London for post-production, then on to Dublin when word came from Jack Donnelly that Harmay was seriously ill. After an unsuccessful operation she died. Donnelly and Harris, brothers in spirit, were equally distressed. Death was never far from Harris's thoughts and he mourned his sister volubly, lamenting the curse of the Harris womenfolk, all taken prematurely, but rejecting the spiritual soother of a return to Catholicism. 'It would be hypocritical,' he told a friend. 'I live life as I believe it. You must be honest with yourself.' Part of him refused to accept Harmay's passing. In his notebooks he wrote:

When I see in my feel
the picture of your history
fade with the sailboats of my mind . . .

When I feel
what you have felt

When I see what you have said
Then I will believe you are dead.

Dublin and Limerick found him more temperate than usual. Questioned about his love life, he expressed obdurate indifference. Someone 'interesting' would be nice, for companionship only. Hollywood women were 'Dreadful, dreadful, dreadful'. He despaired of finding someone who could absorb him, but 'I had dinner with Romy Schneider in Tel Aviv a few weeks ago. We began eating at eight o'clock and we finished at four. When we finished I suddenly realized, "Christ! We've been talking together for *eight hours*!" That's the first time in my life I've *ever* spoken to a woman for eight hours.' Schneider, happily married to German actor-director Harry Meyen, was just a pal and he stressed that he was no longer on the lookout for love. 'I've found that I like living on my own. I like being able to do what I want when I want. I will never marry again . . . I will never again put myself in a position where I can be faulted after ten years. The one tragedy for me is that I haven't got a daughter. I shall never have one now and I would have loved one to spoil. I would have brought her up so well. Sons can make their own way in the world.'

Deirdre Lloyd, the old friend from the Ennis Road, was jokingly blamed for his lack of a daughter. 'He said it was *my* fault,' says Deirdre. 'It dated back to a dark night in Limerick in the early fifties when I was walking down a laneway with a girlfriend. I heard a rush of footsteps and suddenly this big man was on top of me, shouting rape. I turned round and gave him my knee where it hurts. He rolled in agony on the ground – and of course it was Dickie, trying to scare us. He told everyone I damaged his marital prospects and denied him a daughter.'

In a long *Sun* interview Harris unveiled his uncensored new philosophy: 'Sure, making love is good for you. Just

like satisfying any bodily appetite. You feel hungry? – eat.
You're thirsty? – drink. You feel frustrated? – make love. But
don't fall in love. That's too time-consuming. It saps your
energies.' All reference to Liz and the past was avoided. He
would not comment on the union with Harrison. But the hurt
was clear and it clouded his attitude to all women: 'Most of the
women I've had affairs with in the past are my friends now. But
people are so dishonest to one another in bed. They sustain
one another's illusions with half-truths. Women play games
when they're making love. Just as they do all other times. The
trouble with women is that women need men. Women are far
more in search of the reassurance that a man can provide than
vice versa – even in this day of supposed equality.'

The chauvinism masked the pain. 'To be honest he felt
deserted,' says one close friend. 'He can be very childish.
He expected Liz to wait by his side forever, but of course
she had her own needs. [That period] almost destroyed him.
Losing Harmay added to it. If he wanted to get off the booze,
it certainly wasn't a conducive situation.'

Bloomfield took his mind off his loneliness. It all felt too
hurried, too money-starved, but he gave it twenty hours
a day. Two young Limerick songwriters, Billy Whelan and
Niall Connery, had submitted demo tapes to Limbridge the
year before and one featuring a ballad called 'Denise' excited
Harris. On impulse he commissioned a soundtrack. He also
called in Lindsay Anderson to ask his editorial opinion of the
film. Kevin Connor, himself soon to graduate as a director
in children's fantasies like *The Land That Time Forgot*, was
assigned as editor and he sat patiently as Harris employed a
computer-cum-invited-audience 'safety check'. The rough-cut
assemblage was shown to Anderson and the computer-linked
audience, who pressed buttons when they were bored or felt
the movie was over-running. All opinions tallied and Harris
recut his film to suit. Otto Heller, the veteran cameraman
whose advice had helped Harris through Tel Aviv, died during
this editing phase, adding to the sombreness of Harris's mood.
But he was revived by an ever-improving movie – and a new
love affair with British actress Linda Hayden.

Dermot Foley was then president of the Limerick branch
of the International Lions Club, the 900,000-strong worldwide

charity organization. When he read about Harris's first 'personal film' he called him in London and asked about the chances of a special premiere in Limerick. 'I called him and asked him straight. It's the way Dickie likes it. He was always a quick decisions man. I asked. He said, "No trouble."'

Before the November premiere, *A Man Called Horse* and *Cromwell* opened side by side in London to superlative business. In combination with the still-running *Camelot*, they knocked all opposition flat. Richard Harris was on hoardings and in window displays everywhere. Columbia Pictures spent what was then a colossal £25,000 on London store displays alone, saturating Oxford Street with images of Cavaliers and Roundheads. Selfridge's was taken over, with tie-in displays on all floors and a Cromwellian banquet room built to serve traditional period dishes to any of the daily twenty thousand punters who felt like playing the game. The music charts, too, were assaulted with another Harris pop venture, this one called 'The Ballad of a Man Called Horse'. It failed to make an impact.

The movie campaigning paid off brilliantly, beating competitors like *Woodstock* and Lerner and Loewe's *Paint Your Wagon*. In its first seven days *Cromwell* took almost £20,000 in receipts at the Odeon, Leicester Square, then an all-time record for Columbia. A mile away at the Plaza, *A Man Called Horse* averaged £8,000 a week, almost double the average. Harris's personal reviews were also impressive. For Marjorie Bilbow, Harris's Cromwell was 'an unforgettable performance that demonstrates once again that he is at his magnificent best in a role that demands both strength and sensitivity'. The same week *Photoplay* classed him 'a superb actor' in *A Man Called Horse* and speculated excitedly on his next move.

That next move, said Limbridge, would be directorial. A stage play, *Dylan*, had been acquired and Harris would direct a million-dollar film version. Many other small-budget movies would follow. A Limerick acquaintance said: 'Dermot was over the moon for Dickie. They all felt *Bloomfield* would put him in a different league. Dermot told me: "Dick is only starting. Watch what happens next."'

Lions president Dermot Foley recalls Harris's Limerick homecoming 'with his baby' as a cross between a religious visitation and the Keystone Cops. Foley had asked Harris to muster whatever star guests he could and Harris had enthusiastically obliged, laying on a charter flight from Heathrow for Roger Moore, *Avengers* star Honor Blackman, Bee Gee Maurice Gibb and his then singer wife Lulu, actress Imogen Hassall and a score of others. Harris booked his special guests into luxurious Dromoland Castle and a weekend of riding, golf and general revelry was promised. Events unfolded dramatically. At Heathrow the premiere party was delayed forty minutes because of a bomb scare on the plane. For Lulu this was 'a little disconcerting'. Finally they arrived at Shannon for a quick transfer to Dromoland and thence to the Savoy Cinema of Harris's brawling youth.

Hundreds of screaming Limerick youngsters crowded the streets outside the Savoy to watch Harris, in floor-length suede coat and hippie scarf, follow fifteen hundred guests, among them the Minister for Posts and Telegraphs and the Minister for Justice, into the cinema. Harris was modesty triumphant, expertly relishing the role he had long dreamed of: the ultimate Limerick conquest. The bomb scare had been 'Just great fun'.

Once in the auditorium everyone settled expectantly for the momentous twitching of the curtains . . . but then the dimmed lights went up and a stern announcement was made: a male caller to Williams Street Police Station had given a warning that a bomb had been planted in the cinema. The mass evacuation, led by the Minister for Justice, took everyone's mind off movies. One hundred Gardai and Special Branch officers combed the cinema before the all-clear was given and Harris and his tribe returned. Linda Hayden looked pale and shaken. Harris kept smiling. Limerick, which knew about these things, gripped its sides in suppressed hilarity.

Bloomfield drew massively contradictory reviews. Though it earned a Golden Globe nomination, the American critics generally savaged it. The *Hollywood Reporter*, never a Harris fan, accused the actor of unforgivable self-love and baldly called the movie a failure: 'The story basks in its own self-importance since the actor-singer-poet-director (and soon to be novelist) at the helm has again allowed his prodigious energy to be refracted through a project which misses the mark as significant dramatic experience and panders to obvious moral truths.' The erudite *Monthly Film Bulletin* in Britain poured scorn on 'an embarrassing debut for Richard Harris as director', and *Films and Filming* concluded: 'Unremittingly, lumberingly awful.'

The death of *Bloomfield* – booed off screen at the Berlin Festival, where Harris booed back – spelt the death of one facet of the public Richard Harris. Already wary of himself in the mirror of the press, he now slammed the door on candour in his artistic movie aspirations. No more were the hopes of *Hamlet*, *Dylan* or a possible *Borstal Boy* movie discussed. In their place came an offhand brashness in relation to movies and, concurrently, the growing insularity of a long-haired poet. 'He was totally fucked off by it,' says a friend. 'He said to me, "No one *saw Bloomfield*". They had Dick Harris up to here for twenty years. Dick Harris offered them his throat, and they cut it wide open.'

Sandy Howard found Harris bent but not broken. 'Richard isn't a quitter. You learn that very quickly when you really get to know him. I had *Man in the Wilderness* and it was exactly right for him. My friend Jack De Witt had again written the script and Richard was taking a break from everything in Tunisia, so we decided to fly out and talk him aboard. I'd come across the idea, about this trapper left for dead in the wilds of primitive America, when I was hunting locations for something in the Dakotas and some locals told me the tale. I knew it was perfect for Richard, the strong loner theme and all that . . .'

En route to Tunisia Howard and De Witt were briefly distracted by 'a bit of rumpus up the front of the plane'. They didn't think twice about it. 'Which goes to show how Jack and I – and Richard, by the way, when it was his turn – sank ourselves into everything we did. Yes, it was a hijack attempt. But it didn't take our minds off this great picture we were planning.'

Harris embarked on *Man in the Wilderness* almost as an exorcism. It was the ideal project for his mood: well developed, staffed by genuine professionals, short on dialogue. 'I think it helped that I made him a partner on it,' says Howard. 'He was a great partner. Not just in taking the bucks, I mean.

He was a great collaborator, a very giving man. I know it's a cliché, but he was first on set in the mornings, and last to go home. What was my reasoning in making him a partner? Well, it made certain that he showed up each day!' Howard laughs.

The shoot in Almeria, Spain, was among Harris's easiest, though the physical trials of Zachary Bass – 'His real name was Hugo Ass, but we changed it to protect ourselves because it *is* a true story' – were heavy going. Harris didn't mind. 'I like it, I like Bass because he doesn't beat nature, he joins it. There is no fight to survive today as there was once in the old West.'

His fighting form roused again, in May, without a break, he took Paul Gallico's special invitation to star in his adaptation of his own novel *The Snow Goose*, a wartime classic about a hunchback Dunkirk fisherman who gets involved with a shy girl and the wounded goose which become symbolic of British courage. Gallico had had offers of a film version of his 1941 story throughout the years. 'But the other producers wanted to do their own *Snow Goose*, not mine.' Then the American Hallmark Hall of Fame made its approach, in a co-production arrangement with the BBC. It would be Harris's first large-scale TV movie but the attraction of Gallico's blessing was too good to sidestep. Innes Lloyd, the BBC producer who oversaw the production, is in no doubt that Gallico lured Harris. 'But it was more than that. What appealed to Richard too was the image of the cloth-capped gypsy outsider. The man outside normal life, doing his own thing. I think it was, in the phrase, *where he was at* at that time. But my experience of him was nothing other than very pleasant. He did not contribute to the screenplay. The director Patrick Garland and Paul Gallico did all that. But Richard gave himself to us very adeptly, very willingly.' During the six-week shoot at Frinton on the East Coast of England Harris was hard-working – but quiet and reflective. 'We had no booze problems,' says Lloyd. 'What I remember most is his one excitement: rugby. I remember being on the train with him coming to Frinton, and all he really wanted to get fired up on was rugby.'

Both *Man in the Wilderness* and *The Snow Goose* earned Harris good reviews. 'A work of simplicity and purity,' said the *Los Angeles Times* of *Man in the Wilderness*, commending the 'authority' of director Richard C. Sarafian and Harris's 'eloquence in what is virtually a mime performance'. *The Snow Goose* – 'deeply satisfying' for Gallico and Garland, according to Innes Lloyd – also received qualified raves. Cyril Cusack called it, 'Undeniably one of the best things he ever did.'

Harris wasn't appeased. The departure of Liz, the loss of Harmay and the death of *Bloomfield* gnawed at his peace and his confidence. Throughout the remainder of 1971 he drank like he had never drunk, brawled as in the sixties – and occasionally quietened himself to write poems and songs. In October he recorded 'My Boy', a poignant, personal-statement tear-jerker penned for him by Derry songwriter Phil Coulter and Bill Martin. The song spoke of failing marriage and a man's fervid, hopeless devotion to his son. It was entered in the Radio-Tele International Grand Prix at Luxembourg in late October and Harris sang it live, representing Britain. When the *Irish Times* questioned the likelihood of his representing Ireland somewhere, say in the Eurovision Song Contest, he blithely dismissed the implied criticism: 'They know wiser over there. They know I cannot sing.'

He continued to sing, jigsawing together a new album in the absence of Jimmy Webb's support. *My Boy* was one of his best-realized popular albums, a reasoned blend of catchy tunes like his self-penned 'All the Broken Children' and Webb's 'Beth', and labyrinthine symphonies like 'Requiem', another Webb mini-epic that Harris today calls his all-time favourite song. *My Boy* was, by his design, 'a concept album about a marriage' and remains the nearest expression of autobiography that Harris has ever given his fans. 'Beth' might easily be Elizabeth; 'Why Did You Leave Me?' is a self-explanatory, bare plea; 'This is the Way', the aggressive defence philosophy that rejects angst. This last song, by his new musical guru Johnny Harris (no relation) and J. Bromley, possesses an almost frightening primal energy that obliterates the lingering taste of romantic Webb:

> *I have lied, cheated when I could*
> *And worse than this, it felt so good . . .*
>
> *Fighting is just a way of life with me*

Jesus is just a word I use to swear with
This is the way I live my life . . .

The sleeve notes, written by Harris as song preludes, are succinct though stained with a fluttering self-pity that echoed the indulgent aspects of *Bloomfield*. Their uncompromising honesty – warts and all – provides a sampler for the richer, less commercially attuned poetry to come.

Limbridge was by now attracting submissions from aspiring songwriters all over the world, and Harris had his pick of superb, widely ranging material. Dermot carefully shuffled through it all, selecting, editing, arguing possibilities with arranger Johnny Harris. Among their finds was young hip Canadian Tony Romeo, who supplied a second concept album, *Slides*, based on the holiday adventures of a gypsy-like teacher who loses his job because of his radical, nature-loving teaching style. *Slides* was the purest pop, delivering three near-perfect ballsy ballads in 'I Don't Have to Tell You', 'How I Spent My Summer' and 'I'm Coming Home', as well as yet another Webb-style slice of neo-romance in the title track. But the album, on ABC Dunhill's subsidiary Probe label, failed to make the charts and Harris called it, 'Rubbish, misconceived. I hated it. It was a ballad style that was Barry Manilow, not me.' The singers he then revered, apart from the perennial Sinatra, were Tom Jones and Kris Kristofferson.

The court appearances resulting from pub brawls continued. There were no serious consequences and then Harris pulled himself together and put a touring pop show on the road. 'It was something he needed,' says journalist friend Trevor Danker. 'And something he needed *to get out of his system*. He wasn't a kid, but he had the kid pop image still going. Knowing Dick, he said to himself, "Let's take this out on the road and have a laugh with it." And that's what he did.'

After a try-out in the English provinces Harris took his show to the major American venues, playing Chicago, Minneapolis, Columbus, LA and other cities. With four big albums – and *Camelot* – to draw from, there was no shortage of material to fill a two-hour solo show, though Harris admitted at the time that he was 'terrified', as he had been in the solo hours of *Diary of a Madman*, facing the lonely spotlight. Dermot, a couple of chummy London journalists and a variety of girlfriends kept him company in the short days and long nights. A journalist friend recalls: 'Those were raving mad days, you can imagine. It was no different from any rock band scene, with the star being mobbed and sucked up to. Dick enjoyed it, and he especially enjoyed the women.' In one incident, another writer recalled, Harris missed his on-stage cue. The band started playing the opening chords of 'MacArthur Park', but the spotlight raked an empty stage. Panicking, the stage manager sent the writer on an urgent errand to 'Find Harris, for Chrissake!' The writer did find Harris – in his room, naked, with 'a priceless beauty' on hands and knees before him, giving him oral sex. The writer grabbed Harris and hurried him into jeans and kaftan as the pulsating orchestral strains hammered the floor under them. Harris finally made it on stage – a good five minutes into 'MacArthur Park' – pulling up his zip.

'The younger fans stormed the stage after the performance in St Louis,' wrote Richard Evans of the London *Evening News* who followed the journey. 'And in the more sedate setting of New York's plush Philharmonic Hall they lined up three deep at the foot of the stage, hands outstretched, to acclaim and touch their bearded hero.' Afterwards, Evans said, the star took a group of the faithful to a nearby bar – appropriately, the Ginger Man.

'Why?' Evans asked a swooning band of teenage Kansas City girls who had hired a bus to make the pilgrimage. 'Is it because he's a movie star?'

'It's just *him*,' was the reply. 'He's *real*. He's a human being. There's nothing phoney about him. He's someone you can identify with because he doesn't give you all that showbiz schmaltz.'

But Evans, like most critics, was still flummoxed. Harris's songs and the poems he read on-stage in the frequent chatty intermissions were hardly teen-dream stuff. They were songs and poems of divorce, of death and of politics. One poem, 'There Are Too Many Saviours on My Cross', was pointedly political, decrying the violence of Northern Ireland and damning *both* sides. Inevitably, though he had naively not imagined it, the cynical brigade – largely the gutter press he had once indulged – turned on him. In the poem the author, through the voice of a dying Jesus, disowns those 'lending their blood to flood out my ballot box with needs of their own'. A special seven-inch recording of the poem was cut and released, with much hype, on his return to London. At the Limbridge press conference he announced that the proceeds would go to 'the victims of injustice' in Northern Ireland. The reporters weren't impressed: more than one wanted to know if Harris was taking into account the 'other side' in the Ulster struggle. Harris was white-faced in rage: 'Are you questioning for one second the motive of all this? Are you doubting me? Are you looking for an argument? This money will go to *all* families of people who have been killed.'

The moment was significant. Harris had played the game of commerce and landed in a hole. The movie world had let him down. There would be no more games. Now he would say what he felt, write it, broadcast it everywhere. Overnight he became a political crusader, spilling the instincts, prejudices and half-education of thirty years in every direction. Boldly he told the world he supported the IRA in its battle for a unified Ireland. He sent his poetry to Downing Street (to no response) and issued a statement that he was preparing a film on internment-without-trial in Northern Ireland – 'an exposure of British Nazi-style brutalities'.

Ablaze in his Irishness he returned to Dublin at Kevin McClory's request to mount a one-man show at the Gaiety, old home of the Ginger Man, in aid of the Dublin Central Remedial Clinic charity. This homecoming presented yet another Richard Harris, a man vastly changed from the hippie *Bloomfield* kind. During 1972, he told a press conference, he had turned down twenty-two movies, all rubbish. 'I can't be bothered. I have bigger fish to fry.' Later, in a quieter setting, he told a journalist: 'I really hate journalists. They always write the story *they* want to write. They steer the conversation *their* way. You can't win.' Still, he had juicy gifts for them: his new love affair, he confessed, was with Nina Van Pallandt, former half of the Danish singing duo Nina and Frederick. She had stayed in LA to complete her film acting debut in

Robert Altman's *The Long Goodbye* with Elliot Gould, but they would be back in each others' arms soon. 'Marriage is archaic,' he hissed, but: 'This is not just a case of being just good friends – it's a lot more than that.'

After the triumphal Gaiety night – designed by Sean Kenny and mostly self-directed – Harris was, for the first time since *Bloomfield*, ready for the overdue public autopsy. Seated in front of a half-pint of Guinness in Neary's he admitted that, yes, he would love the chance to direct again. Journalist Kay Kent observed 'his eyes lighting up with enthusiasm for the first time that day'. But there was also fair objectivity: 'I never want to act as well as direct again. I was *terrible* in *Bloomfield* . . . *and* in the direction. Although I knew what I wanted to do, I just didn't have the time to prepare properly. I like the idea of directing because I love the poetic expression you can get with movies.'

Random House, the American publishers, issued his first book of poems, *I, in the Membership of My Days*, late in 1973. It consisted of thirty-eight free verse pieces with a binding theme of defiance in the face of imperfection, disillusionment and death. The best of the poems were his musings on the death of Ivan and Harmay – and the Rabelaisian appreciation of crippled Christy Brown, author of *My Left Foot*. The *New York Times* admired them; but Limerick, says Harris, 'couldn't make head nor tail of 'em'. In the first few weeks the book sold twenty-two thousand copies, rendering it, in the publishers' eyes, 'a comprehensive success'. Harris had been paid, he said, 'a six-figure sum' for the work, plus the option of a collection of short stories and the novel *Flanny at 1.10* which was 'almost complete'.

A short time later he was wriggling away from the promise of his new books – and the autobiography Random House was angling for. 'I will not write the sort of thing Random House approached me about. They wanted all the smut and the bed-hopping. But a lot of the women I knew in those madcap years are married with children now and I just wouldn't do it. I despise those sort of books anyway. They do no one any good. Even the money people make from them disappears, or causes trouble.

'I believe there's a balance in everything and a reason for

everything, and the bad and the good you do all comes back to you. It's a sort of boomerang effect. I may have caused a lot of unhappiness with my bad temper and my drinking and my wildness in the past, but at least none of it was deliberate; and no one has to stick around to be a victim and accept the sort of nonsense I gave out.

'Yes, I think people get what they ask for in a strange sort of way. And I'm glad that no one can do anything to me. Because I'd never allow myself to be anyone's victim, however fond of them I might be.'

13

Ann

Booze and continual one-night stands kept his equilibrium (the Nina affair was over inside a year), but still, addictively, he worked. Rod Taylor, firmly among the Harris friends, recalls the Mexican location for the Harris comeback movie, *The Deadly Trackers*: 'It was convivial, let's say. I think Richard had the hots for one of the native actresses, Isela Vega, but he didn't get anywhere. Not to worry – we enjoyed the friendly local hostesses to the full.'

Taylor had stumbled on to the movie – as ambitious a piece of metaphorical morality as any of Harris's westerns – when the production, with a different cast, collapsed in Spain. Then it had been Sam Fuller's picture and Harris had a different antagonist in the simple, lurid tale of a sheriff's pursuit of an outlaw who murders his wife and son. Disputes between Fuller and Harris, equally strong-minded people at equally tipsy stages of their respective careers, sank the movie after four weeks. Fouad Said, innovative photographer of the cult sixties' TV comedy-thriller series *I Spy* and later producer of various good movies like *Across 110th Street*, shifted the remnants to Mexico, abandoned Fuller's script (called *Riata*) and industriously rebuilt the production, keeping Harris happy by allowing him generous creative participation. Said's ally Barry Shear, a 'boy genius' TV director, was elected to the director's chair with Harris's approval; and Sam Manners, production manager, suggested his pal Rod Taylor as the perfect screen enemy for sheriff Harris. Harris and Taylor met at a party at Zsa Zsa Gabor's and, says Taylor, 'fell in love'. The 'near disaster' of *The Deadly Trackers* was taken in hand by both actors who flew to Mexico City and then to the Cuernavaca location, and worked 'religiously' to reconstruct an original chase western. Taylor thought the script 'awful in parts' and stresses that one of the main attractions was Harris. 'He was really a darling, no matter what his own troubles. He went on his knees before me and paid compliment to my work on *Young Cassidy*. He forgave this Aussie imposter doing O'Casey because I was great, he said.'

A paid-up member of the Screenwriters' Guild, Taylor was quick to contribute new scenes to invigorate the hatred between hero and villain: 'I think that's what the story lacked – a decent account of the villain's villainy. So I wrote in these scenes, with Richard's blessing.' Harris – not rookie director Shear, and certainly not Said – was the principal creative force, Taylor makes it clear. 'Richard dominated and I provided what was expected of me as the co-star antagonist. We had our ego clashes – but in the course of fighting creative battles, not personality clashes, ever. I knew Richard jumped on some people's asses, because that's the way he is. That's the way *I* am, come to think of it: I fight with two fists when someone hasn't done their homework. And on the movie there were occasions when people needed to be . . . straightened out.'

Harris was, says Taylor, 'like myself off the piss from Monday to Friday', though, close as they became, Taylor did not see much of the emotional inertia that others observed. 'He was . . . *lively*. Every Monday morning we had this secret code. We held up four fingers to each other. On Tuesday it was three. On Wednesday, two. On Thursday it was one. Which really meant we had just one day till the piss-up started on Friday night. It was a grand time – from Friday till dawn Monday. We put down some booze. But we never let the tequila interfere with the work on the battlefield.' Harris had, Taylor saw, a self-checking mechanism that revealed his professionalism. 'On those weekends, whether we were enjoying the locals or the tequila or not, we worked. On that script. It was the only time we got really, because the locations were gruelling enough and we had a lot to get done.'

To their credit, and Sam Manners's, the production remained on time and on (reduced) budget. Warners covered finance and Harris went on to supervise a tricky, cost-restricted post-production that had clips and out-takes from existing movie soundtracks glued on as a counterfeit musical score. Segments from Jerry Fielding's *The Wild Bunch* score, Pat Williams's *Hardcase* and Richard Markowitz's *The Last Tomorrow* gave the movie a cobbled-together, fragmented aura that Taylor and Harris did their best to ignore. 'Considering what we started with, and the project's history,' says Taylor, 'I liked the end result. Richard should have been proud of himself too.'

Nobody agreed. The *New Yorker* billed the movie as 'an incoherent, blood-soaked chase story'. Praise went only to the technical ingenuity of Said's 'Cinemobiles' – all-in mobile studios used for the first time on foreign location work in *I Spy*. (Said won a Special Oscar in 1974 for his technical contribution to the industry.)

For Harris personally the movie was – almost – his directorial follow-up to *Bloomfield*, and as such its failure cut deeply. Critic Tony Rayns noted an obstinate aping of Brando – 'complete with Method pauses, grunts and flailing arms'. He also disdained the star's evident self-direction: 'Harris swamps the rest of the film with his studied machismo and Shear is left to trail along behind, his function reduced to recording.'

In limbo, Harris started *Gulliver's Travels* for Bond director Peter Hunt at Pinewood. It was a sweet, childlike script – but destined for trouble from the start. The Little People of the story were to be animated in Belgium. Costs there over-ran and the producer filed for bankruptcy. *Gulliver* stopped in mid-production, enraging the star.

In the opinion of Harris's business associates his loyalty to his audience stayed intact while a violent cynicism about the industry and its so-called pacemakers began to show itself. Harris was quoted as saying: 'I can tell you the next Steve McQueen movie, whatever it is. I can tell you how he's going to play it . . . the same way he's been playing it for fifteen years. In the motion picture business you can't have tremendous artistic ambition. And that's why I couldn't care less . . .' An associate says: 'He really couldn't. In an elevator with him you felt it. You felt he was saying. "Fuck this star crap. Fuck the studio time call. Fuck the 'suits' with their rip-off deals. Fuck the box-office. Let me get back to the jungle."'

Harris sat down with Dermot and their accountants for a re-evaluation. He no longer wanted to be dependent on 'some fat-ass producer offering a crumb or two'; a new scheme for future financial security was needed. With the proper strategy and a little luck, that scheme might even some day allow him to make his own films – to make *Hamlet*. As a result of the discussions Harris divested himself of most of the material trappings he had gathered over the years. The rarely used lodge in Kilkee was sold for £14,000. Tower House, the haunted Arthurian folly (he claimed the ghost of a boy pestered him), went for £350,000 – to Jimmy Page of Led Zeppelin. The plan was to shift this money into a wide range of upwardly mobile properties around the world – houses in unlikely areas where the price tags were on the move. As Harris tells it, he and Dermot had concluded that this life would not last. 'We decided to put 50 per cent of every future film fee into property around Los Angeles.' The scheme was enough to restore him, temporarily at any rate, to movie-making.

A new home was sought, and found. Kevin McClory had been living in the Bahamas since the settlement of his court action against Bond creator Ian Fleming had made him a very wealthy man.[1] His six-bedroom home, Pieces of Eight, was on tax-free Paradise Island, formerly owned by Nassau millionaire Huntington Hartford. McClory repeatedly advised Harris to consider Paradise as a home base, but Harris's restless lifestyle prevented him from coming to any decision. Finally McClory found Harris drunk in a Dublin gutter and put him on a plane to Nassau. Harris dried out at Pieces of Eight – and succumbed. With McClory's assistance he searched out and bought a ten-bedroom clapboard house on three acres in the shadow of the Holiday Inn. It was, literally, paradise: rolling lawns surrounded by sweet-scented bougainvillea and cabbage palms, a white beach, a private jetty with a power boat to take him across to the amenities of Nassau, ten minutes away. The purchase price was £200,000. At first Harris told his friends he would be bored to death in the isolation of the Bahamas, but very quickly he adjusted. In fact it was the salvation he needed, the haven in which to hide his smarting creative soul.

---

[1] Kevin McClory disputed the copyright of the Fleming novel, *Thunderball*, the storyline of which he claimed to have co-written. In an out-of-court settlement McClory was granted film rights to *Thunderball*.

Lazy lobster lunches at open-air Captain Nemo's prepared him for Dick Lester's *Juggernaut*, shot with a guest star-heavy cast at Twickenham, and John Frankenheimer's *99 and 44/100% Dead*, scheduled for shooting around LA. Though Harris liked Lester and had always admired Frankenheimer's work, the true *raison d'être* of these films was, as he and Dermot agreed, the procuring of investment cash. There were bonuses. Frankenheimer planned to co-star Harris with Jacqueline Bisset, an actress whom Harris adored from afar. At the last minute, however, the director called to tell Harris of a change of plan. Bisset had dropped out. Frankenheimer had someone altogether new in mind.

There are, in classic Harris style, at least two accounts of the circumstances of his meeting with Ann Turkel, the twenty-six-year-old brunette whom he adopted as acolyte, then substitute daughter, then lover, then wife. In the popular account (recorded by Simon Kinnersley in the *Daily Mail*) Harris was flying to LA on a jumbo when 'the girl in seat 2B caught his attention'. By the time the plane had crossed Newfoundland they had agreed to meet for a private dinner. After that, said the *Mail*, 'their relationship quickly blossomed'.

The alternative version is less romantic. Frankenheimer screen-tested a variety of newcomers for the part of Buffy, the object of the hero's sexual dalliance in *99 and 44/100% Dead*. Part-time model Turkel from Scarsdale in New York State, inexperienced but strikingly handsome, he liked best. On the phone he told Harris, who objected. The role of schoolmarm Buffy, said Harris, was too substantial for a new actress. On top of that the girl suggested – Turkel – was 'everything I deplore in a female'. Harris told *Photoplay*: 'She's too tall, too thin, and a brunette. I've always favoured blondes. She's also not very sociable . . .' When Harris finished the Lester sea rescue movie he flew to LA and watched the Frankenheimer screen test. He was more sure than ever that Turkel was a dud: 'I saw it through and was convinced it was a classic case of casting couch business. I gave Ann ten days of hell while she waited to find out whether or not she was going to be in the picture.'

Frankenheimer – whose casting instincts had proved resoundingly right in his hit films like *The Manchurian*

Candidate (1962) – finally convinced Harris and filming started, with Turkel working overtime to try to impress the star. What made matters harder for Turkel was her hero-worship of Harris. *Camelot* was her favourite movie and, she told crewmen quietly, she had revered pin-up King Arthur for years. Harris detected her sincere commitment and swung to the polar extreme in his behaviour towards her: 'Once we began filming, through guilt, I became attentive and helpful, explaining camera angles, how to read her lines and so forth. I must say she was a good student. But . . . there was no hint of romantic notions.'

Turkel was at sea. She had long fantasized about getting into movies but had doubted her chances with Frankenheimer. Once she tested, her friends promised, she would be cast and adopted by Hollywood for ever. Turkel was less confident, but kept her hopes. According to her, she knew of Harris's bad press and expected the worst. But day by day the working relationship improved. Late night shooting recaps became late night candlelit dinners. Harris squinted inquisitively, and smiled, and relaxed. She was good company, dutiful, beautiful – but uncommunicative. Harris knew she liked him but their intimacies were restrained, guarded. After a couple of weeks they found themselves seated by the pool of Harris's rented LA home, perusing script pages.

Harris asked her: 'Annie, do you think there's something going on between us that we don't know about?'

Ann replied blushingly, 'I think there might be.'

'I was one surprised Irishman,' said Harris later, insisting that the relationship was 'the most unlikely of my life'. Prior to Frankenheimer's offer, Ann Turkel had been 'almost married' to David Niven Jr, head of Paramount's European arm, and heading for the life of a Hollywood society beauty; such a background ill prepared her for coping with poetic, disenchanted, hard-boozing Harris. But the chemistry worked – especially so when Harris introduced her to his sons on holiday in the Bahamas at Christmas. Ann got on well with all the boys – she was closer in age to Damian than to Damian's dad – and described her Bahamian baptism as 'love at first sight'. The islands would be a perfect future home for them, and she can have been excused for thinking that introductions to the family suggested lofty intentions on Harris's part. But he wasn't ready for another marriage. News of Liz's life with Rex Harrison depressed him – though he wished her happiness by whatever means, 'because I love her'. Early in their relationship Harris told Ann of his mistrust of the institution of marriage, stressing that he couldn't see the point any more. Instead, he proposed, they would go on as they had started, in a mutually edifying partnership where he played tutor and she was confidante, companion, comforter. 'I believe you're born alone,' was his favourite comment of the time. 'I don't believe any two people can adapt to suit one another. That idea is a complete fallacy. You've got to work out your own rhythms, and if someone doesn't fit in you've got to say, "Right! That's finished!" and then move on.'

Nevertheless Ann's arrival changed his life, though he was slow to admit it. His motivation – property investments apart – suddenly returned and he had a meeting with Sandy Howard to formalize a venture partnership for a number of new movies. In all Howard was planning a $25 million slate of production, expanding his existing independent production group by taking on high-fliers like executive Terry Morse and distribution experts Charles Boasberg and Milt Goldstein. Howard proposed eight new feature films, four to star Harris – on a fifty-fifty profits split. Among the new movies, over which Harris would have creative supervision, would be *Return of a Man Called Horse*, budgeted at $3.5 million, and *The Last Castle*, a Canadian co-production whose financing scheme necessitated shooting in Nova Scotia. Actor-turned-director Don Taylor was retained by Howard to direct this small-scale weepie (released as *Echoes of a Summer*) and found Harris 'excited by what he was facing up to, very interested and demanding and unwilling to leave stones unturned'. Taylor flew to northern Canada with Howard to scout locations as Harris – to universal surprise – suddenly talked of impending marriage.

Gossip columnists swooped when the news was leaked: Harris would be marrying Ann in April. The follow-my-leader routine began again, with reporters tagging him – and Ann – everywhere. The experience was a new one for Ann, whose

family background was the relatively tame, formal world of
fashion houses and designer launches (her father was a cloth-
ing manufacturer), and whose brief time with David Niven Jr
had kept her firmly in the background.

In April Harris flew to London to record the album of *I, in
the Membership of My Days* under the direction of producer Terry
James and arranger Johnny Harris. All his sons contributed,
reading poetry from his book, and the prose was beefed
up with a number of slight songs, some traditional, others
(notably 'I Don't Know') gracefully penned by Harris himself.
This was turnabout time again: this album, like the spoken
Jonathan Livingstone Seagull which would win him a Grammy
at last, was a move away from mass-market pop. Apart from
compilation rehashes, Harris's chart-oriented musical career
was over.

The *Daily Express*, among many, haunted Harris and Ann
Turkel at the Savoy Hotel, seeking details. Would they wed?
Where? When?

The expected date passed without announcement and
finally Harris met the press in his suite and gruffly said
the marriage was off. 'The postponement is partly because
of filming and recording schedules,' said Harris. 'But it has
also dawned on me that, although we've been around together
for six months or so, we don't really know each other. Until now
I've seen Ann only for a few minutes in the morning before I go
filming. Then for a few minutes in the evening, before I go to
the recording studios. And for another few hours in between,
in the lulls.'

The *Express* pressed him on the change of heart, but Harris
was adamant that they would eventually get married. He
had even told her father, in a telephone conversation – and
cautioned him at the same time: 'I've made no bones that I'm
not good news for any girl. I told him, "If I was in your place
I'd have a contract out on Harris's head in five minutes." All
he did was laugh. But as it was a phone conversation I don't
know if it was through clenched teeth.'

His reasons for marriage were straightforward: 'Ann is an
old-fashioned girl who wants it, and I'd like a daughter.' When
the *Express* met him Harris was nursing 'the worst hangover
in his life'. A brandy, port and soda (mixed) was prescribed

to sort him out, and he went for it with enthusiasm. Still he would not name the day. 'But I'm taking off five months to hole up in the Bahamas and we'll see how we get on being in each other's pocket twenty-four hours a day.'

At the time of Harmay's death Jack Donnelly had been managing the Wicklow Hotel in central Dublin. Now he was back in the sticks, in Cashel, Co. Tipperary, managing the luxurious Cashel Palace, the upper-crust inland staging post for Dublin–Shannon travellers. Harris took time off here with Ann to peruse Don Taylor's movie script. At that time Jack Donnelly described Harris's routine to me: 'He likes his own company, and he likes a quiet time. All day long he lies on his bed reading – westerns are a particular favourite. He'll go out on the town for a big party meal, but most of all he and Ann like to be private. This [the Cashel Palace] is like the Bahamas. Nowadays he likes to escape the treadmill.'

While Ann held her breath, Harris worked on Taylor's movie. 'We saw it the same way from the outset,' says Don Taylor. 'There were no arguments, not even heavy debates. Bob Joseph, who wrote the stage play on which it was based, and I flew to Nassau for a few days of constructive talks with him – and then we went and did it. It was as good as that.' Taylor had discovered an exceptional child star some years before and cast her in his *Tom Sawyer*. Now he wanted to use her again, as the dying girl around whom the story revolved. Her name was Jodie Foster. 'Richard adored her,' says Taylor, 'and he adored the little boy we had, Brad Savage. His way with children showed the scope of his sensitivity, the side of him people try not to see.'

Taylor tackled the booze issue without delay. 'It turned into no problem at all,' he says. 'We sat down and talked about it at the start and he gave me an undertaking. His word was good. When we flew to Canada to do it, we did it without troubles. And, let me say, it was a small film, not much money in it at all, including actors' fees. We did it because we all loved the subject. Bob Joseph, the writer, was an old friend; and I'd worked on a movie called *Jack of Diamonds* for Sandy. Richard was comfortable too with the people. It was a family experience, and a good art-house end result.' Taylor recalls the contentment of the cast and crew, and their

satisfaction with 'an objective achieved'. He remembers the
first showings to Sandy Howard's distribution team: 'When
the movie ended and the lights went up it was obvious that
everyone was moved. This simple, tragic everyday story of a
dying kid shook everybody. The distribution guy said, "It's
a jewel – but do we know how to release it?"'

Echoes of a Summer was many months in post-production
and limped into market release after a premiere at the Cork
Film Festival in June 1976. It achieved no co-ordinated cinema
release in Britain and was not widely seen until its TV premiere
seven years later. It took its place alongside *Juggernaut* and
99 and 44/100% Dead as one of Harris's major box office
flops. *Juggernaut* fared best of the bad lot, grossing well for
a few weeks in London, then disappearing overnight. It was
a tense, seagoing thriller, in which Harris woodenly played
a bomb-disposal man hoisted on to a transatlantic liner to
do his stuff. Frankenheimer's movie was yet another thriller,
land-based but all at sea in terms of suspense and dénouement.
Harris played Harry Crown, a charmless thug engaged by
mob man Uncle Frank (Edmond O'Brien) to ensure the election of Big Eddie (Bradford Dillman) as underworld *capo*.
Frankenheimer himself called it 'probably the worst movie I
ever made'. Charles Champlin of the *Los Angeles Times* met it
with optimism, and was flattened: 'What I think was intended
by Robert Dillon's script was a fast, stylish send-up of the
gangster movie, entertaining in a carefree, lighter-than-air
sort of way. It was meant to produce bubbles, not lather . . .
[The movie] is incalculably slow-going and within 56/100% of
being totally humourless.' Much of the blame went to Harris –
'mournfully laconic beneath a blonde wig'. Ann Turkel barely
merited mention. She was 'photographed as moonily as if what
we had here was classical romance on-screen as well as off'.
Britain's Tom Milne rated it 'distressingly faceless' and granted
Harris 'a pallid Michael Caine imitation' without comment on
Ann Turkel.

Among the vocal admirers of Ann Turkel, actress, was
one David Niven Jr. After a private preview he commented
chivalrously: 'Considering it was her first film, she was very
good and is sure to get future parts. I thought she looked
lovely.'

Harris marked his satisfaction with Ann's performance by giving her a gold, enamel and diamond butterfly – her favourite symbol – on a neck chain. In June, without prior announcement, he followed up by marrying her in a private ceremony in Los Angeles. Harris was unusually tight-lipped about the occasion: 'She is a good talker. When we exchanged our marriage vows the magistrate asked, "Do you take this woman to be your lawful wedded wife?" And before I could utter a word Ann said, "*He does!*"'

Yet another 'new' Richard Harris temporarily emerged, inspired by the resilient young energy of Ann who refused to be dejected by her first failure in films. Those who doubted he had changed had only to listen to him talk about the intensive therapy course he and Ann had joined. 'Neither of us needed it,' he hastened to add, 'but we're so individualistic. We said, "Let's go examine transactional analysis", which I became an absolute freak on . . . but there are no answers.'

The binding force was the individualism, and their kindred gypsy spirits. Both loved to travel at the drop of a hat. Both, said Harris, were 'excitement freaks' prone to bouts of boredom and ever-ready to tackle them. Paradise Island became their home, but Ann insisted on keeping a flat in Scarsdale on the thirtieth floor of a slick apartment building. 'We had a contract,' Harris explained. 'And one of the things she insisted on was her apartment in New York because it kept her family ties. Her grandmother is here, her mother and father, brothers and sisters. And being Jewish they have a tremendous affinity.'

The new Richard Harris spurred himself to keep up with his active young bride. She was, he says, 'a girl with the energies and interests of ten and the days were never long enough for her'. Her interest in modelling continued – she advised Damian's girlfriend on how to get taken on by *Vogue* – and she began planning a record, possibly with her own rock band: 'It's funny because I was discovered for *Vogue* singing. A college friend asked me to sing at a Mary Quant fashion show and an editor from *Vogue* called me afterwards and asked if I'd thought of modelling . . . [Now] I'd like to do an album with Peter Frampton.'

Supported by Sandy Howard's trust in him, Harris flung

himself back into mainstream movies with a new impetus: 'Now if a picture I do fails it will be because *I* failed in the conception or some element, not because some studio has changed its mind.' In this frame of mind, keeping pace with Ann, he returned to Dick Lester's side for *Robin and Marian* with Sean Connery, playing Robin Hood's tormentor King Richard in an oddly muted monotone; then Sandy Howard's *The Return of a Man Called Horse*, directed by Irvin Kershner in Dakota, Mexico and Wiltshire; followed by George Pan Cosmatos's unsuccessful *The Cassandra Crossing*, with Sophia Loren, in Rome and Geneva.

Each of the movies had some qualities; above all they paid well. *Robin and Marian* scored on its Connery audience, and on Audrey Hepburn's comeback as Maid Marian. *The Return of a Man Called Horse*, while profoundly praised in America ('Hauntingly beautiful,' said the *Los Angeles Times*; 'one of the best performances of Harris's career') failed at the cash till. 'It was too gratuitous,' says producer Howard. 'Kershner cast it with Jews and made too much of a play on the graphic violence of the Sun Vow ceremony. I didn't like what I saw. But the critics were generous and I suppose that helped Richard.'

Helpful too was the revival of the abandoned *Gulliver*. Josef Shaftel, the producer, found a new funding deal with Jersey-based Transatlantic Productions and the animation, stopped in mid-stream, started again. It had originally been announced for an Easter 1974 release; now Shaftel told Harris that the movie would be completed and distributed by July 1976. (It was, and failed badly at the box office.)

The initial outward signs couldn't have been better. Ann, too, had been cast in *The Cassandra Crossing* and another co-starring movie was in negotiation. The marriage was harmonious but both of them longed for a baby – a girl – to supplement their Paradise future. 'Ann certainly wasn't calming for him,' says a friend. 'If anything she drove him, day and night. It was good to see it. He laughed a lot with her and doted on her, like a father. That was the affectionate phrase he often used: "My Little Girl". He stopped gallivanting because she put a ten-mile limit around him. What she wanted was a proper decent married life.'

During the Cinecitta shooting of *Cassandra* the couple

sneaked away for a romantic weekend in Paris where Ann saw an African fertility talisman in a shop window. It was woven from elephant's hair that allegedly ensured that the wearer would become pregnant. She urged Harris to buy it for her and she wore it – 'round my waist, because that's nearer to the womb'. The charm worked. By the time they flew back to Rome Ann was pregnant.

Back in the Wilderness

Italy had never been lucky for Richard Harris, and his return to Italian-based film-making maintained the tradition. *The Cassandra Crossing* was a bandwagon plague-on-a-train disaster movie overwhelmed by stars – Loren, Harris, Martin Sheen, Ava Gardner, O.J. Simpson, Burt Lancaster, John Phillip Law, Lee Strasberg – and over-eagerly mounted by Lew Grade and co-producer Carlo Ponti. In Ponti's description Cosmatos, his protégé, was 'a moving movie encyclopaedia'. Cosmatos, with a background as assistant on *Exodus* and in making New York commercials, said: 'Everything I know about directing I learned from watching movies.' The movie had a strained plotline and indifferent performances all round. Harris himself dismissed it when I questioned him: 'I never saw it through. I never saw any of those seventies pictures. I only did them for Ann, because she wanted a screen career.' 'Let's say it was honest,' says John Phillip Law. 'With honest mistakes.'

Ann played Susan, a student hippie innocent infected by deadly germs brought aboard the Stockholm-bound Trans-continental Express by a runaway terrorist. She cuddles her boyfriend, played by Ray Lovelock, sings a song, falls ill, shudders and sweats. Her performance is grand, the part limpidly not. During the shooting of her scenes Ann fell ill for real with stomach pains that worsened over the course of a fortnight. She put on a brave face, but Harris became seriously worried and took action: 'I put her on a plane from Rome to New York and got her back to her gynaecologist. But she miscarried on the airplane. I knew it was coming because she was in such agony for about fourteen days. It was horrible.'

The devastating disappointment momentarily flung them closer than ever. All Harris's close associates echo his urgent desire for a daughter to justify this marriage; but all similarly speak of his devotion to Ann. His hurt was magnified by her loss, and his understanding of her need to satisfy him. It was a circle of pain that neither of them could break out of.

Harris comforted Ann by devoting himself to the preparation of projects exclusively for her. He had already signed with his old employer Mickey Anderson for *Orca – Killer Whale* and there was no suitable role for Ann. But he jumped at Alistair Maclean's *Golden Rendezvous*, on condition that she was cast prominently alongside him. After that he turned to writing his own screenplays for her. In a short space of time no fewer than four were chalked up. 'I'll produce them myself,' Harris told *Photoplay*. 'The first is called *The Case of Patrick Silver*, which will be made with Ann and me [it was never made]. The next one is tentatively titled *Hit Me* and I'll produce with Ann and, I hope, Kris Kristofferson [never made]'. Kristofferson had become something of an obsession for both him and Ann: 'I somehow feel a kinship with him . . . I find his life and mine have parallels. We started off big, were very productive, highly intelligent people. I had a book of poetry, had songs published, gold records and acting. But I lost it all consuming my passions . . . I damaged a talent because I couldn't come to grips with the disappointments that were laid upon one by producers and heads of studios. There'd be two years would go by and I'd think, "What happened to my picture . . .?"'

Even Sandy Howard, he felt, let him down. Harris had always been a very vocal promoter of his own work, but as far back as *The Molly Maguires* he had been arguing about the lack of producer support in pushing his name and his movies. *The Molly Maguires* evolved into an open trade fight. Paramount boss Robert Evans accused Harris of indifference to sales campaigning, declaring him 'aloof to any promotional ideas that might have helped box office'. Harris angrily denied this: as far as he was concerned Evans had 'dumped' the movie. 'They told me they planned for a premiere in New York and asked me to indulge the promotional gimmick in which [his pal Malachy] McCourt and I would go on a drunken binge . . . [Dermot] rang to find out where I'd stay and Paramount informed him that the premiere had been cancelled. Paramount had lost faith in the picture.'

Sandy Howard strenuously denies that he let Harris down over promotion of *Echoes of a Summer*. 'Richard is wrong. Yes, we had distribution difficulties, but that's the film world. You live with it. I did five pictures with Richard and only argued once on any account. That was on *Echoes*. He insisted on singing the title song and he sang it flat. I kept saying it was flat, but he kept saying otherwise. He's a strong-willed fellow. But he sang it flat – he murdered it.'

The remedy for what Harris saw as financiers' duplicity was to do his own scripts and make his own films from scratch. Dermot was all for it, as was Ann. Inspiration came too from his eldest son's progress. Damian, now eighteen, was at London's National Film School and doing well there. 'My son talks about all the great things he's going to do, and I hear myself at that age,' said Harris. 'I suddenly realize I haven't set out to do what I wanted to do [*sic*]. I think I'd better start now.'

'Inventing Ann' became his focus. Under his advice she turned down minor parts in *Rollerball*, *The Man with the Golden Gun*, *Rafferty and the Gold Dust Twins* and *The Bank Shot*. 'I'm sort of tutoring her,' Harris admitted. 'I give a lot of time now to guiding her acting career . . . Lee Strasberg, who's supposed to be the bastard talent-spotter, did a scene with her in *Cassandra Crossing* and he says she's the best raw talent he's seen. And I agree.' Twenty years earlier Strasberg had singled out Harris on *Borstal Boy*, so there seemed real reason for optimism. 'When I married Ann I seemed to get custody of a child. Now the maturity and strength she's bottled up before is all coming out. We have terrific fun together. The basis of our marriage is friendship. The husband is often the stranger in many marriages, spending his time in pubs and so forth. But Ann and I can talk.'

'Richard says I have to establish my own identity,' Ann told the *Guardian*. 'He said he couldn't be married to anyone who couldn't *produce*. At the moment photography is my own form of creativity. I didn't start off to be a photographer, but I knew something about it from modelling. Then Richard started looking so incredible I had to shoot him. Now I'm hooked on shooting him. *Time* magazine even published one of my pictures of him.'

The nomadic life resumed, centred on Paradise Island but freewheeling across the globe when the slightest opportunity afforded itself. *Orca – Killer Whale* took them to Canada and a long, snowy shoot in Arctic waters. A *Jaws* spin-off of fair calibre, it was developed by writer-producer Luciano Vincenzoni whose extensive research fired up Dina De Laurentiis, who in turn sought top-name stars and high financing ($6 million from EMI and Paramount) in the hope of producing a box-office-buster. Harris rejected the idea of using stunt doubles wherever possible, and gallantly relished his role as the tough whaler determined to capture or kill *Orca orcinus* – the killer whale – for financial reward. He resisted comparisons with *Jaws* valiantly: 'I get really offended when people make the comparison. [In *Orca*] the characters are real people, three-dimensional people whose lives become inexorably laced into that of a brace of mammoth mammals of the sea . . . It must never be dismissed as just another disaster or frightener movie . . . The end result is more breathtaking than either director Michael Anderson or Luciano Vincenzoni or I and Charlotte [Rampling, his co-lead] ever imagined.'

When the picture transferred to the gentler climes of Malta, for shooting in the gigantic movie tank at Rinela, Ann stayed in Hollywood. Harris lovingly kept in touch, with daily, sometimes thrice-daily, calls. The separation was a stressful five and a half weeks. 'It was dreadful,' said Ann. 'Our phone bill was astronomical, over ten thousand dollars *a week*! Once we were on the phone for four hours from Los Angeles to Malta. After I'd hung up the operator called me and said, "I just wanted to let you know that you've beaten Richard Burton and Elizabeth Taylor's record on the phone."'

Both *Cassandra Crossing* and *Orca* benefited from Harris's eloquent support – *Orca* significantly, taking a record $3,546,500 in its first weekend of American release. Neither film, however, swayed the critics and, though Harris loudly professed himself indifferent, there was evidence of artistic stirrings that just would not lie down. In the autumn of 1976 Warner Brothers threatened legal action against him for reneging on a verbal agreement with the producers of *The Squeeze*, finally shot in

London with Stacy Keach under Michael Apted's direction. The movie was a fast-paced gritty gangland yarn, but Harris had his sights set considerably higher. At the same time he had negotiated himself onto Ingmar Bergman's *The Serpent's Egg*, to be shot in Sweden. The rush of optimism died fast: weeks before Bergman's picture was due to shoot Harris collapsed and returned to Ann in Los Angeles to recuperate in time for *Golden Rendezvous* in February. 'It was a critical chance missed,' says film writer Tony Crawley. 'He could have reversed a trend. He had money, whatever financial framework he wanted. But he was also on the dead-end movie street. This film – one fell swoop – was his chance to reorientate. But he missed it.'

The specific nature of Harris's late 1976 illness eluded doctors for years. Diagnosed loosely as 'a bug', it seems more likely to have been another flare-up of his hyperglycaemic disorder that remained, despite exhaustive check-ups from the world's best doctors, undiscovered. The *Guardian* had him happily consuming a breakfast fry-up and still drinking heavily, though Ann's influence had, he said, reduced his intake. Still, in *Return of a Man Called Horse* at forty-five, he could appear impressively lithe when shirtless. The counter-evidence of his durable stamina remained, so no one took the hastening breakdowns seriously enough.

Alistair Maclean's *Golden Rendezvous* Harris again rates as 'rubbish'. Seventeen seagoing weeks and $6 million were spent shooting this creaky hijack tale, and though producer André Pieterse started out singing the praises of the Harris–Turkel teamwork ('They resemble the way Humphrey Bogart and Lauren Bacall act together') the movie ended in a fury of bickering and litigation. When post-production was completed at Pinewood no one could make head nor tail of the plot, so an additional six-minute explanatory opening sequence was shot. Harris tried to put the grim experience behind him, but it wouldn't go away. A year later producer Euan Lloyd booked him for a genuinely electric adventure yarn, *The Wild Geese*, for shooting in Pieterse's native South Africa. No sooner had Harris and Turkel landed in Johannesburg than Pieterse's lawyers pounced. *Golden Rendezvous* was under investigation anyway for alleged misuse of government monies originally intended to support the building of a black cinema industry.

In his evidence Pieterse told Rand Court Judge King that Harris was to blame for delaying the production by forty-four days and adding an extra £800,000 to the budget in consequence. Harris had been moody and obstructive, consuming a bottle of vodka a day during the confined shooting on a ship in the Indian Ocean. Harris refuted the claims, countering that Pieterse, not he, owed money. Pieterse had yet to pay him £25,000 of the agreed salary. The claims about Harris's boozing constituted an 'absolutely defamatory' statement.

The two men settled out of court and Harris moved on to *The Wild Geese*, a film about which he expressed more enthusiasm than most for the simple reason that at last it gave him the chance to work with Richard Burton, his post-Brando idol. 'You must remember,' says Ronnie Fraser, also cast alongside Burton, Roger Moore, Stewart Granger, Jack Watson and Helmut Berger, 'that we were all friends. Most of us grew up together in the theatre and movies of the time. There was a competitiveness, yes. But there was also the great shared warmth of friends on an outing.' The outing was to Tshipise, a town in the northern Transvaal on the Rhodesian border, where the unit took over a vast, self-contained township peopled by black actors. Temperatures soared to 110 degrees and the much-voiced fear was that Harris, Burton and Fraser, chummy drunks when the mood took them, would stymie the production. Fraser said: 'The producer was going around worrying, saying, "I know Harris can be a bit of a nuisance and Burton can put back a few too. And Fraser might have a few as well! We could be in trouble here!"' Euan Lloyd's first choice casting had been Burton, Robert Mitchum, Richard Widmark and Roger Moore – 'an altogether safer shower' – but the volatility of the current bunch, properly directed, promised fascinating on-screen sparks. Andrew McLaglen was charged with the directing, using a script by *Twelve Angry Men* author Reginald Rose. 'All the material was there for a great picture,' says Fraser. 'It was just *us* that was the problem.'

As Harris tells it on the talk show circuit, he kept his promise to Euan Lloyd and stayed sober. Coached by decently disciplined Roger Moore he in turn watched over Burton, telling him, 'Whenever you feel like a drink, do like I do, jump up and down.' For the remainder of the production, says Harris, he and Burton were to be seen daily in all sorts of unlikely situations, hopping like kangaroos. A cast member remembers more: 'We had a couple of rented houses in the complex, with nice gardens. My gardener was mowing the lawn and came in with five or six bags of cuttings. I said to him, "What the hell are you doing, bringing this stuff into the house? Take it outside." But he said, "It's not for burning. It's the stuff you roll in paper."'

Harris, Burton and friends indulged, rolling 'deadly joints of Durban Poison, which was blissful!' The high-powered grass gave a totally new complexion to the grilling heat, the flies, the reckless-action mercenary-attack plot. 'We were all so happy,' says the actor. 'The producer was looking at us, wondering: "These guys should be trouble, but they're all angels!"'

The long, hot shoot was for Harris the most fun of all his seventies' films, marred only by the unshakeable illness which confounded him as it confounded the unit doctors who frequently looked him over. *The Wild Geese* was best remembered by Harris as the film on which his tentative acquaintanceship with Burton – hitherto conducted in fleet-ing moments on planes and in hotel lounges – solidified to friendship. The movie itself – about an assault mission led by Burton to free an imprisoned leader of a central African state – was unoriginal but successful enough in its middle-market targeting to inspire talk of a follow-up (though Harris would not have been involved since his character, Rafer Janders, died in the movie).

The spur of Ingmar Bergman forgotten, Harris returned to the Bahamas, refused to take stock and forged on, jumping at the cheques – and the opportunities to fan Ann's career. Whatever qualms he felt he covered with booze and a new indulgence – top-quality cocaine. In the late seventies cocaine became a social necessity for him. By his own admission he spent a fortune on it, and it almost killed him. An actor friend very close to him recalls: 'He knew he wasn't well and he was constantly going into these comas. It was a long time before the doctors sorted all that out. But the first step was getting him off the drink. So he was told to stop drinking and that would relieve the comas. No drink, no drugs . . . and the comas would stop.' But, despite a radical temporary cut-back in drinking, Harris still suffered deep-sleep collapses from which no one could rouse him. The actor friend says, 'He went back to this doctor to sort it out. He said, "What's the fuckin' trouble here? I'm not drinking and still the comas. What's wrong? I want it sorted out." The doctor asked him did he take drugs and Richard said, "No, never touch the stuff." And the doctor is bewildered, he cannot sort this out . . .'

The comas went on, and the doctor came back and questioned Harris again. 'What do you do in place of alcohol?' the doctor asked.

'Oh, I use that white stuff, put it up me nose. And sometimes I do the hash, smoke a joint, you know . . . But I never touch sleeping pills, or all those terrible drugs, no, not even aspirin.'

Another journalist friend says, 'Dermot and he were bad influences on each other. Dermot had a huge capacity for careless drinking, day and night. I think it was the booze that brought down Dermot's marriage [to Cassandra, who later married the actor Pierce Brosnan]. And I think Richard tried to keep up with him, but just couldn't manage it.'

The comas – and sometimes fits – worsened. During a stopover in LA to prepare for Roy Boulting's flop *The Number* (released as *The Last Word*) Harris went into a serious coma that Ann mistook for a heart attack. Once again he was rushed to the Cedars of Lebanon Hospital, just as he had been at the start of *Major Dundee*. The cardiograms showed a sound heart, but there was clearly something chronically wrong that needed urgent diagnosis. As Harris awaited the results of further tests he returned to his rented Beverly Hills mansion and flushed $6000 worth of cocaine down the toilet. Inside eight years Dermot would be dead, from a heart attack induced by heavy drinking. Harris already saw the signs and knew he must change his lifestyle. 'Dermot had more guts than me,' he said later. 'I didn't want to go through drink and drugs.'

On holiday in the Bahamas at Christmas a doctor friend of Elizabeth's urged Harris to check into a New York clinic for more blood tests. It was here, finally, that the life-threatening hyperglycaemia, the root of years of suffering, was revealed. Hyperglycaemia is the reverse of diabetes – too much sugar in the blood – and requires a similar diet-and-medication treatment. Harris was immediately told to cut his drinking, to eliminate all fat and sugar from his meals and start a daily routine of vitamin supplements. Over-ripe mashed bananas, oatmeal and Evian water would be the new staple. Harris was, initially, relieved that the mystery of his bad health was cracked, but it would be two more years before he took the condition seriously and eliminated alcohol from his life.

A process of mopping up began and Ann was the first victim. For some weeks there had been rumours of Harris's annoyance at her reputed involvement with a twenty-two-year-old gym teacher. The relationship was denied but the aching reality could not be: the marriage was failing. 'Actually it was very sudden,' says a friend. 'In her eyes it was salvage-able, but he seemed to want to move on. He hated Beverly Hills and she liked it. Most of the time he stayed there it was just for her. It was probably her influence that brought about the move from Allembic House [the Limbridge offices on Victoria Embankment that were closed up] and the resiting in LA. But Dickie loathed all the falseness of that place.'

Ann tried repeatedly to break through the stone wall that Harris suddenly built round himself, but all she found was the die-hard loner that all his lovers ultimately got to see. He was aggressive in his unease – a mode of behaviour adopted whenever he wished to cease negotiations in any area. The man who had said, 'I function best by myself' was reverting to form, sloughing off the skin of marriage, pushing her away. The tripwires of the failure were clear: the baby hadn't happened; her career was, at least tentatively, up and running; there was little more, apart from friendship, that they could offer each other.

In Harris's opinion selfishness ended his first marriage, selflessness his second. He had, he said, become just a minder for Ann, and her need to stay up late and boogie through the night just exhausted him. The music she listened to, the books she favoured, bored him. As did her image of him. She had fallen in love with King Arthur, then woken up one day to find a tired, middle-aged actor in bed beside her. She couldn't come to grips with a man addled by himself and by the limitations of his artistic potential.

A Bang Not a Whimper, the movie that would have co-starred Ann and Kris Kristofferson (it was apparently retitled from *Hit Me*), was abandoned. In April 1979, just five years after the wedding, the undoing began. Harris consulted Raoul Feider, one of New York's top divorce lawyers, and a flat $1 million pay-off offer was allegedly made to Ann. She refused point-blank and asked Harris to try again. She loved him, and she would do her best to be the wife he wanted.

The separation had already begun. While Ann stood her ground in Beverly Hills Harris stayed at Manhattan's Regency Hotel to prepare for a clutch of good-wage movies that would keep him busy. Already in the can was *The Ravagers*, a post-holocaust romp that no one, least of all Harris, noticed. Ann featured in it and it was their final shared movie. Next up was *Highpoint*, a slap-bang-wallop thriller by Peter Carter, to be shot in Toronto with his first wife Elizabeth's ex, Christopher Plummer. Harris was happy just to get out of town, get on a plane and shake off the scandal-hunters. Many versions of the break-up were now in circulation. Britain's *Daily Mail* blamed it on Ann's affair with Shaun Cassidy, twenty-year-old brother of singer David. 'All the gossip said one thing,' says a friend. 'They were leading different lives – there was no more point pretending.'

Harris skipped the option of confrontation after *Highpoint* and flew back to South Africa on producer Phillip Baird's invitation to do *Game for Vultures*, based on Michael Hartmann's controversial novel about sanctions-busting. American James Fargo, director of Clint Eastwood's popular *Every Which Way But Loose*, also enticed Harris, and the presence of Joan Collins, whom Harris liked and worked well with, was another bonus. The script was good and Harris's best endeavours were briefly aroused. With Fargo, Baird and Collins he participated in long round-table discussions to add humour and punch up the political aspects. Joan Collins recalled: 'My character is really not an essential part of the story but a lot of humour grew from the improvisation with Richard Harris. Nicolle was the main woman and I wondered how I could make her more interesting . . . I think Richard and I succeeded in bringing a touch of deeper characterization to these roles.'

Game for Vultures, despite all its political chances, failed miserably, just like *High Point*. In the *Monthly Film Bulletin* Tom Milne billed it 'ludicrous' and called the final scene, in which heroic Harris and black guerilla Richard Roundtree are shown in split scene fighting on for the cause, 'a strong candidate for the silliest image of the decade'. Worse, Harris's performance – as in *Highpoint* – had the qualities of an assiduous ham.

The one real opportunity of professional redemption might have been Roy Boulting's LA movie, but Harris was edgy and Boulting elderly and jaded. *The Last Word* boasted elements of *It's a Wonderful Life* – in it Harris tackles City Hall in an effort to stop the demolition of a ramshackle apartment block – but script-by-committee, the notorious Hollywood cancer, destroyed it. Three B-picture writers, Michael Varhol, Kit Carson and Greg Smith, muddled Horatius Hareberle's fetching original and Boulting and Harris never recovered. Financed on a shoestring and inadequately post-produced, *The Last Word* never achieved international cinema release and further emphasized Harris's ailing career.

By the end of 1979 Harris was still drinking heavily despite strenuous doctors' orders, and was viciously bad-humoured. A fellow actor says, 'The big names were Stallone, Travolta, and in Britain Connery and Caine. No one spoke about Harris any more, unless it was in terms of the high society scandals. For such a fine artist it must have been frustrating.'

The distracting problem of Ann lingered, but now Harris was travelling alone and talking of her in an emphatic past tense: 'When you marry a girl so much younger than yourself you start to lose your identity in trying to be what they want you to be, and in trying to keep up. My relationship with Ann was very Pygmalion. She was only a very naive young girl when I met her but she grew into a mature woman . . . In the end she was demanding so much of me that it was threatening my own career. I quit singing and my acting was sliding . . . But I got sick of being a part of her life rather than my own. I couldn't be bothered to keep acting out the parts she wanted me to play at home. She was taking me for granted. I'm too big for that. So I took a walk and left her.'

He told journalist Simon Kinnersley: 'I've changed a lot recently. I'm not prepared to take on the responsibility of someone else any more. But I'm quite willing to share. I wouldn't mind going back to a series of hot, traumatic affairs . . .' He was speaking from the location of his newest movie, an off-beat psycho-sexual *mélange* that started filming in Paris, the city of dreams.

15

Your Ticket Is No Longer Valid

The love of cinema, once an inferno in Harris's heart, was almost dead. *Your Ticket Is No Longer Valid*, prophetically titled, fired the killing shot.

Marty Baum, Harris's LA agent, found the project, being developed from an obscure Romain Gary novel by Canadian producers Robert Lantos and Stephen Roth, and sent the screenplay to Harris in Toronto during *Highpoint*. Harris quite liked shooting in Canada – the bitchy phoniness of Hollywood was a universe away – and he liked the core of the proposed story, all about male impotence. In a careful gesture that was a throwback to the meticulous sixties he asked to see the original novel and hunted it down himself when the producers failed to deliver it. As Lantos and Roth had pitched it, the movie was slight; but Harris saw possibilities for the first time in years. With tugging, pushing and a lot of imagination the movie might, just *might*, measure up to a mini-*Sporting Life* – or at least undo the damage of *Bloomfield*. Lantos spoke of the picture as a kind of *Last Tango in Paris* and Harris was further enthused. He met the producers and George Kaczender, who would direct. Here again, Harris's approach was reminiscent of the Lindsay Anderson era. He researched Kaczender, whom he had never met, and watched a copy of his major film, *In Praise of Older Women*. Harris only half-liked Kaczender's picture: 'It appeared to me to have fragments of such cohesion and then such sloppiness. I had to put it down to editing problems.' Kaczender explained that the film had been taken out of his hands in post-production and he too was unhappy about it. According to Harris, Lantos said there and then that his *Ticket* script, for shooting in Paris, Nice and Canada, was not complete. Harris's creative contributions were very, very welcome.

Harris had still not given a final commitment because he couldn't make up his mind whether the story, and the people, measured up. To help his decision he sent the script to Eugene Landy, the radical LA psychologist famous for rehabilitating troubled Beach Boys genius Brian Wilson. Harris then took the trouble to meet Landy and compile fifty-two pages of notes. These he handed to Kaczender and the producers – separately. The essential teamwork he requested was faulty from the start, but it didn't prepare him for what he later described as Lantos's betrayal of his trust.

Harris agreed to do the movie provided that Lantos, Roth and Kaczender accepted his suggestions for revisions and his usual recent contract clause of cast approval. Lantos then informed Harris that George Peppard, the *Breakfast at Tiffany's* star, would be cast as his co-lead. Harris liked Peppard, whom he had met while Peppard was shooting *The Blue Max* at Ardmore in Ireland years before. 'A good friendship was quickly made,' says Peppard today. 'We got blind drunk together, that's what I remember. But I had great regard for Richard, who is a masterful actor, an actor of the first order. I was attracted to this film because of him. But, to be truthful, my career was in the gutter at that time. No one in Hollywood would touch me with a stick . . . so I was pleased when these producers came along with a script that had good potential.' The key casting in the script, Peppard makes clear, was that of the 'highly charged sexual magnet' who resolves Ogilvy's (Harris's) sexual neuroses. Harris was anxious that this part be carefully cast. Lantos showed him three photographs of prospective young actresses, among them a newcomer called Jennifer Dale. After a discussion, Harris settled for Dale in the role of Laura, the twenty-year-old Brazilian dressage rider heroine. What Lantos neglected to tell Harris was that Dale was his own girlfriend, and that she had already been cast. When Harris found out he confronted Lantos and asked why he had been lied to. Lantos defended himself by claiming that Dale was an ex-mistress. But that wasn't the case.

Your Ticket Is No Longer Valid began shooting under the nervous direction of Kaczender – 'a man who doesn't like

to go to war', according to George Peppard – in the autumn
of 1979. After several days Harris had his first scenes with
Dale where, after encountering her out riding, they attempt
to make love. Harris, already depressed by the apparent
insincerity of the producer, was horrified to find the actress
suggesting direction. 'The young lady, carried away by her
position maybe, began to explain to me in front of the entire
company what the scene was about and where the camera
would be put. All my fears came out in that one moment, that
her situation with Lantos was not over. It was an intolerable
situation for me. I blew. No question about me letting off
steam. I told her that she may be a very, very brilliant director
and a very brilliant young lady, but I signed a contract with
Mr Kaczender to direct the picture . . . And I walked away
to my caravan.'

George Peppard had no scenes with Dale but he became
quickly aware of Harris's unease. 'The producer called me
aside after a few days of shooting and had the girl with him,
and told me Richard was being a problem, that he really was
the trouble with the movie. They begged my ear and expected
me to agree. I think they were a little surprised when I told
them I was on Richard's side. He was very professional . . .
and it was obvious immediately to me that the girl was all
wrong for the story. She was the wrong casting, exuding none
of the sexual energy the part called for.'

The film degenerated into a parody of film-making. Lantos
attempted to placate Harris, agreeing to a series of rewrites.
But the producer's insistence on promoting his girlfriend above
all else deeply offended Harris. True, Harris himself had more
than once gone out on a limb to push Ann's career – he
agrees that most of his movies with her were 'rotters' – but
in this instance a potentially important movie, with alleged
high ambitions all round, was being grievously undermined
by wrong casting. It was unforgivable.

Harris says he worked his hardest on *Ticket*, sometimes as
much as eighteen hours a day. But Kaczender's control was
questionable and the collusion of the others sickened him.
When Ann came to visit the Canadian location in an attempt
to discuss their marriage deadlock Harris was relieved by the
distraction. But the visit went awry. Harris told *Cinema Canada*:

'The hotel room had a winding oak stairs to the bedroom. Lantos called to talk to me . . . and heard a noise from the bedroom and accused me of having somebody up there listening to our conversation. I told him there was a lady up there. He said I had somebody there listening to our conversation for evidence. I asked him, "For what evidence?" He then accused me of tape-recording the conversation. He said the atmosphere wasn't congenial to discussion about the script because of that. I shouted up to Ann and she eventually came down and introduced herself as my wife.'

The paranoia destroyed any qualities that the movie might have yielded. George Peppard is in no doubt of that: 'Richard showed no signs of lethargy but the film he signed to do, the film I signed to do, wasn't the one that got made. It was a genuine shame.' Harris retreated and saw a chance go up in smoke. He rallied, however, when, along with Marty Baum and the British Columbia Pictures chief John Van Eyssan, he saw a rough assemblage of the film. Van Eyssan embraced him and applauded the genius of his performance against the odds. 'You are going to win an Academy Award,' said Van Eyssan. 'It is stunning. I have never seen a performance like it.'

Three months later a public test screening was held in Montreal. Lantos was already hot on the promotional trail, celebrating Canadian co-financed film-making and boasting about his wonderful new movie. 'It's a breakthrough film,' he was quoted in Films and Filming. 'I think a lot of people will hate it but absolutely no one will walk out of the theatre after seeing it and be indifferent towards it, or not talk about it. Because for the last half-hour you are going to be in a state of shock.'

The test audience wasn't so sure – but certainly Harris was in a state of shock. The screening was of a film he hardly recognized. Lantos had radically recut and George Peppard perceived 'a mess. This is the kind of movie you can't jazz up. You have to let it run its time. It's not like a big commercial film where everything jumps along. It needs depth and space. It could have been wonderful, the subject was good, but they turned it into a film centred around that girl.'

The emphasis on Ogilvy's sexual identity problem had

been elbowed out in favour of an unblemished projection of Pin-up Dale. Harris explained to *Cinema Canada*: 'I had this wonderful idea about the end of the picture. At the end my character decides to commit suicide. Before he does he takes off his hairpiece and he looks like a grotesque caricature of a human being, with the little band-aids that keep the hairpiece in place . . . The director wondered whether the scene would be advisable, given my image. I didn't care about that. He said [my idea] was staggering. But apparently Lantos had objections. It transpired he objected to the [implied] homosexuality and the grotesquerie at the end. His objections were that it would lower Jennifer's appeal to the audience. It would make them question her. He said that a beautiful woman like Jennifer would not fall in love with a man who wears a hairpiece and high-heeled shoes.'

Harris tried to buy back the film. It had cost $6 million, of which his fee was his now regular $1 million. Marty Baum supported Harris, promising to raise $5 million to reacquire 'every bit of footage, soundtrack, continuity sheets, everything'. Harris's $1 million would make up the difference. Lantos resisted the purchase offer because, he said, he had total faith in the film.

'I was destitute,' said Harris poetically. 'I rang them time and again, begging to go back to that other cut. I offered to fly to Montreal at no cost and that I would pay for the editing if they gave me the opportunity to assemble the picture that we saw in its original form . . . and I could still take out fifteen to twenty minutes of it.'

When Lantos was away in Europe on business Roth gave in and invited Harris back to Montreal. The film editor was contrite. 'I asked him what went wrong.' Harris said. 'He said Lantos had stood over his shoulder, bullying, screaming, intimidating.' They re-edited quickly. Roth approved. He threw his arms around Harris. 'You saved me,' he proclaimed. 'Thank you, thank you so much.'

But the day wasn't saved. Lantos returned from Paris, saw that his baby had been meddled with – and 'went berserk'. The film that finally went on release – to appalling notices and almost zero box-office business – was Lantos's 'Jennifer' version. Lantos later told *Cinema Canada* magazine that Harris had sabotaged his movie. Harris belatedly heard of this attack and fisted his way back into the fray, taking three pages in the magazine to state his case. The 'brutalization' of the movie sickened him. He had done his best against loaded odds, and an opportunity had been lost.

Much more than that was lost. *Ticket* might well have been Harris's reissued passport to committed movie endeavour. But now, with finality, he saw movie-making as a rip-off commercial circus where all that mattered was the buck.

An 'act of friendship' brought him to John and Bo Derek's *Tarzan, the Ape Man*, shot in the jungles of Sri Lanka the following year, 1981. 'I love the Dereks,' was his all-embracing explanation of his involvement. John Phillip Law co-starred and witnessed some strange goings on. 'I didn't like Bo as much as Richard evidently did,' he says. 'But I had a lot of time and respect for John, who is a fair dealer. John's approach to making the movie was to take a needle and stick it right through the globe of the world and see whereabouts is the absolute polar extreme from LA. He wanted to get as far away from Hollywood as he could. I think Richard rose to that too. That part, for me, was fine. I'm one of those outdoorsy camper types who'll muck in and go native anywhere. But Bo tried to bring western civilization with her. Food was brought from LA – which of course went bad *en route* and poisoned everyone. Then one day I opened a door beside the make-up room in one of the unit bases and I'm looking at five hundred rolls of department store paper! That was Bo's private stock of LA toilet paper. It was crazy.'

John Derek was ostensibly director, but Law watched Bo take charge. 'She was on a roll with *10* and all that, and cashing in. But John let her and Richard get out of control. Richard *hugely* overplayed his part. I hugely underplayed. In between was room for Bo to do what she wanted – to be the dazzling star.'

Harris, says Law, couldn't shake the booze. 'He was such a good guy and so well liked by the natives. But every now and then he'd hit the bottle and be really, really ill. Production was held up once or twice when he just overdid it. It was quite worrying, but then he'd pull himself together and we forged on.'

'I kept a diary during that movie,' says Harris. 'I was contracted for forty-two days' work. And I look back on the diary and it reads: "Forty-one days to go till completion . . . only forty days to go . . . only thirty-nine days left . . . I realized it was the end of the line. I didn't want to make movies any more. The whole process just annoyed and bored me.'

Tarzan cost $8 million – though an actor involved says, 'I'll be damned if I saw more than $3 million spent. They must have dug a hole and done something with the rest.' Harris was amply rewarded. Law says, 'He and I came out very well, that was the reason for doing it in the first place.' After shooting was over, Harris was delighted to be back on a plane for New York.

The divorce application, on the grounds of incompatibility, had already been filed in Nassau. For that reason Harris wanted temporarily to avoid the confrontations of the Bahamas or Beverly Hills. But then a call came from a most unlikely quarter, begging him to come out urgently to LA. The touring production of *Camelot* was in trouble and the producers reckoned that Richard Harris, celluloid Arthur, might be their salvation.

Richard Burton was the problem. Since the previous June he had been back on the road with the show in a revival of his 1960 creation. But his health had been doubtful all along. Apart from fighting the bottle he had continual agonizing pain in his right arm, diagnosed as a pinched nerve. Most of the time on stage he could not lift the sword Excalibur and his arm swung, lifeless, by his side. In April the tour arrived at the Pantages Theatre, but Burton survived only six performances. He was admitted to St John's Hospital in Santa Monica, where two days of tests revealed a degenerative condition of the cervical vertebrae in the spine. Surgery was advised and Burton, underweight and exhausted, was sent to bed to build himself up for the operation. It was clear that his touring days were over, but the show still had a packed schedule. The producers thought immediately of Harris as a replacement – allegedly on Burton's prompting – but Harris at first declined. 'I'd had it,' he says. 'I was forced to think long and hard, and then I said, "If Richard asks me, I might do it."' Burton put in a personal call and the favour was granted.

Harris flew to LA on 3 April and held a press conference to introduce himself as the new King Arthur. In view of the production crisis the tour director, who had long since departed for London, was summoned back. Frank Dunlop, founder of the Young Vic, was forced to address the show from scratch. Harris said: 'Richard [Burton] and I approached the part in a totally different way. He played it as a man born to greatness. I play it as a man with greatness thrust upon him. It is fundamental, but vital.'

Rehearsals were, surprisingly for Harris, invigorating. Though he was prone to fainting spells he lapped up eight five-hour work-throughs and seven two-and-a-half-hour musical sessions, harmonizing well with Meg Bussert as Guinevere and Richard Muenz as Lancelot. The grace and grandeur of the old battlehorse came back to him. King Arthur was his pop heyday; it was good to relive it. Burton underwent his operation successfully and flew back to his home in Switzerland to recuperate, bidding adieu to *Camelot* forever. Harris opened, wrung with anxiety but bang on schedule, on 13 April. It was his theatrical comeback after an absence of nearly twenty years.

Variety, among many others, loved the rejigged show and approved of the new King Arthur: 'Harris plays the role for laughs and is a more pixieish king than either Richard Burton or William Parry [Burton's understudy, who would remain Harris's understudy].' Credit for the new *zing* wasn't all Harris's, though. 'Perhaps the best thing that has come out of the problems caused by Burton's illness was the fact that director Frank Dunlop came back for more rehearsals. Aren't road directors supposed to keep an eye on the show even if the star doesn't get sick?' The criticism seemed petty against the obvious triumph: crammed houses, standing ovations, flocks of stage tour offers, new play offers . . .

Harris signed with a new British agent during *Camelot*, indicating a reborn theatrical impetus. Arrangements were made to extend the tour to London, and the Apollo Victoria was booked for a limited season the following year. Talks of other London stage work began. In his recent years on the road Harris had written a stage play called *Miscast in Carrickfergus*, and he wanted his agent to find a venue so that he could bring it to London. It was, it seemed, vintage heyday Harris – 'about me, and Dylan Thomas and Richard Burton and Peter O'Toole, about a kind of corruption, where somebody is born with a gift which was native to their environment in Wales or Ireland and then, to express it, they have to emigrate and be absorbed by another culture, a more sophisticated society, where there's a chipping away of that gift.' Personal experience apart, he was perhaps inspired by the announcement of the first play from Liz's hand – 'about neither of my husbands' – due to open shortly in supper theatre in London.

After seven weeks at the Pantages Theatre *Camelot* hit the road for a gruelling summer tour fractured by Harris's health problems. The success merited Broadway, where Harris had never played, and a venue was at last found at the Winter Garden, with a concurrent deal for Home Box Office, the cable giant, to shoot the 'live' performance for transmission. Harris was ecstatic, but jaded. On stage in Detroit in August he collapsed in mid-performance. The call was made from the stage: 'Is there a doctor in the house?'

Harris said, 'Twenty-eight doctors queued up, examined me and asked for my autograph.' But the hospital test results that followed didn't give cause for amusement. The doctors were blunt: Harris's hyperglycaemia had critically deteriorated. If he kept on drinking he had only eighteen months to live.

On 11 August 1981 at the Jockey Club in Washington Harris ordered two bottles of vintage Château Margaux and shared them joyously with friends. 'They tasted', he says, eyes shut tight to the memory, 'like nectar.' He doesn't recall the year or the price of the wine (he has never been a connoisseur). All he knows is it was the last and best alcohol he ever consumed. A close associate says: 'People often don't believe it, but it's true. For Richard, painfully true. He stopped that night and never ever again took *as much as a sip*. It has been impossibly hard for him. It has driven him to despair at times.' Harris himself told the *Indianapolis Independent News*: 'I could sail the QE2 to the Falklands with all the liquor I drank. I'm off the liquor now, and I'm a very dull man.'

Burton's revival of *Camelot* had started at the Lincoln Center in New York. Harris's return outpaced it in ticket sales and reviews. In the middle of the run, in January, HBO recorded its special. Cathy Fitzpatrick, the associate producer for HBO, remembers: 'The show was a nightmare. First and foremost was the row with Don Gregory, the tour producer who came in to see what we were doing and clashed head-on with Richard. For a minute it looked like someone might get killed.'

Harris, Gregory and Mike Merrick, the other tour producer, had been on bad terms since the summer. Cathy Fitzpatrick says: 'Richard was to me personally very charming, but he was ill during the production, that was obvious. It was freezing winter, to make things worse. The incident of the flare-up happened when Richard appeared late for a run-through call. He had requested the time off, but Gregory called him anyway, since he was needed for camera checks or whatever. They argued backstage. The director, Marty Callner, wasn't very effective coming between them. The next thing, Richard and Gregory were at each other, throwing punches. Then Richard walked out and refused to proceed with the shooting – some of which was before a limited live audience – unless Gregory was removed.'

Harris and Gregory avoided each other for the duration, Gregory attributing Harris's behaviour to 'actor's rhetoric'. 'He was very, very tired, though,' says Cathy Fitzpatrick, 'and his voice failed. We lost quite a few days with him, and that necessitated new set-ups and a schedule that over-ran considerably.' Harris delighted in HBO's patience with all this. Michael Fuchs, the HBO chief, called to cast an eye on the settling storm and professed himself confident in Harris and in the quality of the production, the richest-ever live show for HBO. 'Whatever Richard didn't get done vocally in the Winter Garden he caught up with in dubbing in LA,' says Cathy Fitzpatrick. 'I watched him work there and was impressed by his great care in creating the vocal mood for songs like "How to Handle a Woman". It was mesmerizing to see his concentrated professionalism.'

Marty Callner, with 125 TV specials behind him for the likes of Steve Martin, Diana Ross and Victor Borge, experimented as best he could within the confines of four-square theatre and limited budget. One hundred and twenty camera filters were tested to find the perfect "softness" for a mystical story shot on video. Eventually a $2 pair of ladies' tights did the job. Forty thousand pounds of dry ice was employed to achieve a constant effect of misty romance. A multi-camera set-up was staged, though the single-lens viewpoint of movie-making was striven for. In the end the unedited footage ran to 116 hours, which was finally cut to two and a half hours. Family-rated in the American way, *Camelot* was approved for family viewing by the National Education Association and recommended for schools. When it was put out in September, Harris's honing and heroism were seen to pay off. Viewer ratings were high and the *New York Times* applauded 'a memorably majestic and troubled king . . . [Harris] skilfully elevates a serviceable musical to surprisingly moving drama'.

The moving drama of his personal life raged on. Ann resisted divorce but absorbed herself in a new business partnership with director Barbara Peeters, whom she had met during the low-budget Roger Corman flick *Beneath the Darkness*, in which she featured. M & J Productions, said Ann, would concentrate on self-scripted films, starting with *Brother, Sister*, written jointly by Barbara and her. With great self-assurance she sidestepped questions from friends about the inevitability of a final split with Harris. On the contrary, she let it be known, Richard would star for her in Barbara's *The Indian Who Sold Brooklyn Bridge*.

Harris's viewpoint was different. He had had enough and, though the Bahamian courts requested they try for a reconciliation, he dismissed the possibility. After 421 performances of *Camelot* – 'to 421 standing ovations of fifteen or twenty minutes' – he ended in a blaze of glory and returned to the Bahamas. Ann visited him briefly but there was no peace pact. He told journalist William Marshall: 'I have given Annie a new plan for our marriage. From now on I'm dedicated to living my life as Richard Harris, egomaniac. I have told her we will spend roughly one week out of four together. If she doesn't like that it's the end of our marriage.'

It was. In September the divorce was finalized, once again with an undisclosed settlement for Ann. Harris celebrated as only Harris would – cheekily and dangerously. Back in London for talks with Dermot and his new agent, Terry Baker, he ran into Susie Burton, who was in the process of divorcing Richard. 'I asked her out for a date,' said Harris. 'But she refused me, saying she didn't think it would be proper. I said, "Why not? I'm used to replacing Richard."'

Harris was, he told everyone, 'given a new lease of life' with *Camelot*. Certainly the industry offers became more flattering. A big-budget tour of James Hilton's *Goodbye, Mr Chips* and a musical cable special of Dickens's *A Christmas Carol* both interested him (though he later dropped out of both). The combined fee would be $3.5 million. 'I can't do that well in movies,' he told the *Los Angeles Herald Examiner*. Inspired, he started negotiations to purchase the touring rights of *Camelot* from Alan Jay Lerner. 'I thought: "I've given a chunk of my life to this King Arthur. I've been good to him. It's time for him to be good to me."' The deal was one of the best of Harris's life. In subsequent touring *Camelot* would earn $92 million – outdoing Rex Harrison's box office for *My Fair Lady* – of which Harris personally grossed nearly $8 million. He took great pride in this stroke of business genius, and today tells friends and strangers alike with equal candour about his multi-million *Camelot* rewards.

Before opening *Camelot* with a new British cast at the Apollo Victoria in November 1982 Harris took Sandy Howard's invitation to join a third *Horse* movie in Mexico. The script was of little interest, and the resulting film shows Harris's extreme apathy towards movies at this time. 'It was a mistake,' says Sandy Howard ' – for both of us. I let Richard down with *Triumphs of a Man Called Horse*. It was misconceived, and I put the wrong people on it. The source material was sound – Jack De Witt wrote it shortly before he died – but most of the other people were wrong. John Hough, the director, did his best. But we had the wrong screenplay, and we misused Richard Harris, and I feel sorry for that.'

Harris equally misused the movie. His performance, scarred by visible stage tricks, is his worst ever on film.

Triumphs – rightly – made no money and finished the cycle of *Horse* movies. Harris didn't care. He opened *Camelot* in London to good notices but very poor business. Announced to run till May, the play folded after a couple of weeks. Harris pocketed his fee and jetted back, alone, to Nassau.

The house was lonelier now, mostly stripped of Ann's possessions. But he had all the company he needed in his staff – and Jamie's 'drunk and disorderly' charge hung framed on the porch beside his favourite wicker chair.

16

Don't Let It Be Forgot

These months of Bahamian seclusion – uninterrupted by romance or booze – represented one of the longest periods of reflection since the start of Harris's hectic career. Genuine reassessment, not the usual bullying reaffirmation, was the order of the day. 'He was immediately a different man without the drink,' says actor Godfrey Quigley. Many other friends echo this. Undeniably he matured and looked at his life without prejudice. To friends and foes he confessed that there was much of the past that was unknown to him. Burton, for instance, had told him of their three encounters before *The Wild Geese*; Harris could only recollect one. It had all been great fun, good laughs – but at whose expense? It struck him that he had lived most of his drunken life not for himself, but for an audience. He had overplayed the game expected of him. 'After all, your life is your memories. So what life have I had?'

The excitement of owning *Camelot* put him back on the road in a series of gruelling tours through Australia, North America and Japan. A lesser spirit might have been crippled with the boredom of early morning flights from town to town, the same faces in the company, the same old hoarse songs. But Harris took endless pride in it. All the same he would not, he claimed, 'work it to death like Yul Brynner did with *The King and I*'. When the magic was gone he would stop.

This time the press weren't all on his side. The contradictions of the limelight years – and his media naivety – came back to haunt him. In 1973, during his poetry period, he had professed himself a supporter of the IRA. He had planned an anti-internment movie, but thought twice, deciding to give elbow room to the newly formed political Assembly intended to restore order in Ulster. But he wouldn't lie down. When Tory Opposition leader Edward Heath visited Nassau Harris and McClory took a full page in the *Nassau Tribune* to demand an end to internment without trial and also a free vote by Irishmen to determine their own future. Heath called a press conference and told Harris and McClory to 'ask their friends to stop murdering people'. Harris released an incensed statement through Associated Press, damning 'a deliberate policy of discrimination enforced in the British-occupied areas of the artificial state'.

Shortly afterwards his attendance at a dinner for NORAID – an American fundraising organization for the IRA – drew severe criticism. The repercussions spilled into his professional life. Negotiating a role in Jack Higgins's *The Eagle Has Landed*, in which he would play a wartime IRA man dropped into Britain to kidnap Churchill, Harris was suddenly warned off. Anonymous calls to executive producer David Niven Jr – Ann's ex – indicated disapproval at Harris's participation. Harris was vexed. He pointed out that he was not a NORAID supporter, but withdrew from the movie anyway.

Then came the Harrods Christmas bombing in 1983. Asked to comment by a Florida newspaper, Harris shambled into a minefield of contradictions. The IRA action was 'horribly wrong but understandable'. In his view 'that arrogant lady the British Prime Minister' wanted to keep the trouble going. 'You think she gives a shit about those innocent people getting killed? She says, "Perfect, great, now they're [the IRA] going to lose support in America."'

This tactless flag-waving resulted in an avalanche of hate mail. Harris was horrified, and tried to fight back. But many newspapers including former champion the *Daily Mirror*, attacked him head on.

When the *Republican News*, the Sinn Fein propaganda sheet, advertised Harris's endorsement of the IRA, Harris finally took a stand. He was not, he announced, an IRA supporter. 'The Harrods bombing put an end to all that.' In former years he had been hoodwinked into attending a NORAID dinner, but he had long since lost any sympathies for the cause. 'I could never condone or excuse IRA violence in any form.'

The legacy of courting the press and shooting from the hip wasn't buried so easily. As recently as 1989 Harris arranged bodyguards from the Irish Special Branch to accompany him in public in Dublin. 'There have been phone call threats,' one of the armed officers told me. 'So he asks us to keep him company when he's in town.'

After a year of self-questioning and facing up to reality, the need to repair the swansong disaster of *Triumphs of a Man Called Horse* put him into another small movie, *Martin's Day*, again in Canada. An exquisitely photographed road-movie about a simple-minded criminal who kidnaps a boy (Justin Henry from *Kramer vs. Kramer*) and goes in search of his childhood, the exercise was hardly rewarding. 'Timid,' said *Variety*; few other reviewers ever saw it. Once again, no co-ordinated British cinema release was granted and it was clear that British movie-goers, the ones who had first discovered him, had now all but forgotten his name.

Harris didn't appear concerned. The 1986 Richard Harris seemed unassailably rich, reformed and self-assured. But the background story was different. Liz's divorce from Rex Harrison and subsequent marriage to Lord Beaverbrook's grandson Peter Aitken – an unstable union from the beginning – drew her back to his side. Their friendship warmed up, vitally, at a time when Jamie, the youngest son, admitted his heroin addiction. Harris had bought an apartment for Jamie and furnished it for him, but Jamie sold everything to support his drug habit. Both Richard's and Liz's preoccupation for many long months was Jamie and the mammoth task of helping him get well. 'It's a decision he had to make himself ultimately,' said Harris. 'You can support, give love, but the addicted person has to choose, himself, to quit. Fortunately Jamie did.' Comfort came in the happy progress of the other boys. Jared started with ambitions to study law and attended university in the USA, but the acting bug bit. He joined a theatre group in London and found a place with the Royal Shakespeare Company. Damian, as he had promised, graduated from film school and made his debut as a movie director with fair success on Martin Amis's *The Rachel Papers* in 1989.

In the winter Harris and his brother Dermot put *Camelot* back on the road in America. During a visit to Scranton, the university town in Pennsylvania, they had dinner with and befriended Father Panuska, the Jesuit president of the university. A real affinity was established. Despite their personal educational ups and downs, the Harrises had a special place in their hearts for the benefits of Jesuit teaching methods. Dermot had been educated at Rockwell College in Tipperary, another Jesuit stronghold. The brothers both agreed they had no regrets and wished more young Irish students had access to Jesuit education. Dermot was fervent and articulate about the tragedy of Irish youth battling a school class system and low income standard that made higher education impossible for so many.

The tour moved on to Chicago, where Harris's King Arthur had another rapturous welcome. Dermot loyally followed the show, rarely missing a tour performance. But in Chicago he felt ill, and complained of chest pain. He returned to his hotel to rest, but his condition deteriorated and he was rushed to hospital late in the evening. When Harris took his curtain call he was told of Dermot's collapse. He grabbed a coat and hurried to the hospital, his make-up still in place. By the time he reached Dermot's bedside in the intensive care unit it was too late. Harris said later, 'I collapsed at the hospital. I couldn't bear to see him. I took one look at him . . . and asked them to draw the curtain. Then I sat with him for an hour, with the curtain drawn.' Nothing could be done. The heart attack had been massive, the damage irreparable. The doctors fought, but Dermot slipped away during the night.

'He was a different man when he came back to Limerick,' says Len Dinneen. 'More into himself, more remote. In Limerick he was always just plain Dickie. But it was like he'd forgotten how to be just plain Dickie. Maybe he thought time stands still. And it doesn't.' The funeral mass at Our Lady of the Rosary church on the Ennis Road, not far from the family home, was well attended, though Harris told Dinneen he was disappointed at the absence of old school friends. Liz flew in from London, and Dermot's two children by his marriage to Cassandra were there. A number of Old Crescent pals turned out, and a few old girlfriends. Harris later told me of the impact of the occasion and the poignant sense of the passage of time.

A girl he once dallied with came up to him to express her condolences and he warmly shook her hand. 'But she wasn't a girl any more. She was an old lady. And I was an old man. She stood there before me, all wrinkled and aged, her hands, her belly, all shrivelled and I'm thinking, "Look at her. I once hungered for those lips." And she's looking at me thinking, "Look at him. His hair is dyed, his skin is sagging, he is an old man."'

The crushing blow of Dermot's loss took the fizz out of touring *Camelot*. With his friend and manager removed from his side, Harris no longer wanted to be gypsying on the road. After the funeral he took Concorde back to New York and worked out his contract, but he had lost the passion.

In December he launched a scholarship fund for Scranton University in his brother's memory.[1] Fr Panuska was surprised, but delighted. 'I am moved by this remarkable intention by a person whose acquaintance with Scranton and the University of Scranton is so recent,' he said. Harris, for his part, expressed his gratitude to Scranton for its recent hospitality and for the rallying of his new friends at the time of Dermot's death. They had taken it on themselves to look after the funeral arrangements. Dermot, like himself, owed a debt to the Limerick Jesuits and he had recently donated a portion of land to Old Crescent for a school extension.

The Scranton Fund would pay the fees of at least one Irish scholar's attendance every year. The first student would be a Limerick boy, from the Crescent. After that the students would come from all over Ireland, North and South. 'It is good for education and for the arts,' said Fr Panuska. 'Mr Harris is truly a generous man.'

The philanthropic Richard Harris, comprehensively reformed, gravitated back to Ireland in search of the $500,000 needed to perpetuate the Dermot Harris Scholarship. He had little trouble finding supporters, and persuaded Irish Prime Minister Charles Haughey to pledge himself as a patron, along with prominent Irish businessmen and the Archbishop of New York, Cardinal O'Connor. He was also reported to be

[1] The Dermot Harris Foundation, University of Scranton, Pennsylvania 8510-2192, USA.

courting American Vice-President George Bush (evidently having warmed to Reagan and his Republican administration), and actors Carroll O'Connor and Gene Kelly. Discussions with Rod Stewart about a promotional concert were afoot, and he had canvassed Aer Lingus, the Irish national airline, for air fare allowances.

He was, he said, 'a born again Catholic' with a mission to accomplish in honour of his wonderful brother, who had been 'like a son to me'. He went on: 'There is no doubt that I've trod an exceedingly immoral path, a Rabelaisian drunken life, through non-belief. Now I have become so Catholic you wouldn't believe it. I've become a traditional conservative Catholic. I believe the dogma should not be changed. I believe in what Pope John Paul advocates. I don't believe in the ordination of women. I don't believe in abortion. Contraception I would argue about. I don't believe the Church should change in this almost Sodom and Gomorrah world.'

Comprehensively reformed? Journalist Lise Hand of the *Sunday Independent* went to interview him at the Berkeley Court Hotel, new management home of Jack Donnelly. Armed with a brace of modified questions as befitted 'Richard Harris Mk 2', she found herself wriggling round his suite instead. She wrote: 'Some things never change. Once a rogue, always a rogue, despite all protestations to the contrary.' The interview was tough going – 'only because it is difficult to take notes when a big, strong man keeps trying to wrestle you to the couch or insists that you haven't seen the whole suite until you've seen the bedroom.' In the best traditions of journalism, Hand made her excuses and left. 'Richard Harris may no longer be a wildcat, but he is certainly not a pussycat. Perhaps the description, amiable tiger, will do.'

Resignation replaced re-evaluation. 'We are all unfulfilled,' he told the *Times*. 'Look at Olivier: all he ever wanted to be was the world's greatest actor. Yet privately he always envied Richard Burton's life – the women, the waste. And all the time Richard and I were envying his discipline.'

The jaded surrender foreshadowed *Maigret*, a TV movie comeback of sorts, shot in Paris, London and Tenerife by HTV in association with an American producer/financier. Harris apparently met the challenge with enthusiasm, declaring himself a fan of Maigret and author Georges Simenon ever since John Huston had introduced him to the books on the set of *Man in the Wilderness*. Harris had read, he said, sixty of the 104 Maigret novels and had always fancied himself in the role. The movie was small-budget, just $3 million, but Harris's presence, still undeniably charismatic and starry, elevated it above the run-of-the-mill TV movie. George Weingarten, the American producer who launched the project, had a childhood dream of introducing Simenon properly to America (where the books sold 'only 300,000 a year'). Mutual friend of both Weingarten and Simenon, Graham Greene made the introduction but Georges Simenon, ever cautious of bastardized versions of his hero, resisted at first. Then Weingarten told the author of the guaranteed American screening, and the prospect of Richard Harris playing Maigret – with a unique wardrobe selected by Harris consisting of duffel coat, crushed soft hat . . . and size 15 shoes for his own size $9^1/_2$ feet. Harris's theory had been to reconstruct Maigret 'from the feet upwards'; the oversize shoes would force him to walk in a cumbersome shuffle, the tread of a tired-out gumshoe. Simenon told Weingarten: 'I would never have thought of him in a million years. My favourite was Jean Gabin in France, who made seven films. But now you say it, I can see him.' Weingarten told Harris his salary was beyond the scope of the budget, but Harris replied: 'There is no salary. If I like something I'll do it for nothing.'

Public response to *Maigret* was bad, though Harris was aggressively defensive of his style of portrayal, which presented a short-tempered family man delivering all his lines in a hoarse whisper. 'Ersatz,' said the *Western Mail*. 'Awful,' said the *Saturday Post*. The *Daily Mirror* poured scorn on Harris's Oirish brogue. After trampling Maigret, they ventured, 'How about Sherlock O'Holmes? Paddy Mason? Hercule Guinness?' The *Express* spelled it out: 'Some actors in their frenzied endeavours put on a funny nose, wear a silly hat and adapt a limp. The role springs to life. Others struggle with the inner workings of the character through rehearsals. Harris . . . appeared to be in anguished conflict between the two styles of approach. The result was catastrophic to behold.' Harris didn't listen. 'Who cares about critics?' he told me. 'They don't read sixty Simenon books. What do they know?'

Bouncing between his suite at the Savoy Hotel and his suite at the Berkeley Court in Dublin, Harris continued to defuse his boredom in a mercenary single-mindedness dedicated to preserving Dermot's memory. Already he had $100,000 in the Scranton Fund. Shuffling the pennies was all that interested him. For a while he toyed with offers of action scripts, including *The Limerick Key* (written by Walter and Celeste Gottel and myself). James Coburn had committed himself to this film, for United Artists release, and Walter Gottel had offered a lead role to Ann Turkel. Harris later told me, 'I was only interested in doing that for Ann. I don't want action pictures. I'll do it for Ann, or if it helps the fund.'

Very quickly he signed for Menahem Golan's adaptation of *The Threepenny Opera*, called *Mack the Knife*, to co-star Raul Julia and Julie Walters. Then, again for HTV, *King of the Wind*, a Christmas market period piece in which he played King George II. Asked about his involvement, he puffed at a Benson and Hedges and rattled, 'I've no idea about my character. They put a wig on me and said, "Your name is George", and here I am. I really only came [to London] to go to the theatre. I went to a preview of Dustin Hoffman's *Merchant of Venice*.'

The insouciance was genuine. 'I'm bored' – the eighties' staple – found a persuasive corollary: 'What's the point?' Brief pleasure came with his very personal student production of *Julius Caesar*, preceded by a month-long drama class at Scranton. He called it *A Work in Progress* and donated the door takings to the Dermot Harris Scholarship, already serving its first Limerick student. That the world of theatre still had a place in his heart was evinced by the fact that during *Maigret* he had spent his free time rereading – again – *Hamlet*. By now, he said, he had read the text fifty-seven times and understood precisely the undiscovered subtext. It seemed a wild long shot, but he told writer John McEntee that he still could do the play – 'with José Ferrer and Cyril Cusack as Horatio: you get the idea of what I'm after? It could be tremendously exciting.' But few producers were keen to listen. Dubliner Noel Pearson, the successor to 'Mr Showbiz' Louis Elliman, was one who did. Pearson wasn't interested in *Hamlet*, but his reputation was for staging inventive, oddball productions – and taking good receipts. He liked Harris and refused to see him, as some did, as a has-been. Pearson had many meetings with him and various theatrical ventures were mooted, the most likely being a lavish version of T. S. Eliot's *Murder in the Cathedral*, co-starring Paul Scofield, at St Patrick's in New York. Harris thought the concept fabulously crazy, and wanted to do it. But Pearson failed to find the backing.

In truth, the casting opportunities were fading. Harris's reputation as a tough man with a resolute creative attitude hindered more than helped. One producer summed him up to me in a word: 'Awkward.' On top of that, Harris had – unlike Sean Connery – resisted the metamorphosis of middle age. He was, to be sure, nearly sixty, celebrating his birthday on 1st October 1990. Yet the official promotional material of his productions still had him at fifty-six or fifty-seven. He was, undeniably, trim and light on his feet. But his face had the hollows of age and his eye spoke of elderly experience. Only in *Maigret*, perhaps, did he allow himself to embrace the inevitable. In it he exchanged kisses with a portly, late middle-aged Madame Maigret (Barbara Shelley) and emphasized a rheumy, arthritic slowness that acknowledged its years.

By the spring of 1989 Richard Harris seemed adrift. He told John McEntee he studiously avoided Limerick because of the drinking trap: there were too many memories there, too many friends. 'I miss my old pals. I miss old Charlie St George, the only member of the Young Munster team of the thirties left. I used to go to Charlie's pub up the canal bank. An amazing place. That's where I learned my Bernard Shaw and my republicanism.' Dermot Foley said of Harris, 'He seemed to give up on us as time went on. Not a betrayal of old friendship and trust, but a kind of sad withdrawal.'

Ann's love affair with up-and-coming South African tennis professional Gary Muller, in his early twenties, didn't upset him. He wished her the best, as he had wished Liz with Rex Harrison and Peter Aitken, and kept in touch by telephone, always bubbling with encouragement for her projects.

He had a girlfriend in New York – 'a wealthy, self-sufficient lady whom I see regularly' – but kept close contact with Liz, currently operating a PR agency whose main clients included the new, star-attracting Halcyon Hotel in London where he sometimes stayed. On Liz's birthday in 1989 he surprised her with a special gift. 'I love giving her surprises. After she'd opened her birthday presents I suggested we go to a hotel for a meal. Liz was moaning, saying we'd have to get a taxi because we wouldn't all fit in her old banger, a knackered Renault. When we got outside I let two taxis pass – I love winding her up – and she started to get her temper up, accusing me of being an idiot. I waited until she was about to explode and handed her the keys to . . . the Mercedes.' The gift, a gleaming black Mercedes 190, stunned Liz. She said: 'Richard has always been a generous man, but he has a wicked sense of humour. I wasn't quite sure whether it was all a big joke.'

Nigel Dempster and the Fleet Street gossips started speculating on a permanent reunion, even remarriage. Harris said no. 'I'm a modern example of the feudal lord. I'm the caretaker, the overlord of these people. I'd kill to protect my family. I'd smash their opponents. I don't impose my will, I'm not creating a dynasty, but I watch over them. That includes Elizabeth. Anything I have, she can have. I'm not as close to my second wife, Ann. I don't feel the same sense of protection towards her. She never became a Harris because she is Jewish.'

Even now he took joy in the brawling yarns. When he had read of Rex Harrison throwing a glass of wine into Liz's face during a marital row he phoned Harrison immediately. 'I hear you threw wine at my wife?' he snapped, seemingly oblivious to the ten-years-plus separation.

'She's my wife, not yours,' Harrison barked back.

Harris went for the jugular: 'If you ever do that again I'll come round to your house and knock your hairpiece off.'

I lunched with him in October 1987 and again in the spring of 1989. In between were the lukewarm movies, the scholarship fund-raising, murmurs of the undying dream. In the space of eighteen months he appeared hardly to have moved forward at all. The on-again-off-again book of new poems and the novel, now called *Saul G*, were all he truly enthused over. There were possibilities wafting from the wings, possibilities, possibilities. He wasn't reflective, had no time for the half-remembered past. Mostly his happy talk was of rugby and real life. I once asked him whether he felt detached from reality by virtue of his five-star lifestyle. 'Not at all,' he droned in the tone favoured to frighten the questioner. 'Why would I be? I walk down in the streets, I mix with the people.' And indeed he did. As I spent a little more time with him I found him blissfully relaxed in public, neither self-conscious nor arrogant, merely *normal*. He liked to walk, liked to hum Sinatra songs, to return the fond hellos of the Irish passers-by who always, inevitably, stopped and asked for autographs.

His patience with fans was impeccable; up to a point. During one of our constitutionals, when his mouth was bloody and wired following dental surgery that had been widely reported in the Irish press, a group of beery evening revellers descended on him. One or two drunken women reached for his mouth and poked carelessly. He didn't instantly snap. Instead he recoiled stonily, utterly frozen. He walked on fifty yards, sheltered by myself and two friends. Ahead, at the gates leading into his hotel, was another group of autograph-hunting fans. They surged. He snapped. Without acknowledging the existence of the crowd he bulleted through, venting the foulest expletives in a stentorian rage. I saw the fans pull away in delighted horror. Here, I mused, was the Harris they craved.

At a time when the game seemed past, the battles over, the dreams spurious, Richard Harris rose like a phoenix. In the middle of 1989 when this book started to take shape it seemed to some an epitaph, the story of a star risen . . . and set.

Noel Pearson, Pirandello and the undying dream changed all that.

POSTSCRIPT

Field of Dreams

All nature is but art, unknown to thee:
All chance, direction which thou canst not see . . .

Alexander Pope, *An Essay on Man*

Chance brought Richard Harris back as a viable artist and
star. By his own admission Noel Pearson had offered him
just a walk-on in his movie of the Irish stage classic *The Field*,
to be shot on location in Galway by director Jim Sheridan
whose debut, *My Left Foot*, was the current 'ethnic' toast of
Hollywood, the modern-day *Chariots of Fire*. Just as *Chariots*
launched David Puttnam and Hugh Hudson internationally,
the multi-award success and big box-office of *My Left Foot*
placed the Pearson–Sheridan team on the big production map
and gave them clout. Sheridan had great visions of slick
thrillers – 'My idea of a decent European director in Hollywood
is *Robocop*,' he told me – but Pearson approached the steps of
the ladder with a savvy caution. Immovably Dublin-based,
Pearson knew that a local movie of quality, expanding in
psychology as opposed to thrills, was the right successor to
My Left Foot. '*The Field* was brought to us by Ray McAnally,'
says Jim Sheridan, 'who always believed in it as a movie.
We had him in *My Left Foot*, but in *The Field* he was to be
the star.'

John B. Keane's play was about a land dispute in which
the loutish Bull McCabe – McAnally – exercised dangerous
wiles to procure a plot of ground he believed was his rightful
heritage. The play had its theatre premiere in Dublin with

McAnally starring in November 1965, and had since been a regularly revived crowd-puller. But its construction was, as theatre demanded, claustrophobically narrow. Sheridan, writing his own screenplay, 'opened it' and introduced an American contender to challenge the Bull.

McAnally's professional position for a major starring movie could not have been sounder. Having served his apprenticeship in Irish theatre and British TV over thirty years he had finally won international acclaim with his Oscar-nominated role in *The Mission* and the BAFTA-winning tour de force *A Very British Coup*. Deeply intellectual, McAnally never wavered in his pursuit of thespian theory. He was sixty-three when he approached *The Field* in its film version but his excitement, says John B. Keane, 'was that of a first-timer'.

Richard Harris, who at his best shared a finicky integrity in flushing out perfect technique, wasn't happy about the casting offer down the billing from McAnally. Thirty years before, on *Shake Hands with the Devil*, he had pipped McAnally and his subsequent career had been undeniably starrier. But he cannot have been surprised by the offer. He was drifting, and his reputation as an abrasive star echoed from recent movies like *Maigret*, where the rows on set were legend. Harris didn't apologize for his on-set reputation: 'I've seen these so-called *nice* actors. Very able fellows like Ian McKellen and Kenneth Branagh. But they're like bank managers. So sweet and careful. Who needs it? We are suffering from a plague of good taste. Give me Sean Penn and Mickey Rourke any day. They project *danger*. That's what makes an actor interesting.'

Ray McAnally's death from a heart attack at his Wicklow cottage in June threw Pearson and Sheridan into turmoil. 'It was terrible,' says John B. Keane. 'Everything could have gone so wrong from then. Ray was perfect for Bull, but then this disaster!' Harris saw an opportunity, but he was not – still – the front-runner for the lead role. Harris: 'They said they didn't want me. They said I was old hat. They wanted Brando or Connery. Brando's make-up man, whom I had known for years, actually rang me on Marlon's behalf and asked who these Irish people were. I told them they were a bunch of layabouts who couldn't be trusted. I did everything in my power to stop them getting someone else.'

Pearson – slowly – kowtowed. Sheridan agreed. Harris was in.

His sharp intake of breath at this critical casting was distinctly audible. When Tom Berenger was announced as the American antagonist Harris brooded warily. 'Some of the backers in Britain didn't know who the hell he was,' he told me. His voice was spiky with apprehension. 'They have John Hurt too . . . but it's going to be wonderful, wonderful – it's the best thing I've ever read.' Some weeks before, just after the announcement of his casting. I had been with him as he scoured the bookstalls of a hotel for research reading. He chose books of photographs of the West of Ireland, Peg Sayer's bestselling and classic Irish diary and an armful of academic paperbacks. 'I want the mood,' he said. 'It's all down to mood.'

The Field began shooting in October in the village of Leenane on the Galway–Mayo border, in a mood described by assistant director Kevan Barker as 'pure hell'. Barker, whose recent credits included work with Merchant–Ivory and a host of first-rank stars from Maggie Smith to Julie Christie, found Harris to be everything his bad press implied. 'Maybe it was profound insecurity, but it made life a nightmare for all of us.' On Day One Harris fell out ill, suffering a hyperglycaemic attack after consuming the unit chef's lasagne. 'He threw a tantrum just as he was about to settle down to important scenes with Sean Bean, the excellent young British actor. He did a wobbly and accused the chef of putting sugar in the lasagne, which drove the chef through the ceiling, of course.'

Director Jim Sheridan, mild of manner and open to the prompting voice of experience, struggled to keep the peace. 'It was endless uphill work,' says Barker. 'Tom Berenger just walked away when Richard did his thing, guffing off every which way.' In Barker's opinion Harris contested Sheridan's direction and strove to put over his own directorial concept.

John B. Keane, however, was 'delighted' with Harris's furious energy. Harris was bright-eyed when he told the author he had been looking for years for 'a script to measure up to this'. Elsewhere he bragged that at last he had found his divinely tailored role, the role he was born to play. A crew member says: 'Richard lived Bull McCabe. Yes, he was obnoxious. But so was the Bull. It wasn't just hell-raising crap, or the illnesses that caused us to lose some days. It was his total absorption in a very loud and angry part.'

The Field cost $7 million (part paid by Granada TV, who had scored on *My Left Foot*), of which Harris's fee was a relatively paltry £100,000 plus. No actor on the film was paid more than Harris and that seemed apt, a sign of his genuine return to form. At the crew wrap party Harris forked out £1000 for booze – but stayed doggedly dry. 'I have to say he was generous,' says Barker. 'If he hadn't been so stupidly anti-Brit and hypochondriacal he would have been quite nice actually.'

It was clear immediately that Harris had swung the crucial coup. Morgan O'Sullivan, managing director of Ardmore Studios, gave the post-production grapevine word: 'He pulled it off. Everyone who has seen the first cut [of the movie] says it brings him back to the class of *This Sporting Life*. It is his professional rebirth.' Many predicted he would win the elusive Oscar; even Kevan Barker conceded that his presence was 'often gigantic'. George Peppard asserts: 'If he does get his Oscar it's simply overdue. He is, in a word, the professor. A fine, fine actor with many great performances behind him – and ahead of him, I'll bet.'

Elated though 'utterly fagged out' after *The Field*, Harris chose not to back-pedal. His usual Christmas vacation on Paradise often spilled long past New Year. This time he was up and at it as soon as the festivities were out of the way. By mid-January he was back in the newspapers, embroiled in a row with the Glasgow Citizens Theatre, with whom he had promised to appear in a play that was intended to take him back to the West End stage. Theatrical impresario Duncan Weldon was the one who offered Harris his return ticket, welcoming any play of Harris's choice. Harris mulled long over Anouilh's *Ring Around the Moon* and *The Lion in Winter* before finally remembering Pirandello's adventure in madness, *Henry IV*. Forty years earlier, the play had delighted and inspired Harris. He had promised one day to perform it. Now he would fulfil that promise.

The dispute with the Citizens Theatre centred on Harris's rejection of the proposed Pirandello translation. He had his own translation (by Julian Mitchell) which he wanted to do; but director Peter Prowse insisted on his resident writer's version. 'I hated it,' says Harris. 'They updated the play and it was very camp. I withdrew.' Prowse decided to go ahead without him, recasting in a hurry. 'All hell broke loose,' Harris told the *Evening Standard*. 'The press said I failed to turn up, I'd let them down, it was all my fault . . . but I didn't get into a public row.'

This heroic statement suggested a true rebirth – at last a disciplined, non-meddling attitude towards the media. In the succeeding months the very noticeable comeback would be distinguished by Harris's modesty. No more than two or three major interviews were granted, mostly to highbrows like the *Times*.

Under the direction of David Thacker, his chosen new man, Harris began rehearsing his own *Henry IV* in an atmosphere of confidence that recalled pre-*Bloomfield* days. A woman friend, Greek actress Aliki Michael, described him to me during the February build-up as 'Quite emphatically self-assured, very much his old self, very deep and inward-looking'. In due course the play started touring, opening in Cardiff to generally good notices. But Harris wasn't pleased yet. More and more he assumed the authorial voice, more and more he was the self-director of old. The ride grew bumpy, but he was unwavering in his sense of purpose. 'He is just determined to come back into London in triumph,' said the friend. 'With *The Field* and Pirandello he has just turned the clock back to 1963 in one fell swoop.'

Sarah Miles, Harris's co-star in *Henry IV*, withdrew in mid-April, claiming personal reasons. By the end of the month David Thacker was gone, to be replaced by Harris's new choice, Val May. Thacker's departure was 'for artistic differences only'. Whether he liked it or not Harris found himself fighting a rearguard action in the press: 'No, I didn't lock myself in my dressing-room and refuse to come out . . . but the set *was* wrong . . . I registered my objections by going on stage and ranting and raving . . .' he told the *Evening Standard*.

In May, conclusively, Richard Harris retook the 'legitimate' West End. The *Standard* celebrated a return to 'sparkling form' and all the leading reviews concurred. 'What was especially fascinating about it', says a producer, 'was Harris's self-restraint. In previous years a victory like this would have bored you to death with Harris blaring how wonderful he was. This time he just let the work speak for itself.' John McEntee of the *Standard* agreed: 'He seemed to just want to quietly bask in the achievement.'

The bushfire talk of imminent awards became rampant. A mid-1990 call to reshoot part of the completed *Field* suggested that Harris was in full creative charge, leaving no stone unturned. 'It is extraordinary,' said a producer. 'A dormant side of him has reawakened. He is frantic. He *will* get his Oscar nomination, wait and see.'

In truth, Harris probably cared less. His vanity has always been off-centre, confounding in its highs and lows. When I questioned him about his pride in past awards he dismissed them abruptly and genuinely. He had no idea where the various citations, gold records and statuettes had ended up. Certainly they weren't at home in the Bahamas. 'I don't care about these things,' he said. 'An actor acts, that's all there is to it.'

The real trophies in his life, the objects he truly values, reveal the heart of Richard Harris. His *Snow Goose* director Innes Lloyd says, 'Rugby ignites him.' *King of the Wind* director Peter Duffell says, 'Get him talking rugby and you've cracked him.' Dermot Foley says, 'Dickie Harris is a rugbyman, not an actor. His whole career has been in the scrum pack.' Harris himself cherishes his true prizes: 'I've already got Moss Keane's [rugby] shirt, and Tony Ward gave me Phil Bennett's jersey. I've got Ireland, New Zealand, Wales and South Africa. All I need now are England, Scotland and France . . .'

Ultimately, as he himself articulates it at sixty, the Richard Harris story is an unbroken circle that, despite defiant revivals, defies a sense of climax. He was always noticeable and noticed (except by Ivan); he was always entertaining; always ambitious; always daring; always, in his eyes with room for no one to disagree, a star. No publicist alive could have showcased him better, no manager could have honed a bigger career. The Oscar, finally, becomes redundant. He has what he wants – and the historical record of the fattest press file of the century to bear witness.

The climax of fulfilment seems impossible because all his life has been a kind of climax. The 'dual nature' of his Limerick boyhood developed quickly into a double life of performing and promotion. It was a relentless scrum battle, in which he bare-knuckled and roared his way to success. The layers beneath – the real man – escaped detection for so long because of the din. Richard Harris, one suspects, enjoys best the victory of his own confusing legend. He prefers to hide himself because he knows what he knows – and he understands the brutality of the games field, where the best man doesn't always win. The genius of his game plan is: keep 'em guessing.

The true Richard Harris is a restless, inquisitive, sensitive, adventurous gypsy whose emotional detachment is his lodestar. His ability to isolate himself from everything – from friendship, home, failure and success – is the secret of his achievement, and his unease. 'He is always explosive,' says his brother Noel. 'Sometimes it gets him what he wants, mostly it hurts him. I always wish he could be more objective, more reasoned. But he's just Dick, who always just flew off the handle . . . but then always gave us something to laugh about.'

'The key to Richard is easy,' says Rod Taylor. 'He wants it *right*. He wants the Garden of Eden. We all do. Richard is just one of those guys who, no matter how you shake him, won't stop trying.'

The child-man emerges, obsessed with the perfection of the game, his feet still rooted in the wilds of Kilkee, in the all-things-possible past. He is, in that sense, truly a *barnac* – a colourful unputdownable barnacle who clings forever to the undefined Glad Day dream. And meanwhile indulges the sporting life.

Filmography

Including TV performances (see note at end)

Alive and Kicking (Associated British-Pathé, Great Britain, 1958)
Director: Cyril Frankel. *Producer:* Victor Skutezky. *Screenplay:* Denis Cannan. *Photography:* Gilbert Taylor. *Editor:* Bernard Gribble. *Music:* Philip Green. *Assistant director:* Robert Jones. *Running time:* 94 minutes. *Cert:* U. In black and white. *Production company:* ABPC/A Victor Skutezky Production.

Dora	Sybil Thorndike	*Russian Captain*	Eric Pohlmann
Rosie	Kathleen Harrison	*Birdwatcher*	Colin Gordon
Mabel	Estelle Winwood	*Solicitor*	John Salew
MacDonagh	Stanley Holloway	*Old Man*	Liam Redmond
Matron	Joyce Carey	*Old Woman*	Marjorie Rhodes

Richard Harris uncredited in most production notes.

Shake Hands with the Devil (United Artists, Eire, 1959)
Director: Michael Anderson. *Producer:* Michael Anderson. *Executive producers:* George Glass and Walter Seltzer. *Screenplay:* Ivan Goff and Ben Roberts, adapted by Marion Thompson from the novel by Rearden Conner. *Photography:* Erwin Hillier. *Editor:* Gordon Pilkington. *Music:* William Alwyn. *Production designer:* Tom Morahan. *Running time:* 111 minutes. *Cert:* A. In black and white. *Production company:* Troy Films, in association with Pennebaker Inc.

Sean Lenihan	James Cagney	*Mary Madigan*	Marianne Benet
Kerry O'Shea	Don Murray	*Michael O'Leary*	Niall MacGinnis
Jennifer Curtis	Dana Wynter	*Terence O'Brien*	Richard Harris
Kitty O'Brady	Glynis Johns	*Paddy Nolan*	Ray McAnally
The General	Michael Redgrave	*Liam O'Sullivan*	Noel Purcell
Lady Fitzhugh	Sybil Thorndike	*Colonel Smithson*	Christopher Rhodes
Chris Noonan	Cyril Cusack		

The Wreck of the Mary Deare (MGM, United States, 1959)
Director: Michael Anderson. *Producer:* Julian Blaustein. *Screenplay:* Eric Ambler from the novel by Hammond Innes. *Photography:* Joseph

Ruttenberg and Fred Young in Cinemascope. *Editor:* Eda Warren. *Assistant directors:* Hans Peters, Paul Groesse. *Special effects:* A. Arnold Gillespie and Lee LeBlanc. *Music:* George Duning. *Running time:* 104 minutes. *Cert:* U. In Metrocolor. *Production company:* Blaustein-Baroda.

Gideon Patch	Gary Cooper	*Janet Taggart*	Virginia McKenna
John Sands	Charlton Heston	*Higgins*	Richard Harris
Nyland	Michael Redgrave	*Mike Duncan*	Ben Wright
Sir Wilfred Falcett	Emlyn Williams	*Gunderson*	Peter Illing
Chairman	Cecil Parker	*Frank*	Terence de Marney
Petrie	Alexander Knox		

A Terrible Beauty (United Artists, Great Britain, 1960)

Director: Tay Garnett. *Producer:* Raymond Stross. *Screenplay:* Robert Wright Campbell, based on the novel by Arthur Roth. *Photography:* Stephen Dade. *Editor:* Peter Tanner. *Art director:* John Stoll. *Music:* Cedric Thorpe Davie. *Musical director:* Dock Mathieson. *Running time:* 90 minutes. *Cert:* U. *Production company:* A Raymond Stross-DRM Production.

Dermot O'Neill	Robert Mitchum	*Kathleen O'Neill*	Eileen Crowe
Neeve Donnelly	Anne Heywood	*Sergeant Crawley*	Geoffrey Golden
Don McGinnis	Dan O'Herlihy	*Father McCrory*	Hilton Edwards
Jimmy Hannafin	Cyril Cusack	*Quinn*	Wilfred Downing
Sean Reilly	Richard Harris	*Malone*	Christopher Rhodes
Bella	Marianne Benet	*Corrigan*	Eddie Golden
Ned O'Neill	Niall MacGinnis	*Tim*	Joe Lynch
Patrick O'Neill	Harry Brogan		

The Long and the Short and the Tall (Warner-Pathé, Great Britain, 1960)

Director: Leslie Norman. *Producer:* Michael Balcon. *Executive producer:* Hal Mason. *Screenplay:* Wolf Mankowitz, based on the play by Willis Hall. *Photography:* Erwin Hillier. *Editor:* Gordon Stone. *Music:* Stanley Black. *Assistant directors:* Terence Verity and Jim Morahan. *Special effects:* George Blackwell. *Running time:* 105 minutes. *Cert:* X. In black and white. *Production company:* Michael Balcon/Associated British.

Private Bamforth	Laurence Harvey	*Private Whitaker*	David McCallum
Corporal Johnstone	Richard Harris	*Private Smith*	John Meillon
Sergeant Mitchem	Richard Todd	*Private Evans*	John Rees
Lance Corporal Macleish	Ronald Fraser	*Tojo*	Kenji Takaki

The Guns of Navarone (Columbia, Great Britain, 1961)

Director: J. Lee Thompson. *Producer:* Cecil F. Ford. *Executive producer:*

Carl Foreman. *Associate producer:* Leon Becker. *Screenplay:* Carl Foreman, based on the novel by Alistair MacLean. *Photography:* Oswald Morris in Cinemascope. *Additional photography:* John Wilcox. *Editor:* Alan Osbistron, with Raymond Poulton, John Smith and Oswald Hafenrichter. *Music:* Dimitri Tiomkin. *Assistant director:* Geoffrey Drake. *Special effects:* Bill Warrington and Wayy Veevers. *Running time:* 157 minutes. *Cert:* A. In Technicolor. *Production company:* Open Road.

Mallory	Gregory Peck	*Baker*	Allan Cuthbertson
Miller	David Niven	*Weaver*	Michael Trubshawe
Andrea	Anthony Quinn	*Grogan*	Percy Herbert
Brown	Stanley Baker	*Sessler*	George Mikell
Franklin	Anthony Quayle	*Muesel*	Walter Gotell
Pappadimos	James Darren	*Nicholai*	Tutte Lemkow
Maria	Irene Papas	*Commandant*	Albert Lieven
Anna	Gia Scala	*Group Captain*	Norman Woodland
Jensen	James Robertson Justice	*German Gunnery Officer*	Christopher Rhodes
Barnsby	Richard Harris	*Cohn*	Bryan Forbes

Mutiny on the Bounty (MGM, United States, 1962)

Director: Lewis Milestone. *Producer:* Aaron Rosenberg. *Screenplay:* Charles Lederer, based on the novel by Charles Nordhoff and James Norman Hall. *Photography:* Robert L. Surtees in Ultra Panavision 70. *Editor:* John McSweeney Jr. *2nd unit photography:* James C. Havens. *Art directors:* George W. Davis and J. McMillan Johnson. *Set decoration:* Henry Grace and Hugh Hunt. *Assistant director:* Ridgeway Callow. *Music:* Bronislau Kaper. *Choreography:* Hamil Petroff. *Special effects:* A. Arnold Gillespie, Lee LeBlanc and Robert R. Hoag. *Running time:* 185 minutes. *Cert:* A. In Technicolor. *Production company:* Arcola.

Fletcher Christian	Marlon Brando	*Michael Byrne*	Chips Rafferty
William Bligh	Trevor Howard	*Samuel Mack*	Ashley Cowan
John Mills	Richard Harris	*John Fryer*	Eddie Byrne
Alexander Smith	Hugh Griffith	*James Morrison*	Keith McConnell
William Brown	Richard Hadyn	*Minarii*	Frank Silvera
Edward Young	Tim Seely	*Graves*	Ben Wright
Matthew Quintal	Percy Herbert	*Staines*	Torin Thatcher
Edward Birkett	Gordon Jackson	*Chief Hitihiti*	Matahiarii Tama
William McCoy	Noel Purcell	*Maimiti*	Tarita
John Williams	Duncan Lamont		

This Sporting Life (Rank, Great Britain, 1963)

Director: Lindsay Anderson. *Producer:* Karel Reisz. *Executive producer:* Albert Fennell. *Screenplay:* David Storey, based on his novel. *Photography:* Denys Coop. *Editor:* Peter Taylor. *Music:* Roberto Gerhard. *Musical director:* Jacques-Louis Monod. *Art director:* Alan Withy. *Production manager:* Geoffrey Haine. *Assistant director:* Ted Sturgis. *Running time:* 134 minutes. *Cert:* X. In black and white. *Production company:* Independent Artists/A Julian Wintle-Leslie Parkyn Production.

Frank Machin	Richard Harris	*Dentist*	Frank Windsor
Mrs Hammond	Rachel Roberts	*Doctor*	Peter Duguid
Weaver	Alan Badel	*Waiter*	Wallas Eaton
Johnson	William Hartnell	*Head Waiter*	Anthony Woodruff
Maurice Braithwaite	Colin Blakely	*Mrs Farrer*	Katherine Parr
Mrs Weaver	Vanda Godsell	*Lynda*	Bernadette Benson
Judith	Anne Cunningham	*Ian*	Andrew Nolan
Len Miller	Jack Watson	*Riley*	Michael Logan
Slomer	Arthur Lowe	*Hooker*	Murray Evans
Wade	Harry Markham	*Gower*	Tom Clegg
Jeff	George Sewell	*Cameron*	John Gill
Phillips	Leonard Rossiter	*Trainer*	Ken Traill

Deserto Rosso (The Red Desert) (Academy/Connoisseur, Italy/France, 1964)

Director: Michelangelo Antonioni. *Producer:* Antonio Cervi. *Executive producer:* Angelo Rizzoli. *Screenplay:* Michelangelo Antonioni and Tonino Guerra. *Photography:* Carlo di Palma. *Music:* Giovanni Fusco. *Electronic music from compositions by:* Vittorio Gelmetti. *Singer:* Cecilia Fusco. *Costumes:* Gitt Magrini. *Production manager:* Ugo Tucci. *Assistant directors:* Giovanni Arduini and Flavio Nicolini. *Running time:* 116 minutes. *Cert:* X. In Eastman Colour. Print by Technicolor. *Production company:* Film Duemila/Cinematografica Federiz (Rome)/Francoriz (Paris).

Giuliana	Monica Vitti	*Max*	Aldo Grotti
Corrado Zeller	Richard Harris	*Valerio*	Valerio Bartoleschi
Ugo	Carlo Chionetti	*Workman*	Giuliano Missirini
Linda	Xenia Valderi	*Workman's Wife*	Lili Rheims
Emilia	Rita Renoir		

and with Beppi Conti, Giulio Cotignoli, Giovanni Lolli, Hiram Mino Madonia, Arturo Parmiani, Carla Ravasi, Ivo Scherpiani and Bruno Scipioni. With subtitles.

Major Dundee (BLC/Columbia, United States, 1964)

Director: Sam Peckinpah. *Producer:* Jerry Bresler. *Screenplay:* Harry Julian Fink, Oscar Saul and Sam Peckinpah. *Photography:* Sam Leavitt in Panavision. *Editor:* William A. Lyon with Don Starling. *2nd unit photography:* Cliff Lyons. *Production manager:* Francisco Day. *Assistant to producer:* Rick Rosenberg. *Music:* Daniele Amfiteatrof. *Title song by:* Daniele Amfiteatrof and Ned Washington. *Sung by:* Mitch Miller's Singalong Gang. *Costumes:* Tom Dawson. *Special effects:* August Lohman. *Assistant directors:* Floyd Joyer and John Veitch. *Running time:* 134 minutes. *Cert:* A. In Eastman Colour. *Production company:* Jerry Bresler Productions.

Major Amos Dundee	Charlton Heston	*Wiley*	Slim Pickens
Captain Benjamin		*Captain Waller*	Karl Swenson
Tyreen	Richard Harris	*Sierra Charriba*	Michael Pate
Lieutenant Graham	Jim Hutton	*Jimmy Lee*	John Davis
Samuel Potts	James Coburn	*Benteen*	Chandler
Tim Ryan	Michael Anderson	*Priam*	Dub Taylor
	Jnr	*Captain Jacques*	
Teresa Santiago	Senta Berger	*Tremaine*	Albert Carrier
Sergeant Gomez	Mario Adorf	*Riago*	Jose Carlos Ruiz
Aesop	Brock Peters	*Melinche*	Aurora Clavell
O. W. Hadley	Warren Oates	*Linda*	Begonia Palacios
Sergeant Chillum	Ben Johnson	*Dr Aguilar*	Enrique Lucero
Reverend Dahlstrom	R. G. Armstrong	*Old Apache*	Francisca Reyguera
Arthur Hadley	L. Q. Jones		

La Bibbia (The Bible . . . In the Beginning) (20th Century-Fox, Italy/United States, 1966)

Director: John Huston. *Producer:* Dino De Laurentiis. *Screenplay:* Christopher Fry. *Script assistants:* Jonathan Griffin, Ivo Perilli and Vittorio Bonicelli. *Photography:* Giuseppe Rotunno. *Editor:* Ralph Kemplen. *Music:* Toshiro Mayuzumi. *Musical director:* Franco Ferrara. *Associate producer:* Luigi Luraschi. *Production supervisor:* Bruno Todini. *2nd unit director* (for 'The Creation'): Ernst Haas. *Art director:* Mario Chiari. *Set decorators:* Enzo Eusepi and Bruno Avesani. *Costumes:* Maria De Matteis. *Choreography:* Katherine Dunham. *Zoological consultant:* Angelo Lombardi. *Assistant directors:* Vana Caruso and Ottavio Oppo. *Running time:* 175 minutes. *Cert:* U. In Technicolor. Print by DeLuxe. *Production company:* Dino De Laurentiis.

Narrator	John Huston	*Hagar*	Zoe Sallis
Adam	Michael Parks	*Lot*	Gabriele Ferzetti
Eve	Ulla Bergryd	*Lot's Wife*	Eleonora Rossi Drago
Cain	Richard Harris	*Abel*	Franco Nero
Noah	John Huston	*Isaac*	Alberto Lucantoni
Nimrod	Stephen Boyd	*Abraham's Steward*	Robert Rietty
Abraham	George C. Scott	*Lot's Daughters*	Adriana Ambesi
Sarah	Ava Gardner		Grazia Maria Spina
The Three Angels	Peter O'Toole		

and with Claudia Lange, Luciano Conversi, Pupella Maggio, Peter Heinze, Angelo Boschariol, Anna Maria Orso, Eric Leutzinger, Gabriella Pallotta and Rosanna De Rocco.

I Tre Volti (Three Faces of a Woman) (Dino De Laurentiis, Italy, 1964)

Directors: Michelangelo Antonioni, Mauro Bolognini and Franco Indovina. *Producer:* Dino De Laurentiis. *Screenplays:* (1) Antonioni; (2) Tullio Pinelli and Clive Exton; (3) Indovina, Alberto Sordi and Rodolfo Sonego. *Photography:* Carlo di Palma and Otello Martelli. *Editors:* Da Roma, Baragli. *Music:* Piero Piccioni. *Running time:* 120

minutes, in three self-contained segments. In Technicolor. *Production company:* Dino De Laurentiis.

(1) *Princess Soraya*	Soraya	*Rudolph*	Jose de Villalonga
Reporter	Ivano Davoli	(3) *Mrs Melville*	Soraya
Photographer	Giorgio Sartarelli	*Armando*	Alberto Sordi
Designer	Piero Tosi	*Agency manager*	Goffredo
American producer	Ralph Serpe		Alessandrini
(2) *Linda*	Soraya	*TV reporter*	Renato Tagliani
Robert	Richard Harris	*TV reporter*	Alberto Giubilo
Hedda	Esmeralda Ruspoli		

The Heroes of Telemark (Rank, Great Britain, 1965)

Director: Anthony Mann. *Producer:* S. Benjamin Fisz. *Screenplay:* Ivan Moffat and Ben Barzman, based on the books *Skis Against the Atom* by Knut Hauglund and *But for These Men* by John Drummond. *Photography:* Robert Krasker in Panavision. *Editor:* Bert Bates. *Music:* Malcolm Arnold. *Art director:* Tony Masters. *Set decoration:* Bob Cartwright and Ted Clements. *2nd unit director:* Gil Woxholt. *Special effects:* John Fulton. *Assistant directors:* John Quested and Derek Cracknell. *Running time:* 131 minutes. *Cert:* U. In Technicolor. *Production company:* Benton Films.

Dr Rolf Pedersen	Kirk Douglas	*Claus*	William Marlowe
Knut Straud	Richard Harris	*Einar*	Brook Williams
Uncle	Michael Redgrave	*Captain of the*	
Anna	Ulla Jacobsson	*Galtesund*	David Davies
Arne	David Weston	*Hartmuller*	Karel Stepanek
Major Frick	Anton Diffring	*Mrs Saundersen*	Elvi Hale
Terboven	Eric Porter	*Erhardt*	Gerard Heinz
Colonel Wilkinson	Mervyn Johns	*German Ski Sergeant*	Victor Beaumont
Sigrid	Jennifer Hilary	*Businessman*	Philo Hauser
Jensen	Roy Dotrice	*Sturmführer*	George Murcell
Professor Logan	Barry Jones	*Mr Sandersen*	Russell Waters
Nilssen	Ralph Michael	*Factory Watchman*	Jan Conrad
General Bolts	Geoffrey Keen	*Major*	Robert Bruce
Doctor at Hospital	Maurice Denham	*Norwegian Naval*	
Knippelberg	Wolf Frees	*Attaché*	Brian Jackson
General Courts	Robert Ayres	*German Official*	Paul Hansard
Gunnar	Sebastian Breaks	*Businessman's*	
Freddy	John Golightly	*Girlfriend*	Jemma Hyde
Oli	Alan Howard	*Galtesund*	Grace Arnold
Henrik	Patrick Jordan	*passengers*	Howard Douglas

Hawaii (United Artists, United States, 1966)

Director: George Roy Hill. *Producer:* Walter Mirisch. *Screenplay:* Dalton Trumbo and Daniel Taradash, based on the novel by James A. Michener. *Photography:* Russell Harlan in Panavision. *Prologue sequence photography:* Chuck Wheeler. *Editor:* Stuart Gilmore. *Music:* Elmer Bernstein. *Song:* 'My Wishing Doll', Elmer Bernstein and Mack

David. *Associate producer:* Lewis J. Rachmil. *Production managers:* Robert Anderson and Emmett Emerson. *2nd unit director:* Richard Talmadge. *2nd unit photography:* Harold Wellman. *Art director:* James Sullivan. *Set decorator:* Edward G. Boyle with Ray Boltz Jr. *Special effects:* Paul Byrd. *Production designer:* Cary Odell. *Assistant director:* Ray Gosnell. *Running time:* 186 minutes. *Cert:* A. In DeLuxe Colour. *Production company:* Mirisch Corporation.

Abner Hale	Max von Sydow	*Kelolo*	Ted Nobriga
Jerusha Bromley	Julie Andrews	*Noelani*	Elizabeth Logue
Rafer Hoxworth	Richard Harris	*Iliki*	Lokelani S. Chicarell
Charles Bromley	Carroll O'Connor	*Gideon Hale*	Malcolm Atterbury
Abigail Bromley	Elizabeth Cole	*Hepzibah Hale*	Dorothy Jenkins
Charity Bromley	Diane Sherry	*Captain Janders*	George Rose
Mercy Bromley	Heather Menzies	*Mason*	Michael Constantine
Rev. Thorn	Torin Thatcher	*Collins*	John Harding
John Whipple	Gene Hackman	*Cridland*	Robert Crawford
Immanuel Quigley	John Cullum	*Micah Hale, aged 4*	Robert Oakley
Abraham Hewlett	Lou Antonio	*Micah Hale, aged 7*	Henrik von Sydow
Queen Malama	Jocelyn La Garde	*Micah Hale, aged 12*	Claus S. von Sydow
Keoki	Manu Tupou	*Micah Hale, aged 18*	Bertil Werjefelt

Caprice (20th Century-Fox, United States, 1966)

Director: Frank Tashlin. *Producers:* Aaron Rosenberg and Martin Melcher. *Screenplay:* Jay Jayson and Frank Tashlin. *Story:* Martin Hale and Jay Jayson. *Photography:* Leon Shamroy in Cinemascope. *Editor:* Robert Simpson. *Aerial photography:* Nelson Tyler. *Music:* De Vol. *Musical director:* Al Woodbury. *Title song:* Larry Marks. *Special photographic effects:* L. B. Abbott and Emil Kisa Jr. *Art directors:* Jack Martin Smith and William Creber. *Associate producer:* Barney Rosenzweig. *Production manager:* Francisco Day. *Assistant director:* David Silver. *Running time:* 98 minutes. *Cert:* A. In DeLuxe Colour. *Production company:* Aaron Rosenberg/Martin Melcher Productions.

Patricia Foster	Doris Day	*Su Ling*	Irene Tsu
Christopher White	Richard Harris	*Inspector Kapinsky*	Larry D. Mann
Stuart Clancy	Ray Walston	*Auber*	Maurice Marsac
Matthew Cutter	Jack Kruschen	*Butler*	Michael Romanoff
Sir Jason Fox	Edward Mulhare	*Mandy*	Lisa Seagram
Madame Piasco	Lilia Skala	*Barney*	Michael J. Pollard

Camelot (Warner-Pathé, United States, 1967)

Director: Joshua Logan. *Producer:* Jack L. Warner. *Assistant to producer:* Joel Freeman. *Screenplay:* Alan Jay Lerner, based on the musical play by Alan Jay Lerner (book and lyrics) and Frederick Loewe (music); itself based on the novel cycle *The Once and Future King* by T. H. White. *Photography:* Richard H. Kline in Panavision 70 mm. *Editor:* Folmar Blangsted. *Production and costume designer:* John Truscott. *Musical director:* Alfred Newman. *Orchestrations:* Leo Shuken and Jack Haynes. *Art director:* Edward Carrere. *Set decoration:* John W. Brown. *Action sequences:* Tap and Joe Canutt. *Assistant director:* Arthur Jacobson. *Running time:* 181 minutes. *Cert:* U. In Technicolor. *Production company:* Warner Bros.

King Arthur	Richard Harris	Lady Clarinda	Estelle Winwood
Guinevere	Vanessa Redgrave	Sir Lionel	Gary Marshall
Lancelot du Lac	Franco Nero	Sir Dinadan	Anthony Rogers
Mordred	David Hemmings	Sir Sagramore	Peter Bromilow
King Pellinore	Lionel Jeffries	Lady Sybil	Sue Casey
Merlyn	Laurence Naismith	Tom of Warwick	Gary Marsh
Dap	Pierre Olaf	King Arthur as a Boy	Nicholas Beauvy

The Molly Maguires (Paramount, United States, 1970)

Director: Martin Ritt. *Producers:* Martin Ritt and Walter Bernstein. *Screenplay:* Walter Bernstein, suggested by the book by Arthur H. Lewis. *Photography:* James Wong Howe in Panavision. *Music:* Henry Mancini. *Traditional songs:* 'Eileen Aroon', 'Cockles and Mussels', 'Garry Owen'. *Production manager:* David Golden. *2nd unit director:* Oscar Rudolph. *Editor:* Frank Bracht. *2nd unit photography:* Morris Hartzband. *Art director:* Tambi Larsen. *Set decoration:* Darrell Silvera. *Technical adviser:* Joseph Lawrence. *Running time:* 125 minutes. *Cert:* U. In Technicolor. *Production company:* Tamm Productions.

James McPharlan	Richard Harris	Frank McAndrew	Anthony Costello
Jack Kehoe	Sean Connery	Father O'Connor	Philip Bourneuf
Mary Raines	Samantha Eggar	Mr Raines	Brendan Dillon
Captain Davies	Frank Finlay	Mrs Frazier	Francis Heflin
Dougherty	Anthony Zerbe	Jenkins	John Alderson
Mrs Kehoe	Bethel Leslie	Bartender	Malachy McCourt
Frazier	Art Lund	Mrs McAndrew	Susan Goodman

Cromwell (Columbia, Great Britain, 1970)

Director: Ken Hughes. *Producer:* Irving Allen. *Screenplay:* Ken Hughes. *Script consultant:* Ronald Harwood. *Photography:* Geoffrey Unsworth in Panavision. *Editor:* Bill Lenny. *Music:* Frank Cordell. *Associate producer:* Andrew Donally. *Production supervisor:* Frank Bevis. *Production designer:* John Stoll. *Costumes;* Nino Novarese. *Special effects:* Bill Warrington. *2nd unit photography:* Wilkie Cooper. *Assistant director:* Ted Sturgis. *Running time:* 140 minutes. *Cert:* U. In Technicolor. *Production company:* Irving Allen Productions.

Cromwell	Richard Harris	John Hampden	Ian McCulloch
Charles I	Alec Guinness	John Pym	Geoffrey Keen
Earl of Manchester	Robert Morley	Richard Cromwell	Anthony May
Queen Henrietta		John Lilburne	Patrick O'Connell
Maria	Dorothy Tutin	General Digby	John Paul
John Carter	Frank Finlay	The Speaker	Llewellyn Rees
Prince Rupert	Timothy Dalton	Prince of Wales	Robin Stewart

Earl of Stafford	Patrick Wymark	*Archbishop*	André Van
Hugh Peters	Patrick Magee	*Rinuccini*	Gyseghem
Sir Edward Hyde	Nigel Stock	*Mrs Cromwell*	Zena Walker
Lord Essex	Charles Gray	*Bishop Juxon*	John Welsh
Henry Ireton	Michael Jayston	*Thomas Fairfax*	Douglas Wilmer
Oliver Cromwell II	Richard Cornish	*Henry Cromwell*	Anthony Kemp
Ruth Carter	Anna Cropper	*Mary Cromwell*	Stacy Dorning
Solicitor General	Michael Goodliffe	*Bridget Cromwell*	Melinda Churcher
General Byron	Jack Gwillim	*Old Man/William*	George Merritt
Hacker	Basil Henson	*Drummer Boy*	George Rowland
Captain Lundsford	Patrick Holt	*Elizabeth Cromwell*	Josephine Gillick
President Bradshaw	Stratford Johns		

A Man Called Horse (Cinema Center, United States, 1970)

Director: Elliot Silverstein. *Producer:* Sandy Howard. *Screenplay:* Jack De Witt, based on the story by Dorothy M. Johnson. *Photography:* Robert Hauser in Panavision. *Editor:* Philip Anderson. *Music:* Leonard Rosenman. *Production designer:* Dennis Lynton Clark. *Art director:* Phil Barber. *Set decoration:* Raul Serrano. *Associate producer:* Frank Brill. *Production manager:* Robert Beche with Gilbert Kurland. *Special effects:* Federico Farfan and Tim Smythe. *2nd unit director:* Yakima Canutt. *Assistant director:* Terry Morse Jr. *Running time:* 114 minutes. *Cert:* AA. In Technicolor. *Production company:* Sanford Howard Productions.

Lord John Morgan	Richard Harris	*Thorn Rose*	Lina Marin
Buffalo Cow Head	Dame Judith Anderson	*Elk Woman*	Tamara Garina
Batise	Jean Gascon	*He-Wolf*	Michael Baseleon
Yellow Hand	Manu Tupou	*Leaping Buck*	Manuel Padilla
Running Deer	Corinna Tsopei	*Medicine Men*	Iron Eyes Cody,
Joe	Dub Taylor		Richard Fools
Bent	William Jordan		Bull and
Ed	James Gammon		Ben Eagleman
Black Eagle	Edward Little Sky	*Striking Bear*	Terry Leonard

and with Sioux Indians from the Rosebud Reservation in South Dakota

The Snow Goose (BBC/Universal, 1971)

Director: Patrick Garland. *Producer:* Innes Lloyd. *Screenplay:* Paul Gallico. *Photography:* Ray Henman and Paddy Carey. *Editor:* Ken Pearce. *Special effects:* Jim Ward. *Costumes:* Ken Morey. *Make-up:* Anna Chesterman and Bill Lodge. *Music:* Carl Davis. *Running time:* 100 minutes approx. In colour. *Production company:* BBC-Universal-Hallmark Hall of Fame Co-Production.

Philip Rhayader	Richard Harris	*Fritha*	Jenny Agutter

Bloomfield (20th Century-Fox, Great Britain, 1971)

Director: Richard Harris. *Producers:* John Heyman and Wolf Mankowitz. *Screenplay:* Wolf Mankowitz, from a story by Joseph Gross. *Additional material by:* Richard Harris. *Photography:* Otto Heller. *Editor:* Kevin

Connor. *Music:* Johnny Harris. *Songs:* 'The Loner' by Maurice Gibb and Billy Laurie, sung by the Bloomfields; 'Hail the Conquering Hero' and 'Homing in on the Next Trade Wind' by Tony Colton and Ray Smith, sung by Heads, Hands and Feet; 'Nimrod's Theme' by Bill Whelan and Niall Connery; and 'Nimrod's Exit from Eirad' by Bill Whelan, Niall Connery and Johnny Harris. *Associate producer:* Maurice Foster. *Production supervisor:* Denis Johnson Jr. *Production managers:* Mati Raz and Arik Dichner. *Production designer:* Richard Macdonald. *Special effects:* Camera Effects. *Titles:* General Screen Enterprises. *Assistant directors:* Ted Morley and John Stodel. *Running time:* 95 minutes. *Cert:* U. In Technicolor. *Production company:* World Film Services/ Limbridge Productions.

Eitan	Richard Harris	Menachem	Reuven Bar Yotam
Nira	Romy Schneider	Nimrod's Father	Zvi Yaron
Nimrod	Kim Burfield	Nimrod's Mother	Beyla Genauer
Yasha	Maurice Kaufman	Bulldozer Foreman	Amnon Bernson
Weiner	Yossi Yadin	Ariana Proprietor	Jacques Cohen
Chairman	Shraga Friedman	1st Committee Man	Mosco Alkalai
Teddy	Aviva Marks	2nd Committee Man	Nathan Cogan
Bank Manager	Yossi Grabber	3rd Committee Man	Morrie Alexander
Eldad	David Heyman	4th Committee Man	Erwin Rigglehaupt
Avraham	Giddion Shemer	Football Commentator	Brian Moore
Sarah	Sarah Moor		

Man in the Wilderness (Columbia-Warner, United States, 1971)

Director: Richard C. Sarafian. *Producer:* Sanford Howard. *Executive producer:* John McMichael. *Screenplay:* Jack De Witt. *Photography:* Gerry Fisher in Panavision. *Editor:* Geoffrey Foot. *Music:* Johnny Harris; 'Zach Bass Theme' by Johnny Harris and John Bromley. *Associate producer:* C. O. Erickson. *Production manager:* Francisco Molero. *2nd unit photography:* John Cabrera. *Production designer:* Dennis Lynton Clark. *Art director:* Gumersindo Andres. *Special effects:* Richard M. Parker. *Assistant director:* John Carlos Lopez Rodero. *Running time:* 105 minutes. *Cert:* A. In Technicolor. *Production company:* Warner Bros/Wilderness Film Productions; a Sanford/Limbridge Production.

Zachary Bass	Richard Harris	Benoit	James Doohan
Captain Henry	John Huston	Potts	Bryan Marshall
Indian Chief	Henry Wilcoxon	Longbow	Ben Carruthers
Fogarty	Percy Herbert	Smith	Robert Russell
Lowrie	Dennis Waterman	Coulter	John Bindon
Grace	Prunella Ransome	Wiser	Bruce M. Fischer
Ferris	Norman Rossington	Russell	Dean Selmier

and with Rudy Althoff and Peggy the Bear, Sheila Raynor, Manolo Landau, William Layton and Judith Furse

The Deadly Trackers (Columbia-Warner, United States, 1973)

Director: Barry Shear. *Producer:* Fouad Said. *Executive producer:* Edward

Rosen. *Screenplay:* Lukas Heller, from a story by Samuel Fuller. *Photography:* Gabriel Torres. *Editor:* Michael Economou with Carl Pingitore. *Music:* uncredited, but segments from the movies *The Wild Bunch* by Jerry Fielding, *The Last Tomorrow* by Richard Markowitz and *Hardcase* by Pat Williams. *Art director:* Javier Torres Torija. *Set decoration:* Ernesto Varrasco. *Associate producer:* David Oliver. *Production executive:* Sam Manners. *Production manager* (Mexico): Alfonso Sanchez. *Assistant directors* (Mexico): Jesus Marin and John Quill. *Running time:* 105 minutes. *Cert:* X. In Technicolor. *Production company:* Ciné Film.

Sean Kilpatrick	Richard Harris	*Teacher*	Joan Swift
Frank Brand	Rod Taylor	*Maria*	Isela Vega
Gutierrez	Al Lettieri	*Deputy Bill*	William Bryant
Choo Choo	Neville Brand	*Priest*	Ray Moyer
Schoolboy	William Smith	*1st Jefe*	Armando Acosta
Katherine Kilpatrick	Kelly Jean Peters	*Bar Customer*	Federico Gonzalez
Kevin Kilpatrick	Sean Marshall	*Banker*	John Kennedy
Deputy Bob	Read Morgan		

This movie began life as *Riata*, directed in Spain by Sam Fuller, in the summer of 1972. It was abandoned after several weeks' shooting and started again in Mexico, directed by Barry Shear. See pp. 174-6 for full information.

Juggernaut (United Artists, United States, 1974)
Director: Richard Lester. *Producer:* Richard De Koker (Richard Alan Simmons). *Screenplay:* Richard De Koker, with additional dialogue by Alan Plater. *Photography:* Gerry Fisher in Panavision. *Editor:* Antony Gibbs. *Music:* Ken Thorne. *Production designer:* Terence Marsh. *Art director:* Alan Tomkins. *Executive producer:* David V. Picker. *Associate producer:* Denis O'Dell. *Production manager:* Roy Stevens. *2nd unit photography:* Paul Wilson. *Aerial photography:* Peter Allwork. *Special effects:* Cliff Richardson and George Richardson. *Technical adviser:* Lieutenant Commander Sidney Walton. *Assistant directors:* David Tringham, Terry Hodgkinson and Vincent Winter. *Running time:* 110 minutes. *Cert:* A. In DeLuxe Colour. *Production company:* UA.

Fallon	Richard Harris	*Junior Officer*	Richard Moore
The Captain	Omar Sharif	*Chief Engineer*	Jack Watson
Charlie Braddock	David Hemmings	*Jerry Kellog*	Bob Sessions
Superintendent		*Laura Kellog*	Liza Ross
John McCleod	Anthony Hopkins	*Mr Fowlers*	Michael Egan
Nicholas Porter	Ian Holm	*The Walker*	Ben Aris
Barbara	Shirley Knight	*Digby*	Paul Antrim
Social Director	Roy Kinnear	*Henning*	Colin Thatcher
Azad	Roshan Seth	*Menzies*	Terence Hillyer
O'Neill	Cyril Cusack	*Hughes*	John Stride
Sid Buckland	Freddie Jones	*Baker*	Michael Hordern
Mrs Buckland	Kristine Howarth	*Bartender*	Norman Warwick

Corrigan	Clifton James	*2nd Radio Officer*	Freddie Fletcher
1st Officer		*Driscoll*	John Bindon
Hollingsworth	Mark Burns	*Susan McCleod*	Caroline Mortimer
2nd Officer	Gareth Thomas	*David McCleod*	Adam
3rd Officer	Andrew Bradford	*Nancy McCleod*	Rebecca Bridge

99 and 44/100% Dead (Fox-Rank, United States, 1974)

Director: John Frankenheimer. *Producer:* Joe Wizan. *Screenplay:* Robert Dillon. *Photography:* Ralph Woolsey in Panavision. *Underwater photography:* Lamar Boren. *Editor:* Harold F. Kress. *Music:* Henry Mancini. *Song:* 'Easy, Baby' by Henry Mancini, Alan Bergman and Marilyn Bergman, sung by Jim Gilstrap. *Associate producer:* Mickey Borofsky. *Production manager:* Melvin B. Dellar. *Underwater director:* Paul Stader. *Art director:* Herman Blumenthal. *Set decoration:* Jerry Wunderlich. *Special effects:* Ira Anderson Jr and Paul Pollard Sr. *Stunt co-ordinator:* Glenn Anderson. *Assistant directors:* Kurt Neumann and Lorin B. Salob. *Running time:* 98 minutes. *Cert:* AA. In DeLuxe colour. *Production company:* Joe Wizan/Vashon.

Harry Crown	Richard Harris	*Clara*	Janice Heiden
Uncle Frank	Edmond O'Brien	*North*	Max Kleven
Big Eddie	Bradford Dillman	*Guard*	Karl Lukas
Buffy	Ann Turkel	*Burt*	Anthony Brubaker
Marvin "Claw"		*Shoes*	Jerry Summers
Zuckerman	Chuck Connors	*Jake*	Roy Jenson
Dolly	Constance Ford	*Driver*	Bennie Dobbins
Tony	David Hall	*Gunman*	Chuck Robertson
Baby	Kathrine Baumann		

Released in some markets as *Call Harry Crown*.

Gulliver's Travels (EMI, Great Britain, 1976)

Director: Peter Hunt. *Producers:* Raymond Leblanc and Derek Horne. *Executive producer:* Josef Shaftel. *Screenplay:* Don Black, based on the novel by Jonathan Swift. *Photography:* Alan Hume. *Animation directors:* Nic Broca, Marcel Colbrant, Vivian Miessen, Louis-Michel Carpentier and Jose Abel. *Editors:* Ron Pope and Robert Richardson. *Production designer:* Michael Stringer. *Art director:* Norman Dorme. *Modeller:* John Burke. *Music:* Michel Legrand. *Songs:* Don Black (performers uncredited). *Running time:* 81 minutes. *Cert:* U. In Eastman colour. *Production company:* Valeness-Belvision.

Lemuel Gulliver	Richard Harris	*Father*	Norman Shelley
Mary Gulliver	Catherine Schell	*Uncle*	Meredith Edwards

and the voices of Michael Bates, Denise Bryer, Julian Glover, Stephen Jack, Bessie Love, Murray Melvin, Nancy Nevison, Robert Rietty, Norman Shelley, Vladek Sheyball, Roger Snowdon, Bernard Spear and Graham Stark.

Robin and Marian (Columbia-Warner, United States, 1976)

Director: Richard Lester. *Producer:* Denis O'Dell. *Executive producer:*

Richard Shepherd. *Screenplay:* James Goldman. *Photography:* David Watkin. *Editor:* John Victor Smith. *Music:* John Barry. *Production designer:* Michael Stringer. *Art director:* Gil Perondo. *Fight arrangers:* William Hobbs and Ian McKay. *Stunt sequences:* Miguel Pedregosa and Joaquin Parra. *Assistant director:* Jose Lopez Rodero. *Running time:* 107 minutes. *Cert:* A. In colour. *Production company:* Raster, for Columbia.

Robin Hood	Sean Connery	*Old Defender*	Esmond Knight
Maid Marian	Audrey Hepburn	*Sister Mary*	Veronica Quilligan
Sheriff of		*Surgeon*	Peter Butterworth
Nottingham	Robert Shaw	*Jack*	John Barrett
King Richard	Richard Harris	*Jack's apprentice*	Kenneth Cranham
Little John	Nicol Williamson	*Queen Isabella*	Victoria Merida
Will Scarlett	Denholm Elliott		Roja
Sir Ranulf	Kenneth Haigh	*1st Sister*	Montserrat Julio
Friar Tuck	Ronnie Barker	*2nd Sister*	Victoria Hernandez
King John	Ian Holm		Sanguino
Mercadier	Bill Maynard	*3rd Sister*	Margarita Minguillon

Working title: *The Death of Robin Hood.*

Echoes of a Summer (United Artists, USA/Canada, 1975)
Director: Don Taylor. *Producer:* Robert L. Joseph. *Executive producers:* Sandy Howard and Richard Harris. *Screenplay:* Robert L. Joseph. *Photography:* John Coquillon. *Editor:* Michael F. Anderson. *Music:* Terry James. *Song:* 'The Last Castle', written and sung by Richard Harris. *Associate producers:* Dermot Harris and Muriel Bradley. *Production supervisor:* Terry Morse Jr. *Production co-ordinator:* Chip Fowler. *Costumes:* Ron Talsky. *Running time:* 98 minutes. *Cert:* A. In Eastman colour. *Production company:* Beata Filmco. A Castle Service Co. feature. In association with Astral Bellevue Pathé, Bryanston Distribution Inc.

Eugene Striden	Richard Harris	*Dr Hallett*	William Windon
Ruth Striden	Lois Nettleton	*Phillip Anding*	Brad Savage
Sara	Geraldine Fitzgerald	*Deirdre*	Jodie Foster

Working title: *The Last Castle.*

Return of a Man Called Horse (United Artists, United States, 1976)
Director: Irvin Kershner. *Producer:* Terry Morse Jr. *Executive producers:* Sandy Howard and Richard Harris. *Screenplay:* Jack De Witt, based on a character from the story 'A Man Called Horse' by Dorothy M. Johnson. *Photography:* Owen Roizman in Panavision. *Additional photography:* Ron Taylor and Jorge Stahl. *Editor:* Michael Kahn. *Production designer:* Stewart Campbell. *Set decoration:* Ernesto Carrasco. *Music:* Laurence Rosenthal. *Costumes:* Dick La Motte and Yvonne Wood. *Special make-up:* Burman Studio. *Make-up supervisor:* Del Armstrong. *Associate producer:* Theodore R. Parvin. *Production co-ordinator:* Lisabeth Plannette. *Production managers:* Hal Galli and Alberto Ferrer. *2nd unit*

director: Michael D. Moore. *Stunt co-ordinator:* Mickey Gilbert. *Assistant directors:* Fred Brost and Mario Cisneros. *Running time:* 125 minutes. *Cert:* AA. In DeLuxe colour. *Production company:* Sandy Howard Productions.

John Morgan	Richard Harris	Moonstar	Ana De Sade
Elk Woman	Gale Sondergaard	Standing Bear	Pedro Damien
Zenas Morro	Geoffrey Lewis	Thin Dog	Humberto Lopez-Pineda
Tom Gryce	Bill Lucking	Grey Thorn	Patricai Reyes Spindola
Running Bull	Jorge Luke	Lame Wolf	Regino Herrerra
Chemin D'Fer	Claudio Brook	Owl	Rigoberto Rico
Raven	Enrique Lucero	Red Cloud	Alberto Mariscal
Blacksmith	Jorge Russek	Brown Dove	Eugenia Dolores

Orca – Killer Whale (EMI, United States, 1977)

Director: Michael Anderson. *Producer:* Luciano Vincenzoni. *Screenplay:* Luciano Vincenzoni and Sergio Donati. *Photography:* Ted Moore in Panavision. *Underwater photography:* Vittorio Dragonetti. *Whale sequences:* J. Barry Herron. *Shark sequences:* Ron Taylor. *Editors:* Ralph E. Winters, John Bloom and Marion Rothman. *Special photographic effects:* Frank Van Der Veer. *Music:* Ennio Morricone. *Song:* 'My Love, We Are One' by Ennio Morricone and Carol Connors. *Production designer:* Mario Garbuglia. *Set decoration:* Armando Scarano. *Art directors:* Boris Juraga and Ferdinando Giovannoni. *Production managers:* Stanley Neufeld and William O'Sullivan. *Post-production supervisor:* Phil Tucker. *2nd unit/underwater director:* Folco Quilici. *Miniature coordinator:* Fernando Valento. *Special effects:* Alex C. Weldon. *Chemical effects:* Rinaldo Campoli. *Mechanical effects:* Jim Hole and Giuseppe Carozza. *Costumes:* Jost Jakob. *Make-up:* Neville Smallwood. *Titles:* Van Der Veer Photo. *Assistant directors:* Brian Cook, Peter Bennett, Terry Needham (*2nd unit:* Rob Lockwood and Flondar Brunelli). *Running time:* 92 minutes. *Cert:* A. In Technicolor. *Production company:* Famous Films. A Dino De Laurentiis Presentation.

Captain Nolan	Richard Harris	Ken	Robert Carradine
Rachel Bedrod	Charlotte Rampling	Paul	Peter Hooten
Umilak	Will Sampson	Priest	Arnold Wayne Heffley
Annie	Bo Derek	Gas Station	
Novak	Keenan Wynn	Attendant	Vincent S. Gentile
Swain	Scott Walker	Dock Worker	Don "Red" Barry

The Cassandra Crossing (20th Century-Fox, Great Britain/Italy/West Germany, 1977)

Director: George Pan Cosmatos. *Producers:* Lew Grade and Carlo Ponti. *Executive producer:* Giancarlo Pettini. *Screenplay:* Tom Mankiewicz, Robert Katz and George Pan Cosmatos. *Story:* Robert Katz and George Pan Cosmatos. *Photography:* Ennio Guarnieri in Panavision. *Editors:* Françoise Bonnot, Roberto Silvi and Cesare D'Amico. *Music:* Jerry

Goldsmith. *Song:* 'I'm Still on My Way' by Dave Jordan. *Aerial photography:* Ron Goodwin. *Additional photography:* Sergio Salvati. *Production designer:* Aurelio Crugnola. *Set decoration:* Mario Liverani. *Models supervisor:* Aurelio Crugnola. *Special effects:* Aldo Gasparri and Roberto Pignotti. *Train effects:* Transacord Ltd. *Production supervisor:* Mara Blasetti. *Production managers:* Cristina Luescher (Switzerland), Jean Pieuchot (France). *Assistant directors:* Joe Pollini, Tony Brandt and Antonio Gabrielli. *Running time:* 129 minutes. *Cert:* A. In Technicolor. *Production company:* Associated General Films (London)/Campagnia Cinematografica Champion (Rome). For International Ciné Productions (Munich).

Jennifer Rispoli Chamberlain	Sophia Loren	*Father Haley*	O. J. Simpson
Dr Jonathan Chamberlain	Richard Harris	*Conductor*	Lionel Stander
Nicole Dressler	Ava Gardner	*Tom*	*Ray Lovelock*
Colonel Mackenzie	Burt Lancaster	*Mrs Chadwick*	Alida Valli
Robby Navarro	Martin Sheen	*Captain Scott*	Tom Hunter
Dr Stradner	Ingrid Thulin	*Swedish Ambulance Driver*	Lou Castel
Herman Kaplan	Lee Strasberg	*Attendant*	Stefano Patrizi
Major Stack	John Phillip Law	*Patient*	Carlo De Mejo
Susan	Ann Turkel	*Katherine*	Fausta Avelli

Golden Rendezvous (Rank, United States, 1977)

Director: Ashley Lazarus. *Producer:* André Pieterse. *Executive producer:* Murray Frank. *Screenplay:* Stanley Price, based on the novel by Alistair MacLean. *Adaptation:* John Gay. *Photography:* Ken Higgins. *Editor:* Ralph Kemplen. *Music:* Jeff Wayne. *Music consultant:* Milton Okun. *Art director:* Frank White. *Associate producer:* Robert Porter. *Production manager:* Douglas Twiddy. *Assistant directors:* Brian Cook, Terry Needham and Peter Bennett. *Running time:* 103 minutes. *Cert:* A. In colour. *Production company:* Fil Trust-Milton Okun Productions/Golden Rendezvous Productions.

John Carter	Richard Harris	*Howard Taubman*	Robert Beatty
Susan Beresford	Ann Turkel	*Benson*	Michael Howard
Charles Conway	David Janssen	*McCloskey*	Ian Yule
Van Heurden	Burgess Meredith	*Captain of Unicorn 1*	Hugh Rouse
Luis Carreras	John Vernon		
Dr Marston	Gordon Jackson	*1st Officer of Unicorn 1*	Ian Hamilton
Preston	Keith Baxter	*Browning*	Richard Cox
Elizabeth Taubman	Dorothy Malone	*Passenger*	Shelagh Holliday
Fairweather	John Carradine	*Agente*	Philip Boucher
Captain Bullen	Robert Flemyng	*Gomez*	Paul Malherbe
Tony Cerdan	Leigh Lawson		

The Wild Geese (Rank, Great Britain, 1978)

Director: Andrew V. McLaglen. *Producer:* Euan Lloyd. *Screenplay:* Reginald Rose, based on the novel by Daniel Carney. *Photography:*

Jack Hildyard in Panavision. *Editor/2nd unit director:* John Glen. *Music:* Roy Budd. *Title song:* Joan Armatrading. *Military and technical adviser:* Colonel Mike Hoare. *Production designer:* Syd Cain. *Costumes:* Elsa Fennell. *Action arranger:* Bob Simons. *Associate producer:* Chris Chrisafis. *Running time:* 134 minutes. *Cert:* AA. In colour. *Production company:* Richmond Film Productions (West) for Varius Entertainment Trading Co. SA.

Colonel Allen Faulkner	Richard Burton	*Mr Martin*	Jeff Corey
Shawn Flynn	Roger Moore	*Jock*	Ronald Fraser
Rafer Janders	Richard Harris	*Tosh*	Ian Yule
Pieter Coetzee	Hardy Kruger	*Samuels*	Brook Williams
Sir Edward Matherson	Stewart Granger	*Keith*	Percy Herbert
RSM Sandy Young	Jack Watson	*Rushton*	Patrick Allen
President Limbani	Winston Ntshona	*Eposito*	Glynn Baker
Jesse	John Kani	*Heather*	Rosalind Lloyd
Witty	Kenneth Griffith	*Mrs Young*	Jane Hylton
The Priest	Frank Finlay	*Sonny*	David Ladd
Balfour	Barry Foster	*Emile*	Paul Spurrier

Game for Vultures (Columbia-EMI-Warner, Great Britain, 1979)

Director: James Fargo. *Producer:* Hazel Adair. *Executive producer:* Phillip Baird. *Screenplay:* Phillip Baird, based on the novel by Michael Hartmann. *Photography:* Alex Thomson. *Editor:* Peter Tanner. *Music:* John Filed and Tony Duhig. *Additional arrangements:* Wilf Gibson. *Art director:* Herbert Smith. *Set decoration:* Vernon Dixon. *Production controller:* Jack Smith. *Production manager:* Ed Harper. *Stunt co-ordinator:* George Leech. *Armourer:* Sam Bartram. *Assistant directors:* Gus Agosti, Iain Whyte and Mike Stiebel. *Running time:* 106 minutes. *Cert:* X. In colour. *Production company:* Pyramid Films. For Caris Enterprises (Zurich).

David Swansey	Richard Harris	*Sergeant Peter Swansey*	John Parsonsno
Gideon Marunga	Richard Roundtree	*Alice Kaymore*	Alibe Parsons
Nicolle	Joan Collins	*Tony Knight*	Neil Hallett
Colonel Brettle	Ray Milland	*Sixpence*	Ken Gampu
Larry Prescott	Bertil Taube	*Ted Mallan*	Victor Melleney
Raglan Thistle	Denholm Elliott	*Ronnie Harken*	Graham Armitage
Ruth Swansey	Jana Cilliers	*Brigid*	Elaine Proctor
Danny Batten	Tony Osoba	*Nyemba*	Simon Sabela

and with Mark Singleton, Patrick Mynhardt, Wilson Dunster, Joe Mafela, Ndaba Mhlongo, Pieter van Dissel, Charles Comyn, Richard Haines, Peter Elliott, John Malherbe, Sam Williams, Elijah Dlamimi, Chris Chittell, Ian Steadman, Mervyn John, Kenneth Hendel, Kevin Basel, John Boulter, Tim Heale, Ryno Hattingh, Alan Smart, Hal Orlandini, Daniel Yeni and Tobie Cronje.

The Ravagers (Columbia, United States, 1979)

Director: Richard Compton. *Producer:* John W. Hyde. *Executive producer:* Saul David. *Screenplay:* Donald S. Sanford, based on the novel *Path to*

Savagery by Robert Edmond Alter. *Photography:* Vincent Salzis. *Editor:* Maury Winetrobe. *Production designer:* Ronald E. Hobbs. *Costumes:* Ron Talsky. *Assistant directors:* Pat Kehoe and Fred Karlin. *Running time:* 91 minutes. *Rating:* PG. In Metrocolour. *Production company:* Columbia.

Falk	Richard Harris	Leader	Anthony James
Faina	Ann Turkel	Brown	Woody Strode
Sergeant	Art Carney	Miriam	Alana Hamilton
Rann	Ernest Borgnine	Blind Man	Seymour Cassel

High Point (ICM, United States, 1980)

Director: Peter Carter. *Producer:* Daniel M. Fine. *Executive producers:* William J. Immerman and Jerry Pam. *Screenplay:* Richard Guttman and Ian Sutherland. *Story:* Richard Guttman. *Photography:* Albert J. Dunk. *Music:* John Addison. *Production designer:* Seamus Flannery. *Associate producer:* Robert J. Opekar. *Production company:* Highpoint Film Productions Inc.

Kinney	Richard Harris	Dietrich	Bill Lynn
James Hatcher	Christopher Plummer	Prisoner/Agent	David Calderisi
Lise	Beverly D'Angelo	Henchman 1	Eric House
Mrs Hatcher	Kate Reid	Model 1	Lynda Mason Green
Don Manzarella	Peter Donat	Man with briefcase	Ken James
Banner	Robin Gammell	Prison Guard	Frank Gibbs
Falco	Maury Chaykin	Freightman 1	Ardon Bess
Centino	Saul Rubinek	Freightman 2	Steve Pernie
Alex	George Buza	Patrolman 1	Bill Starr
Molotov	Louis Negin	Patrolman 2	Jack Van Evera

and with Trent Dolan, Susan Connors, Devon Britton, Kathy Deckard, Sallianne Spence, Margaret Doty, Roger Periard, Dar Robinson and Terry Leonard.

The Last Word (United States, 1980)

Director: Roy Boulting. *Producers:* Richard C. Abramson and Michael C. Varhol. *Screenplay:* Michael Varhol, Greg Smith and L. M. Kit Carson, based on a story by Horatius Hareberle. *Photography:* Jules Brenner. *Editor:* George Grenville. *Music:* Carol Lees. *Production designer:* Jack Collis. *Set decorator:* Dennis Peeples. *Special effects:* Henry Millar. *Running time:* 105 minutes. *No MPAA rating.* In colour. *Production company:* A Variety International Pictures Inc. release.

Danny Travis	Richard Harris	Governor David	Biff McGuire
Paula Herbert	Karen Black	Roger	Christopher Guest
Captain Garrity	Martin Landau	Denise Travis	Penelope Milford
Ben Travis	Dennis Christopher		

Released in some markets as *Danny Travis.* Working title: *The Number.*

Your Ticket Is No Longer Valid (Canada, 1980)
Director: George Kaczender. *Producers:* Robert Lantos and Stephen J. Roth. *Executive producer:* Robert Halmi. *Screenplay:* Leila Basen and Ian McLellan Hunter, from the novel by Romain Gary. *Photography:* Miklos Lente. *Editor:* Peter Sintonick. *Production designer:* Claude Bonnière. *Associate producer:* Wendy Grean. *Production manager:* Lyse Lafontaine. *Running time:* 90 minutes approx. In colour. *Production company:* RSL Films Ltd/CFDC.

With Richard Harris, Jeanne Moreau, George Peppard, Jennifer Dale, Winston Reckert, George Touliatos, Alexandra Stewart. Working title: *Finishing Touch*.

Tarzan, the Ape Man (CIC, United States, 1981)
Director: John Derek. *Producer:* Bo Derek. *Screenplay:* Tom Rowe and Gary Goddard, based on the characters created by Edgar Rice Burroughs. *Photography:* John Derek. *Editor:* James B. Ling. *Music:* Perry Botkin. *Musical supervision:* Harry V. Lojewski. *Music consultant:* Dan Carlin Jr. *Art director:* Alan Roderick-Jones. *Titles:* Burke Mattsson. *Title art:* James L. Michaelson, (Svengali card) Frank Frazetta. *Technical adviser* (mountain climbing): Allan Placko. *Stunt co-ordinator:* Jock O'Mahoney. *Head animal trainer:* Paul Reynolds, assisted by Fess Reynolds, Bill Gage, David McMillan and Joe Campassi. *Production executive:* Eva Chun. *Production co-ordinator:* (Sri Lanka) Chandran Rutnam. *Assistant directors:* Jack Oliver, Michael Lally and Warner Warnasiri. *Running time:* 112 minutes. *Cert:* AA. In Metrocolor. *Production company:* Svengali. For MGM.

Jane Parker	Bo Derek	Riano	Maxime Philoe
James Parker	Richard Harris	Feathers	Leonard Bailey
Harry Holt	John Phillip Law	Club Members	Wilfred Hyde-White
Tarzan	Miles O'Keeffe		Laurie Mains and
Nambia	Akushula Selayah		Harold Ayer
Ivory King	Steven Strong		

Triumphs of a Man Called Horse (VTC, Spain, 1982)
Director: John Hough. *Producer:* Derek Gibson. *Executive producer:* Sandy Howard. *Screenplay:* Ken Blackwell and Carlos Aured, based on a story by Jack De Witt, based on characters created by Dorothy M. Johnson, Jack De Witt and Miriam De Witt. *Photography:* John Alcott and John Cabrera. *Special photography:* Peter Collister and Dwight Little. *Editor:* Roy Watts. *Assembly editor:* John Currin. *Production designer:* Alan Roderick-Jones. *Art director:* Marilyn Taylor. *Special effects:* Frederico Farfan Sr, Jorge Farfan and Frederico Farfan Jr. *Music:* Georges Garvarentz. *Musical director:* Patrick Shart. *Song:* 'He's Comin' Back' by Georges Garvarentz and Buddy Kaye, performed

by Rita Coolidge. *Costumes:* Betty Pecha Madden. *Creative consultant:* Sandra Bailey. *Stunts:* Peter Cox, Cliff Happy, Marguerite Happy, Yolanda Ponce, Larry Randles, David Rodgers, Ben Scott, Joe Stone, Greg Walker and Raul Martinez.

John Morgan	Richard Harris	*Elk Woman*	Anne Seymour
Koda	Michael Beck	*Big Bear*	Miguel Angel Fuentes
Redwing	Ana De Sade	*Eye of the Bull*	Regino Herrera
Captain Cummings	Vaughn Armstrong	*Perkins*	Lauturo Murua
Sergeant Bridges	Buck Taylor	*Durand*	Roger Cudney
Private Mullins	Sebastian Ligarde	*Gance*	Simon Andreu

Martin's Day (MGM/UA, United States, 1985)

Director: Alan Gibson. *Producers:* Richard F. Dalton and Roy Krost. *Screenplay:* Allan Scott and Chris Bryant. *Photography:* Frank Watts. *Editor:* David deWilde. *Music:* Wilfred Josephs. *Production designer:* Trevor Williams. *Set decorator:* Steve Shewchuk. *Costumes:* Lynne Mackay. *Assistant director:* Bill Corcoran. *Running time:* 98 minutes. *Rating:* PG. In Medallion Color. *Production company:* World Film Services production. UA Entertainment of a United Artists presentation.

Martin Steckert	Richard Harris	*Martin*	Justin Henry
Dr Mennen	Lindsay Wagner	*Karen*	Karen Black
Lt Lardner	James Coburn	*Brewer*	John Ireland

Maigret (HTV, Great Britain, 1988)

Director: Paul Lynch. *Producers:* Patrick Dromgoole and Johnny Goodman for HTV; Robert Cooper and Arthur Weingarten for Robert Cooper Entertainment. *Screenplay:* Arthur Weingarten, based on the character created by Georges Simenon. *Photography:* Bob Edwards. *Art director:* Steve Groves. *Production designer:* Caroline Smith. *Running time:* 95 minutes approx. In colour. *Production company:* HTV/Robert Cooper Entertainment.

with Richard Harris, Patrick O'Neill, Victoria Tennant, Ian Ogilvy, Barbara Shelley, Eric Deacon, Andrew McCulloch, Dominique Barnes, Lachelle Carl, Vernon Dobtcheff, Mark Audley, Annette Andres, Don Henderson, Richard Durden, Eve Ferrett and Caroline Munro.
TV distribution only.

Mack the Knife (United States, 1989)

Director: Menaham Golan. *Producer:* Stanley Chase. *Executive producers:* Menahem Golan and Yoram Globus. *Screenplay:* Menahem Golan, based on *The Threepenny Opera* by Bertholt Brecht and Kurt Weill. *Photography:* Elemer Ragalyi. *Editor:* Alain Jakubowicz. *Musical director:* Dov Seltzer. *Choreography:* David Toguri. *Production designer:* Tivadar Bertalan. *Costumes:* John Bloomfield. *Assistant directors:* Avner Orshalimy and Gabor Varadi. *Running time:* 120 minutes. *Rating:*

PG-13. In Magyar Color. *Prints by* Rank. *Production company:* 21st Century Film Corporation.

MacHeath	Raul Julia	*Polly Peachum*	Rachel Robertson
Mr Peachum	Richard Harris	*Money Matthew*	Clive Revill
Jenny	Julia Migenes	*Tiger Brown*	Bill Nighy
Street Singer	Roger Daltry	*Lucy*	Erin Donovan
Mrs Peachum	Julie Walters	*Coaxer*	Julie T. Wallace

King of the Wind (HTV, Great Britain, 1990)
Director: Peter Duffell. *Producers:* Michael Guest, Paul Sarony, Peter Davis and William Panzer. *Executive producers:* Patrick Dromgoole and Johnny Goodman. *Screenplay:* Phil Frey, based on Marguerite Henry's novel. *Photography:* Brian Morgan. *Production designer:* Ken Sharp. *Art director:* Steve Groves. *Running time:* 90 minutes approx. In colour. *Production company:* HTV/Davis Panzer Productions Inc.

with Richard Harris, Frank Finlay, Jenny Agutter, Nigel Hawthorne, Ralph Bates, Neil Dickson, Barry Foster, Jill Gascoine, Anthony Quayle, Ian Richardson, Peter Vaughan, Ben Aris, Dicken Ashworth, Terence Connoley, Susie Cooper, Mark Dawson, John Forgham, Joan Hickson, Nick Gillard, Melvin Hayes, Hilton McRae, David Raine, Richard Ridings, Courtnay Roper-Night, Paul Spurrier, Barry Stanton.
TV distribution only.

The Field (Ferndale Great Britain/Eire, 1990)
Director: Jim Sheridan. *Producer:* Noel Pearson. *Executive producer:* Steve Morrison. *Screenplay:* Jim Sheridan, based on the stage play by John B. Keane. *Photography:* Jack Conroy. *Production manager:* Mary Alleguen. *Art director:* Frank Halligan Flood. *Set dresser:* Josie MacAvin. *Editor:* Pat Duffner. *1st assistant director:* Kevan Barker. *Running time:* 108 minutes. *Production company:* Noel Pearson/Granada Production.

Bull McCabe	Richard Harris	*Father Doran*	Sean McGinley
Bird O'Donnell	John Hurt	*Flanagan*	John Cowley
American	Tom Berenger	*Sergeant*	Malachy McCourt
Tadgh McCabe	Sean Bean	*Dan Peader Andy*	Eamon Keane
Young Widow	Frances Tomelty	*Woman Tinker*	Ruth McCabe
Maggie	Brenda Fricker	*Woman Tinker 2*	Joan Sheehy
Redhead	Jenny Conroy		

Additional Television Work

Richard Harris has appeared extensively on television over the years. Apart from his major TV movie credits listed above, he starred in the Granada TV play *The Iron Harp* (1957), the football documentary *Today Mexico, Tomorrow the World* (1972) and the interview tribute *Lerner and Loewe* (1983).

He has made numerous appearances on talk shows, ranging from

Ed Sullivan, Milton Berle and Johnny Carson in the United States, to Michael Parkinson and Michael Aspel in the UK.

His stage version of *Camelot* was filmed and screened by Home Box Office in the United States in 1982 (produced by Don Gregory and Mike Merrick; directed by Marty Callner; co-starring Meg Bussert and Richard Muenz).

Theatre Credits

Early walk-on parts in Kilkee and Limerick are not listed. Neither is his student production of *Julius Caesar* at Scranton University (see p. 219 for details).

Easter by August Strindberg. At the Playhouse, Limerick, 1947. As Sebastian.

Winter Journey (based on *The Country Girl*) by Clifford Odets. At the Irving Theatre, London, 1956. Directed by Harris.

The Quare Fellow by Brendan Behan. At the Comedy Theatre, London, 1956. As Mickser.

Macbeth by William Shakespeare. At the Theatre Royal, Stratford East, London; Zurich and Moscow tour also, 1957. As Ross.

You Won't Always Be on Top by Henry Chapman. At the Theatre Royal, Stratford East, London, 1957. As Mick.

And the Wind Blew by Edgar de Rocha Miranda. At the Theatre Royal, Stratford East, London, 1957. As Monsignor Gusmao.

Man, Beast and Virtue by Luigi Pirandello. At the Theatre Royal, Stratford East, London, and the Lyric Theatre, Hammersmith, London, 1958. As Paulino.

Love and Lectures (the Bernard Shaw–Ellen Terry Letters). At the Theatre Royal, Stratford East, London, 1958. As Bernard Shaw.

The Pier by James Forsyth. At the Bristol Old Vic, 1958. As Tommy Ledou.

Fings Ain't Wot They Used T'be by Frank Norman and Lionel Bart. At the Theatre Royal, Stratford East, London, 1959. As Sergeant Collins and as George.

The Dutch Courtesan by John Marston. At the Theatre Royal, Stratford East, London, 1959. As Malheureux.

The Ginger Man by J. P. Donleavy. At the Fortune Theatre, London, and the Gaiety Theatre, Dublin, 1959. As Sebastian Dangerfield.

Diary of a Madman by Nikolai Gogol. At the Royal Court Theatre, London, 1963. As Aksenti Ivanovitch.

Camelot by Alan Jay Lerner and Frederick Loewe. United States tour, 1981–2. Apollo Victoria Theatre, London, 1982. Also worldwide tour, including Japan and Australia, 1986. As King Arthur.

Henry IV by Luigi Pirandello. British tour and Wyndham's Theatre, London, 1990. As Henry IV.

Discography

Based on British album and single releases.

Singles

'MacArthur Park'/'Paper Chase'. RCA 1699. Released June 1968.

'How to Handle a Woman'/'I Wonder What the King Is Doing Tonight'. Warner Bros 7215. Released August 1968.

'Didn't We'/'In the Final Hours'. RCA 1733. Released September 1968.

'The Yard Went On Forever'/'Lucky Me'. Stateside SS8001. Released November 1968.

'One of the Nicer Things'/'Watermark'. Stateside SS8016. Released March 1969.

'Fill the World with Love'/'What a Lot of Flowers'. Stateside SS8032. Released November 1969.

'Ballad of a Man Called Horse'/'The Morning of the Mourning for Another Kennedy'. Stateside SS8054. Released July 1970.

'I Don't Have to Tell You'/'How I Spent My Summer'. Probe PRO581. Released March 1973.

Albums

Camelot. Original Motion Picture Soundtrack with Franco Nero and Vanessa Redgrave. Warner Bros. WS1712. Released August 1968.

A Tramp Shining. RCA SF 7947. Released August 1968.

The Yard Went On Forever. Stateside SSL 5001. Released December 1968.

Richard Harris Love Album. Stateside SSL 5025. Released September 1970.

Bloomfield. Original Motion Picture Soundtrack. Pye NSPL 18376. Released December 1970.

My Boy. Probe. SPBA 6263. Released February 1972.

Tommy. Orchestral version produced by Lou Reizner. Ode 99001. Released November 1972.

Slides. Probe. SPBA 6269. Released March 1973.

His Greatest Performances. Probe. SPB 1075. Released August 1973.

Jonathan Livingstone Seagull. CBS 69047. Released August 1973.

I, in the Membership of My Days. Mostly poetry album. ABC. ABCL
5056. Released August 1974.

The Prophet. Atlantic. K50109. Released January 1975.

MacArthur Park. Compilation re-release. Music for Pleasure. MFP50521.
Released January 1976.

Camelot. London stage cast. That's Entertainment Records. TER 1030.
Released April 1983.

Index

THE
SEVEN
MOODS
OF
CRAFT
SPIRITS

THE SEVEN MOODS OF CRAFT SPIRITS

350 GREAT CRAFT SPIRITS FROM AROUND THE WORLD

Dominic Roskrow

8
eightbooks

eightbooks

First published in 2018
by Eight Books Limited
22 Herbert Gardens
London NW10 3BU
info@8books.co.uk
www.8books.co.uk

A catalogue record for this book is available from the British
Library.

ISBN 978-1-9998583-2-2

Printed in China

FSC
www.fsc.org
MIX
Paper from
responsible sources
FSC® C016973

The publisher would like to thank the students and staff at the University for the Creative Arts, Canterbury.
Illustrations:
Ellie Beer, eleanor.i.beer@gmail.com: 29, 31, 33, 34, 36, 38, 42, 43, 44, 45, 46, 50, 67, 69, 71, 79, 81, 84, 85, 86, 87, 149, 153, 166, 167, 168, 169, 172, 173, 176, 177, 178, 179, 180, 182, 186, 187.
Natasha Collins, tashfayecol13@gmail.com: 30, 32, 36, 42, 42, 43, 47, 51, 89, 90, 92, 94, 97, 97, 99, 101, 103, 107, 112, 123, 195, 197, 200, 201, 202, 204, 207, 208, 211, 211, 212.
Panayiotis Drakos, fender81@windowslive.com: 143, 144, 146, 147, 148, 150, 151, 155, 156, 157, 159, 160, 163, 168, 169, 169, 170, 171, 172, 173, 173, 175, 176, 177, 180, 182, 185, 187, 187, 194.
Josh Earles, joshuae007@hotmail.co.uk: 28, 30, 31, 34, 35, 39, 40, 49, 58, 63, 66, 66, 68, 72, 74, 74, 79, 80, 96, 108, 171, 172, 177, 179, 180, 183, 191(all), 196, 197, 200, 201, 204.
Jessica Hallam, jesshallam0527@gmail.com: 28, 30, 33, 35, 39, 43, 51, 62, 65, 66, 75, 76, 115, 118, 122, 123, 126, 128, 143, 145, 147, 148, 151, 151, 154, 160, 163.
Megan G Hampton, meganhampton1@hotmail.com: 12, 13, 14, 15, 16, 17, 18, 19, 49, 58, 59, 60, 69, 72, 74, 75, 76, 80, 88, 89, 88, 92, 94, 95, 95, 98, 105, 106, 64, 67, 81, 107, 109, 115, 118, 119, 120, 124, 124, 125, 129, 131, 134, 134, 137, 142, 142.
Carmen-Alexandra Mitu, carmenalexandra.mitu@yahoo.com: 28, 29, 32, 33, 34, 35, 38, 40, 44, 47, 65, 65, 67, 81, 116, 121, 133, 135, 137, 144, 147, 148, 150, 152, 156, 157, 158, 158, 161, 163.
Rena, iren.r@hotmail.co.uk: 54, 56, 71, 73, 91, 114, 127, 130, 131, 143, 144, 154, 157, 160, 168, 171, 174, 175, 181, 181, 182, 184, 185, 198, 203, 206, 207, 209, 210, 210, 213.
Madison Salgado, maddylmsalgado@gmail.com: 114, 114, 118, 119, 120, 122, 125, 127, 130, 130, 132, 132, 136, 137, 146, 150, 152, 152, 159, 162, 192, 193, 195, 197, 199, 201, 204, 205, 207, 209, 210, 212, 213, 214.
Katy Streeter, illustreeter@gmail.com: 20, 22, 24, 26, 48, 61, 64, 75, 77, 78, 78, 80, 88, 90, 91, 97, 98, 99, 100, 100, 100, 103, 104, 104, 106, 115, 119, 123, 124, 129, 136, 140, 162, 162, 176, 196, 214.

CONTENTS

INTRODUCTION

IN THE MOOD FOR SPIRIT

Craft has become big business, the fashion buzzword of the moment. And the hippest, most stylish, and most sought-after part of the world of craft is craft distilling, or to use its other name, micro-distilling.

Over the many months of talking and tasting all things craft, I asked a string of distillers, brewers, drinks producers, publicists, and fellow writers what craft actually meant, and I was made aware of two contradictory facts. One, absolutely everyone knew what it was and would recognize it if they saw it; and two, nobody could provide a suitable definition for it. The exceptions were those who had concluded that actually there was no such thing as craft.

A micro-distillery is defined by Wikipedia as 'a small, often boutique-style distillery established to produce beverage-grade spirit alcohol in relatively small quantities, usually single batches (as opposed to larger distillers' continuous distilling process)'.

Given that all the single malt whisky made in Scotland, no matter how big the distillery is or who owns it, is made in batches, one must assume that the author of this definition is not

Scottish. And it's clearly nonsense. Distilling in batches on pot stills is what they do at Glenfiddich, and with an output of more than 2 million gallons (10 million liters) a year, that's hardly micro-distilling. Conversely, many of the new American craft distillers are making vodka, gin, and bourbon on continuous stills — which means they are not making batches of spirits.

But there are other big problems with that definition, too. In fact, of all areas of craft, craft distilling is the hardest to define.

The dictionary definition of craft is 'a skill, particularly in a trade'. That works for craft distilling, but it raises another question, to wit: isn't all whisky-making a craft?

One argument says that the answer to that is 'No', because a craft distillery must be 'small'. But what on earth does that mean? Can you really put a figure on it, or are we talking about a more amorphous sense of what small is? All distilling, at whatever level, requires knowledge and skill, and at the big commercial distilleries the finest ingredients are used and the best talent employed to make the world's leading spirits brands. Is a Talisker malt whisky or an Elijah Craig 12 Year Old bourbon any less of a crafted product because they are made on a bigger scale?

Which brings up to the issue of quality.

Quality cannot be part of any definition of what a craft spirit is because, if it were, Bacardi would be a craft rum. How many of us agreed with Diageo when one of its heads claimed that Johnnie Walker was the world's biggest craft product? And conversely, a former lawyer distilling his first bourbon is highly unlikely to make anything even remotely as good as Jim Beam. While researching a book on American craft distilling, I was sent whiskeys by proud producers that were, frankly, shockingly bad. This isn't a subjective view, either. You might like roast chicken, I may like fried chicken, but we would certainly agree that neither of us likes raw chicken. And many of these whiskeys were raw chicken.

So craft isn't about size or quality, although elements of both clearly form part of our understanding of what it is.

We make more progress defining our terms when we look at one of the dictionary definitions of the word 'boutique'. The word can be used to mean 'a business serving a sophisticated or specialized clientele'.

This is much better. The definition nods toward the concept of size, but makes it an issue of demand as well as supply. The word 'business' implies a level of care and professionalism, and by using the words 'sophisticated and specialized clientele', some concept of quality is brought in to the frame.

Not only that, but there is also a strong implication that if there was a surge in demand from that sophisticated and specialized clientele, the business would still be a boutique one even if it correspondingly grew to serve the increased demand.

This is an important point. It means that craft distillers can grow and still be craft distillers, even though they are moving away from one definition of micro-distilling. In other words, they can continue to describe themselves as craft distillers for as long as they do not compromise on the original intentions and ideals laid out when the distillery was first set up.

Perhaps, then, a craft distillery can be defined as 'as any distillery which starts out as an independent boutique operation with the intention of making a bespoke and individual spirit, and which stays true to the ideals of creating premium and quality spirits no matter what happens to it'.

The last bit of this definition might seem to be a little woolly, but it needs to be because it leaves us some wriggle room when we look around the world at craft distilling.

The publishers of this book expressed a wish that the content should be global, but that the focus should be away from the large international companies. That proved easier said than done. There are tiny distilleries in far-flung parts of South America and the West Indies that are funded by international drinks giants, but which are run by the same families that have run them for generations, employing the same fifth-generation distiller as they did before the money men stepped in.

It is also the case that the extra money from big corporations may well have revived and saved a crumbling tequila business in Mexico, or a family rum business in Venezuela. When Rémy Cointreau bought small Scottish island distillery Bruichladdich, it allowed a distillery which had been working flat out to survive the luxury of closing for a few months while new stills were installed. When you drink Havana Club, you are tasting a spirit put together by a collaboration of Cuba's finest rum distillers, but it's in your hands thanks to the distribution network of drinks giant Pernod Ricard.

Ownership is a complicated business. Many rum distilleries operate in exactly the same way as they have done for hundreds of years, but they are distributed by European drinks distributors under licence. Most businesses have shareholders and are not strictly independent at all.

No matter how we choose to define craft spirits, we know them when we see them. They are everything described above, along with pride, provenance, and heritage. They are peppered with innovation and exploration, and prepared to dispense with conventional thinking. They are warm and welcoming. You have a pretty good idea that if you met their makers, you'd find that they were nice folk: enthusiastic, passionate, dedicated, and highly committed to their cause.

We no longer drink one favorite drink. We cherry-pick, and we choose our libations on the basis of the mood we happen to be in. And that's what this book is all about. Every one of the 350 spirits here has been chosen because it's ably equipped to raise your spirit, whatever your mood.

The world of spirits has traditionally been a slow-moving one: the various categories were clearly defined; the way they were consumed was pretty much set in stone. But a perfect storm is changing all that. The renewed interest in cocktail culture, a thirst for knowledge and innovation, a relaxation in laws across the world encouraging a new wave of distilleries, and a desire to seek out craft products of all natures which are unique, localized, and with a good backstory have all contributed to a surge in new distilling operations. It's self-perpetuating, too. As one former policeman or accountant proves that it is possible to live the dream, others are prepared to take the plunge. They're kicking over statues, too, questioning the old ways, and asking why you can't try new methods and create new hybrid spirits. It's exciting, vibrant, and inspiring. And it's not going to come to a halt anytime soon.

I hope this book takes you on a journey, introduces you to new friends, and does justice to all the craftsmen and craftswomen who have dedicated their lives to making us feel good.

Happy drinking. And I don't mind if I do…

Dominic Roskrow

SPIRIT TYPES

ABSINTHE — a potent, aniseed-flavored spirit traditionally made using wormwood.

AKVAVIT/AQUAVIT — normally clear or light spirit made from potatoes or other starchy products. Popular in Northern Europe. May be aged.

ARMAGNAC — a type of brandy traditionally made in Aquitaine in southwest France.

ARRACK — eastern spirit made from coco palm or rice.

BAIJIU — eastern (mainly Chinese) clear spirit made from grain.

BOURBON — American spirit made from a mash bill dominated by corn, but also likely to include wheat, malted barley, and/or rye.

BRANDY — strong spirit distilled from wine or fermented fruit juice. May be aged for long periods.

CACHAÇA — Brazilian white rum made from sugar cane.

CALVADOS — apple brandy made exclusively in the Calvados region of northern France.

COGNAC — premium-quality brandy made in the Cognac region of western France.

GENEVER/JENEVER — Dutch gin. See below.

GIN — spirit distilled from a variety of raw ingredients, including grain and potatoes, infused with botanicals, and with a flavor dominated by juniper berries.

GRAPPA — a form of brandy distilled from the mulch and skins of grapes. Normally bottled young.

HERBAL LIQUEUR — liqueur flavored with herbs and spices, often to an ancient recipe, and often for medicinal purposes. Many recipes are linked to old monastical orders.

LIQUEUR — strong, sweet spirit often used as a mixer or as an after-dinner drink.

MESCAL/MEZCAL — a specific style of Mexican spirit distilled from the juice of the agave plant.

MOONSHINE — traditionally, an illicitly distilled spirit made in the Appalachian Mountains. Now more widely used to describe un-aged American whiskey, particularly corn whiskey.

OUZO — Aniseed-flavored spirit made in Greece.

PISCO — Peruvian white brandy distilled from Muscat grapes.

POITÍN/POTEEN — traditionally an illegal Irish spirit made from anything to hand, but mainly potatoes. The term is applied today to a range of un-aged or very young Irish grain spirits.

POT STILL WHISKEY — Irish style of whiskey made from a mash bill comprising malted barley and another unmalted grain.

RAKI — a strong spirit made in Eastern Europe, Turkey, and the Middle East.

RHUM AGRICOLE — a specific style of rum made in the French Caribbean from freshly squeezed cane juice rather than molasses.

RUM — a spirit distilled from sugar cane molasses or residues.

RYE — in most countries, rye is a whisky made with at least 51 per cent rye in its mash bill. Canadian rye, however, is made with a blend of rye whiskeys and a small amount of another liquid, such as bourbon or fruit juice.

SAMBUCA — an aniseed-flavored Italian liqueur that originated in Civitavecchia. The name derives from the Latin for 'elderberry'.

SCHNAPPS — mid-European strong alcoholic drink made from grain; not unlike gin.

SHOCHU — a Japanese distilled spirit, often made from sake, but can be from a range of spirits. Often very rough.

SINGLE MALT WHISKY — spirit made from malted barley, yeast, and water from one distillery only. In Europe, single malt must be aged in oak for at least three years, but other parts of the world have far looser definitions.

SOTOL — a Mexican spirit like mescal, but derived from a specific type of agave plant.

TEQUILA — the parent spirit to mescal and sotol, and a generic term for a wide range of potent Mexican agave-derived liquors.

VODKA — spirit from the East, particularly Russia and Poland. Normally distilled from rye, wheat, or potatoes.

WHISKY/WHISKEY — a spirit made from grain, yeast, and water. In Europe these are the only ingredients, but American craft distillers describe spirits with flavors and hops as whiskey.

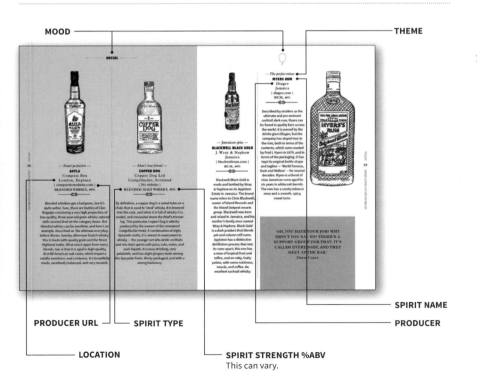

MOOD ——— THEME

PRODUCER URL ——— SPIRIT TYPE

SPIRIT NAME

PRODUCER

LOCATION

SPIRIT STRENGTH %ABV
This can vary.

SPIRITS PRODUCERS

JOHN GLASER
Compass Box
London, UK

John Glaser is a visionary, an artisan, and a pioneer. He has long argued that the age of whisky doesn't matter as long as the product tastes great, and he has been mixing malts into wonderful whiskies for years. He's currently aging whisky and seeking out the very best casks in which to do so.

TIM DUCKETT
Heartwood
Tasmania, Australia

Tim Duckett is sitting on some of the oldest whisky casks in Australia, and he releases them only when he feels they are ready. When he does, they tend to be unforgettable: high-strength, in-your-face power packs with inventive names like Convict Redemption and Vat Out of Hell.

SPIRITS PRODUCERS

ALEX CHASKO
Teeling Whiskey Co.
Dublin, Ireland

Independent whiskey-maker Teeling has changed
the game in Ireland, bringing distilling back to
the capital and introducing a new generation to
Irish whiskey. Alex Chasko has led from the front,
exploring new flavors and creating a portfolio
of outstanding whiskeys that are taking the
category into exciting areas.

MARCEL TELSER
Telser
Liechtenstein

Marcel Telser knew he wanted to make whisky,
but he was determined to do it his own way.
From the strange wooden packaging of early
bottlings to unusual cask maturation, he has
made malt that has improved hugely. He is
now in the vanguard of an exciting new Alpine
whisky movement.

SPIRITS PRODUCERS

TARQUIN LEADBETTER
Southwestern Distillery
Wadebridge, UK

There are scores of people making gin these days, but few do so with the style and panache of Cornwall's Tarquin Leadbetter. The stylish bottles, the blue wax tops, and the delicate taste all make for a unique and excellent gin; he makes a rather superb pastis, too.

DAVID ROUSSIER
Distillerie Warenghem
Lannion, France

France might not be an obvious choice for whisky production, but there are a growing number of distilleries producing good-quality whiskies of different styles across the nation, from the sweet and fruity Brenne of the Cognac region to the peaty and earthy whiskies of Glann ar Mor in Brittany. Perhaps France's finest whisky is Armorik, made by David Roussier at Distillerie Warenghem in Brittany. It has come on in leaps and bounds since David recruited the late Dr Jim Swan, and now can match some of Scotland's finest Speyside and Highland whiskies.

SPIRITS PRODUCERS

RACHEL BARRIE
BenRiach
Edinburgh, UK

Female whisky-makers are no longer a novelty, but Rachel Barrie played a pioneering role in a male-dominated world by consistently making great whisky. She propelled the malts of Glen Garioch into the premier league, turned Bowmore around, and is now making whisky for BenRiach, a rising star of a company.

ANGELA D'ORAZIO
Mackmyra
Gävle, Sweden

Angela D'Orazio is something of a Jekyll-and-Hyde character, creating easy-drinking, sweet, fruity whiskies for export on the one hand, and challenging, innovative, and remarkable limited edition releases on the other. Founded in 1999, Mackmyra was in the first wave of new distillers and grew up very much in the public eye. But the quality of the whiskies it now offers is exceptional, and each release creates excitement in the domestic market and, increasingly, beyond the frontiers of Sweden.

SPIRITS PRODUCERS

DAVID PICKERELL
Freelance consultant
Louisville, KY, USA

Scratch the surface of the American craft distilling industry, and Dave Pickerell's name will come up sooner or later. He was master distiller at Maker's Mark for 14 years, but in 2008 he started offering his distilling skills to some of America's best new distilleries, including Corsair and Whistle Pig.

DARREN ROOK
The London Distillery Company
London, UK

Darren Rook takes his business very seriously indeed. He opened London's first distillery for more than a century, and then set about creating a world-class gin using only organic ingredients. But he has years of whisky experience, and the industry is waiting for his first malt with growing excitement.

TODD AND SCOTT LEOPOLD
Leopold Bros
Denver, CO, USA

Todd and Scott first pooled their expertise to open a brewery in Ann Arbor, Michigan. When that proved a success, they branched out into spirits. In 2008, they moved to Denver, where they now successfully make a range of spirits, including vodka, gin, whiskey, liqueur, aperitivo, fernet, amaro, and absinthe.

SPIRITS PRODUCERS

HEATHER BEAN
Syntax Spirits
Greeley, CO, USA

Heather Bean is a busy woman. After 25 years in the mechanical, chemical, and software industries, in 2010 she started Syntax from scratch, and has since grown the operation so much that in 2018 it had to move to larger premises. She now offers her expertise as head distiller to some of the many newcomers to the business.

PETER BIGNELL
Belgrove Distillery
Kempton, Tasmania, Australia

What's a farmer and renowned sand and ice sculptor doing making whisky? Turning heads is the answer. Peter Bignell makes 100 per cent rye whisky from rye grown on his own land, using a still he made himself and which is fired by biofuel. This is a small but perfectly formed distillery operation.

DR BILL LUMSDEN
Glenmorangie
Edinburgh, UK

Dr Bill Lumsden is another creative master who was producing outstanding whiskies without an age statement many years ago. He has explored old styles of malt whisky, played with maturation processes, and created stunning malts such as Glenmorangie Signet, raising the bar for whisky-makers everywhere.

THESE SPIRITS ARE FUN,
SOMEWHAT FRIVOLOUS, AND
DESIGNED TO SHARE. MANY
OF THEM MIX WELL, TOO, AND
HAVE THE POTENTIAL TO BE
THE LIFE AND SOUL OF ANY
PARTY. THEY ARE LAUGHTER
AND GOOD TIMES IN A GLASS.

SOCIAL

EAST LONDON LIQUOR COMPANY
Bow, London, England
{ eastlondonliquorcompany.com }

East London Liquor Company (above) brings together a collection of young and gifted distillers making vodka, gin, and whisky. There is also a shop stocking exciting craft products, and a bar where visitors can taste cocktails made with the company's distillates; alternatively, they can choose from a rotating selection of draught and bottled beers.

MERCHANT HOUSE
London, England
{ merchanthouse.bar }

The folk behind this stylish and cosy bar reckon that they have the best selection of gins and rum in the country. That may or may not be the case, but certainly the choice is outstanding. The bar is tucked away on Bow Lane in East London, and has a speakeasy feel about it. You'll struggle to find more knowledgable staff anywhere — they know the story behind every bottle on display.

THE POT STILL
Glasgow, Scotland
{ thepotstill.co.uk }

A traditional, single-roomed Glaswegian pub which boasts a floor-to-ceiling selection of world whiskies. Scotch is to the fore, of course, but if it's good whisky, it'll find its way here. Always a good atmosphere, with locals and tourists packed together by the bar or sharing the limited seating space.

THE OLD BELL INN
Saddleworth, England
{ theoldbellinn.co.uk }

The Old Bell Inn not only boasts the largest selection of gins on the planet, it also has the Guinness World Records certificate to prove it. The pub, a few miles from Oldham in northwest England, stocks a remarkable 600 gins in its emporium. Why not book one of its 18 rooms for the weekend and indulge yourself?

THE BRITONS PROTECTION
Manchester, England
{ manchesterbars.com }

Like The Pot Still (above), the Britons Protection is a traditional boozer, and proud of it. It has a number of snug rooms, traditional pub grub, and an ever-changing selection of cask ales. But it is most noted for its huge whisky selection, and the staff pride themselves on keeping up to date with all things whisky.

TROF NQ
Manchester, England
{ trofnq.co.uk }

NQ stands for Northern Quarter, and refers to a particularly trendy area of Manchester in which there are numerous stylish bars offering a great range of craft spirits. Rare bourbons are its specialty, but you'll find all sorts of gems here from around the world.

SEVEN MOODS OF CRAFT SPIRIT   SOCIAL

WHISKYBROTHER
Johannesburg, South Africa
{ www.whiskybrother.com }

Marc Pendelbury already runs a whisky show and owns a whisky shop, so this whisky bar was his next logical step. He teamed up with local businessmen to open Whiskybrother in 2018. Scotch whisky is the main focus — the bar has more than 600 varieties of the liquor — but also has plenty to interest American whiskey fans. The bar has room for 28 covers, and there is a tasting room that can accommodate up to eight people.

ATLAS
Singapore
{ atlasbar.sg }

There are plenty of people who believe that Singapore currently has the best bar scene in the world, but even by these standards Atlas stands out. It graces the ground floor of one of Singapore's most iconic buildings, Parkview Square, and has an extraordinary choice of spirits from across the world, all delivered with panache.

HIMKOK
Oslo, Norway
{ himkok.no }

Oslo? And Himkok (left) doesn't look much from the outside, either. Inside, though, it's packed with rustic charm, it has a micro-distillery making vodka, aquavit, and gin, it specializes in Norwegian craft products, and is renowned for craft cocktails. Himkok was considered one of the world's top 20 bars in 2017.

DICK MACK'S
Dingle, Ireland
{ dickmackspub.com }

Dick Mack's is everything an Irish pub should be, and then some. Over the years, a string of Hollywood greats have graced these premises, and it's not hard to see why. The pub has a superb collection of Irish whiskeys, but it also stocks Scotch whisky and a diverse selection of other spirits.

BABA AU RUM
Athens, Greece
{ babaaurum.com }

Baba au Rum describes itself as the 'House of Spirits', and it certainly offers a strong selection of world drinks. Unsurprisingly, rum features prominently at this friendly and stylish bar, and the cocktails that contain it are of the finest quality. The place is described as a sip and savor bar rather than a party one.

VILLA KONTHOR
Limburg, Germany
{ villakonthor.de }

Limburg is home to one of the world's greatest whisky festivals, so it is fitting that the city should have a bar as good as this one. Villa Konthor specializes in wine, whisky, and…um… chocolate. It's also noted for stocking unusual spirits from independent producers, and has a number of rare and single cask bottlings.

LEYENDA
New York, NY, USA
{ leyendabk.com }

The delightfully named Ivy Mix won Best American Bartender at Tales of the Cocktail in 2017. She and her mentor, cocktail matriarch Julie Reiner, run this Latin bar and restaurant with class. Cocktails are naturally at the core of the operation, but Leyenda (above) also offers a superb selection of tequilas, mescals, other Mexican spirits, and rums.

THE FLATIRON ROOM
New York, NY, USA
{ theflatironroom.com }

A stylish and upmarket bar that stands out in a city with several great spirit-drinking venues, The Flatiron Room stocks more than 1,000 whiskies. It's geared for both the expert and the novice, it has a whisky school, and it allows regulars to keep their bottles tagged and on site so that they can always enjoy their favorite tipple.

JACK ROSE DINING SALOON
Washington, DC, USA
{ jackrosediningsaloon.com }

Jack Rose's is huge, and so is its whiskey collection. In all, there are around 2,400 different varieties from every part of the world. There is a speakeasy downstairs, where tastings are held, there are leather sofas to relax on, and the bar has regular themed promotions. All in all, this is a highly impressive whiskey operation.

DELILAH'S
Chicago, IL, USA
{ delilahschicago.com }

Whiskey bars can be stuffy and superior, but Delilah's is anything but. It's a music venue with a punk heart, more biker bar than high-class style bar. It offers a great beer range as well as spirits, especially whiskey. It has special bar-specific offerings, regularly features live music and other events, and is generally a lot of fun.

MULTNOMAH WHISKEY LIBRARY
Portland, OR, USA
{ mwlpdx.com }

It's called a whiskey library, but in addition to the 1,200 whiskeys there are 600 other spirits. To enjoy them, expect to line up. When you eventually make it through the door, you step back in time in a bar that looks more like the study in a mansion house than a drinking establishment. The bar is so popular that it offers membership packages, but you'll have to wait your turn for one of them, too.

PINTS PUB
Denver, CO, USA
{ pintspub.com }

Pints takes its inspiration from the traditional British pub, and brews its own British-style real ale. It also has a huge collection of whiskies — arguably the largest in the world. There are so many of them that they have to be listed in a whisky book, in the latter pages of which is a fantastic selection of world craft whiskies.

RETAILERS

THE WHISKY EXCHANGE
London, England
{ thewhiskyexchange.com }

The Whisky Exchange is an online retailer offering every type of spirit, and if you're looking for craft spirits it has an outstanding collection, including some 400 plus gins. The team here are dedicated fans of quality spirits who offer informed and intelligent reviews, and welcome customer feedback. The rum selection on offer is particularly impressive. The company also has a shop in Bedford Street, Covent Garden, and stages the hugely successful annual Whisky Show.

LA MAISON DU WHISKY
Paris, France
{ whisky.fr }

La Maison du Whisky is pretty much at the heart of everything that happens with whisky in France. While whisky from Scotland is at the heart of what they do — the French drink about twice as much blended Scotch as any other country in the world, and France is second only to the United States for consumption of single malt — the company behind this shop imports whisky from all over the world. It also organizes a series of whisky events.

MASTER OF MALT
Tunbridge Wells, England
{ masterofmalt.com }

An online retailer with a healthily irreverent, bordering on maverick, streak. Master of Malt offers a wide range of spirits beyond whisky, and provides chatty and friendly tasting reviews, as well as some background on each brand. Many of the drinks are offered in tester sizes, so you don't have to commit to a whole bottle. The company behind Master of Malt also owns the award-winning craft brand Ableforth's.

ROYAL MILE WHISKIES
Edinburgh and London, UK
{ royalmilewhiskies.com }

As the name suggests, the company's principal store is halfway up the Royal Mile in Edinburgh. The premises are a treasure trove (opposite), meeting tourist demands for well-known and respected Scottish single malts, while also offering the discerning whisky fan a choice of whiskies from elsewhere in the world. There is a London store, and in recent years the company has significantly stepped up its online offering.

PARK AVENUE LIQUOR SHOP
New York, NY, USA
{ parkaveliquor.com }

It's amazing how many brands do not make it into the market place in America, but if you're looking for something unusual, chances are you'll find it in New York, and if it's whisky, you could do a lot worse than try here. There are off-the-wall spirits such as mescal, and craft spirits, from Edinburgh Gin to unusual American creations. The shop holds regular in-store samplings and tastings.

BINNY'S BEVERAGE DEPOT
Various locations, USA
{ binnys.com }

It might be a chain, but in 2018 it celebrated its 70th anniversary as an independent, family-owned business. It is based in Chicago, IL. The proud boast of Binny's is that it has as good a choice of wines, beers, and spirits as any store in the United States. If it isn't in Binny's, they say, it probably isn't worth drinking. Another point in the company's favor is that it positively supports independent producers.

— *The breakfast snifter* —
**CROSS BREW COFFEE
LIQUEUR**
Bramble Bar
Edinburgh, Scotland
{ cross-brew.com }
LIQUEUR, 20%

The modern style bar is all
about independence, points
of difference, style, and
creativity, and across the
world there are scores of
young mixologists making
their own bitters, mixers,
and liqueurs. Bramble in
Edinburgh has gone one
further and created a liqueur
to sell. Cross Brew is described
by one online retailer as a
'damn fine coffee liqueur'. It
is made using cold-brewed,
dark-roasted coffee spirits and
a small amount of sugar. It can
be consumed neat over ice or
as a mixer for a longer drink,
making it an exciting and
classy alternative to Kahlúa.

—*Worth the weight* —
**HAAMONII SMOOTH
SHOCHU**
San Francisco,
CA, USA
{ shareharmony.com }
SHOCHU JAPANESE
SPIRIT, 22%

This is promoted as a health
product, because it has half
the calories of the spirit it is
closest to — vodka. Schochu
is an ancient Japanese spirit
that is lighter than vodka but
serves a similar purpose — as
a base for any number of
cocktails. Alternatively, it is
sipped on ice or taken with a
small amount of fresh juice.
Haamonii Smooth Shochu
possesses a distinctly smooth,
pure, and refreshing taste.
Crafted in small batches, it
has won several international
awards, including a gold
medal from the people who
voted Grey Goose the world's
number one vodka.

— *Es tu Bruto?* —
**BRUTO AMERICAN
LIQUEUR**
St George Spirits
Alameda, CA, USA
{ stgeorgespirits.com }
LIQUEUR, 24%

St George in California makes
rather excellent, but unusual
whiskey, and has done so from
way before the current craft
distilling boom. And it's not
averse to experimenting or, as
in this case, getting all retro on
us. This is inspired by distiller
Lance Winters's memories of
growing up in California in the
1970s. Bruto comes in retro
packaging which recalls that
of a traditional Italian liqueur,
and the botanicals in it include
Seville orange, gentian root,
balsam fir, and bark from the
coffee berry bush. It is unusual
in that it is quite sharp and
citrusy rather than over-sweet,
and it works well in a Negroni.

— *Eastern promise* —
JINRO 24
Hite Jinro
Seoul, South Korea
{ en.hitejinro.com }
KOREAN SPIRIT, 24%

The bottle proclaims that Jinro is the world's best-selling spirit, and indeed it tops the charts in China, Japan, and, perhaps unexpectedly, in North America. It is a form of soju, a clear, aromatic Korean liquor that can be made from rice, grain, or potatoes to a variety of different strengths. It is traditionally served neat and chilled, but in recent years it has proved to be a versatile ingredient in cocktails. The manufacturers recommend drinking it with barbecued or grilled meat.

— *The Big Easy one* —
NOLA COFFEE LIQUEUR
St George Spirits
Alameda, CA, USA
{ stgeorgespirits.com }
LIQUEUR, 25%

New Orleans, LA, has a unique coffee culture and a distinctive taste in coffee, and this is St George's attempt to emulate the latter. Created by distiller Dave Smith, it consists of roasted yirgacheffe coffee beans, French chicory root, Madagascar vanilla beans, and organic cane sugar combined to create a coffee liqueur with dimension and depth. 'Just like the city of New Orleans itself, our Nola Coffee Liqueur intrigues, engages the senses, and invites you to let go of expectations and give yourself over to a wholly delicious experience', says the distillery. Hard to disagree.

— Honey delight —

NEW GROVE HONEY RUM LIQUEUR

New Grove

Mauritius

{ newgrove.mu }

LIQUEUR, 26%

— A best zeller —

APPENZELLER ALPENBITTER

Appenzeller

Appenzell, Switzerland

{ appenzeller.com }

BITTERS, 29%

New Grove has been in business on Mauritius for nearly 200 years, and has built an enviable reputation for its wide range of premium rum products. Although much of its output is quite traditional, the company has also diversified into maturing rum in unusual casks, and making different drinks styles. This drink is the first rum liqueur from the island, and it uses home-grown sugar molasses and honey from neighboring Rodrigues Island. It has a light golden tint, and you'll taste spice, citrus peel, grapefruit, and a strong honey influence. Serve as an aperitif or a digestif, on the rocks.

It has been said that bitters are to the spirits world what salt and pepper are to food, but really they're more than that. They are more akin to chili sauces, which come in a range of styles and strengths. Many cocktail-makers create their own, but when there are products such as this, there really isn't any need. Like many bitters, this one comes from Switzerland and was launched more than 100 years ago. The recipe is secret, but this is a natural product made up of 42 different herbs and spices. Popular in its own right, particularly during après-ski.

— You can't refuse —
AMARO AVERNA
Averna
Sicily, Italy
{ amaroaverna.com }
LIQUEUR, 29%

We've described this as a liqueur, but it has much in common with the world of bitters. This, too, has a secret recipe originally formulated by Benedictine monks in Sicily 150 years ago, and unchanged ever since. What sets it apart from its competitors is the way in which the herbs and spices are infused. Amaro Averna has a bittersweet taste, with hints of orange and licorice balanced with notes of myrtle, juniper berries, rosemary, and sage. According to the producers, it stimulates the senses and captures the feeling of Sicily: 'Averna is not just an amaro,' they claim, 'but a true experience'.

— Nice 'n' tarty —
BACARDÍ RAZZ
Bacardí
London, England
{ bacardi.com }
FRUIT SPIRIT, 32%

Bacardí has proved remarkably adept at expanding its product range and keeping its brand name at the forefront of the drinking public's mind and at the front of the bar, in spite of a general downturn of interest in the rum category. Somewhat unfairly, it is not taken seriously by many spirits experts, partly because of products such as this. A shame, because Bacardí Razz is flavored using the finest raspberries, and unashamedly targeted at the younger party crowd. It's sweet, but there's a very appealing tartness to it, too, and it works well drunk neat over ice.

SOCIAL

SEVEN MOODS OF CRAFT SPIRIT

— Fingers-lickin' good —
DEAD MAN'S FINGERS
CORNISH SPICED RUM
The Rum & Crab Shack
St Ives, England
{ deadmansfingers.com }
SPICED RUM, 37.5%

Rum and crab would seem to
be a marriage made in heaven,
and this venue, one of two,
has been successfully trading
in both for a few years now.
The owners created this drink
to add a taste of Cornwall to
Caribbean rum. It's a delicious,
spiced drink in which you'll
find flavors of saffron cake,
caramel, vanilla, cinnamon,
nutmeg, and orange. Available
by the nip at The Rum & Crab
Shack, and by the bottle from
several online retailers, it's
a beautiful example of the
spiced rum style. If you add
cola, make sure it's cola from
Fever Tree.

— Sip slidin' away —
NEW GROVE DARK RUM
New Grove
Mauritius
{ newgrove.mu }
RUM, 37.5%

New Grove is a small artisanal
family distiller operating on
the island of Mauritius. It
uses local produce, and has
focused on premium rum
since before the middle of
the 19th century. Its range
includes aged and higher-
strength rums, and rums
matured highly unusually in
wood. This is one of its more
conservative offerings, but it
is excellent. It's made using an
old family recipe, and is both
smooth and spicy. There are
notes of burned molasses, too,
and it's very rich and fruity.
Sipping rums are becoming
popular in some regions, and
this fits the bill perfectly. One
for warm summer evenings.

— The daddy —
BACARDÍ CARTA BLANCA
Bacardí
Puerto Rico
{ bacardi.com }
RUM, 37.5%

This is the famous expression
of Bacardí, the one that has
conquered the world and can
be seen on back bars pretty
much everywhere. There's a
very good reason for that. It
is said that white rums were
harsh, crude, and unrefined
until they were reinvented by
the company's founder, Don
Facundo, who introduced
charcoal filtration to remove
the rum's impurities, and oak
aging to smooth the raw edges
of the spirit and produce a
mellow, clear, white rum.
This is a straight-down-the-
line, perfectly good product,
although its light, smooth
flavor might not appeal to
serious rum drinkers.

— Devil of a drink —
CLOVEN HOOF
Guilty Libations
Oxford, England
{ clovenhoofrum.com }
SPICED RUM, 37.5%

As its name implies, this is a spicy number with a rebellious heart, a Brewdog for the rum fan. The imagery is suitably diabolical, and the company's mission statement is studiously anti-corporate. And not a nautical reference in sight. But this is still a pretty serious rum. It contains spirit imported from Guyana's Diamond Distillery, and a rum from Trinidad that has a distinctive cough candy smell and taste. In England, cloves and natural spices are added to create an intriguingly palatable beverage. Cloven Hoof is currently on sale only in the South of England, but there are plans to expand.

— Aging gracefully —
BRUGAL AÑEJO
Brugal
Dominican Republic
{ brugal-rum.com }
RUM, 38%

Añejo means 'aged', and when applied to tequila or rum, it means a spirit aged for between one and seven years, normally in an oak barrel. This rum is from the Dominican Republic, and has acquired a premium reputation because of its rounded, smooth mouth feel and taste. Brugal is a family company founded in 1888 by Don Andrés Brugal Montaner and now run by the fifth generation of the Brugal family. This is the family's original rum, and it has been matured in American ex-bourbon casks for up to five years. But the smooth taste is due to the removal of heavier alcohols during distillation.

— Grape expectations —
ASBACH URALT
Asbach
Rüdesheim-am-Rhein,
Germany
{ asbach.de }
BRANDY, 38%

Another spirit with its origins stretching back to the 19th century, this brandy and its sibling, Asbach 3 Year Old, are perennial favorites and have a very loyal following, particularly among Allied ex-servicemen who were stationed in Germany. Produced by a company that makes chocolates as well as spirits, this brandy contains only the finest grapes, and is made up of 25 different distillations, matured for up to three years in French limousin oak casks. The result is smooth and sweet, similar to Cognac, but fuller and fruitier than its French counterpart.

— An Italian job —
MOLINARI SAMBUCA EXTRA
Molinari
Colfelice, Italy
{ molinari.it }
SAMBUCA, 38%

Sambuca is an anise-flavored spirit that may cloud when mixed with water, as ouzo and other spirits of the same kind also do. It is a fine example of a white sambuca, as opposed to the red and black versions of the spirit. It's promoted as a cocktail drink, but it can be served neat. It is arguably most enjoyable when served with a coffee bean — in Italian, that's *sambuca con la mosca'* ('sambuca with the fly'). Other ways to drink it include ice cold from the freezer, and after using it to rinse your empty coffee cup.

— All about apples —
BUSNEL TROIS LYS CALVADOS PAYS D'AUGE
Distillerie Busnel
Cormeilles, France
{ distillerie-busnel.fr }
APPLE BRANDY, 40%

Calvados is a French *appellation contrôlée* for a style of apple brandy made in Normandy, much of it in Pays d'Auge. It is not afforded anything like the same respect as Armagnac or Cognac, and it's been many decades since it enjoyed its golden age when the phylloxera insect all but wiped out the grape harvest in France, and no wine or brandy could be produced. But apple brandy may well be coming back into vogue. A surprisingly complex spirit, Calvados may be made using more than 200 types of apple. Busnel Trois Lys is a sweet, entry-level version with a distinctive vanilla note.

— A great schnapp shot —
HENKES AROMATIC SCHNAPPS
J.H. Henkes
Amsterdam,
Netherlands
GENEVER, 40%

Experimentation has led to a blurring of traditional distinctions between various types of drink. This beverage, for example, has been made for more than 200 years and has always been known as schnapps, but the label states that it's a grain-based jenever, a Dutch form of gin. It's distilled four times, and is regarded as a spirit of fine quality. Bizarrely, it is popular in Nigeria, where it is served at birth, marriage, and death ceremonies. Jenever it may be, but juniper isn't to the fore: expect nuttiness, baked apples, nutmeg, cinnamon, and cloves; it's spiced gin.

— *All that glitters* —
GOLDSCHLÄGER SCHNAPPS
Global Brands
Switzerland
FLAVORED SCHNAPPS
40%

This brand is sold worldwide as a young person's shot drink, and it's instantly recognizable because the bottle contains fine slivers of real gold. The burning question is: why? The brand has something of a chequered past, reducing its alcoholic strength from 53.5% ABV to the current level. Production moved from Switzerland to Italy and back again, and it has had several owners, including Diageo. It's probably the finest example of a cinnamon-based liqueur in the world. Expect a rich, sweet, syrupy spirit with a hot cinnamon kick. Tends to be downed as a shots drink, but can be mixed to good effect.

— *Gentle gin* —
XELLENT EDELWEISS GIN
Diwisa Distillery
Willisau, Switzerland
{ xellent.ch }
GIN, 40%

In 2018, the family behind Diwisa celebrated 100 years of producing fine spirits. In the intervening period, the company has grown from a one-man operation into a business with more than 100 employees. Diwisa is perhaps best known for its fruit liqueurs, but it also makes this excellent gin. The component rye is grown by local farmers on land between around 1,500 and 2,500 feet (500–700 m) above sea level, and irrigated with pure glacier water. Twenty-five Swiss herbs, berries, and flowers are subsequently added to a gentle distillation that ensures a smooth, soft gin.

— *California dreamer* —
ST GEORGE CITRUS VODKA
St George Spirits
Alameda, CA, USA
{ stgeorgespirits.com }
VODKA, 40%

'Citrus' is slightly misleading, and if you think that vodka is an inferior and tasteless spirit, then reappraise right now. The orange flavor of this superb spirit is derived from top-quality fruit imported from Seville and Valencia, Spain. Bergamot is brought in from a family farm in the nearby San Joaquin Valley. Each infusion is distilled separately, then blended to produce a flavorsome spirit with sweet and sour orange notes and a lemony nose. St George Citrus Vodka has won acclaim from leading critics across the world, and with good reason: it's a real sunshine of a summer drink.

— *A devil of a drink* —
666 PURE TASMANIAN VODKA
Pure Distillery Co
Tasmania, Australia
{ 666purevodka.com }
VODKA, 40%

The distillery is called 'Pure' for two reasons.
One, according to local tradition, the fresh rain
falling on Cape Grim at the northwestern tip
of Tasmania is the cleanest in the world. And
two, this vodka is a pure Tasmanian product,
made with locally sourced barley triple distilled
on pot stills before being charcoal-filtered to
remove any remaining impurities. Tasmania
is increasingly famous for its fine whisky.
This vodka shows that the island has other
strengths, too: it is smooth, clean, and…
well… pure.

— *Grape expectations* —
MONSOON GIN
Bass & Flinders Distillery
Victoria, Australia
{ bassandflindersdistillery.com }
GIN, 40%

Bass & Flinders are innovative distillers who are
doing some very exciting things with what they
call gin, but a gin that is unusual because it is
made with grape-based spirit. Varieties include
a pink gin with cherries and raspberries in the
recipe, and Angry Ant gin, which includes…
yep, you guessed it. Monsoon Gin is subtitled
'Eastern Twist', and the unusual Shiraz grape
spirit base is complemented by lemongrass,
ginger, and ginseng. The spirit is distilled in
small batches on an alembic pot still — slowly,
in order to ensure a smooth and dry gin. Try it
with ginger beer, fresh mint, and a couple of
lemongrass sticks.

— *Spuds-u-like* —

OGILVY POTATO VODKA

Ogilvy Distillery
Angus, Scotland
{ ogilvyspirits.com }
VODKA, 40%

One of the most exciting aspects of the micro-distilling or craft distilling boom is that it has injected new life into existing businesses. Given Britain's decision to quit the European Economic Community and the uncertainty that has thereby been caused, that'a great thing, especially for rural communities, where traditional business has struggled. Many of the new distilleries are housed in renovated farm buildings that had lain derelict and ignored for decades. And if you've got potatoes, why not make white spirit? William Chase, founder of Tyrrells potato crisps, now makes superior vodka and gin, and is turning his hand to whisky at the Ogilvy Distillery on a small, family farm in Scotland. The potatoes used to make the vodka are grown on site, and processed on a specially made dinky vodka still named Spud. Once distilled, the vodka is filtered through charcoal for up to a week. The resulting liquor is smooth, with a creamy fruit and vanilla palate and some late spice. This is micro-distilling at its finest.

SEVEN MOODS OF CRAFT SPIRIT   SOCIAL

— Sweet perfection —
ASYLA
Compass Box
London, England
{ compassboxwhisky.com }
BLENDED WHISKY, 40%

Blended whiskies get a bad press, but it's quite unfair. Sure, there are bottles of Clan Bagpipe containing a very high proportion of low-quality, three-year-old grain whisky colored with caramel that let the category down. But blended whisky can be excellent, and here's an example. Described as 'the ultimate everyday, before dinner, Sunday afternoon Scotch whisky', this is made with quality grain and the finest Highland malts. What sets it apart from many blends, too, is that it is aged in high-quality, first-fill American oak casks, which impart a vanilla sweetness and a richness. It's beautifully made, excellently balanced, and very moreish.

— Man's best friend —
COPPER DOG
Copper Dog Ltd
Craigellachie, Scotland
BLENDED MALT WHISKY, 40%

By definition, a copper dog is a metal tube on a chain that is used to 'steal' whisky. It is lowered into the cask, and when it is full of whisky it is sealed, and concealed down the thief's trouser leg. This particular Copper Dog is whisky produced by the owners of the renowned Craigellachie Hotel. A combination of eight Speyside malts, it is aimed at newcomers to whisky — the younger set who drink cocktails and mix their spirits with juice, cola, water, and such liquids. It is easy-drinking, very palatable, and has slight gingery taste among the Speyside fruits. Nicely packaged, and with a strong backstory.

— *Jamaican spice* —

BLACKWELL BLACK GOLD
J. Wray & Nephew
Jamaica
{ blackwellrum.com }
RUM, 40%

Blackwell Black Gold is
made and bottled by Wray
& Nephew on its Appleton
Estate in Jamaica. The brand
name refers to Chris Blackwell,
owner of Island Records and
the Island Outpost resorts
group. Blackwell was born
and raised in Jamaica, and his
mother's family once owned
Wray & Nephew. Black Gold
is a dark product that blends
pot and column still rums.
Appleton has a distinctive
distillation process that sets
its rums apart; this one has
a nose of tropical fruit and
toffee, and an oaky, fruity
palate, with some nuttiness,
treacle, and coffee. An
excellent cocktail whisky.

— *The perfect mixer* —

MYERS RUM
Diageo
Jamaica
{ diageo.com }
RUM, 40%

Described by retailers as the
ultimate and pre-eminent
cocktail dark rum, Myers can
be found in quality bars across
the world. It is owned by the
drinks giant Diageo, but the
company has stayed true to
the rum, both in terms of the
contents, which were created
by Fred L Myers in 1879, and in
terms of the packaging. It has
kept its original bottle shape
and tagline — 'World Famous,
Dark and Mellow' — for several
decades. Myers is a blend of
nine Jamaican rums aged for
six years in white oak barrels.
The rum has a smoky tobacco
nose and a smooth, spicy,
sweet taste.

'OH, YOU HATE YOUR JOB? WHY
DIDN'T YOU SAY SO? THERE'S A
SUPPORT GROUP FOR THAT. IT'S
CALLED EVERYBODY, AND THEY
MEET AT THE BAR.'
DREW CAREY

— Different and distinct —
GOLD OF MAURITIUS
Grays Distillery
Mauritius
{ grays.mu }
RUM, 40%

Consumers: wake up to the fact that rum can be as diverse as malt whisky. This is very much a case in point. Rum was first produced commercially in Mauritius in 1850, and today the island is home to several distilleries. The tropical climate and the rich volcanic soils ensure excellent sugarcane. Every bottle is blended under the supervision of Frederic Bestel, who selects specific un-aged rums from local Mauritian distilleries before conditioning them in South African port casks. The result is a winey, distinctive rum, heavily influenced by the wood in which it has matured.

— Spicy Eastern delight —
OLD PORT EAST INDIAN
Amrut
Bangalore, India
{ amrutdistilleries.com }
RUM, 40%

Indian rum is a potential can of worms, because for years Indian 'whisky'-makers have locked horns with the rest of the world over the definition of whisky. In India, many brands that call themselves whisky are made with sugar molasses — as rum always is, and whisky can never be. Amrut makes fine single malt whisky, so you might expect the company to know what rum is and what whisky is. And indeed, this is a very palatable example of rum which actually sells better abroad than it does in the domestic market. It is sweet, with some spicy and woody notes. Better mixed than sipped straight.

— *Colombian magic* —
DICTADOR 12 YEAR OLD
Destilería Colombiana
Cartagena, Colombia
{ dictador.com }
RUM, 40%

The importance of an age on a bottle of spirits is a constant source of debate, and there is a lot of confusion over what an age actually means. For whisky, it's pretty straightforward: the age refers to the youngest whisky in the bottle, so if you mix 12-year-old, 15-year-old, and 18-year-old whisky, that whisky is a 12-year-old, and it means it has spent at least 12 years in oak. A whisky bottled today after 12 years is exactly the same age as a whisky matured for 12 years in the 1970s. But other spirits producers are less fussy. A Cognac expert recently introduced a Cognac as a 60-year-old because it had been matured for 10 years and then bottled 50 years ago. Rum makers aren't fussy about age. Some of them use the Scottish method. This, though, is an average, and includes rums between eight and 14 years old. Dictador is different for two reasons. Firstly, it is produced through a solera system, with younger whiskies at the top being added to older whiskies lower down, softening the overall palate feel. Secondly, the rum is not made from molasses, but from sugarcane honey. This is because, in Colombia, all cars must run partially on biofuel; biofuel is made from molasses, and molasses are consequently in short supply. The resulting rum is complex and excellent, with a delicate smokiness, oaky tannins, and some attractively fruity notes.

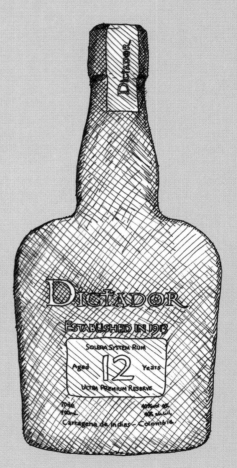

SEVEN MOODS OF CRAFT SPIRIT   SOCIAL

— The guvnor —
BACARDÍ GRAN RESERVA MAESTRO DE RON
Bacardí
Puerto Rico
{ bacardi.com }
RUM, 40%

Bacardí Gran Reserva Maestro de Ron is further proof, if proof were needed, that, despite being a drinks giant, Bacardí can still make fine rum. It was launched in 2014, for travel retail only, in an attempt to kick-start the super premium category of sipping rums. It is said to be inspired by a recipe passed down through generations of master blenders that involves slow-filtering of the blended rum — aged up to three years — through a coconut shell charcoal. The result is smooth, fruity, and floral, with vanilla notes and hints of walnut, oak, and almond.

— Good wood —
PLANTATION XO 20TH ANNIVERSARY
Maison Ferrand
Barbados
{ plantationrum.com }
RUM, 40%

An extraordinary rum which, as its name suggests, was created to mark owner Maison Ferrand's 20th anniversary. Plantation is the company's best and most premium rum range, and, like other expressions, this was initially aged in ex-bourbon barrels in Barbados. Some of the rum has matured for 20 years. It is then shipped to France, where it is further matured in small ex-Cognac barrels for an additional 12 to 18 months. The result is a delight: toasted coconut and vanilla on the nose, and an orange crunchy bar on the palate — milk chocolate, honey and orange zest. The finish is rich and full.

— Mexican fave —
MOCAMBO 10 YEAR OLD
Licores Veracruz
Córdoba, Mexico
{ licoresveracruz.com }
RUM, 40%

Mexican rum? Surely some mistake? Nope, that's what this is, and actually it shouldn't come as a surprise that this is a solid and enjoyable rum. Licores Veracruz is sited near the coast in Córdoba and makes a range of spirits drinks. The Veracruz region has had quality sugarcane since it was introduced by the Spanish Conquistadores in the middle of the 16th century. Mocambo is made up of 70 per cent rum from sugarcane juice, and 30 per cent rum from molasses. The result is full-bodied and bold, with hints of tobacco and green and orange fruit, and some spiciness.

— *The golden touch* —

EL DORADO

Demerara Distillery
Georgetown, Guyana
{ heeldoradorum.com }
RUM, 40%

The legend of a city of gold
ruled by a gilded king
encouraged early explorers to
search the ancient heartland
of Guyana in search of El
Dorado — 'the golden one'.
Demerara Distillery boasts
nine stills, and makes a range
of rums under the El Dorado
name. This 12-year-old is
labeled in the same way as
malt whisky, so all the spirit
is at least 12 years old, and
is a blend of pot still and
coffey still rums. It has been
described as 'great' by online
retailer Master of Malt, and
it has won a large number of
awards. On the palate, you'll
get juicy raisins, cocoa, toffee,
vanilla, and spice.

— *Dressed to kill* —

**DIPLOMÁTICO RESERVA
EXCLUSIVA**

Diplomático
La Miel, Venezuela
{ rondiplomatico.com }
RUM, 40%

Everything about this product
— from the packaging to the
last drop — cries 'quality.'
Diplomático Distillery has
been successful worldwide
ever since it was taken over
by a team of Venezuelan
entrepreneurs in the 1950s.
The distillery is sited at the
foot of the Andes, close to
sugarcane-producing regions
and a pure water source.
Diplomático Reserva Exclusiva
is an elegant and complex
sipping rum, crafted from
pure sugarcane honeys. It is
delicately distilled in ancient
copper pot stills, and aged in
small ex-whisky oak casks for
up to 12 years.

— *Thais that bind* —

SANGSOM

Sangsom Company
Bangkok, Thailand
{ interbevgroup.com }
RUM, 40%

SangSom was launched in
1977, and after a flurry of
medal wins, when it earned
the name SangSom Rianthong
(SangSom Gold Medals) in
Thailand, it disappeared. Then
at the start of the new
millennium it reappeared, and
it is now the most successful
spirit in Thai liquor history.
You'll find it consumed all
over Thailand, often served in
buckets with mixers over ice,
with drinkers drinking
communally through a straw.
It is aged for at least three
years, and has a mellow taste
and an aromatic nose. It is
exported, but only on a very
small scale.

— Strange brew —
JINZU
Cameronbridge Distillery
Cameronbridge, Scotland
{ diageo.com }
GIN, 41.3%

Jinzu is described on the bottle as a 'distinctively crafted gin', but there is much more to it than that. It was created by bartender Dee Davies in Bristol, England, and it won her Diageo's Show Your Spirit award. The multinational then took the brand on, and now produces it in its Scottish grain plant near Edinburgh. The taste of juniper is to the fore, but this drink is made with gin, sake, and cherry blossom, and it is like nothing you have ever tasted before. It's an elegant and stylish spirit, and the bottle is beautiful, too.

— Give me a Bruk —
BRUKSWHISKY
Mackmyra
Gävle, Sweden
{ mackmyra.com }
SINGLE MALT WHISKY, 41.4%

Mackmyra was in the vanguard of the world whisky revolution that began in the early part of the new millennium. Its early whiskies were distinctive and difficult to love, but in recent years it has stuck to a two-pronged attack of exciting, innovative, and big-flavored malt whiskies and lighter, sweeter, easy-to-drink alternatives. Brukswhisky is a core expression that sits between the two types, with plenty of fruit, and hints of apple pie and custard, as well as some red berries and oaky spice. It's not like a Scottish single malt, and it doesn't want to be. A confident, complex, and assertive whisky.

— No grain, no gain —

GLENDALOUGH DOUBLE BARREL

Glendalough Distillery
Glendalough, Ireland
{ glendaloughdistillery.com }
GRAIN WHISKEY, 42%

Ireland is in the midst of a whiskey renaissance.
The country once had 200 distilleries, but that
number fell to just a handful in the 1960s,
when the survivors came together to form
Irish Distillers, which defined Irish whiskey as
blended, 40% ABV, non-peated, and triple-
distilled — distinctly different from Scottish
single malt. That definition wasn't true to the
taste and diversity that had previously existed,
but at the time no one wanted all that. Then
along came Cooley, who brought back a range
of styles. Now, in the second decade of the third
millennium, there has been a huge revival, and
the new wave of distilleries means that Dublin
is becoming a whiskey city once more. In time,
the Irish capital may even have a whiskey trail
similar to the one for bourbon in Louisville,
Kentucky. Glendalough Distillery was one of
the first of the new builds, and this whiskey is
a stylish advertisement for the next generation
of whiskey-makers, showing clearly that the
emerging practitioners aren't interested in
'me too' Irish whiskeys. This product has a
mash bill made up of barley and corn; it is
matured in bourbon casks for three and a half
years, and then in oloroso sherry casks for
a further six months. The result is a rich and
creamy whiskey that has butterscotch, honey,
and dried fruit notes.

— Cool sippin' whiskey —
MICHTER'S US1 STRAIGHT RYE
Michter's
Louisville, KY, USA
{ michters.com }
RYE WHISKEY, 42.4%

Rye whiskey has been in and out of fashion
more times than denim jeans with holes in the
knees, and in recent years it has become the
spirit of choice for scores of cocktail-makers.
Michter's is one of the better examples of the
style. Rye must have at least 51% rye in its mash
bill, and this is a straight rye, which means that
it has been matured for at least two years. This
is also a single barrel whiskey, so flavor from
barrel to barrel will vary. But it is made to the
original 18th-century recipe, so expect a citrusy,
plummy, and not overly spicy sipping rye.

— A top Tom tipple —
BATHTUB OLD TOM
Ableforth's
Tunbridge Wells, England
{ ableforths.com }
GIN, 42.4%

Old Tom is a traditional style of gin from the
18th and 19th centuries. It is sweeter than
conventional gin. There are various theories
about where the name comes from, but the
most common explanation is that cat-shaped
plaques were hung outside shops selling gin.
It has even been claimed that customers put
their money in the cat's mouth, and that the gin
was dispensed from a lead pipe beneath the
cat's paws. This particular style — with juniper,
orange, and citrus flavors — was neglected for
many years until Ableforth's responded to a
request from The Handmade Cocktail Company.
It makes a superb gin and tonic.

— *Northern lights* —
TYCHO'S STAR
Spirit of Hven
Sankt Ibb, Sweden
{ hven.com }
SINGLE MALT WHISKY, 42.8%

— *Shipshape whisky* —
THREE SHIPS 10 YEAR OLD
James Sedgwick
Wellington, South Africa
{ threeshipswhisky.co.za }
SINGLE MALT WHISKY, 43%

Hven (or Ven) is a small island between Sweden and Denmark that is best known as a holiday destination. It is home to around 400 people, including Henrik Molina, who has a highly methodical and studied interest in spirit production. His distillery is sited within a four-star hotel that has an award-winning restaurant, pub, and wine bar. Whisky production began in 2008, and from the very start the malt whisky has been outstanding. This whisky is named after Tycho Brahe, the 16th-century Danish astronomer. It is complex and contradictory, with soft candy bouncing up against a range of spices over a peaty under-carpet.

The Three Ships range features malt and grain whiskies, both varieties of which are created at the same location in the Western Cape. This is unusual; the normal practice is for distilleries to produce only one type or the other. This award-winning product has a rounded, Speyside-like fruitiness, a touch of earthy peat, and some spice from the wood tannins. In 2013, James Sedgwick's parent company, South African drinks conglomerate Distell, expanded further into whisky-making with the purchase of the three Scottish distilleries formerly belonging to Burn Stewart.

SEVEN MOODS OF CRAFT SPIRIT   SOCIAL

— Evan in a bottle —

EVAN WILLIAMS 1783

Heaven Hill
Louisville, KY, USA
{ evanwilliams.com }
BOURBON, 43%

At the start of the current millennium, bourbon was treated as something of a dirty little secret by the Louisville tourist authorities. Bottles of it languished on top shelves, and had you suggested that some of city's top restaurants would promote it within a decade, and offer tasting flights as well as dishes made with it, you'd probably have been laughed at. Now the spirit is promoted there with pride, its role in the success of the State is recognized, and the Louisville tourist folk have created a bourbon trail through the city. Heaven Hill, which owns the Evan Williams brand, was for a long time one of the few distillers that produced whiskey in Louisville; Whiskey Row, where bourbon had once been created and traded, had ceased to be anything more than a name. But today the Evan Williams Bourbon Experience in the center of the city is one of Kentucky's most popular tourist attractions. The 1783 in this brand's name refers to the year Williams established the State's first distillery on the banks of the Ohio River. The modern drink has remained fairly close to the original recipe. It is a classic sharing bourbon — not too demanding, with notes on the palate of buttered sweetcorn, vanilla, honey, and oak.

— *A perfect match* —
DALMORE CIGAR MALT
Dalmore
Alness, Scotland
{ whyteandmackay.com }
SINGLE MALT WHISKY, 44%

A fine example of people power in action.
Whyte & Mackay, the parent company of the
Dalmore Distillery, seemed to have bowed
to social trends and the anti-smoking lobby
when they scrapped their Cigar Malt, stating
as their reason for doing so the fact that it
was no longer permissible to enjoy the luxury
of a smoke and a malt in a large number of
licenced premises. Whisky and cigar lovers were
outraged by this decision, and fought
successfully to have the brand restored. Good:
it's a fine drink (though not cheap), even when
unaccompanied by a smoke. Expect oak, toffee,
orange, and red berries on the palate. The finish
includes spice and burned orange peel.

— *Irish gold* —
ROE & CO
Diageo
Dublin, Ireland
{ roeandcowhiskey.com }
BLENDED IRISH WHISKEY, 45%

The launch of a premium blended whiskey by
drinks giant Diageo, which has significant roots
in Ireland, tells us two things: firstly, that the
boom in Irish whiskey is no passing fad; and
secondly that the growth in new distilleries has
to a large extent been ground-upward. Diageo
was slow to pick up on the latter point: in 2014
it swapped its Bushmills distillery for Don Julio
tequila, an odd thing to do when just a few
years later the company would be building a
new distillery and launching a new Irish
expression. Some people are cynical about
the Roe & Co blend, but it is rich, sweet, and
creamy, with sweet apple, vanilla, and pear.

— Hitting the spot —
YELLOW SPOT
Irish Distillers
Dublin, Ireland
{ jamesonwhiskey.com }
POT STILL WHISKEY, 46%

Pot still whiskey is a specific style peculiar to Ireland, and, in somewhat typical Irish fashion, the name doesn't have anything to do with the fact that it's made in a pot still, as most malt whisky is. It refers instead to the grain mash bill — a mix of malted barley and another unmated grain. The resulting whiskey is high in fusel oils, and has a distinctive, complex, and spicy taste. Until very recently, the only pot still whiskeys available to any great extent were Redbreast and Green Spot, with the occasional special bottling of Midleton. All those whiskeys are owned by Irish Distillers, and some time around 2010 the company committed to a program of releasing a new pot still whiskey twice a year for a decade. The move has revived pot still whiskey, and made it a much sought-after style. The Redbreast range now has four expressions.

This is the second in the 'Spot' series, and in theory has been produced specifically for Dublin retailer Mitchell & Son. The name refers to the whiskey sellers' habit of using a different daub of colored paint on casks of different ages, and yellow represents 12 years old. Yellow Spot has been matured in three different types of cask: ex-bourbon, ex-sherry, and, most crucially, ex-Malaga wine casks, which give it a sweetness not found in other pot still whiskeys. Expect dried berries, fleshy, fruity, and fresh stone fruits, bourbon vanilla, and caramel.

— *The local one* —
WILD TURKEY 101
Wild Turkey
Lawrenceburg, KY, USA
{ wildturkeybourbon.com }
BOURBON, 50.5%

— *Proceed with caution* —
STROH 80
Stroh
Klagenfurt, Austria
{ stroh.at }
RUM, 80%

The American proof system is exactly double the internationally used Alcohol By Volume system, so this is a weighty 50.5%. It's seen as the real deal by many bourbon fans, not least blue-collar workers in Kentucky itself. To reflect modern tastes, there's now a Wild Turkey 81, but don't bother with that. This is how Wild Turkey is meant to be tasted, in a tumbler and over ice, ideally while waiting for a barbecue while the sun is setting. It has been aged for at least six years, so you get big oak and cigar box notes, vanilla, sandalwood, toffee, honeycomb, and, finally, pepper and chili spice.

Yes, you read that right; it's not a misprint. This is a mighty 80% ABV, and, according to the people who make it, it's so strong that biker gangs in South Africa have included it in their initiation ceremonies. But the Austrian producers are much happier to discuss the positive uses for this highly distinctive alcohol: from its color to its taste, there is nothing even remotely like it. Stroh suggest that you use it in all or any of the following ways: in cocktails and hot drinks; as an accompaniment for Austrian delicacies, such as Gugelhopf and Kaiserschmarren; in baking; or for flambés.

WHEN IT COMES TO THE NEW
WAVE OF CRAFT DISTILLERS,
ALL SORTS OF WONDERFUL
DRINKS ARE MAKING THEIR
WAY TO MARKET. SOME ARE
TOTALLY NEW, OTHERS ARE
TWISTS ON OLD CLASSICS, BUT
ALL HAVE A STORY TO TELL.

ADVENTUROUS

ABHAINN DEARG
Isle of Lewis, Scotland
{ abhainndearg.co.uk }

Abhainn Dearg is Scotland's most westerly distillery, and is located on the Isle of Lewis in the Outer Hebrides. It is a tiny distillery, and its malt, matured in sherry or bourbon casks, will always be limited in quantity, serving the local community, distillery visitors, and a select number of Internet 'friends.'

STRATHEARN
Methven, Scotland
{ strathearndistillery.com }

A Scottish micro-distillery operating from one room since 2013, when it started producing gin. Owner Tony Reeman-Clark has experimented with casks made from other woods, calling the spirit Uisge Beatha, but he stopped in 2017 when he ran in to trouble with the European Union. What now, with Brexit?

ARBIKIE
Inverkeilor, Scotland
{ arbikie.com }

Arbikie is a micro-distillery on a Highland farm owned by the Stirling family. It is a single estate distillery, in which all the ingredients are grown on the same property, and all production takes place there. The distillery was founded in 2013, and has made gin and vodka.

COTSWOLDS
Shipston-on-Stour, England
{ cotswoldsdistillery.com }

In 2014, distillery owner Daniel Dzor launched a gin. By the time he launched his malt in 2017, the gin boom had happened, and he was an award-winning gin-maker. His first malt is made up of 70 per cent spirit matured in red wine casks, and 30 per cent from ex-bourbon wood (opposite).

WALSH WHISKEY
Royal Oak, Ireland
{ http://walshwhiskey.com }

Bernard Walsh has an excellent reputation, producing Writer's Tears and The Irishman. His distillery is one of several whiskey-making establishments creating a new and exciting era. It's a purpose-built distillery on the estate of an 18th-century house, and there is an air of expectation as the whiskey is matured.

WORLD WHISKY DISTILLERIES

BOX
Bjärtrå, Sweden
{ boxwhisky.se }

Box is a located in a remote region of northern Sweden in an old sawmill beside a lake. It makes malt whisky at various peating levels and in a range of different wood types, including Hungarian oak. It has started bottling its whiskies; they are all excellent and have huge potential.

STAUNING
Skjern, Denmark
{ stauningwhisky.com }

Denmark's Stauning Distillery was founded by a group of friends who knew they were in business when Jim Murray compared their early distillate to classic Ardbeg. Their whiskies are challenging, chaotic, and fun. Someone must approve, because the company is expanding and moving into a new distillery.

KENTUCKY PEERLESS
Louisville, KY, USA
{ kentuckypeerless.com }

It's brave to open a distillery in Whiskey Row in the heart of bourbon country (left), and then to mess with the accepted production process for bourbon and rye. But that's what Peerless is doing, having re-established a link to the family's distilling heritage. The rye is exceptional. The bourbon is maturing.

LA ALAZANA
Chabut, Argentina
{ laalazanawhisky.com }

Argentine Patagonia might not seem a likely whisky-producing region, but all the ingredients are there. La Alazana is a farm distillery, producing its first whisky in 2014. From the off, the distillery team got it right, and although the malt wasn't very sophisticated, it had a light and fruity charm about it.

TEELING
Dublin, Ireland
{ teelingdistillery.com }

Stephen and Jack Teeling worked with their father, John, at Cooley before setting up Teeling and building a distillery in the depressed Liberties area of Dublin, bringing whiskey production back to the city. The company has produced a range of award-winning whiskeys, including some excellent special cask finishes.

CHICHIBU
Chichibu, Japan
{ one-drinks.com }

Ichiro Akuto is the grandson of the founder of the Hanyu distillery, and he has built a cult following for his whiskies, having successfully opened a tiny, labor-intensive operation around 70 miles (100 km) from Tokyo. The distillery makes a range of malt whiskies with passion and commitment.

— *Let's go bananas* —

JOSEPH CARTRON BANANA LIQUEUR

Joseph Cartron
Nuits-Saint-Georges,
France
{ carton.fr }
LIQUEUR, 25%

Joseph Cartron is a family company that has been making fruit liqueurs and fruit spirits since the 1880s. It is currently run by the fifth generation of the family from the heart of the wine-producing region of Burgundy. And we're not talking a handful of fruit products either — the company makes dozens of them, and has won a reputation for sourcing the finest fruit and making outstandingly fresh and vibrant spirit drinks. The bananas for this liqueur are sourced from Ecuador.

— *A fruity delight* —

ABLEFORTH'S CHERRY BRANDY

Ableforth's
Tunbridge Wells,
England
{ ableforths.com }
LIQUEUR, 26.4%

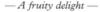

Pretty much every drink made by Ableforth's is a gem, and this cherry brandy is no exception. Cherry brandy tends to have a poor reputation, because it often becomes cloying and sickly, so getting the taste spot-on is no mean skill. The key here is that, instead of taking neutral grain spirit and flavoring it, as many producers do, Ableforth's has taken a simpler approach, combining fine XO and VSOP with top-quality cherries, as well as some plums and damsons. The resulting spirit has a fresh and lively palate, with allspice and cinnamon to round it off.

— *The party spirit* —

SAGATIBA CACHAÇA PURA

Sagatiba
Rio de Janeiro, Brazil
{ sagatiba.com }
CACHAÇA, 38%

There are very few spirits that are more associated with good times and partying than cachaça, the distinctive Brazilian cousin of rum. Made from fermented sugarcane juice, it is the national drink of Brazil, and has been steadily growing in popularity after it was heavily promoted during the 2014 World Cup and the 2016 Olympics. This is the brand that led the way in Europe: it's a premium version with a substantial kick. It works best in cocktails, particularly a full-flavored caipirinha when mixed with lime and sugar.

— *A rare delight* —

HACIENDA DE CHIHUAHUA ANEJO SOTOL
Vinomex
Chihuahua, Mexico
{ vinomex.com.mx }
SOTOL, 38%

Sotol is often described as a form of tequila. Certainly it is distilled from agave plants, but it is produced by the much rarer Dasylirion or Desert Spoon agave, which, unlike the Blue Weber Agave used for tequila, germinates from seeds that are often destroyed by the harsh climate. It takes 12 to 15 years for the plant to grow fully, and there are strict rules and restrictions on harvesting it. This liquor is top-quality, though something of an acquired taste. It is matured for 24 months in French oak barrels.

— *Top notch tequila* —

1800 ANEJO TEQUILA
Beckmann Family
Mexico
{ 1800tequila.com }
TEQUILA, 40%

For some years, there has been talk of tequila coming into vogue as a spirit, and Diageo's decision to swap its Bushmills Irish whiskey brand for a leading tequila gave substance to the rumor. Tequila fans point out that the spirit has as much diversity as single malt whisky, and, while it's an acquired taste, it's no more challenging than Scotch is. This one, named after the year tequila was first created, is at the super-premium, high end of the category. Most of the spirit is aged in French oak barrels for more than a year, and some of it is matured for three years in American oak.

60

— *Shine on, you crazy uncle* —
CRAZY UNCLE MOONSHINE
Whippersnapper Distillery
Perth, Australia
{ whippersnapperdistillery.com }
MOONSHINE, 40%

Whippersnapper is the first urban distillery in
Perth, Western Australia, and it makes a whisky
called Upshot. The distillery is a tribute to two
World War II pilots who loved whisky and set
up a moonshine operation in Perth after the
conflict. Crazy Uncle Moonshine has a mash bill
made up of Australian corn, wheat, and barley.
It is distilled on a special still. It's often hard
to get too excited about un-aged moonshine,
but this one has a delicious vanilla note and a
clean, crisp taste. It's beautifully packaged, too,
with an unusual and original award-winning
label. Currently hard to find outside Australia,
but give it time.

— *Gin genius* —
BLACKWATER NO 5
Blackwater Distillery
Co Waterford, Ireland
{ blackwaterdistillery.ie }
GIN, 41.5%

The founder of this craft distillery is Peter
Mulryan, a no-nonsense Irish whiskey expert
and writer, so it is no surprise to find that
Blackwater is taking a meticulous approach to
making spirits. The whiskey is still some way
away, but this gin is a beauty. The distillery's
location, on the bank of the Blackwater River,
is pretty special, too. No 5 is created totally by
hand and eye, a slow, labor-intensive process,
and the botanicals come from the distillery's
own monastic garden. The result is a floral gin,
with distinctive sweet lemon notes. Master of
Malt described it as 'a yummy gin-shaped time
machine'. Bang on.

— *East meets West* —

JAPANESE GIN
The Cambridge Distillery
Cambridge, England
{ cambridgedistillery.co.uk }
GIN, 42%

The Cambridge Distillery is one of the world's most innovative and is prepared to try new and even controversial projects in the interests of finding new directions. This spirit takes traditional gin botanicals such as juniper and combines them with Japanese ones. There is now a Japanese gin distillery in Kyoto, but Cambridge Distillery was the first to combine East and West in this fashion. Each botanical is hand-distilled in tiny volumes under vacuum. Low-temperature distillation is employed to maximize the flavors, which are imparted by shiso leaf, a Japanese culinary herb used for seasoning and in wasabi; sesame seed, which is so common to Japanese cooking that the country is now the world's biggest importer of it; sanshō, which gives rootsy, earthy characteristics; and yuzu, which has an aromatic zest and replaces lemon in the final gin's taste. This is a premium spirit, and it's packaged beautifully in bottles printed using silkscreen printing techniques. The gin has won a number of awards, and can be found at top Japanese restaurants such as Nobu. The gin combines spiciness, clean cucumber, and lemon zest on the palate, and the finish is lemony. If that's not enough for you, try Watenshi. Using this Japanese gin, the distillery is able collect the spirit normally lost to evaporation by distilling at half the pressure found on top of Mount Everest and at a temperature lower than the coldest day in the South Pole.

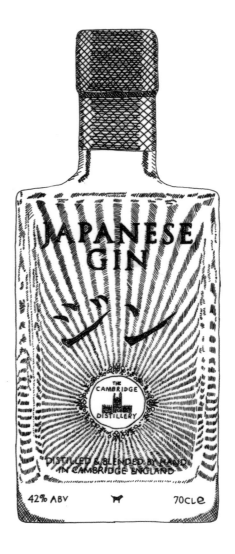

— *Water of life* —

ACQUAVITE DI VINACCIA BACCO PER VENERE

Nannoni Grappe

Castagno, Italy

{ nannoni.net }

GRAPPA, 42%

Acquavite, aquavite or aqua vitae are generic terms that may be used to describe a range of distilled spirits. In this case, acquavite refers to a delicate and fragrant, award-winning member of the grappa family. Grappa is immensely popular in Italy, where there is a passion for any young spirit, especially a fresh and fruity one like this. Like grappa, it's made with grapes — the whole grape, including skins, seeds, and stems — crushed into a young wine and then distilled. The relatively low alcoholic strength (grappas can be as strong as 60% ABV) means that this makes a refreshing aperitif that can be enjoyed with antipasti and olives.

— *A Mars a day…* —

MARS MALTAGE COSMO

Mars Shinshu

Kamiinagun, Japan

{ tokiwaimports.com }

BLENDED MALT WHISKY, 43%

Mars Shinshu is one of Japan's lesser-known distilleries, and one that has had a chequered and difficult history. But with the recent trend toward Japanese whisky, it is now once more enjoying an upsurge in its fortunes. Mars Maltage Cosmo is a blended malt, which means that it is a mixture of malts from different distilleries. The combination includes some products from Scottish distilleries, although the identities of these contributors are not disclosed to the public. Not everyone approves of this approach, but Cosmo maintains Japan's high standards. It has some pleasant vanilla and red berry fruits on the nose, and a taste that mixes orange, oak, and milk chocolate.

— A star is born —

STARWARD

New World Distillery
Victoria, Australia
{ starward.au }
SINGLE MALT WHISKY, 43%

Australian whisky is flourishing at the moment, although you might not notice if you live outside Australia or Southeast Asia, since much of it never leaves those parts of the world. Starward is an exception. Much of the fuss about the ever-improving malts from Down Under revolves around Tasmania, where several distillers are situated. But there are some great distilleries on the mainland, too, and this is one of them. The New World Whisky Distillery is the brainchild of entrepreneur David Vitale. The name of the business says it all — this is an attempt to bring a new twist to traditional single malt. Vitale proudly points to the fact that his team took nine years to tweak and change its formula before deciding on this recipe. Its taste will strike a chord with established malt lovers, but it will not be overfamiliar to them: it departs from the norm by using Australian malted barley and by aging the spirit in Australian apera (fortified wine) casks. The result is an excellent whisky that bears favorable comparison with Scottish single malt. It is rich and sweet, with a spicy finish. And it was good enough to attract investment from drinks giant Diageo as part of its program of funding up-and-coming small distilleries around the world.

SEVEN MOODS OF CRAFT SPIRIT   ADVENTUROUS

— Aged to perfection —
TAKETSURU
Nikka
Yoichi and Miyagikyo,
Japan
{ nikka.com }
BLENDED MALT WHISKY,
43%

There are two reasons this whisky finds itself in the 'adventurous' category: one, because you're going to have to travel far and look hard to find it; and two, it has an eye-watering price in the retail sector and a considerably inflated one when it comes out of someone's cupboard and finds its way to auction. The blend contains malts from Nikka's two distilleries. It's not as lively as some of Japan's other whiskies, but it is a delight, with earthy, almost mushroom-like notes, rich stewed fruit, and traces of both sherry and peat. Wonderful whisky-making.

— Fancy a cuppa? —
COFFEY GRAIN
Nikka
Tochigi, Japan
{ nikka.com }
GRAIN WHISKY, 45%

No, it doesn't have any coffee in it; neither does it taste of coffee. But the name certainly piques the interest of consumers curious about the Japanese whisky category in general. Actually 'coffey' is another name for the column or continuous still used in the making of grain whisky. This brand is made up mainly of corn, and corn brings with it a sweeter note. If that's your thing, this is a cracker, and it's more readily available than in the past, since Nikka has tried to fill the gap created by shortages of its single malts.

— Norse magic —
AALBORG TAFFEL AKVAVIT
Aalborg
Aalborg, Norway
{ aalbogakvavit.co.uk }
AKVAVIT, 45%

Akvavit is an alcohol spirit flavored wth herbs and spices and distilled mainly in Scandinavia. It has a history stretching back 500 years. With alcoholic bitters, herbal spirits, and well-made liqueurs gaining traction in the marketplace, akvavit might win new followers. Taffel refers to a specific style of the spirit, which is matured in casks, though this one is slightly unusual insomuch as it is golden, rather than clear. This is a premium drink, created in 1946 to celebrate the centenary of Aalborg Taffel Akvavit. It is described as smooth, flavorsome, and spicy.

— Irish delight —

DUNVILLE'S VR 10 YEAR OLD

Echlinville Distillery
Newtownards,
Northern Ireland
{ echlinville.com }
SINGLE MALT WHISKEY,
46%

There has been a resurgence in Irish whiskey in recent years, both in the southern Republic and in northern Ulster. Dunville was once one of the best-known names in Irish whiskey, and a version of it has now been revived by the Echlinville Distillery in Northern Ireland. Finished in Pedro Ximénez casks, this Very Rare 10 Year Old is an extraordinary achievement and a sumptuous treat: its flavor may take a little while to open up, but when it does it reveals a delightful apple-pie-and-custard of a whiskey, with some charming and memorable fruit candy notes.

— Eastern promise —

WHITE OAK AKASHI

Eigashima Shouzo
Akashi, Hobnshu, Japan
{ No website }
BLENDED WHISKY, 46%

Japanese whisky is dominated by two big producers, but there are a scattering of others. White Oak — or Eigashima — Distillery is primarily a sake- and shochu-producing plant, and its relationship with whisky has been a stop-start one. Only in recent years has the company responded to world demand for Japanese whisky and exported this product. The domestic version of Akashi, made with molasses, should be avoided, but the export version, with grain and malt, is a fine example of quality blended whisky, with some vanilla, cherry, and sweet spice in the mix. Not easy to find, but worth the search.

— Capital spirit —

PREMIUM GIN BATCH 1

East London Liquor
Company
London, England
{ eastlondonliquorcompany.
com }
GIN, 46%

East London Liquor Company is the meeting of minds of a group of young and passionate spirit-makers. The business operates from an old factory on Bow Wharf, and the site boasts a spirits shop and a cool bar with a perspex screen at the back through which you can watch distilling take place. Quality is key here, and while this first batch of gin stays close to the classic, juniper-led, traditional gin blueprint, it has a full citrus-driven flavor, and offers an affordable alternative to some of the better mainstream gins.

— *For the many…* —
FEW BARREL GIN
FEW Spirits
Evanston, IL, USA
{ fewspirits.com }
GIN, 46.5%

FEW Spirits is one of the bigger and better known of the American craft distilleries that are now scattered across the United States. This gin is one of the stars of its range. As the name implies, it is matured in charred barrels, and the result is a sweet, full-flavored sipping gin that online retailers Master of Malt have described as 'stunning'. And they're not lying. There are citrus, clove, juniper, and cherry notes here. It's irreverent, playful modern, and inventive, and has many of the finest properties of both bourbon and genever.

— *The Chosen Few* —
FEW SINGLE MALT
FEW Spirits
Evanston, IL, USA
{ fewspirits.com }
SINGLE MALT WHISKY, 46.5%

Why FEW? This is the first distillery at Evanston, Illinois, since Prohibition, and Frances Elizabeth Willard was a leading member of the local Temperance Movement. One of the most significant trends in the current American craft boom is the development of single malt whisky, a style that was rarely made in America. Much of it is truly horrible, but this is top notch. It's got a soft, chocolatey taste with some dusty smoke courtesy of cherrywood. Don't expect anything like Scotland — this is a new and exciting category for whiskey, and FEW is at the very forefront of it.

— *Love it to Death* —
DEATH'S DOOR GIN
Death's Door
Washington Island,
WI, USA
{ deathsdoorspirits.com }
GIN, 47%

The name refers to the corridor between Washington Island and the Door County peninsula, and there is something truly exciting about this company's range of premium spirits. The team here strive to work with local producers. Death's Door gin is made from Death's Door vodka, which in turn is made from three grains — red winter wheat, malted barley, and corn. The gin is simple, with just three botanicals — fennel, coriander, and Washington Island's own wild juniper berries — but powerful and flavorsome enough to hold its own in any cocktail.

— *Go ape* —

MONKEY 47

Monkey 47

Schwarzwald, Germany

{ monkey47.com }

GIN, 47%

One of the fascinating things about the resurgence of interest in gin is how different distillers approach the flavor profile. Juniper is meant to predominate, and some gins (such as Death's Door) use just two or three botanicals to highlight it. Other gins seem to include juniper as a footnote by adding scores of botanicals. This one does both. It is not only 47% ABV, it also has 47 botanicals, including cranberries. But juniper's still there, and Monkey 47 is outstanding. Expect pine and citrus notes from this complex and highly original gin.

— *Out of Africa* —

KOVAL SINGLE BARREL BOURBON

Koval

Chicago, IL, USA

{ koval-distillery.com }

BOURBON, 47%

One of the craft industry pioneers, Koval — set up in 2008 — is an example of how quality and innovation can be combined to provide exciting and adventurous new whiskey styles. The law requires that bourbon must have a mash bill made up of at least 51 per cent corn. The rest is normally a mix of barley, rye or wheat. Here, though, millet, is used instead, and the corn double whammy works superbly. Gluten-free, organic, and unfiltered, this bourbon has a rich orchard fruit and marmalade orange taste, with a spicy late tang and some charred oak in the finish.

— *Turkish delight* —

YENI ALA RAKI

Yeni

Istanbul, Turkey

{ yenirakiglobal.com }

RAKI, 47.3%

Raki is the traditional national drink of Turkey, and it has been made for centuries. It can be rough and badly produced, but this is from the premium end of the spectrum, and is pleasant neat or with chilled water. The drink is traditionally served at the raki table, where it is consumed with mezze, which includes salad, olive oil, meatballs, stuffed vegetables, and fried food. Yeni Ala Raki is made through a complex and time-consuming distillation process using sun-dried grapes — juicy raisins — and distills them three times before aniseed is added.

— Full sail ahead —

MACKINLAY'S SHACKLETON THE JOURNEY

Whyte & Mackay

Glasgow, Scotland

{ whyteandmackay.com }

BLENDED MALT WHISKY, 47.3%

In 2007, a stock of Mackinlay's whisky that belonged to Ernest Shackleton was discovered in one of the bases he set up in Antarctica in 1916. Brand owners Whyte & Mackay were permitted to remove a bottle and take samples before putting it back again. Then, from that sample, whisky-maker Richard Paterson set out to recreate Shackleton's whisky. It was bottled and sold, raising £250,000 ($350,000) for the Antarctic Heritage Trust. This is a second version of that whisky, released in 2016 to mark the centenary re-enactment of Shackleton's epic journey. Shackleton's Mackinlay's is thought to have been mainly or even completely made up of whisky from the now defunct Glen Mhor Distillery, and at the core of this new version is a rare 1980 Glen Mhor cask. The remake also includes a peated version of Dalmore that is unavailable commercially, as well as malts from at least eight other distilleries, including Glenfarclas, Ben Nevis, Jura, and Aultmore. This is a whisky that shows what can be achieved in the underrated blended malt category. Genuinely different and unusual, its distinctive orange, toast, sweetcorn, and citrus notes combine on the nose, and it is a real treat on the palate, with orange fruits surfing over the rich and earthy base, and tannins and spices giving the malt a complex overall taste.

— *The personal touch* —
SANTO DOMINGO ALBARRADAS MEZCAL
Del Maguey
Albarradas, Mexico
{ delmaguey.com }
MESCAL, 48%

Del Maguey produces a range of single village mescals, all of which come in attractive green bottles with labels bearing the name of the settlement in question. This mescal comes from the Mixe region of the southern part of Oaxaca, an area described as a 'high-altitude tropical zone similar to parts of Hawaii'. It is the work of Esperidion Morales Luis, who has been making the spirit since the 1950s, and his son Juan. It has a light nose, with strong citrus notes. On the palate, the initial taste is of tropical fruits with spicy and woody notes. If you can't find this one, any of the Single Village range warrants exploration.

— *Fox in the box* —
WASMUND'S SINGLE MALT
Copper Fox
Sperryville, VA, USA
{ copperfox.biz }
SINGLE MALT WHISKY, 48%

Wasmund's is another fine example of how American single malt whisky is developing into a truly exciting new whisky category, and is doing so by exploring new ways of making the spirit — ways that are not always within the rules laid down by Scotland and Europe. The barley is hand-malted at the distillery, and dried over applewood and cherrywood — the only distillery anywhere to use this method. Maturation takes place in used bourbon barrels, with applewood and oak chips added. The result is a rich, full-bodied, smoky malt with orange, pepper, spice, and fruit chutney notes.

—*Wild rover* —
BÁN POITÍN
Echlinville Distillery
Newtownards, Northern Ireland
{ ban-poitin.com }
POITÍN, 48%

Search for the website for this brand, and the words 'Ireland's most notorious spirit' come up. Click on the link, and you reach an all-but-empty holding page with the words 'Watch this space…'. Not sure what to make of that. Thankfully, the spirit itself isn't quite so enigmatic. Poitín was once the staple Irish spirit distilled from whatever its makers could get their hands on. It is associated with the lawless rebel heart of Ireland, and its illicit production was seen as a stance against the oppressive establishment that the country endured over the centuries. Often extremely potent and potentially dangerous, poitín was outlawed for many years and, when it was permitted once more, all sorts of spirits were passed off under its name, including a sweet toffee-like spirit and a distilled single malt spirit — known to most of us as 'new make'. Today, there is a range of different tasting poitins, made from a host of different base ingredients. This one is made from potatoes, malted barley, and sugar beet. It is stylishly packaged, and has a firm, spirit-rich flavor. It can be drunk neat, but it is particularly good as a substitute for whisk(e)y in cocktails.

— For the masses —
RED STAR BAIJIU
Red Star Company
Beijing, China
{ redstarwine.com }
BAIJIU, 50%

— A barrel of fun —
REBEL YELL SINGLE BARREL 10 YEAR OLD
Lux Row Distillers
Bardstown, KY, USA
{ rebelyellbourbon.com }
BOURBON, 50%

In 2016, 100 million gallons (five billion liters) of baijiu were consumed, making it the world's most popular spirit. The vast majority of this, of course, was in China, but nevertheless it is a significant world spirit, and although it is similar to other spirits, such as vodka or Japanese shochu, its higher strength sets it apart. It can be made from a range of grains, but is normally distilled from sorghum. This one is produced in huge volumes, and was designed to give the average Chinese citizen quality baiju at an affordable price. The Chinese drink it warm and with food, but it can also be consumed from shot glasses.

Rebel Yell has unsavory links with the American Civil War, and when this liquor was launched it came complete with Confederate flags and a music tape featuring the likes of Lynyrd Skynyrd. The brand has since changed hands, and its current owners play up the rebel side of the brand rather than the yell part. Visit the website, and it's all motorbikes and road trips. This is an anomaly, then: an upmarket 10-year-old whiskey from one cask — and 10 years is very old for bourbon. But it's a total delight, with the soft, sweet, wheated nature of the core liquid offset by tannins and spice from the barrel.

— *Spice attack* —
BATAVIA ARRACK VAN OSTEND
Alpenz
Amsterdam, Netherlands
{ alpenz.com }
ARRACK, 50%

— *The 'Untamed One'* —
SÄNTIS DREIFALTIGKEIT EDITION MALT
Locher
Appenzell, Switzerland
{ saentismalt.com }
SINGLE MALT WHISKY, 52%

Batavia Arrack originates from Java, and in the great days of the spice trails from the East it was much sought-after as a key ingredient for making punch. Its attraction lies in the fact that, when used as a cocktail or punch ingredient, it elevates spices and citrus notes. It has played a crucial role in the world of cocktails, and is popular with chocolatiers and pastry-makers. This specimen is made from sugar molasses and local red rice, and is a fiery and robust spirit neat. It's an acquired taste, with a strange grapey note, and it sits somewhere between light rum and grappa.

Switzerland has been playing catch-up in the world of whisky, because until 1999 spirit distillation was banned there. But two decades later, the country has started to produce some great expressions, and Säntis has been at the heart of the action. This family brewery has been established since the 1880s, and at the turn of the new millennium Karl Locher started making single malt whisky. This is a smoky, peaty beauty. The malt is smoked in three different ways: in beech, in oak, and in peat. Some sweet fruit and spice notes are weighted into the mix, too, making for a highly distinctive and world-class whole.

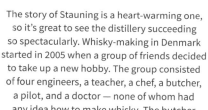

— *West coast wonders* —
STAUNING PEATED
Stauning
Skjern, Denmark
{ stauningwhisky.com }
SINGLE MALT WHISKY, 54%

The story of Stauning is a heart-warming one,
so it's great to see the distillery succeeding
so spectacularly. Whisky-making in Denmark
started in 2005 when a group of friends decided
to take up a new hobby. The group consisted
of four engineers, a teacher, a chef, a butcher,
a pilot, and a doctor — none of whom had
any idea how to make whisky. The butcher
suggested that they convert his old abattoir into
a mini-distillery. The floor of the old cold store
was used as a floor malting, an old mincer was
turned into a grain mill, the pickling vat was
used for fermentation, and the oven — which
still smelled of smoked bacon — was fed with
grain instead of meat. They got peat from the
nearby Klosterlund Museum, where they exhibit
and work with peat, as people in Denmark have
done since the Iron Age. The distilling project
subsequently went from strength to strength:
the team have moved to a new site, and are
currently building a larger distillery with the
backing of drinks giant Diageo. Stauning's
peated whisky is made in batches, so there
is some variation, but the distillery style is a
sophisticated mix of milk chocolate, grain, and
smoke. This is a business that is going places.

74

— Green magic —

BERGER, VERT & VIF ABSINTHE

Marie Brizard
Bordeaux, France
{ mariebrizard.com }
ABSINTHE, 55%

Absinthe is misunderstood.
What little people know about
it involves hallucinations,
green fairies, and drinking
rituals that are reminiscent
of opium dens and crack
smoking. It was made illegal
100 years ago, and many
producers turned to pastis.
But it is a wonderful and
extraordinary spirit. Now that
production is again permitted,
quality absinthe is enjoying a
renaissance. This version was
originally a Dutch product
made in the 1830s by Charles
Frédéric Berger. It is now
owned by French liqueur-
maker Marie Brizard, and
combines star anise, licorice,
and Artemisia pontica extract.

— Kentucky belle —

PIKESVILLE 6 YEAR OLD RYE

Heaven Hill
Louisville, KY, USA
{ pikesvillerye.com }
RYE WHISKEY, 55%

Rye whiskey fell badly out of
favor at the back end of the
last millennium, but it is now
the darling of the mixology
world, its spicy characteristics
regarded as the perfect base
for innovative and exciting
cocktails. At the premium end,
it's a pretty fine drink in its
own right. Pikesville was
originally produced in
Maryland, but is now made
in bourbon country. This
is a spicy, sweet treat, best
enjoyed straight as a
sharpener. With only 51 per
cent rye, it just scrapes in
to the rye category, but you
wouldn't know it from the
strong spice attack. Pleasant,
woody notes in the finish, too.

— Full-bodied —

PAUL JOHN CLASSIC SELECT CASK

John Distilleries
Goa, India
{ pauljohndistillery.com }
SINGLE MALT WHISKY,
55.2%

India is in constant dispute
with Europe, especially
Scotland, over its whisky.
Most 'whisky' from India is not
recognized because it is made
with molasses, not grain. India
retaliates by imposing punitive
tariffs on European whiskies.
John Distilleries is one of the
few Indian merchants
profitably exporting their
whiskies, and this liquor is at
the root of its success. It's a
full-bodied, fruity malt that
can hold its own with the
world's finest. Its sprightly and
fresh taste is due in part to its
youth, and partly to an Indian
climate that ensures
accelerated maturation.

— *No-nonsense rum* —

ORD RIVER OVERPROOF RUM

Hoochery Distillery
Kununurra, Australia
{ hoochery.com.au }
RUM, 56.4%

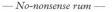

Ord River Overproof Rum is the brainchild of Raymond 'Spike' Dessert III, an American farmer who set up a seed business in the Ord River valley in The Kimberley, Western Australia. The region is ideal for producing sugarcane, and when the industry was booming, Spike hit upon the idea of making rum. Hoochery Distillery is the oldest distillery in Western Australia, and was the first to produce rum. In recent years, this has swept the board in Australian spirits awards. Despite its strength, it can be enjoyed neat: its spiciness and vanilla and chocolate notes make for a great sipping rum.

— *Incendiary spirit* —

WOOD'S 100 OLD NAVY

Wood's
Guyana, West Indies
RUM, 57%

The 100 in the name of this rum refers to 100% proof under the British proofing system — that's 57% ABV, the strength a spirit needs to be before a match will ignite gunpowder soaked in it. This was the strength at which it was served to seamen, making it a genuine, old-fashioned, naval rum. It is taken from the contents of three separate drums from Guyana, each of which contains spirit made with rich sugarcane from the banks of the Demerara River. It has a rich, syrupy taste, and is remarkably smooth, with toffee and spice notes. It makes a strong cocktail base, too.

— *Pot lucky* —

REDBREAST 12 YEAR OLD CASK STRENGTH

Irish Distillers
Cork, Ireland
{ irishdistillers.ie }
POT STILL WHISKEY, 57.7%

Redbreast is probably the best-known expression of pot still whiskey, a style unique to Ireland made from a mash of malted barley and another, unmalted grain. Irish Distillers committed to releasing 20 new pot still whiskey expressions over 10 years and this, the cask strength version of the popular standard 12 year old, was one of the first. It is everything a pot still whiskey should be: earthy and oily, with a complex but powerful mix of red berry and stewed fruits, vanilla, and chewy distinctive spices. This is right up there with the world's very best whiskies.

— An Aussie institution —

BUNDABERG OVERPROOF

Bundaberg Distillery
Bundaberg, Australia
{ bundabergrum.com.au }
RUM, 57.7%

Bundaberg's standard rum is an Australian
national institution, its distinctive square bottle
and white bear logo instantly recognizable.
The distillery has a history stretching back
to the 1880s, and its rums are increasingly
being exported, winning new fans across the
world. The high-strength Overproof version
is produced on a much smaller scale than
the standard version, but shares many taste
characteristics with its sibling. The difference
is due to extra aging and the added alcoholic
strength helping to make Overproof a fruity,
easy-drinking, and rounded rum with extra
intensity and bite.

— Finest craft gin —

THE WEST WINDS GIN THE BROADSIDE

The West Winds
Melbourne, Australia
{ thewestwindsgin.com }
GIN, 58%

Australians must be fed up with being portrayed
as brash, loud, and aggressive. Their country
boasts some of the most sophisticated and
refined food and drink on the planet, and here's
some of the evidence. The West Winds was set
up by four friends in 2010 to create damn fine-
quality craft gin. Two of their early creations —
The Sabre and The Cutlass — achieved that, but
then they came up with this superb overproof
number. Sea parsley and sea salt are used in the
recipe, and a spicy juniper hit, delicious citrus,
and a distinctive saltiness make this one of the
best drinks in an already strong sector.

— Battle-hardened —

BOWER HILL BARREL STRENGTH
Bower Hill
Louisville, KY, USA
BOURBON, 59.4%

Smoke and mirrors abound in the American whiskey industry; things are often not what they seem. The Bower Hill range of bourbons is steeped in mystery, and it's almost impossible to trace the brand's owners. We know that it is distilled and matured in Louisville, Kentucky, but it has purported links to a distillery in Ohio that turns out to be non-existent. The simplest and most likely explanation for this is that it is bourbon distilled under licence by one of Louisville's small band of distilleries and bought by a group of investors who have concocted a marketing backstory. But no matter: what we have here is a very fine bourbon. The name of this liquor refers to an incident during the Whiskey Rebellion of 1794. After the American War of Independence, a tax was imposed on spirit production to clear the enormous war debt, and unhappy distillers resisted and refused to pay. Whiskey-making was particularly hard hit by the tax. A gun battle at Bower Hill led to several deaths before the uprising was finally crushed. This is a fiery, spicy, and oaky bourbon, with strong cinnamon notes, sugar molasses, and a sweetcorn and butter taste.

— Full-bodied rye —
THE BOSS HOG 14 YEAR OLD
Whistle Pig
Middlebury, VT, USA
{ whistlepigwhiskey.com }
RYE WHISKEY, 60.3%

Whistle Pig is a whiskey producer that is pursuing the dream of selling whiskey made with rye from the farm, matured in barrels made from farm-produced oak. That dream started to become reality in 2015, when a rye distillery was opened on the site. To plug the gap, Whistle Pig buys in its rye, and with the help of whiskey expert and distiller David Pickerell, matures it in special casks. This is matured first in new oak American barrels, then in used bourbon ones, and finally in Scottish hogsheads. The result is a powerful, spicy, and earthy rye of outstanding quality, with hints of oak and smoke.

— Burn, baby, burn —
LIMEBURNERS SINGLE MALT SHERRY CASK
The Great Southern Distilling Co.
Albany, Australia
{ distillery.com.au }
SINGLE MALT WHISKY, 61%

The Great Southern Distilling Company is one of Australia's whisky pioneers, and it has grown up in the public eye. Since the early part of the millennium, it has made malt whisky that has evolved from ordinary to extraordinary. The distillery does a number of cask strength whiskies in small batches. Getting hold of them isn't easy, but this one is well worth seeking out. It's matured in second-fill bourbon casks, then transferred to a very small sherry cask. The result is a complex whisky that demands water, which, once added, unleashes a fresh, grainy malt with honey, raisin, and soft toffee in the mix.

— A Jamaican giant —

J. WRAY & NEPHEW WHITE OVERPROOF

J. Wray & Nephew
Jamaica
{ jwrayandnephew.com }
RUM, 63%

— Allowed to breathe —

JADE TERMINUS OXYGÉNÉE ABSINTHE SUPÉRIEURE

Jade Liqueurs
New Orleans, LA, USA
{ bestabsinthe.com }
ABSINTHE, 68%

— Dark and daring —

PLANTATION OFTD

Maison Ferrand
West Indies
{ plantationrum.com }
RUM, 69%

J. Wray & Nephew is now part of the ever-growing Gruppo Campari, which includes whisky distilleries in Scotland, Ireland, and the United States. Despite its size, the company has made a considerable effort to maintain the finest aspects of local crafted products. White Overproof is the world's biggest-selling over-strength rum comprising a special blend of spirits from Wray & Nephew's estates. It has a fruity, natural aroma with overtones of molasses, and the palate is complex, with molasses, exotic fruits, and banana. It's fiery and spicy, with a long, spicy finish.

Jade Liqueurs was founded in 2000 by scientist T A Beaux. The company is deadly serious about its absinthes, re-creating authentic recipes from the Belle Epoque. This one's unique selling point lies within the word 'Oxygénée'. It refers to a special hot oxygenation process designed to sterilize the spirit, and thus destroy potentially harmful properties it may contain. It is made exactly as the original would have been, and includes a species of wormwood from the foot of the Alps. It a creamy, powerful, and medicinal absinthe and the strongest expression in the Jade range.

Plantation is owned by French drinks company Maison Ferrand, but its range is made up of quality West Indian rums. OFTD, which stands for Old Fashioned Traditional Dark, is a blend of rums from Guyana, Jamaica, and Barbados. It was added to the company's portfolio at the end of 2016, when it was selected by a panel that included American drinks expert David Wondrich and the owners of some of the world's best bars, including Trailer Happiness in London and Latitude 29 in New Orleans. OFTD bursts with flavor, including raisins, nutmeg, oak, vanilla, molasses, and honey.

— *Blast from the past* —

**JADE ESPIRIT EDOUARD
SUPÉRIEURE**

Jade Liqueurs

New Orleans, LA, USA

{ bestabsinthe.com }

ABSINTHE, 72%

This was the first of Jade's
re-creations of authentic
vintages made before the
century-long absinthe ban.
Edouard Supérieure is a Swiss
absinthe made with all the
finest ingredients, including
Andalusian anise and fennel of
Gard. In spite of the very high
alcohol content that often
gets this spirit its maverick
reputation, this is a million
miles away from some of the
cheap, commercial absinthes.
There is a strong herbaceous
note here, together with an
earthiness, and each mouthful
has a long, clean finish.

— *Tiks all the boxes* —

OLD J TIKI FIRE

Admiral Vernon's

St Lucia

RUM, 75.5%

Admiral Edward Vernon is
famous for reducing the
strength of Royal Navy rum in
the 18th century, and when
the ships' crews complained
about the poor-quality grog,
he suggested that they should
add limes and sugar to make
the drink more palatable. It's
lime, vanilla, and sugar that
mark out this rum, as well
as a strong spicy note. Old
J Tiki Fire is a high-strength
version of Old J Spiced Rum,
and the additional kick
enables Old J Tiki Fire to make
its presence felt in a whole
host of rum-based cocktails.
Obviously not a drink to be
consumed neat.

— *A fine balancing act* —

**GOSLING'S BLACK SEAL
151 PROOF**

Gosling's

Bermuda

{ goslingsrum.com }

RUM, 75.5%

Gosling's has a history
stretching back more than 200
years, and its establishment as
'the Spirit of Bermuda' came
about by happy accident.
James Gosling had set out for
America in 1806 with £10,000
of merchandise. But after 91
days in becalmed waters, his
ship's charter expired, and
he was forced to dock at the
nearest port — St George's,
Bermuda. Since then, the
company's rums have
become world-famous.
This expression is a big,
brash vanilla-and-caramel-
flavored mixing rum.
The signature serve is a
Dark 'n' Stormy — this rum
mixed with ginger beer.

— *Needs water!* —

SUNSET VERY STRONG

St Vincent Distillers
Saint Vincent and The
Grenadines
{ sunsetrum.com }
RUM, 84.5%

This distillery was originally
built to take advantage of
the island's sugar, of which
there was once a plentiful
supply. But no longer: the
refinery has shut, and the
island's main export is now
bananas. The distillery was
taken over for a while by the
island's government, but it is
now again privately owned.
This extraordinarily strong
rum is the favored spirit on St
Vincent, although for obvious
reasons it is mixed with other
ingredients. Designed as a
powerful cocktail base, it has
buttered toast and tropical
fruit notes when heavily
diluted. Some ginger spice is
in the mix, too.

— *Potent and powerful* —

KNOCKEEN HILLS POTEEN
EXTRA STRENGTH

Knockeen Hills
Tiverton, England
{ irish-poteen.com }
POTEEN, 90%

The spelling might be
confusing, but this is the
same basic spirit as the poitín
written about elsewhere,
even though it is made in
Devon. Ninety-nine per cent
of the ingredients are Irish,
though, and they have to be
because poteen is recognized
as a heritage-based spirit, and
protected by its European
Geographical Indicative status.
This is quadruple-distilled,
and not for consumption
neat. It has a deceptively
soft and fruity nose, and a
fiery, peppery taste. Fruit
comes when water is added
in quantity. The company also
offers lower strength poteen.

— *Cold comfort* —

COLD DISTILLED ABSINTHE

Ableforth's
Tunbridge Wells,
England
{ ableforths.com }
ABSINTHE, 91.2%

The strongest spirit in the
'adventurous' section was
always going to be an absinthe
or a poitin — and it's an
absinthe. It's also English.
Ableforth's is part of online
retailer Master of Malt, and
Professor Cornelius Ableforth
is a fictitious eccentric spirits
creator. This is a serious drink,
though. 'Cold distilled' means
vacuum-distilled at room
temperature. This is a much
gentler process than pot-still
distillation which preserves
the freshness and vitality of
the ingredients. The amount
of oil carried over is lower, too,
so there is very little cloudi-
ness when water is added.
Excellent with LOTS of water.

———— ❦ ————

CAN A SPIRIT REALLY BE
POETIC? EACH ENTRY HAS
BEEN INCLUDED BECAUSE IT
IS AN ORCHESTRA IN A GLASS:
BALANCED, DELICATE, AND
IN PERFECT HARMONY. TO
DESCRIBE EACH IS TO SEEK
SUPERLATIVES AND TO WAX
LYRICAL.

———— ❦ ————

POETIC

WHISKY FESTIVALS

WHISKY LIVE
Various countries
{ whiskylive.com }

Whisky Live is an event owned by top spirits periodical *Whisky Magazine*. Effectively it is a franchise, with organizers in each territory staging the event with the marketing support of the publication, including the option of having a representative to host tastings and master classes. Some Whisky Live events, such as those in London, Tokyo, Paris, Cape Town, and Johannesburg, have been held annually for many years now, but there have also been occasional events in Dublin, Tel Aviv, Warsaw, Manila, Auckland, and Sydney. Whisky Live is normally a two-day show.

SPIRIT OF SPEYSIDE FESTIVAL
Scotland
{ spiritofspeyside.com }

The Spirit of Speyside — held over the long Bank Holiday weekend at the beginning of May — has grown into a major event supported by a great number of the 60 or so distilleries in the region. It features dinners, competitions, open days, distillery tours, and lots of entertainment. Highlights in recent years have been getting access to distilleries that don't normally allow public tours, such as Mortlach and Longmorn, and special festival bottlings.

The Festival has become increasingly professional and well organized, with information points and transport links.

FEIS ILE
Scotland
{ islayfestival.com }

This is the Islay Festival, held over eight days at the end of May every year since 1986. Originally a music and whisky festival, it also includes events on Jura, the neighboring island. The distilleries throw open their doors for a week of tours, master classes, tastings, and events, and each of the distilleries has its own special day. In recent years, it has become customary to release a special festival bottling, and fans of the local distilleries, which include Lagavulin, Laphroaig, Bowmore, and Ardbeg, will form a line for these releases, which immediately become collectors' items.

LONDON WHISKY SHOW
England
{ whiskyshow.com/london }

The London Whisky Show claims to be the United Kingdom's finest and largest whisky festival. And with some justification: it has undoubtedly become one of the key dates in the whisky lover's diary. It takes place over one weekend at the end of summer, with a third, media day on the following Monday. It's held at Old Billingsgate, the historic former fish market in the heart of London, and has consistently increased in size year on year, with more and more world distillers joining the biggest Scottish names. A second show featuring old and rare whisky is held every spring in Glasgow.

WHISKY FESTIVALS

MALTSTOCK
Overasselt (near Nijmegen),
Netherlands
{ maltstock.com }

Not so much a festival, more a cross between
a gathering of the clans and a scout camp
with alcohol. Described as 'a relaxed whisky
weekend', the inclusive package includes
two nights' accommodation, two breakfasts
and dinners, snacks, and at least two master
classes. Many of the producers stay for the
event, so guests can chat to them at will.
There's a midnight café for dancing, and a
bonfire and tastings both evenings. Musicians
are encouraged to join in, too. Revelers are
asked to bring whisky, which is pooled and
shared. The whole thing is Dutch magic.

INTERNATIONAL WHISKY FESTIVAL NETHERLANDS
Grote of Sint-Jacobskerk, The
Hague, Netherlands
{ goo.gl/JbYYJo }

As whisky has become more fashionable,
numerous new whisky festivals have sprung
up, and groups such as The Whisky Lounge
run tours of these events around the United
Kingdom. The International Whisky Festival
is one of the oldest of its kind, and it attracts
the world's top producers and whisky lovers.
The event functions in much the same way as
Whisky Live, with guests wandering past the
exhibitors' tables, trying a range of whiskies.
The venue — a deconsecrated 16th-century
church — is most impressive.

LIMBURG WHISKY FESTIVAL
Limburg, Germany
{ festival.whiskyfair.com }

Limburg Whisky Fair has been growing ever since it was first launched in 2002, and today it is the biggest event of its kind in the world. There are several reasons for that. Germany has some of the most committed whisky fans, so that helps, but perhaps more importantly, the Limburg show succeeds in being all things to all people, with rare and old bottlings alongside new releases, and large, established distilleries rubbing shoulders with recently established micro-distillers. As the event has grown, fringe attractions have sprung up, and groups of friends now meet and share whisky in bars and restaurants across the town.

SAN FRANCISCO WHISKY FEST
San Francisco, CA, USA
{ whiskyfest.com/san-francisco }

San Francisco Whisky Fest celebrated its 20th anniversary in 2017, and during those two decades it has grown into a fantastic occasion, not just for tasting wonderful whiskey, but also for meeting the people who make it. It attracts a star-studded list of distillers and whiskey-makers. Bourbon features prominently here, and in 2017 three generations of the Russell family — Jimmy, Eddie, and Bruce — were pouring Wild Turkey, while Julian and Preston Van Winkle were pouring at their ever-popular stand. If you're going, do some research — smart folk aim straight for the rarer whiskies to make sure they don't miss them.

SEVEN MOODS OF CRAFT SPIRIT   POETIC

— Squash for adults —
JOHANNIS BEERE BLACKCURRANT
Berentzen
Echtland, Germany
{ berentzen.de }
SCHNAPPS, 18%

Berentzen makes a wide range of low-alcohol products, schnapps and liqueurs, and has achieved great success with its apple-based drinks. The logical next step was to produce flavored schnapps. Schnapps is a generic term, but in German production it refers to a type of eau-de-vie made with fruit must. The Berentzen range is now Germany's most popular schnapps. Johannis Beere Blackcurrant is a delightful, gentle, and full-flavored drink made from a base of wheat spirit. It is fresh and summery, and has sufficient alcohol to give it a pleasant, adult bite.

— Bramble on —
MORRISON & MACKAY BRAMBLE GIN LIQUEUR
Morrison & Mackay
Aberargie, Scotland
{ mandmwhisky.co.uk }
GIN LIQUEUR, 26.5%

Morrison & Mackay is an independent Scotch whisky merchant based in Perthshire. Its brands include established names, such as whisky spirit-based drinks Bruadar and Columba Cream, and Ginger Tam's, a winter-warming alcoholic ginger liqueur. Bramble Gin Liqueur is one of the company's fruit liqueurs. It combines fresh and juicy brambles with London dry gin. This is a natural product: there are no artificial flavorings or colourings. It is sweet and fruity, and makes a great summer drink over ice after a meal — perhaps instead of dessert?

— Near purr-fection —
PUSSER'S 15 YEAR OLD
Pusser's
Guyana and Trinidad
{ pussersrum.com }
RUM, 40%

The history of Pusser's is linked closely to that of the British Royal Navy. The sailor's daily tot of rum was handed out by the ship's purser; 'purser' became corrupted in speech to 'pusser': hence the name. This is a blend of rums from Guyana and Trinidad made in century-old wooden stills. The rum is created in open vats, where natural yeasts ferment the sugars in a three-stage process that takes 72 hours. The rum is then aged for 15 years in oakwood barrels. The full, rich taste is all natural: no flavoring agents are added. This is a big, syrupy rum, with large amounts of spice and vanilla.

— *Germanic harmony* —

BLAUE MAUS SINGLE CASK

The Fleischmann family

Eggolsheim, Germany

{ fleischmann-whisky.de }

SINGLE MALT WHISKY, 40%

Blaue Maus was established by Robert Fleischmann, and is now run by his son, Tomas. The distillery makes a range of whiskies, among the most notable of which are Green Dog, Black Pirate, and Spinnaker. But perhaps the best of the distillery's produce is reserved for the Blaue Maus (Blue Mouse). Single cask bottlings vary from cask to cask, but the constant theme here is a light, herbal, and fruity liquid. Most single casks are bottled at cask strength, but the 40% ABV works with the lighter malt. There is some soft pear and overripe apple in this unusual mix. Don't expect Scotch, but do expect a mouthful that trips deftly across the tongue.

— *Gin with bite* —

GREYLOCK GIN

Berkshire Mountain Distillers

Sheffield, MA, USA

{ berkshiremountaindistillers.com }

GIN, 40%

Making an everyday and accessible gin to pass the time while you wait for a whisky to mature is a common enough practice, but there is an increasing number of small craft distillers who see the gin as a destination in its own right. So it is with this delicate and sophisticated offering from Berkshire Mountain Distillers. The highly respected spirits and cocktails writer Gary Regan described Greylock as 'absolutely kickass', and it has been reviewed favorably by top magazines, including *Imbibe*. This is a clean, crisp, juniper-led gin, with plenty of licorice and citrus notes, as well as a distinctive herbal undertow.

SEVEN MOODS OF CRAFT SPIRIT   POETIC

— Quality sipping rum —
GOSLING'S FAMILY RESERVE
Gosling
Bermuda
{ goslingsrum.com }
RUM, 40%

—A sweet delight —
MORTON'S OVD
Matthew Clark
Guyana
{ matthewclark.co.uk }
RUM, 40%

Gosling is best known for its Black Seal range, written about elsewhere in the present volume, but this is something of a hidden gem, and well worth seeking out. It is the same blend as Black Seal, but is matured for much longer. The result is an aged rum that bears favorable comparison with fine brandy or single malt. The bottles are hand labeled, dipped in wax, and presented in stylish boxes. But it's the taste that you'll be waxing eloquently about: it's rich, full, oaky, and with layer after layer of dried and stewed fruits. As good as sipping rum gets, this a must for all rum fans.

In the first half of the 19th century, many entrepreneurs sourced products from across the world as trade routes were established and the British Empire flourished. Among the leading importers and bottlers was George Morton, who began shipping this rum from Guyana in 1838. OVD stands for 'Old Vatted Demerara', and this sweet, dark rum became highly successful in Scotland, where it remains the number one drink of its type. It is matured in oak casks, and has a rich, creamy taste with complex toffee notes and a mellow finish. It can be sipped neat, or added to a number of mixers, including peppermint cordial.

— *The Queen of gins* —
DARNLEY'S VIEW
Wemyss
Edinburgh, Scotland
{ darnleysview.com }
GIN, 40%

Every man, woman, and dog seems to
be making gin these days but Wemyss —
pronounced 'weems' — is an independent
whisky bottler that introduced this award-
winning spirit long before the deluge. It's
named to celebrate the moment when Mary
Queen of Scots first saw her future husband,
Lord Darnley, from a courtyard window of the
family seat, Wemyss Castle. This gin contains
just six botanicals, including elderflower, and
each is perfectly balanced with the others.
There are distinctive floral and citrus notes, but
this gin is elegant and understated, and, despite
its lightness, there's enough juniper to ensure
that it works well with a range of mixers.

— *Total luxury* —
BELVEDERE
Belvedere
Warsaw, Poland
{ belvederevodka.com }
VODKA, 40%

It seems a long time ago now, but before the
world of vodka got ridiculous with its marketing
stories, Belvedere was one of the first
companies to try to reposition itself in the
marketplace from a standard spirit to a luxury
one. The owners focused on the brand's Polish
heritage, a vodka-making tradition of more
than 600 years, and the strict rules governing
Polish vodka production which require, among
other things, that only locally produced
raw materials are used. The result here is a
quadruple-distilled, crisp, clean rye vodka of
the highest quality. Belvedere is a style bar
favorite, and remains a brand leader in spite of
intense competition.

— Bounty bar rum —
SUNSET CAPTAIN BLIGH XO
Sunset
Saint Vincent and The
Grenadines
{ sunsetrum.com }
RUM, 40%

Captain William Bligh is best
remembered for the 1789
mutiny on his ship, HMS
Bounty, but that wasn't the
only major incident in his life.
Fifteen years later, he was
appointed governor of New
South Wales, with orders to
clean up the corrupt rum
trade. But his harsh rule led
to a rebellion which saw him
deposed. Sunset Captain Bligh
XO is an award-winning, easy-
drinking rum that has been
matured for about a decade
in ex-bourbon barrels. The
taste balances vanilla and oak,
and has a delightful coconut
aftertaste.

— A man's dram —
LUKSUSOWA
Poznan, Poland
{ luksusowa.com }
VODKA, 40%

This is vodka with a sense of
humor. At least, we think it
is. 'The manly guide', states
the website. 'We know that in
today's world it can be hard to
remember what truly makes a
man, a man. That's why we've
created this compendium of
wisdom to help you live like
a man was made to. Join us
on our continuing mission
to Save The Male — if not for
ourselves then for our sons'.
Right. Meanwhile, Luksusowa
has a history stretching back
to 1928. It is Poland's first and
only potato vodka, and the
name means 'luxury'. It lives
up to the billing, with a rich
and creamy taste, a slight
herbal edge, and an overall
sweetness.

— Delightfully zingy —
CHASE SEVILLE ORANGE
Williams Chase
Hereford, England
{ chasedistillery.com }
GIN, 40%

Chase is William Chase, an
English potato farmer who
used some supermarket-
rejected potatoes to make
chips, and ended up with a
multi-million-pound company
named Tyrrells. He next turned
his hand to potato vodka,
and he now has a range of
stunning spirits such as this
one. Made with botanicals
including juniper, orange peel,
licorice, elderflower, and bitter
almonds, this gin is given a
final infusion of raw peel from
Seville oranges to provide a
crisp, zingy, citrus finish.
The producers suggest mixing
it with rosewater and honey
to make an Orange Blossom
Fizz cocktail.

— *The real deal* —

THE REAL MCCOY 5 YEAR OLD
Four Square Distillery
Barbados
{ foursquare.com }
RUM, 40%

The Real McCoy is named after Bill McCoy, who built his reputation for quality spirits during the Prohibition era in the United States early in the 20th century. He would pick up stocks of Cutty Sark whisky from Bermuda and quality rum from Barbados, then sail to New York, where he would set up a floating liquor store to sell his products from three miles offshore, in international waters. His customers included folk who ran the illegal and hidden speakeasy drinking dens. Unlike other traders, who diluted their spirits or traded in inferior rums, McCoy never interfered with his wares. The bad spirits became known as 'hooch' or 'booze', but McCoy's rums and whiskies became known for their superior quality, and visitors to speakeasies would seek them out, asking for the Real McCoy. This rum, which is absolutely outstanding, has no added sugars, perfumes or flavorings, and is made with pure spring water and the finest sugarcane. There are three rums in this range, aged for three, five or 12 years in heavily charred ex-bourbon barrels, and they taste as good as a fine bourbon or a single malt whisky. The five year old is fabulous value for money, and I strongly recommend you mix it with nothing. It is rich in vanilla, caramel, and spice, with dried raisins, some treacle, and lashings of oaky tannins. It is neither sweet nor cloying, and if whisky is your thing, it is well worth exploring. It's the Real McCoy all right.

— *Affluence in a glass* —
RUSSIAN STANDARD PLATINUM
Russian Standard
St Petersburg, Russia
{ russianstandardvodka.com }
VODKA, 40%

If you want a sense of how big the vodka market has become, check out Milan, Italy, where Russian Standard has its flagship bar. There, the world's best cocktail-makers are invited to demonstrate their skills. It's extremely impressive, and a tad decadent. Just like this vodka. Russian Standard is Russia's number one premium vodka, and this is the premium version of that premium beverage. The producers have a unique silver filtration system that further refines the vodka to make it extraordinarily silky smooth and ultra-clean. Its sharply defined citrus note makes it ideal as a shot or served neat over ice.

— *A fine Italian job* —
MALFY CON LIMONE
Torino Distillati
Moncalieri, Italy
{ malfygin.com }
GIN, 41%

Torino Distillati at Moncalieri, near Turin, produces a wide range of alcohol products, including grappas, brandies, and liqueurs. It was owned by Seagram at one point, but is now run by Carlo and Piera Vergnano and their children. If you think that Italian gin sounds like an oddity, the Vergnanos beg to differ. They claim that gin was invented in Italy in the 11th century by monks on the Salerno coast. Whether that's the case or not, this is a fine blend of juniper and citrus. The lemons — freshly harvested from Italy's coastal regions — supply rich and zesty citrus notes, and give the gin a delicious bite.

CAORUNN SMALL BATCH
Inverhouse Distillers
Cromdale, Scotland
{ caorunngin.com }
GIN, 41.8%

The boom in gin is a recent
phenomenon, and it would
be easy to link Caorunn with
it. But it would be unfair to
do so, because it has been
producing the spirit since
2009, long before the current
craze. It's made in the heart of
the Scottish Highlands at the
Balmenach distillery, which
has been producing single
malt whisky for nearly 200
years. Caorunn is personally
crafted by Simon Buley using
pure grain spirit, Scottish
water, and 11 botanicals,
including ones produced
locally. It is made in small
batches and quadruple-
distilled. There are some
attractive floral and herbal
notes. Described as 'great' by
Gin Foundry.

— *Labor of love* —

ROCK ROSE
Dunnet Bay Distillers
Thurso, Scotland
{ dunnetbaydistillers.com }
GIN, 41.5%

In a country world-famous for
its single malt and blended
whiskies, Dunnet Bay is almost
the definition of a small craft
distillery. It is situated in the
stunning far northeast of
Scotland, an area that has
inspired poets, writers, and
artists for generations. The
distillery makes vodka and
gin, and there is a definite
link between Rock Rose
Gin and its environment,
including the wild and rugged
coastline. The botanicals used
in its creation include sea
buckthorn, *Rhodiola rosea*,
and rowan berries. The result
is full-bodied, rounded, and
balanced. Well worth seeking
out if you can find it.

'NOT EVERYONE WHO DRINKS
IS A POET. SOME OF US DRINK
BECAUSE WE'RE NOT POETS.'
DUDLEY MOORE

SEVEN MOODS OF CRAFT SPIRIT   POETIC

— Cornish cream —
TARQUIN'S HANDCRAFTED
Southwestern Distillery
Wadebridge, England
{ southwesterndistillery.com }
GIN, 42%

The tiny Southwestern Distillery is situated in
a small village near Wadebridge on Cornwall's
north coast. In addition to this gin, it makes
a pastis — the first distillery in Britain ever
to do so. That shouldn't come across as too
much of a surprise, because Cornwall has
strong historical, cultural, and linguistic ties
with Brittany. Southwest is as traditional as
a distillery gets. The copper pot still, named
Tamara, is fired by flame, and cuts are judged
by eye. The botanicals are selected by sight
and feel. The bottles are all individually filled,
corked, sealed, labeled, numbered, and waxed
by hand. And the spirits are rigorously tested by
nose and taste. Tarquin, the distiller, says that
the botanicals are taken from around the world
with the exception of one — Devon violets.
'They come from my garden', he says. 'From
these I take the delicate leaves, which add a
vibrant green freshness to the gin, and create
something deliciously unique. We like to think
the result is comparable to stumbling upon a
beautiful orange blossom field in the middle
of a crisp, dry pine forest'. This gin has won
gold medals at the San Francisco World Spirits
Competition, and in the International Wine and
Spirits Competition. It's delicious, with a nose
of orange blossom, cardamom, and very clean
and fresh pine notes, lots of orange blossom,
and some enjoyable spice notes.

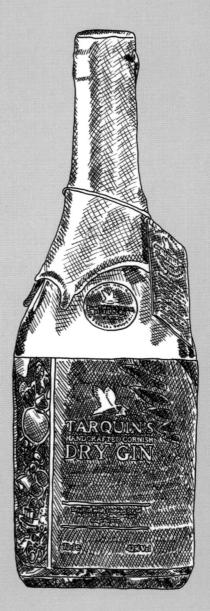

— *Aromatic oils* —

GIN MARE

Global Premium Brands
Guadalajara, Spain
{ ginmare.es }
GIN, 42.7%

The producers of this excellent
and unusual gin describe one
of the key ingredients, the
arbequina olive, as its liquid
gold. It is the only olive to have
its own Designation of Origin,
and it plays a key role in taking
Spanish gin into new and
original territory. The distillery
is located in an ancient fishing
village between the Costa
Brava and the Costa Dorada,
but this isn't an altogether
Spanish project. Described
as Mediterranean Gin, Mare
includes basil from Italy,
thyme from Greece, rosemary
from Turkey, and citrus fruits
from Spain. The result is an
award-winning, savory and
herbal drink that has become
a bar favorite.

— *Garda honor* —

PUNI NOVA

Puni Distillery
Glorenzo, Italy
{ puni.com }
SINGLE MALT WHISKY, 43%

You may not readily associate
Italy with malt whisky, but
this distillery lies in the north
of the country, at the head
of Lake Garda and the foot
of the Alps. It's a region with
strong Teutonic connections,
and Puni fits in nicely with
the whiskies of Switzerland,
Austria, and Germany. The
distillery is an archaeological
curiosity, purpose-built within
a strange brick cube. Puni
Nova is unusually made with
malted rye and malted wheat,
as well as malted barley. It's
full-flavored for a three-year-
old malt, and appeals to the
Italian penchant for younger
spirits. The palate includes
pepper, spice, fruity rye, and
green fruits.

— *Wax lyrical* —

MAKAR

Glasgow Distillery
Glasgow, Scotland
{ glasgowdistillery.com }
GIN, 43%

The name is a medieval
Scottish word for a poet, and
when distilling returned to
Glasgow in recent years, this
Makar was the first product.
It is a vibrant, juniper-based,
handcrafted spirit that has
been successful in
numerous international
competitions, including the
Global Gin Masters for three
years running — in 2015,
2016, and 2017. It comes in a
heptagonal bottle to reflect
both the number of times the
liquid is distilled in Annie, the
company's copper pot still,
and the number of carefully
selected botanicals that
complement the finest juniper
berries from which the core
flavor is derived.

SEVEN MOODS OF CRAFT SPIRIT   POETIC

— *Black beauty* —

BLACK SHUCK

The Norfolk Sloe
Company
Fakenham, England
{ blackshuckltd.co.uk }
GIN, 43%

— *Highland glory* —

**BALVENIE DOUBLEWOOD
17 YEAR OLD**

William Grant & Sons
Dufftown, Scotland
{ williamgrant.com }
SINGLE MALT WHISKY, 43%

— *Brand of hope and glory* —

THE ENGLISH — ORIGINAL

The English Whisky
Company
East Harling, England
{ englishwhisky.co.uk }
SINGLE MALT WHISKY, 43%

Black Shuck is the name given
to a ghostly and fearsome
huge black dog with fiery red
eyes that folklore suggests
prowled the East Anglian
region, terrorizing and killing
anyone it came across. Or is it
folklore? In September 2017,
archaeologists discovered the
skeleton of a seven-foot (2 m-)
'dog' buried in a shallow grave
in an ancient Suffolk abbey.
This premium gin comes from
a family company on Norfolk's
north coast, and it combines
traditional botanicals, such as
juniper, coriander, and bitter
orange peel, with Norfolk's
own lavender and sea
buckthorn. It is available from
selected Norfolk outlets.

William Grant is best known
for its Glenfiddich single
malt, but it also owns one
of Scotland's finest malt
producers — Balvenie, next
door. Virtually all Balvenie
expressions are world-class
but, in a distinguished lineup,
this one still stands out.
Whisky rarely gets any better.
As the name suggests, this has
been matured in two different
types of cask, and the taste is
all about honey and vanilla.
The 17 years in wood create
some oaky notes and gentle
spices, but this really is pure
luxury in a glass. A 12-year-old
version of this is also well
worth seeking out.

The English Whisky Company
was founded and established
by the Nelstrop family, farmers
from Norfolk, and it is the first
new English distillery for over
100 years. With more than 10
years of continuous distilling,
the whiskies are now among
the very best of the new wave.
The distillery, St George's, uses
pure water from an
underground water table.
Recently repackaged, The
English — Original is the
distillery's core malt. It's a
refreshingly nutty and malty
whisky, with some orange and
citrus notes, hazelnut, and
vanilla. Beware, though — it's
very moreish.

— The class of 58 —

58 GIN

Mark Marmont

London, England

{ 58gin.com }

GIN, 43%

58 Gin is based in Hackney
Downs in East London, and
the distillery is one of a
number that now offer you
the chance to make your own
gin, selecting the botanicals,
and bottling the finished
gin in a wax-sealed bottle,
complete with personalized
label. Chances are you won't
manage anything as good
as this, though. It is created
by respected distiller Mark
Marmont on an alembic still
using British wheat and
botanicals including juniper,
pink grapefruit, lemon,
coriander, orris, vanilla,
bergamot, cubeb pepper, and
angelica. The result is a solid
juniper-and-citrus delight with
a late surge of pepper. Classy.

— Perfect harmony —

HIBIKI HARMONY

Beam Suntory

Tokyo, Japan

{ whisky.tokyo.com }

BLENDED WHISKY, 43%

Hibiki contains no fewer than
10 different malts and grain
whiskies made at Suntory's
two distilleries, Yamazaki and
Hakushu. The whiskies are
drawn from five different cask
types. Hibiki was first made in
1989 to mark Suntory's 90th
birthday. Its older expressions
are among the world's most
prized (and prize-winning)
blended whiskies. This one
was introduced as a non-age
statement product to meet
the ever-escalating demand
for Japanese whisky. It's a
peach: sweet, with notes of
white chocolate, fruit candy,
orange, and some toasted
oak. As we've come to expect,
it's beautifully balanced, and
exquisitely blended.

— Molecular engineering —

**YAMAZAKI DISTILLER'S
RESERVE**

Beam Suntory

Tokyo, Japan

{ whisky.tokyo.com }

SINGLE MALT WHISKY, 43%

Japan has some of the most
advanced distilleries in the
world. The nation's two
biggest producers have only
two each, so they have to
make dozens of different
whiskies at each of them to
service their blended whisky
operation. This means an
array of stills, several yeasts,
and maturation in casks that
have been used for a number
of different wines and spirits.
This whisky is classified as
a single malt because all
the whiskies in it are from
Yamazaki. But is a collection
of various whiskies, and therefore something of a greatest
hits package with lots of fruit,
and some light, oak notes.

— *A coming of age* —

APPLETON ESTATE 21 YEAR OLD

Appleton Estate
Jamaica
{ appletonestate.com }
RUM, 43%

Age isn't necessarily all it seems on a bottle of rum or brandy, but in this case the age statement is the same as it is for whisky, and the number 21 means that the youngest rum in this mix of Jamaican spirits is at least that number of years old. Most of the rum has been stored in American oak casks, and the result is a fine sipping rum that combines vanilla, cocoa, and orange. The time in the oak gives it depth, with some tannin and oak notes. It doesn't need mixing, and has been described as 'just brilliant' by online retailer The Whisky Exchange.

— *Full and fun* —

BACARDI SUPERIOR RON HERITAGE

Distell
Puerto Rico
RUM, 44.5%

Bacardi is, of course, a giant of a rum producer. But this special limited edition bottling is of such quality that it deserves to be given 'craft' status. It was released in 2009, and there were only 7,500 cases, so finding it will take some doing. 2009 marked the 100th anniversary of the Daiquiri arriving in America. This was a cocktail created using Bacardi when the company was still based in Cuba. This rum is contained in a replica of the original bottle from that time. It is a richer, fuller rum than Bacardi's standard product, and is bottled at the same strength as it was in 1909.

— *An Old favorite* —

VERY OLD BARTON

Sazerac
Bardstown, KY, USA
{ sazerac.com }
BOURBON, 45%

If you're taking a bottle to a party in Kentucky, take this. It is an all-rounder of a bourbon that is a real crowd-pleaser. It's made at the Barton Brands distillery on the edge of Bardstown, the unofficial bourbon capital of the world, and home to the annual Kentucky Bourbon Festival. Very Old here means six years, which is a good age for a bourbon, but not really very old these days. Barton bottles this liquor at various strengths, but this is the one to go for. It has a high corn content, and is a chewy, fruity, sweet delight with the spice and tannins from the oak giving it depth.

— A joint effort —
HAVANA CLUB SELECCIÓN DE MAESTROS
Pernod Ricard
Cuba
{ havanaclub.com }
RUM, 45%

A very special rum indeed. Havana Club's Selección de Maestros reflects the close-knit nature of the Cuban rum industry, since it is made by a collaboration of all of the members of the guild of Maestros del Ron Cubano. Led by the acclaimed rum-maker Don José Navarro, the group meets first to select the finest and most exceptional aged rums from the island. The selected rums are blended and further aged. Then the guild picks the rums that have matured the best. The finished rum is exceptional, with leather, cigars, orange, coffee beans, and cedarwood. Beautifully packaged, too.

— Mixing with the best —
MICHTER'S US*1
Michter's
Louisville, KY, USA
{ michters.com }
BOURBON, 45.7%

US*1 refers to the fact that Michters' original distillery was the first in the United States, and this bourbon is one of a range that includes rye whiskey and American whiskey. Each is made in small batches of no more than a dozen barrels, because, according to the makers, it ensures that no bad barrels can be blended in to a big run, so the highest quality is consistently maintained. The original distillery is closed, and the operation has moved to Louisville. This is a quality bourbon, with vanilla, caramel, and fruit jostling for attention. It is very popular with the bar trade because of its outstanding mixing qualities.

'THE LIGHT MUSIC OF WHISKY FALLING INTO GLASSES MADE AN AGREEABLE INTERLUDE.'
JAMES JOYCE, *DUBLINERS*

SEVEN MOODS OF CRAFT SPIRIT POETIC

— Brothers in arms —
TEELING 13 YEAR OLD REVIVAL
Teeling Whiskey Co
Dublin, Ireland
{ teelingwhiskey.com }
SINGLE MALT WHISKEY, 46%

No one should ever underestimate the contribution the Teeling family has made to the renaissance in Irish whiskey. Before John Teeling launched his Cooley company, Irish whiskey was being kept afloat by Jameson and Bushmills. Teeling resurrected long-forgotten Irish whiskey brands, and defied his critics to launch whiskeys that did not conform to the national style — peated single malts, grains, double-distilled whiskeys, and cask strength whiskeys. When John finally sold the company, his sons Stephen and Jack left to form the Teeling Whiskey Company. They brought whiskey-making back to Dublin, with a new distillery and visitor center in the Liberties area of the city. Other companies have now also opened distilleries in the city, again mainly in the Liberties district, and in 2017 the Dublin Whiskey Festival was launched, demonstrating that Ireland's capital has whiskey flowing through its veins once more. This whisky is called Revival for obvious reasons, then. It was released to mark the opening of the distillery, and the whiskey has been matured for 12 years in ex-bourbon barrels, and then for another year in ex-Calvados casks. It's a limited edition release of just 10,000 bottles. The apple spirit reinforces the classic Irish notes of apple pie and custard, and there is plenty of toffee sweetness here, too. But it twists unexpectedly late on, when the sweet apple turns a little sharper, and spices come through, enhancing the all-round taste of this enchanting whiskey.

— Let's get High —
HIGH WEST RENDEZVOUS RYE
High West Distillery
Park City, UT, USA
{ highwest.com }
RYE WHISKEY, 46%

High West is one of the American companies
that was ahead of the curve, starting to distill
in 2007 at a time when it was not yet
fashionable to do so. By making this rye
one of its core products, this modest Utah
operation has since expanded to four sites, and
has established an international reputation for
high-quality American whiskeys. Rendezvous
Rye is a no-age-statement blended rye that
won gold at the San Francisco World Spirits
Competition. It has a very high rye content, and
it's a bittersweet affair, with a massive wave of
hot spices. Just as rye should be.

— The legacy lives on —
BARRY CROCKETT LEGACY
Irish Distillers
Midleton, Ireland
{ irishdistillers.ie }
POT STILL WHISKEY, 46%

Named after Midleton master distiller Barry
Crockett and released in 2011, this was one of
the first new pot still whiskeys introduced by
Irish Distillers as part of their drive to restore
a distinctive style to its rightful place among
the world's finest whiskeys. Released in
small batches annually, this product has won
numerous awards. It falls at the sweeter end of
the pot still whiskey spectrum, and in addition
to the expected fluffy apple and pear notes,
there all sorts of exotic fruits and spices to give
it a complex and satisfying taste. The long,
fruity finish is particularly impressive.

— The story continues —

CHAPTER 14
St George's Distillery
East Harling, England
{ englishwhisky.co.uk }
SINGLE MALT WHISKY, 46%

Although St George's Distillery produces single malt whisky in a similar style to the single malts of Scotland, there are distinctive differences between this Norfolk product and its North British counterparts. The Chapter system is one such difference. Each bottling from the very young spirit onward was given a chapter heading to show the evolution of the malt from its very beginning to seven and eight years of age and beyond. Chapter 14 is one of the distillery's very best bottlings. It contains six-year-old malt spirit — maturation is faster in eastern England than in Scotland — and is packed with intense, sweet fruitiness and Danish pastry notes.

— An American dream —

HIGH WEST AMERICAN PRAIRIE RESERVE
High West
Park City, UT, USA
{ highwest.com }
BOURBON, 46%

The Great Plains have played a crucial role in the development of America. They are or were home to Native Americans and countless animals, including the great buffalo. Their vast expanse has sustained ranchers and farmers for generations. Major investment is needed to preserve the wilderness, and High West has a mission to help preserve it. Ten per cent of after-tax profit from the sale of this bourbon goes to the American Prairie Reserve, a nonprofit organization committed to creating the largest nature reserve in the continental United States. The whiskey is a blend of two bourbons and is earthy, with toasted oak, cherries, honey, and sweet spice.

— A crime not to —
JOHN E FITZGERALD LARCENY
Heaven Hill
Louisville, KY, USA
{ larcenybourbon.com }
BOURBON, 46%

John E Fitzgerald enjoys legendary status as the man who built a distillery on the Kentucky River in the 1870s, and then sold his bourbon to workers on the railroads and steamships, and to private clubs. That's the legend. But the reality probably is that he was a bonded treasury agent, and as such the only man at the time allowed to carry warehouse keys. And he used them to take barrels from the warehouse. He was thought to have had great taste, and his barrels became known as 'Fitzgerald Barrels'. When Julian 'Pappy' Van Winkle acquired the business, he named his Old Fitz whiskey after the former owner. This spirit went on to become the first great wheated bourbon. The present bottling was released by Heaven Hill to pay tribute to the lawless agent with a great palate. Larceny is bottled at a weighty 92 proof, 46% ABV, and the barrels for it were selected by the distillery's master distillers. It is six years old, and with wheat the second grain instead of rye, the finished whiskey is smooth and mellow. There is butterscotch and toffee on the nose, and the whiskey is rich and chewy in the mouth, and laced with caramel and buttery notes. Larceny was released to widespread acclaim, picked up a double gold medal at the San Francisco World Spirits Competition, and was chosen as one of the world's top 20 spirits in the world by *Spirit Journal*.

— Wizard of Oz —
BAKERY HILL CLASSIC
David Baker
Melbourne, Australia
{ bakeryhill.com }
SINGLE MALT WHISKY, 46%

David Baker is one of Australia's most experienced distillers, and his distillery is a long way from any other, so he had to make up a lot of his working practices as he went along. Broken equipment? He had to fix it himself. New taste profiles? It was his job to test them all out perosnally. He has made some fabulous whiskies, both peated and unpeated, for many years now, and it's becoming harder to get them outside Australia because of growing domestic demand. Classic is the distillery's unpeated staple release, and in it you'll find big cereal flavors, appealing malty notes, honey, and eucalyptus. A cask strength version can also be purchased.

— Swiss on a roll —
LANGATUN QUINTA DO ZAMBUJEIRO CASK
Langatun
Langenthal, Switzerland
{ langatun.ch }
WHISKY, 49.1%

The Alpine countries have a long, distinguished history of distilling, but the production of brandy, genever, and fruit spirits seldom sits comfortably with that of whisky and, with few exceptions, whisky from the region struggled before 2010. In recent years, though Germany, Austria, and particularly Switzerland have got their acts together. In 2011, the excellent Swiss distiller Langatun poured its spirit into casks from Portugal's Swiss-owned Quinta do Zambujeiro winery. It was bottled at slightly under six years old in 2017, and in 2018 it topped an Alpine tasting ahead of several Scottish single malts. No wonder. Lots of fresh, clean, grapey notes with sweet apple and pear.

— *Aged to perfection* —
STARKA 25 YEAR OLD
Starka
Szczecin, Poland
VODKA, 50%

One consequence of the worldwide craft revolution has been a blurring of traditional boundaries between different drinks categories. Many of the new players are finding fertile land at the margins between gin, vodka, genever, and whisky. When you start aging vodka and gin, you step into murky and choppy waters. Starka pre-dates the craft boom, but it is a rarity: an aged vodka. It is produced from 100 per cent Danskowkje rye aged in oak barrels in deep cellars. The result is an exquisite, oak-enriched and spicy vodka best served chilled over ice.

— *Explosively strong rum* —
PUSSER'S GUNPOWDER PROOF
Pusser's
Guyana and Trinidad
{ pussersrum.com }
RUM, 54.5%

54.5% was the strength of the rum that was handed out to sailors in the British Royal Navy between 1655 and 1970 — more than 300 years. Life was eye-wateringly tough on warships in the 17th and 18th centuries. The invigorating rum ration was the highlight of the day, and this expression is as close as it's possible to get to the way it would then have been served. This modern reincarnation was praised by the editors of *Forbes* magazine as 'the single malt of rum', and named as one of their top 10 rums in the world. It is rich in stewed and dried berry fruits, syrupy, and with malt-like tannins.

'BEER BOTTLES, WHISKEY BOTTLES, BROWN GLASS, GREEN. THEY FELL TO THE LAWN AND I'D FEEL SERENE. ADAM WAS KING TO MY STILTED QUEEN.'
KATE BERNHEIMER, *THE COMPLETE TALES OF KETZIA GOLD*

SEVEN MOODS OF CRAFT SPIRIT POETIC

— *Boy George* —
STAGG JUNIOR
Buffalo Trace
Frankfort, KY, USA
{ buffalotracedistillery.com }
BOURBON, 66.05%

George T Stagg built the most dominant
bourbon distillery during what has become
known as The Gilded Age of Bourbon, and it's
fitting that two stunning whiskeys are named
after him. Why two? This bottling has an older
brother that is as rare as hen's teeth because
it is widely regarded as one of the world's very
greatest whiskeys. Jim Murray awarded it 97.5
in his *Whisky Bible*, the highest score he has
ever given. It is released in batches toward the
end of each year, along with special bottlings
of some of Buffalo Trace's finest old whiskeys,
including 17-Year-Old Eagle Rare, and Sazerac
Rye. It is immediately snapped up by fans,
and when you taste it — neat, even though its
strength is at the top end of the 60s or early 70s
— you'll find out why. It is off the charts. Stagg
Junior isn't far behind it, though. It's Junior
because younger whiskey has been used. The
idea behind its release is to make a version of
Stagg more readily available. If you're expecting
George T Stagg Lite, then think again: this has
a very weighty 66.05% strength, and it packs a
memorably powerful punch. It is not as complex
as its older sibling, but it's a total delight
nevertheless. Batches vary in strength and
taste, but not by much. What we have here is
chili, dark chocolate, cloves, sandalwood, and
red berry fruits. By George, indeed! It is
Stagg-eringly good.

— A barrel of laughs —
ELIJAH CRAIG BARREL PROOF
Heaven Hill
Louisville, KY, USA
{ elijahcraig.com/barrel-proof }
BOURBON, 69.4% (VARIABLE)

Elijah Craig was a Baptist preacher who
was imprisoned several times in Virginia for
preaching without a licence. He built a distillery,
and, notwithstanding claims that he invented
bourbon, he probably made the same form
of rye whiskey as everyone else. It has also
been claimed, again probably falsely, that
Craig was the first person to put whiskey in
charred barrels. Elijah Craig Barrel Proof varies
in strength from barrel to barrel, but you can
expect a strength in the high 60s. The bourbon
is 12 years old — very old for a drink of its kind
— and is described by online retailer Master of
Malt as 'an intense and awesome bit of whiskey
deliciousness.'

'IT HAPPENS TO BE A
FACT THAT NEARLY
EVERY WRITER OF
FICTION IN THE
WORLD DRINKS
MORE WHISKY
THAN IS GOOD FOR
HIM. HE DOES IT
TO GIVE HIMSELF
FAITH HOPE
AND COURAGE. A
PERSON IS A FOOL
TO BECOME A
WRITER. HIS ONLY
COMPENSATION
IS ABSOLUTE
FREEDOM.'
ROALD DAHL, *BOY: TALES
OF CHILDHOOD*

POETIC

SEVEN MOODS OF CRAFT SPIRIT

———— ❧ ————

'BUCOLIC' MEANS 'RELATING TO A RURAL IDYLL', AND I HAVE CAST A WIDE NET, TO THE DISTILLERIES OF THE WEST INDIES, AUSTRALIA, AND SOUTH AMERICA. THIS IS ALL ABOUT NATURAL AND FULL FLAVORS.

———— ❧ ————

BUCOLIC

CRAFT SPIRIT DISTILLERIES

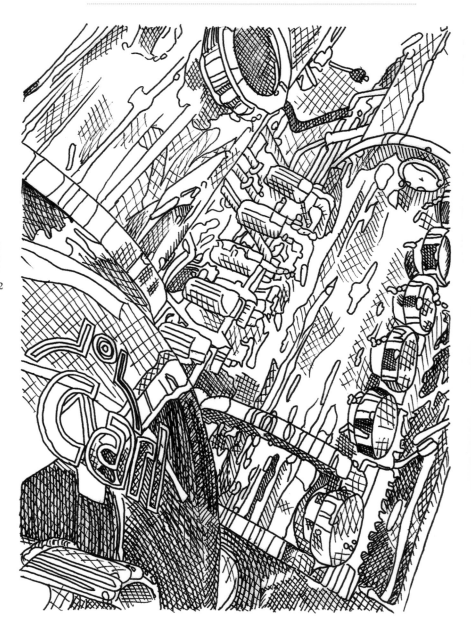

KI NO BI
Kyoto, Japan
{ kyotodistillery.jp }

Ki No Bi (left) is something of a rarity in two ways: one, it is a dedicated gin distillery; and two, it is a dedicated gin distillery in Japan. It was launched in 2016, and it makes gin with local ingredients, such as yuzu hinoki wood chips, red shiso leaves, bamboo, and green sanshō.

DÀ MHÌLE
Llandysul, Ceredigion, Scotland
{ damhile.co.uk }

Dà Mhìle is an organic distillery on an organic farm that makes the world-famous Telfi Cheese. Its name is Welsh for '2000', and its first whisky was made organically for it by Springbank Distillery in Scotland to celebrate the millennium. Dà Mhìle now makes, gin, brandy, and malt and grain whiskies.

SOMERSET CIDER BRANDY CO
Martock, Somerset, England
{ somersetciderbrandy.com }

Somerset is cider country, and this distillery is an offshoot of Burrow Hill Cider Farm, which specializes in real cider. Owner Julian Temperley offers a range of apple products, but the pick is his 20-year-old cider brandy, a batch of which is released every year on Apple Day, October 21.

HOUSE SPIRITS
Portland, OR, USA
{ housespirits.com }

House Spirits is probably best known for its Westward single malt whiskey, which is now available internationally. But it also has an aquavit that won best aquavit in the world at the San Francisco World Spirits Challenge. It also regularly produces 'developmental' spirits designed to push traditional boundaries.

FOUR PILLARS
Healesville, Yarra Valley, Australia
{ fourpillarsgin.com.au }

Four Pillars makes gin with a difference. The range includes Pure Kisumé, which captures the flavors of modern Japan in Australia; yuzu, nashi, and sake. Its Christmas Gin smells like Yuletide, and is based on a recipe for Christmas pudding.

BAINBRIDGE
Bainbridge Island, WA, USA
{ bainbridgedistillers.com }

Bainbridge Distillery makes one of the most unusual and exciting whiskeys in the world of craft distilling. Bainbridge Yama Mizunara Cask is a single grain whiskey, matured in Japanese mizunara wood, which is sourced directly from Japan, and then made into small casks. It imparts an exotic, incense-like spiciness.

SEVEN MOODS OF CRAFT SPIRIT   BUCOLIC

— Ship shape —
ADMIRAL VERNON'S OLD J SPICED
Admiral Vernon's
St Lucia
{ oldjspicedrum.co.uk }
SPICED RUM SPIRIT DRINK, 35%

The spiced rum market is crowded, and to stand out in it takes some doing. This manages it. It's not strictly a rum, because it is under 37.5% ABV, so it must be described as a spiced rum spirit drink. When Admiral Vernon lowered the strength of navy rum, he suggested to his disgruntled men that they should add lime and sugar to it. This does just that, but the drink has a modern twist, with vanilla and Persian lime riffing off classic rum notes and toffee and spice. Regarded as one of the best offerings in the spiced rum category.

— Jet setter —
KOKO KANU COCONUT
Gruppo Campari
Kingston, Jamaica
{ kokokanu.com }
FLAVORED RUM, 37.5%

Some spirits just scream 'fun times' at you, and this is one of them. It is made with Jamaican white rum, a style noted for its big flavors, at the legendary Wray & Nephew Distillery. The rum is mixed with fresh coconut essence, and the resulting drink is delicious and rich in every aspect. It is well made, and free of the artificial additives that sometimes mar spirits of this nature. It's a versatile, adaptable, party drink that can be consumed either neat or as a mixer. It goes well with fruit juices, and tastes great at barbecues on warm summer evenings.

— Feisty flagship rum —
REBELLION SPICED
Dutch Spirits
Trinidad
{ rebellion-rum.com }
SPICE RUM, 37.5%

Rebellion Spiced was introduced by drinks giant Metaxa a few years ago to give customers a fuller, more powerful, spiced rum, but the brand has moved homes and it is now part of a company based in Amsterdam, Netherlands. It is made of rum from a 200-year-old distillery in Trinidad, mixed with cloves, ginger, cardamom, pepper, vanilla, cinnamon, and orange. Don't be put off by the *Pirates of the Caribbean*-style bottle: this is one of those rums that can be enjoyed neat, but which is at its best when served with cola, ice, and a squeeze of fresh lime.

— *Collective spirit* —
SANTIAGO DE CUBA AÑEJO RUM
Cuba Ron
Santiago, Cuba
{ cubaron.com }
RUM, 38%

There was considerable speculation about what the world of rum would look like if Cuba was allowed to trade freely. What would it mean for the indigenous producers, or for Cuban rum-makers in exile, like Bacardi? We will not discove for as long as the United States discourages normalization of relations with the island. A shame, because this rum, from a state-owned distillery, is classy. *Añejo* means 'aged', and this rum has been matured in white oak barrels for five years, resulting in a drink that is rich in vanilla, caramel, and coffee flavors.

— *A walk in the woods* —
J J WHITLEY NETTLE GIN
Halewood International
London, England
{ halewood-int.com }
GIN, 38.6%

Some serious thought has gone into this unusual and exciting nettle gin. It is distilled to 38.6% in homage to Dmitri Mendeleev, father of chemistry, who recommended to the Tsar of Russia that alcohol and water molecules combine perfectly at that ABV. It contains eight botanicals, with juniper and citrus peel to the fore, together with coriander, elderflower, and licorice. But the stars here are the nettles, which rediscover a classic style of gin, inspired by British gardens and hedgerows. This is an unusual, punchy, and herbaceous gin, with damp forest and chopped basil working alongside the juniper hit.

— *A splash of color* —
SHARISH BLUE MAGIC
António Cuco
Monsaraz, Portugal
GIN, 40%

Sharish is a range of gins created by Portuguese distiller António Cuco, a teacher of tourism who helped out in his parents' restaurant. He amassed a collection of gins behind the bar, and became so enamored of the drink that he decided to have a go at making it himself. At first, he used his pressure cooker to make two and a quarter gallons (15 liters) of gin a week, but his business has expanded since. This is bright blue due to the presence of a botanical named blue pea. Add water, and it turns pink. Other botanicals include strawberries and ginger; the latter gives the spirit a distinctive spicy flavor.

SEVEN MOODS OF CRAFT SPIRIT   BUCOLIC

— *Royal flush* —
VICTORIA'S RHUBARB
Warner Edwards
Harrington, England
{ warneredwards.com }
FLAVORED GIN, 40%

Warner Edwards is a farm-based craft distillery
in Northamptonshire in the heart of rural
England. The aim of the company is to make
products that are made on site, hand-finished,
and steeped in provenance. The water source
is just over 300 yards (300 m) from the old
barn that houses the gin distillery. The gin is
made in batches, and the small team behind
the operation is proud of the fact that every
bottle is hand-crafted, from the filling to the
wax seal and labeling. All distillers like to say
they put a huge emphasis on quality, but in this
case it's absolutely true, as witnessed by the
large number of awards its gins have received.
The main gin, named Harrington after the
nearest village, contains botanicals gathered
from surrounding fields and hedgerows.
It was originally distilled on Curiosity, the
company's German still. (The company now
has a second still named Satisfaction.) Victoria
Rhubarb gets its name from the fact that it is
made using rhubarb that grew in the gardens
of Buckingham Palace when Queen Victoria
was on the throne. The juice of the rhubarb is
extracted by putting it through an original fruit
press. Then it is blended with Harrington gin
to produce an attractive pink gin. The rhubarb,
along with cardamom and black pepper, create
a tangy and outstanding drink that Master of
Malt described as 'excellent and enjoyable'.

— A perfect match —
PINK GRAPEFRUIT GIN
Williams Chase
Hereford, England
{ chasedistillery.co.uk }
GIN, 40%

Williams Chase is the distillery
owned by William Chase, a
potato farmer whose small-
scale, hand-made potato chip
business rapidly expended
into the multi-million pound
Tyrrells Crisps Company. In
2004, he turned to making
first vodka and then gin, using
potatoes as the source of the
spirit. The distillery is based
on his original farm, all the
potatoes used in the spirit
are grown on site. This is the
distillery's most renowned
gin — an elegant and very dry
spirit which, when combined
with pomelo and pink
grapefruit becomes just what
you might expect — zesty, tart,
fresh, and very drinkable.

— Single estate tequila —
MUCHOTE TEQUILA
REPOSADO
Vivanco Family
Los Altos, Mexico
{ muchote.com }
TEQUILA, 40%

The key to making ultra-
premium tequila is planting
agave plants in the best soil
and climate. Muchoté Tequila
is made from agave grown
in the Los Altos region or
highlands of Jalisco, an area
with acidic, iron-rich, red soil,
which yields large agaves
with a high sugar content.
It takes between 10 and 12
years for the agave to mature.
The jimadors (local farmers)
select and harvest the plants
by hand to make sure that
the whole harvest consists of
nothing other than Weber azul
(blue) agave, the finest form
of the plant. The tequila is
aged in American oak casks for
seven months for a smooth,
sweet, rounded flavor.

'YEP, GIN AND BRANDI. CALL
ME CRAZY, BUT NAMING YOUR
DAUGHTERS AFTER ALCOHOLIC
BEVERAGES IS JUST ASKING FOR
TROUBLE.'
KELLEY ARMSTRONG, *WAKING THE WITCH*

BUCOLIC

SEVEN MOODS OF CRAFT SPIRIT

— *Coming up roses* —

STRATHEARN HEATHER ROSE

Strathearn Distillery
Methven, Scotland
{ stratherarndistillery.com }

GIN, 40%

Strathearn is one of Scotland's smallest whisky distilleries, but it also makes a range of gins, of which this is the prime example. Heather Rose is made with botanicals that include juniper, coriander seeds, orange peel, lemon peel, licorice root, rose petals, and purple heather flowers. The gin is produced in two stages. First, vapor is infused using a 110-gallon (500-liter) pot still. Then the botanicals are added. With rose and heather in the mix, the gin takes on a Prosecco-like character. The color changes to pink when topped up with tonic. Fragrant, floral and light; sweet, yet spicy.

— *Grape expectations* —

G'VINE

Jean Sébastien
Robicquet
Cognac, France
{ gvine.com }

GIN, 40%

G'Vine is produced at Maison Villevert on a family estate in the heart of the Cognac region. Its creators say they have attempted to combine the heritage of the Charente region, the avant-garde attitude of Paris, and the effortless chic of France's Southwest. It is certainly unusual. It is distilled by company founder Jean Sébastien Robicquet, and its base spirit is made from grapes and 10 botanicals, including the rare vine flower. This makes for a unique gin that has a grapey smell and taste, with the fruit adding sweetness to a product with strong citrus and ginger notes.

— *Sugar and spice* —

STRAWBERRY & BLACK PEPPER GIN

Bullards
Norwich, England
{ bullardsspirits.co.uk }

GIN, 40%

Strawberry & Black Pepper Gin was created to capture summer in a glass, and it's another outstanding release from Bullards, a distilling company based at The Ten Bells public house in the center of Norwich. The distillery hasn't been in business long, but the team are quick learners because the company's dry gin won Best Dry Gin in the World at the World Gin Awards. Here we get a double whammy of strawberries, which feature both in the distillation and the infusion. Pepper is then added as a restraining influence to prevent the product from becoming excessively fruity.

— Proudly individual —
ANGOSTURA 1787
Angostura
Trinidad
{ angosturarum.com }
RUM, 40%

The people at Angostura are proud that all their rum comes from just one distillery. Thus, they say, it is the same as single malt whisky, but only in kind; not in quality — they claim their rum is better.

That's some boast, and although it's not comparing like with like, one taste of this will demonstrate that they have something of a case. It was released in the second half of 2016, and is a hefty 15 years old. You can taste the oak in the rum, and there are some impressive tannin and spice notes. There are some exotic and dried berry fruits on the palate, too, as well as toffee. It's balanced, rounded, and thoroughly excellent.

— A high flyer —
TWO BIRDS LONDON DRY GIN
Two Birds
Market Harborough,
England
{ twobirdsspirits.com }
GIN, 40%

If you want a definition of artisanal or craft distilling, look no further than Two Birds. The company, set up by Mark and Lyn Gamble using stills Mark built himself, stemmed from a love of gin and some experimentation. Only 100 bottles are made at a time, and they are all hand-filled, labeled, and checked. This London dry gin has won countless awards, and is something of a juniper monster, with just four other botanicals in the recipe Two Birds also makes an innovative and unusual range of flavored vodkas.

— Top of the world —
ANTIGUO DE SOLERA
Santa Teresa
Estada Aragua,
Venezuela
{ ronsantateresa.com }
RUM, 40%

Regarded by many as the finest South American product of its type, this is an aged rum produced through a solera system, in which rum is taken away for filling from the bottom of the solera, and new rum is then added at the top. The distillery is unique. It rehabilitates former gang members when they are released from prison, and encourages them to work hard to turn their lives around — and it encourages them to play, of all things, rugby. This rum is extraordinarily complex and rounded, with notes of tobacco smoke, leather, dark chocolate, and honey.

— *Flower power* —

FLOR DE CANA 12 YEAR OLD

Compania de Licorera
Managua, Nicaragua
{ flordecana.com }
RUM, 40%

Flor de Cana is produced by a company with its roots going back to the 19th century, although this range of rums was introduced in the 1990s. The company makes both white and dark rums, and has has established a reputation for well-crafted and outstanding whiskies. The rums are matured in former bourbon white oak casks, so oaky tannin notes are present, as well as toffee and vanilla from the wood. What sets this spirit apart is the delightful apple note that is present in the taste. Few spirits drinks have won as many awards internationally as this one.

'DON'T WORRY ABOUT NEGATIVE TEMPERATURES BECAUSE MINUS TIMES MINUS EQUALS PLUS. IF YOU ARE NOT VERY GOOD AT MATHS, THEN PUT SOME RUM IN THE TEA.'
Ljupka Cvetanova, *The New Land*

— *From deepest Peru* —

LA CARAVEDO PISCO

La Caravedo
Ica, Peru
{ lacaraverdo.com }
PISCO, 41%

The national spirit of Peru, pisco is made to a stringent set of rules. It is a white spirit distilled from any combination of eight grape varietals. It must be produced in small batches, crafted on copper pot stills, and left unpaged and unaltered, which means that not even water can be added to it. Established in 1684, La Caravedo is believed to be the oldest distillery in the Americas. This pisco is made from the strongest of the approved grape types, Quebranta, around eight pounds (3.6 kg) of which go into every bottle of this oily and highly unusual drink.

DÀ MHÌLE SEAWEED
Dà Mhìle
Llandysul, Wales
{ damhile.co.uk }
GIN, 42%

Dà Mhìle is a Welsh farm operation making only organic products. It is best known for Telfi, a range of artisanal cheeses that it makes by traditional methods from locally sourced raw malt. Its Celtic Promise is Britain's highest-awarded British cheese. The farm's link with the world of spirits stretches back to 1992, when the Savage-Onstwedder family looked to find an organic whisky. Dà Mhìle is Gaelic for two thousand, and the plan was to release an organic whisky for the new Millennium. Using barley from the Springbank Distillery in Campbeltown, Scotland, the farm produced enough organic malt whisky to fill 15 hogsheads. (The capacity of one hogshead is 64 gallons/238.5 liters.) Much of this was duly released as a seven-year-old in the year 2000, but some of it was held back until 2017, when the whisky reached 25 years old. The farm applied for a distilling licence in 2010, and unlike lots of other potential distillers in the United Kingdom, had relatively few problems in getting one. The distillery started producing spirit in 2012, and is now run by the son of the founder, John-James Savage-Onstwedder. First released in 2014, Seaweed gin includes marine algae from the Newquay coast of West Wales and the West Coast of Ireland, and it is this ingredient that gives the liquor its green hue. The gin is triple-distilled, and has, perhaps unsurprisingly, a slightly tangy, salty taste. It is designed to be drunk while eating seafood.

122

— Crisp apple delight —

SOMERSET CIDER BRANDY 5 YEAR OLD

Somerset Cider Brandy Co

Martock, England

{ ciderbrandy.co.uk }

APPLE BRANDY, 42%

Pass Vale Farm at Burrow Hill grows apples in what is widely regarded as one of the best regions in the United Kingdom for producing fermenting apples. As a county, Somerset is known as a strong cider-producing region, and this farm uses 40 apple varieties to produce Burrow Hill Cider. It started producing apple brandy from its ciders in 1987 on two copper continuous tower stills named Josephine and Fifi. The brandy is matured in small oak casks. Expect a crisp, refreshing, and highly tasty apple brandy. Somerset Cider Brandy has Protected Indication, and is recognized as a controlled style in European law.

—A taste of Africa —

WHITLEY NEILL RHUBARB & GINGER

Halewood International

Liverpool, England

{ halewood-int.com}

GIN, 43%

Whitley Neill Rhubarb & Ginger is one of the many great gins in which sweet fruitiness is balanced by spicy ginger. It's a treat. The distiller here is John Neill, a direct relative of the family that set up the famous northwestern English drinks giant Greenall Whitley. He has brought traditional distilling techniques to innovative styles of gin like this one. He has a highly developed sense of adventure, so he went looking for unusual botanicals, with a penchant for Africa well to the fore. This gin consequently features baobab fruit, which resembles a cross between an orange and a grapefruit. This gin is utterly irresistible.

— *A Black art* —

ARBIKIE KIRSTY'S GIN

Arbikie Distillery
Arbroath, Scotland
{ arbikie.com }
GIN, 43%

Kirsty is Kirsty Black, the distiller at Arbikie Distillery, and Arbikie is a micro-distillery on a farm in Angus on Scotland's east coast. This is a field-to-bottle operation making whisky and vodka as well as gin, and Kirsty works alongside three brothers to produce small batch spirits. The botanicals in this gin include kelp, blaeberry, and carline thistle. The base spirit is made from three varieties of farm-grown potatoes. A surprisingly large number of people recommend that it should be consumed on its own or with a very small amount of tonic. It has a creamy richness, and is very well made.

— *Feisty flavors* —

BENROMACH 15 YEAR OLD

Gordon & McPhail
Forres, Scotland
{ benromach.com }
SINGLE MALT WHISKY, 43%

Until the micro-distillery boom took hold, Benromach could lay claim to being among the smallest whisky distilleries in Scotland. It's a remote distillery that had closed down before spirits merchants Gordon & McPhail took it over, and the company has stayed true to its traditional roots. There is virtually no mechanization here at all. G & M have done a great job with their whiskies, making traditional and earthy Highland-style spirits and experimental whiskies with all sorts of different flavors. This 15-year-old is a beauty, rich in orange and red fruits, and with cinnamon, nutmeg, plum, and some charred smoke.

— *Taste of rural Norfolk* —

THE ENGLISH – ORIGINAL

The English Whisky
Company
East Harling, England
{ englishwhisky.co.uk }
SINGLE MALT WHISKY, 43%

Established in the early part of the new millennium, the English Whisky Company produced the first English whisky for more than 100 years when it launched a peated and an unpeated malt named, respectively, Chapter 6 and Chapter 9. That somewhat confusing Chapter system has since been dropped, as has the original reference to St George's, the name of the distillery. This is an updated version of Chapter 6, and it has its eyes firmly on the export market. It has a clean and fresh vanilla-driven taste, with tropical fruits and some nutty notes. It's very nicely packaged, too.

— *English new boy* —
COTSWOLDS SINGLE MALT
Cotswolds Distillery
Shipston-on-Stour,
England
{ cotswoldsdistillery.com }
SINGLE MALT WHISKY, 43%

The Cotswolds Distillery
bottled its first malt whisky
in late 2017, and, during the
three-year wait for its malt
to mature, launched a highly
successful gin. This whisky
fulfils a dream for distillery
owner Daniel Szor, who has
worked closely with the local
community to produce a malt
worthy of this pretty region
of England. The distillery is a
sizeable one, and no expense
has been spared to create
whisky in Scottish pot stills
and mature it in quality oak
casks. An interim tasting at
32 months promised that the
finished product would be
a fruity, sweet, and easy-
drinking whisky.

— *Norfolk 'n' good* —
THE NORFOLK FARMERS
The English Whisky
Company
East Harling, England
{ englishwhisky.co.uk }
**SINGLE GRAIN
WHISKY, 45%**

Norfolk Farmers
demonstrates that the
English Whisky distillery is
developing something of a
sense of humor. The label
has a sketch of a cat wearing
a bowler hat — for no other
reason than that the bowler
hat was invented in Norfolk,
apparently. It also marks a
departure from established
practice — it's a grain whisky
made with eight different
grains. But since it's all made
at St George's Distillery, it's
a single grain whisky. The
product is as sweet as you
might expect, with some
chili spice and lots of caramel
and chocolate.

— *Maritime marvel* —
ROCK OYSTER
Douglas Laing & Co
Glasgow, Scotland
{ douglasliang.com }
**BLENDED MALT
WHISKY, 45.8%**

Another outstanding whisky in
Douglas Laing's blended malt
repertoire, Rock Oyster joins
the Big Peat and Scallywag
on their bucolic journey. This
one contains malts from the
islands of Jura, Arran, Orkney,
and Islay, and has distinctive
island characteristics: sea
salt, peat, smoke, honey, and
pepper. All in all, it's further
proof that the blended malt
category can be dynamic,
and bring disparate malt
tastes together in an oral
supergroup. The company's
master blender, Fred Laing,
says: 'If I could select one
dram to transport the whisky
enthusiast to the islands of
Scotland, it would be this'.

ARMORIK DOUBLE MATURATION
Distillerie Warenghem
Boutill, France
{ distillerie-warenghem.com }
SINGLE MALT WHISKY, 46%

Although France is known for wine and brandy, it has a wide range of other drinks that it's pretty good at, too. Cider and apple brandies are made in Normandy, and Brittany has a strong tradition of beers as well as whiskies. Distillerie Warenghem is among a growing number of French distilleries making whisky, and is arguably the best of them. Owner David Roussier employed the late Scottish whisky troubleshooter Dr Jim Swan to tighten up production, and he's making fine malt now. This is matured initially in locally made casks and finished in oloroso sherry casks. It is a dusty, honeyed, and grainy delight.

— *Top dog* —

SCALLYWAG
Douglas Laing & Co
Glasgow, Scotland
{ douglaslaing.com }
**BLENDED MALT
WHISKY**, 46%

Douglas Laing is a Scottish independent bottler, which means it buys whisky casks and bottles them under its own labels. It is also part of a small group of companies that mix together different malt whiskies to produce whiskies such as this. A few years ago the company launched an Islay blended malt called The Big Peat and this is his new pet — a little fox terrier. Here the company has taken several whiskies from Speyside, a region associated with sweet, fruity, non-smoky whiskies. This has some big and bold sherried malts in the mix, but there's a healthy dose of spices, including ginger.

> 'THE GIN AND TONIC HAS SAVED MORE ENGLISHMEN'S LIVES, AND MINDS, THAN ALL THE DOCTORS IN THE EMPIRE.'
> WINSTON CHURCHILL

— *Grain to glass* —

THE BOTANIST
Bruichladdich Distillery
Port Charlotte, Isle of Islay, Scotland
{ thebotanist.com }
GIN, 46%

Bruichladdich — pronounced 'brook-laddy' —
is a small island distillery that was reopened
by an independent consortium a few years
back and has enjoyed legendary status ever
since. It's known for an eclectic mix of malt
whisky styles, and for its somewhat rebellious
and non-conformist approach to the whisky
business. It has now been sold to Campari,
but the new owners have allayed any fears
about the future by investing in the distillery
to make it even better and stronger. And they
have stood aside and allowed the creative and
somewhat scientific powers that be to get on
making highly respected single malt whisky.
The distillers here are very keen to explore
provenance and terroir, and have been making
malt whisky with barley from a selection of
fields, both local and in other parts of Scotland.
Then, when it came to making a gin, the
distillery turned decisively to its local
environment, setting out to capture Islay's
unique terroir in a spirits drink. The Botanist
includes 22 foraged island botanicals, hand-
picked locally, and sustainable by the
distillery's botanical scientists. These include
such exotic delights as cicely seeds,
dabberlocks, and steeping ferns, along with
better-known fruits such as rhubarb, lime, and
pear. A further nine, more traditional,
botanicals are also used. These are distilled
in Ugly Betty, an old Lomond still, and the
resulting gin is astounding, with strong floral,
citrus, and menthol notes all much in evidence.

126

— Two worlds collide —
BERKSHIRE BOURBON SMOKE AND PEAT
Berkshire Mountain Distillers
Sheffield, MA, USA
{ berkshiremountaindistillers.com }
AMERICAN WHISKEY, 46%

— Remote paradise —
THE SPIRIT OF LEWIS
Abhain Dearg
Uig, Isle of Lewis, Scotland
{ abhaindearg.com }
SINGLE MALT WHISKY, 46%

As is often the case with the new wave of American distillers, Berkshire Mountain is being a bit naughty with its use of the term bourbon here. In truth, this is a groundbreaking American whiskey from an innovative and exciting producer set up in 2007. The liquor is distilled and initially matured in the traditional bourbon style, and then transferred into casks that formerly contained smoky and peaty whisky from the Scottish island of Islay. The result is exactly what you would expect: an enjoyably smoky but quite subtle taste that complements the candy, vanilla, and toffee notes of the bourbon.

Gaelic names: don't you just love them? This one — pronounced 'aveen jarrik' — means 'Red River'. Established in 2008, this distillery is the first on Lewis for almost 200 years. Its initial three-year-old release came in two small casks, one of which went on tour to Germany, the other to a bar in Glasgow. Both quickly sold out; so, too, did a subsequent product named The Spirit of Lewis. In 2018 distiller Mark (known as Marko) will release this 10-year-old. It's included here because, if it's anything like the first release, but more mature, it will be as rugged and robust as the island it comes from. Packed with taste, too.

SEVEN MOODS OF CRAFT SPIRIT   BUCOLIC

— *The Powers of love* —
POWERS JOHN'S LANE
Irish Distillers
Midleton, Ireland
{ irishdistillers.ie }
POT STILL WHISKEY, 46%

One of the iconic brands of Irish whiskey, Powers was once produced at a distillery on John's Lane in Dublin. It was one of the few surviving distillers which formed Irish Distillers back in the 1960s. Irish whiskey had not only lost its dominant position in the world of whisky over the course of the 20th century: it had almost been wiped out altogether. So Jameson, Powers, Bushmills, and Paddy formed Irish Distillers. But the decline of Paddy and Powers continued, due to the fact that both were seen as old men's drinks consumed in rural back bars. It took the arrival of Teeling in the late 1980s to shake up the Irish whiskey scene, and although Irish Distillers was slow on the uptake, it eventually responded to its new competitor with an energetic and impressive investment in its pot still operation. Pot still whiskey, once the heart and soul of Irish whiskey, had become scarce, with just Redbreast and Green Spot keeping the light on. Irish Distillers' promise to launch 20 pot still whiskeys in 10 years not only created huge excitement, it lit the touch paper for a new wave of craft distilling, and Ireland is now thriving again. Powers John's Lane was one of the first of the new pot still whiskeys, and it's great. Oily but rapier sharp, it has flavors of red berries, vanilla, dark chocolate and Camp coffee. A spicy treat.

— *To kill for* —

MACHIR BAY

Kilchoman Distillery
Isle of Islay, Scotland
{ kilchomandistillery.com }
SINGLE MALT WHISKY, 46%

Kilchoman was the first new distillery for generations to open on Islay, off Scotland's west coast, and, in keeping with the island's reputation for peaty whiskies, its products are smoky and phenolic. They're also getting better by the year. Machir Bay is named after the most spectacular beach on the island. The distillery is relatively small, so this, its flagship product, is made only in small batches — and the 2017 release was the sixth. It has been matured predominantly in ex-bourbon casks, but with some oloroso ones, too, so there are buttery, fruity notes, and some hints of butterscotch in amid the smokiness. All in all, a worthy addition to Islay's malt offering.

— *West coast wonder* —

SPRINGBANK 15 YEAR OLD

Springbank Distillers
Campbeltown, Scotland
{ springbankwhisky.com }
SINGLE MALT WHISKY, 46%

Campbeltown is the peninsula running parallel to Glasgow on the west coast of Scotland. It was once home to a great number of distilleries. But the owners got greedy, produced poor-quality whisky, and its demise was spectacular. It took independent family distillers J & A Mitchell to save the region from losing its whisky trade altogether. Springbank enjoys iconic status, and this 15-year-old is one of its staples. There are tropical fruit elements at work here, but the trademark Springbank earthiness, some tannins from the cask, and a healthy wave of chilli make for an unforgettable dram.

> 'MY MAIN AMBITION AS A GARDENER IS TO WATER MY ORANGE TREES WITH GIN, THEN ALL I HAVE TO DO IS SQUEEZE THE JUICE INTO A GLASS.'
> W. C. FIELDS

— Close to pastis —
IRISH POT STILL GIN
Echlinville Distillery
Newtownards,
Northern Ireland
{ echlinville.com }
GIN, 46%

Echlinville Distillery has
big plans to make great
whiskey. Determined not to
be diverted from its quest by
the uncertainty surrounding
Britain's departure from the
European Union, it aligns itself
with the Republic of Ireland's
distillery boom. Irish Pot Still
Gin is made with barley grown
and malted by the distillery.
It is the first gin to bear the
Echlinville name, and it's a
beauty. Seaweed from
Strangford Lough and
indigenous whin bush petals
combine to give the gin its
character, says the distillery,
and what seems to be a liberal
dash of aniseed gives the drink
a distinctive pastis-like flavor.

— A taste of honey —
THE HIVE
Wemyss
Edinburgh, Scotland
{ wemyssmalts.com }
**BLENDED MALT
WHISKY, 46%**

The blended malt category
— quite different from the
huge blended whisky category
— gives independent bottlers
such as Wemyss the chance
to break with convention,
and to bring a more modern
approach to whisky retailing.
Here, that involves naming the
whisky to reflect the taste. The
Hive is made up of more than
10 signature malts from the
Speyside region of Scotland so
that the taste is honey-sweet,
with citrus and floral notes
making for a clean, fresh
mixture of malts. In late 2016,
a cask strength version of each
of the three blended malts in
the range was released.

— Sweet with peat —
LONGROW 18 YEAR OLD
Springbank Distillers
Campbeltown, Scotland
{ springbankwhisky.com }
SINGLE MALT WHISKY, 46%

Springbank is effectively
three distilleries in one.
The eponymous whisky
has a distinctive earthy and
oily taste, but the site also
makes a triple-distilled, very
sweet, easy-drinking whisky
named Hazelburn. And it
also produces this, a full-on
peated whisky, originally
made as an experiment, but so
popular that it is now a regular
offering. In the past, it has
been released at younger ages
but this one is great — damp,
autumnal forest and some
charcoal on the nose, followed
by a big wave of chill, kippers,
barbecue, and sweetness,
all delivered on a clinging,
oily base.

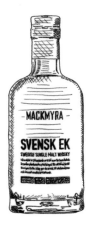

— Feisty and sherried —
GLENDRONACH 18 YEAR OLD ALLARDICE
Glendronach Distillery
Forgue by Huntly, Scotland
{ glendronachdistillery.co.uk }
SINGLE MALT WHISKY, 46%

Glendronach is a Speyside distillery, so you'd expect a rich, sweet, fruity whisky. And for a long time, that's what you got. But the distillery had been neglected for a long time, and had lost direction. Then Billy Walker and his team bought it, and everything changed. A war cemetery at the back of the distillery has been spruced up, the aging buildings have been given a facelift — and Walker has restored the liquid in the bottle by taking the rich, fruity flavors and adding a traditional, earthy, meaty, and sulfur-flecked sherry influence. The oak and the bold flavors make this a classic sherry cask whisky.

— Great Swede —
SVENSK ESK
Mackmyra
Gävle, Sweden
{ mackmyra.com }
SINGLE MALT WHISKY, 46.1%

Mackmyra was set up by a group of friends after a whisky-fueled conversation during a skiing trip. They funded the company by issuing shares, so their business is collectively owned. Early efforts left a lot to be desired, but the whiskies have improved immensely over the years, and now cover a range of styles, from the very smoky to the cleanest, sweetest malts from ex-bourbon casks. The name means 'Swedish oak', and that's what this malt has ben matured in. It makes for an earthy, dusty, spicy malt whisky with some nutty and chocolate notes. It is distinctly not Scottish, and justly proud of the fact.

SEVEN MOODS OF CRAFT SPIRIT   BUCOLIC

— *A malty monster* —

TIMOROUS BEASTIE
Douglas Laing
Edinburgh, Scotland
{ douglaslaing.com }
BLENDED MALT WHISKY, 46.8%

A sense of humor and a whiff of irreverence are welcome additions to Scotland's often straight-faced whisky industry. This is another blended malt from independent bottler Wemyss, and it takes its name from Robert Burns's wonderful poem 'To A Mouse'. This whisky, however, is anything but timorous — the company describes it as 'not for the faint-hearted'. It is a mixture of Highland malts, including Dalmore, Glen Garioch, and Glengoyne, and is rich, oily, chewy, and assertive. On the palate, there are green fruits and aniseed, as well as an intriguing combination of coastal brine, moor heather, and sherried berries.

— *In a field of its own* —

PORT CHARLOTTE ISLAY BARLEY
Bruichladdich
Port Charlotte, Isle of Islay, Scotland
{ bruichladdich.com }
SINGLE MALT WHISKY, 50%

One of whisky's hottest debates surrounds the question of whether the coastal conditions on an island such as Islay influence the final taste of a malt whisky matured over several years. Salty rain lashes the shores during lengthy winters, and salt cakes the walls of the island's warehouses. This whisky is not heavily peated, and it has a distinctive salty tang, supporting the contention that coast affects taste. It is a young, zesty, assertive, and stylish drink in which there's a lot going on. Smoky yes, but so much more. It's clean, well made, and a very exciting taste sensation. It epitomizes all that's good about the island it comes from.

— Creative brilliance —

FLOODWALL
Copper & Kings
Louisville, KY, USA
{ copperandkings.com }
APPLE BRANDY, 50%

Is this the world's coolest distillery? Owner Joe Heron called it Copper & Kings because it sounds like a rock band. He puts cool music on his website, and hosts art exhibitions, sausage parties, and band evenings either in the performance area or on the roof. The purpose-built distillery, in the fashionable Butchertown Market area of Louisville, is decorated in modern orange and brown, and every spare bit of land has been turned over to nature, to provide sanctuary for the rare butterflies that were once plentiful in the region. Brandy is the predominant spirit made here, but there is also an excellent absinthe, and a number of experimental spirits. Heron extends his rock-'n'-roll credentials to the drinks he makes, too. He even has a brandy called Jacket, after Louisville's finest sons, My Morning Jacket. Floodwall is named after the barrier constructed after the great flood of 1937, when the Ohio River burst its banks and caused the deaths of 385 people. This apple brandy is distilled in copper pot stills, and matured in ex-bourbon barrels and oloroso sherry casks. It is a minimum of four years old. The overall taste is subtle and sophisticated, and not dominated by apple at all. Heron says that brandies with a predominantly apple taste have had flavors added, and that his products are all entirely natural. This is a fantastic spirit.

SEVEN MOODS OF CRAFT SPIRIT   BUCOLIC

SEVEN MOODS OF CRAFT SPIRIT — BUCOLIC

— Great Scot —

ORGANIC SCOTTISH BARLEY

Bruichladdich
Port Charlotte,
Isle of Islay, Scotland
{ bruichladdich.com }
SINGLE MALT WHISKY, 50%

Bruichladdich — pronounced 'brook laddie' — is arguably the most opinionated distillery in Scotland, and it practices what it preaches. It has turned to the history books for clues as to how traditional whisky was made, and uses its mainly Victorian-era equipment to produce great malts the old-fashioned way. The distillery notes that, before industrialization, all barley was farmed organically, and so here it is working with three farmers to source barley in the same way. The aim is to make fresh, exciting whisky, and this one definitely works: it is a creamy, syrupy malt, with green fruit and citrus notes, sweet lime, honey, and an endearing maltiness. Artisan whisky at its finest.

— Swarthy and seductive —

ARDBEG UIGEADAIL

Ardbeg
Port Ellen,
Isle of Islay, Scotland
{ ardbeg.com }
SINGLE MALT WHISKY, 54.2%

Pronounced 'oog-a-dall', this is one of the finest single malts in the world, even though it's a peated battering-ram of a whisky, and very much something that you either love or hate. Ardbeg is a quirky and characterful distillery, and this malt epitomizes what it does. The name means 'dark and mysterious place', and that's a perfect description — stewed fruits and zingy grain are subjected to wave after wave of industrial smoke, heavy tar, strong black coffee, and coastal brine. It's so chunky you can almost chew it. It's almost everything an Islay whisky should be.

'WHEN LIFE GIVES YOU JUNIPER BERRIES, MAKE GIN!'
LAURIE BUCHANAN, PhD

— A storm in a glass —
TEMPEST
Bowmore
Bowmore, Isle of Islay, Scotland
{ bowmore.com }
SINGLE MALT WHISKY, 55.6%

If the southern Islay distilleries of Ardbeg, Lagavulin, and Laphroaig are the Maiden, Metallica, and Motorhead of Scottish single malt whiskies, then the core range of Bowmore is Bon Jovi — a metal-lite, peaty pop version of the heavy metal trio. It's not that the standard Bowmores aren't good — they are — it's merely that, if you're a fan of big, phenolic, smoky whiskies, then at Bowmore you're living on a prayer. Bowmore can surprise, though: the distillery contains a warehouse that takes a battering from the fierce waves that crash against it every winter, and here malt magic happens. The walls are caked with sea salt, and the air is damp and cool. The distillery has bottled whisky of pure gold, aged for decades, and each bottle fetches tens of thousands of pounds when it surfaces periodically at auction. The distillery's owners have also green-lighted a series of special releases, which have shown that Bowmore has many strings to its bow. This is the fifth edition of Tempest, a cask strength series that has flipped from heavily peated malts in the first three to fruit-rich bottlings. The last two have been produced by the excellent distiller and blender Rachel Barrie, and this one packs a punch through its fruitiness: lime, tropical fruits, and orange fruits mix it up with sea-spray saltiness. Loud and very proud.

SEVEN MOODS OF CRAFT SPIRIT   BUCOLIC

— Flight of fancy —
REDBREAST 12 YEAR OLD CASK STRENGTH
Irish Distillers
Midleton, Ireland
{ irishdistillers.ie }
POT STILL WHISKEY, 57.2%

For many years, the standard strength
Redbreast 12 year old kept the Irish pot still
category from extinction. Although Jameson
was the main focus for Irish Distillers, the
company kept producing the uniquely Irish
whiskey style for dedicated aficionados. So
when it announced a new generation of pot still
whiskeys, a cask strength version of Redbreast
was greeted enthusiastically. It doesn't
disappoint. This is distinctly different from
the standard bottling — it's a weightier, oilier
version of the whiskey, with a complex array of
orange and berry fruits, delicious wispy spices,
and hints of sherry. This has won countless
awards, and with good reason.

— Packing a punch —
OCTOMORE SCOTTISH BARLEY EDITION
Bruichladdich
Port Charlotte, Isle of Islay, Scotland
{ bruichladdich.com }
SINGLE MALT WHISKY, 59.5%

Octomore began life as one of those pub 'What
if?' conversations, and has evolved from that
conjectural beginning into the world's most
peated whisky, delivered at a strength powerful
enough to propel an automobile. It is named
after the farm behind the distillery, and while
the concept is a bit gimmicky, the malt certainly
isn't. The distillery describes it as an iron fist
in a velvet glove, and while it holds peat and
power to its heart, there are gentler, more
complex aspects to it. All bottlings are five
years old, and matured in ex-bourbon barrels.
Don't be put off by the age — peat makes a
livelier young whisky.

— *Bit of an animal* —

OLD DEER
Langatun
Langatun, Switzerland
{ langatun.com }
**SINGLE MALT
WHISKY, 62.1%**

The Alpine regions of Switzerland, Austria, Germany, and Liechtenstein have a long and proud tradition of distilling. Trouble was, while they produced great brandies, genevers, and liqueurs, their attempts at whisky were dodgy in the extreme. In the early part of the millennium, however, that began to change. Distilleries such as Langatun started to produce characterful malts like this one. It's triple-distilled, matured in ex-Chateauneuf-du-Pape casks, and bottled at cask strength. This is as big as whisky gets, with orange peel, orchard fruits, and clean vanilla in the mix.

— *Bear essential* —

OLD BEAR SMOKY
Langatun
Langenthal, Switzerland
{ langatun.ch }
**SINGLE MALT
WHISKY, 62.4%**

Old Bear Smoky pays tribute to the founder of the Langatun brewery and distillery, who began making beer at his farm in 1857. A bear appeared on the brewery's logo. This is normally bottled at 40% ABV, but this cask version takes the malt to another, higher level. It is made exactly the same way as Old Deer, but smoked barley is used. The result is an unusual malt whisky with fresh smoke on the nose, and an earthy, smoky taste, as well as rich grapes, wood smoke, milk chocolate, and toffee. Approach this whisky with an open mind, and it may well become a firm favorite.

— *Give me a T…* —

TEXAS BLUE CORN BOURBON
Balcones
Waco, TX, USA
{ balconesdistillery.com }
BOURBON, 64.9%

The United States has been undergoing a craft distilling revolution in recent years, although not all the new distillers are producing quality drinks. Some, though, are taking whiskey into new and exciting areas, and Balcones is one of them. Its excellent single malts have received most of the attention, but this bourbon is wonderful. It is the first bourbon made with blue corn, which creates a full-bodied, rich, and oily bourbon with baked apple and vanilla ice cream flavors. It opens out significantly with the addition of water, which brings toffee, cereal, and fruits to the fore.

HERE CRAFT DISTILLERS
LET THEIR IMAGINATIONS
OFF THE LEASH, QUESTION
ESTABLISHED GROUND RULES,
AND ENTER THEIR OWN
PERSONAL WONDERLANDS.

IMAGINATIVE

SACRED
London, England
{ sacredspiritscompany.com }

Distilling doesn't get much more micro than Sacred (left). The gin is made in the residential home of Ian Hart. He uses vacuum distillation, and used to test his distillates each Sunday in the local pub, eventually settling on Recipe 23 for his first bottling. That was in 2009, and Sacred has since launched eight different gins.

TWO BIRDS
Market Harborough, England
{ twobirdsspirits.co.uk }

Two Birds Spirits was founded in 2013 in a quaint English country town. It started as a fun quest to make quality gin, and grew into an award-winning distillery. Spirits made now include an indulgent salted caramel vodka and a devilishly potent absinthe.

ADNAMS COPPER HOUSE
Southwold, England
{ adnams.co.uk }

Adnams is a privately owned brewery that has produced fine ale since the 1870s. Its distillery has made award-winning gins, absinthes, and vodkas. This grain-to-glass operation makes single malt, triple malt, and a rye malt, using rye from land belonging to company chairman Jonathan Adnams.

MCQUEEN GIN
Callander, Scotland
{ mcqueengin.co.uk }

McQueen produces and bottles naturally-made and award-winning gins at its distillery in Perthshire. No flavor elements are added. Its standard products are great, but it really comes into its own with its chilli gin, spiced chocolate orange, chocolate mint, mocha, and sweet citrus gins.

WRECKING COAST
Tintagel, England
{ thewreckingcoastdistillery.com }

Most distillers like to look back to tradition and heritage, and work by hand on ancient lambic stills. Not Wrecking Coast. It searched long and hard for a futuristic still with which to make a gin that tasted like Cornish clotted cream. It found it in Dutch company iStill. The results are daringly different.

WARNER EDWARDS
Harrington, England
{ warneredwards.com }

Warner Edwards are Tom Warner and Sion Edwards, who met on their first day at agricultural college in 1997 and soon became firm friends. The distillery opened in 2012, and has been in the vanguard of the craft movement ever since. Their gin is made in a 200-year-old converted barn.

IMAGINATIVE

SEVEN MOODS OF CRAFT SPIRIT

— In the hand —

TWO BIRDS SALTED CARAMEL

Two Birds

Market Harborough, England

{ twobirdsspirit.co.uk }

FLAVORED VODKA, 37.5%

Two Birds is among the best of the new wave of craft spirit producers, having hit on formulas for its gins and vodkas that have resulted in a string of awards in blind tastings. The packaging is exceptional, too, and here the team shows its creative side with an excellent vodka.

The distillers admit that not everything they try works out, but it certainly did here. The vodka is infused with a particularly rich caramel. The level of salt is fairly restrained, but sets off the caramel perfectly. Great to serve alongside desserts, or over ice with tonic and a slice of apple.

— Raise a toast —

EUREKA LEMON MARMALADE VODKA

Williams Chase

Hereford, England

{ chasedistillery.co.uk }

VODKA, 40%

Farmer William Chase has taken to spirit-making like the proverbial duck to water, and, having established his potato-based spirits, he has shown a commendable penchant for innovation. His distillery has made a number of imaginative spirits, and this is one of his best.

Here he has distilled his vodka with lemon marmalade. The spirit is then marinated with Eureka lemon peel for a further three days. The result is a rich yellow vodka that has obvious citrus notes, but that's not the whole story: it is pleasantly rich and creamy, and the vanilla notes are reminiscent of lemon sorbet.

— Have it large —
MANCHESTER VIGIL GIN
Zymurgorium
Manchester, England
{ zymurgorium.com }
GIN, 40%

Manchester Vigil Gin is produced by Aaron Darke, a proud Mancunian who loves science (hence the name of his business), making alcohol, and nature. His website bears the working bee symbol that represents the city. He has given this gin the strap line 'Stay strong our kid, emergency edition' and has donated all profit from it to the charity appeal in response to the 2017 Manchester bombing. It is made with wild juniper, strawberries, cherries, redcurrants, blackberries, raspberries, angelica, caraway, orris root, orange blossom, lime blossom, and vanilla. It is hard to find, but worth looking for.

— Hang in there —
STONE PINE DEAD MAN'S DROP
Stone Pine
Bathurst, Australia
{ stonepinedistillery.com.au }
RUM, 40%

Stone Pine is run by Bev and Ian Glen, whose roots are deeply Scottish. Bev ran various Edinburgh pubs; Ian holds a postgraduate diploma in Brewing and Distilling from Heriot-Watt University, and has spent his entire career in the malting, brewing, and distilling industry. In 1830, 19 members of the infamous Ribbon Gang were publicly hanged for murder, bushranging, and horse thieving. This was the first such execution in Bathurst. Dead Man's Drop evokes the spirit of that era, marrying barrel-aged rum with orange peel, vanilla, ringwood, and cinnamon myrtle.

— Buy some… —
ZUBROWKA BISON GRASS
Zubrowka
Poland
{ facebook.com/ zubrowkauk }
VODKA, 40%

Widely regarded as one of the finest Polish vodkas on the market, now or ever, Zubrowka has a unique taste, and has carved itself a comfortable niche in a very crowded sector. It is distilled from rye, and flavored with bison grass, which grows in Polish forests and gives the liquid a yellowish hue. Every bottle has a stem of bison grass in it: traditionally, this was supposed to impart a dry, herbal note, but today it is more for appearance than taste. The flavor of the product is described as having woodruff, vanilla, coconut, and almond notes.

— Hot hot hot —

GREEN CHILE VODKA

St George Spirits

Alameda, CA, USA

{ stgeorgespirits.com }

VODKA, 40%

Not to be confused with
the English distillery of the
same name, St George Spirits
started out in 1982 as a
one-man operation, and is
now a thriving business that
sits contentedly between the
old-established American
distilleries and the new wave
of craft ones. With this drink,
the label tells you everything:
crushed jalapeño peppers,
lime peel, and base spirit are
distilled; four types of peppers
(Serrano, habanero, red and
yellow sweet bell peppers) are
infused separately, and then
blended with the spirit. The
result is a challenging vodka
that is ideal for making a
top-notch Bloody Mary.

— Dive right in —

SPYTAIL BLACK GINGER

Spytail

France

{ spytailrum.com }

SPICED RUM, 40%

Spytail's website is enigmatic
and vague, but claims that
this spiced rum is *the* spirit of
adventure. There's a confusing
maritime and travel theme to
it, but the brand is French and
it's hard to follow the logic. No
matter: this is an absolutely
fabulous spiced rum. It's made
to a centuries' old method
of macerating fresh ginger
root and an array of spices
with the rum in the cask.
The ginger and other spices
dominate the taste, but there
are some delicious tropical
fruit notes, some honey, and
a twist of toffee. It works
well in cocktails or with fruit
juices, but can equally well be
consumed on its own.

— A roast to toast —

**SPIT-ROASTED
PINEAPPLE GIN**

That Boutique-y Gin
Company

Tunbridge Wells, UK

{ www.masterofmalt.co.uk }

FLAVORED GIN, 40.1%

That Boutique-y Gin Company
is part of Master of Malt, the
online spirits retailer, and
Spit-Roasted Pineapple Gin
is one its several unusual and
inspired individual bottlings.
According to the distributors,
pineapple gin was popular
in the 1920s, but later went
out of fashion and eventually
disappeared. Here, pineapples
covered in demerara sugar
are roasted on the spit until
they are caramelized. They are
then combined with gin. It's a
surprisingly gutsy pairing, with
the zing and sweetness of the
pineapple working with the
botanicals of the gin.

— Acid attack —

ANTY GIN
Cambridge Distillery
Cambridge, England
{ cambridgedistillery.co.uk }
FLAVORED GIN, 42%

The Cambridge Distillery is one of the more enterprising and explorative distilleries in Britain, and is quite prepared to go where many others might not venture. This gin is a case in point. It's a joint venture with the Nordic Food Lab, and it marks the point where the enjoyment of drinking clashes with some pretty highbrow science. It is made with formica rufa (red wood ants), a common species in Northern Europe. According to the distillery, these creatures communicate using a host of pheromones, and they defend their complex communities by producing formic acid. This acid is responsible for a range of aromas, so if you distill gin with the ants, all sorts of taste compounds come to the fore. A colony of some 6,000 red wood ants has been nurtured in Kent in England, and an average of 62 ants — not 60 or 65, 62 — make up each bottle of Anty Gin, but that's not all that makes this product unusual. Some of the botanicals are pretty left-field, too: to support the distinctive flavor of the wood ant distillate and the characteristics of Bulgarian juniper berries, wild springtime botanicals have been added, including wood avens, nettle, and Alexanders. The base alcohol is made of 100 per cent organic English wheat, and every distillation is carried out just one liter at a time. You might struggle to find this, since it's made in very small batches. It's definitely an imaginative spirit.

145

146

— Real venom —

TIGER SNAKE SOUR MASH

The Great Southern Distilling
Company
Albany, Australia
{ distillery.com.au }
WHISKEY, 43%

Sour mash is the process used by American
distillers to produce bourbon and Tennessee
whiskey. At the end of a distillation, there is
a residue of spent grains with all the sugars
stripped out to make alcohol (hence 'sour'),
and this is used in the next distillation because
it regulates bacteria. Tiger Snake Sour Mash
is an Australian take on bourbon (which is
a controlled term, and can be used only in
America). This drink is made predominantly
of corn, but also contains malted barley and
rye. There are American whiskey notes here,
but this is fruitier, and has some nuts and oats
alongside the main vanilla and honey themes.

— Mighty oak —

OAK CROSS

Compass Box
London, England
{ compassboxwhisky.co.uk }
BLENDED MALT WHISKY, 43%

Describing this whisky as coming from London
is misleading. Compass Box is a London-based
company creating highly palatable whiskies,
but the whisky comes from Scotland, and
under recent legislation the whisky must be
bottled north of the border, too. It's called Oak
Cross because the mixture of malt whiskies
is matured in an American oak cask with new
French oak heads. Even under normal
maturation, this would have been wonderful —
all stewed fruits, baked apple, and toffee. But
the virgin oak brings spices to the party, and
there are hints of ginger and Christmas cake in
the mix, too, to make it even better.

— *Tea-licious* —

DRUMSHANBO GUNPOWDER

P J Rigney
Drumshanbo, Ireland
{ goo.gl/m84bGu }
GIN, 43%

This is a curio: a gin made with oriental botanicals and gunpowder tea in a small shed in a tiny town in the heart of rural Ireland. The label bears an image of the jackalope, a mythical cross between a jackrabbit and an antelope -- the idea is that these two creatures have come together in the same way as gin and tea have been united in this drink. The gin is the creation of P J Rigney, and it includes kaffir lime, Chinese lemon, oriental grapefruit, and meadowsweet. The tea is distinctive, but so too are some pleasant citrus notes, and the finely balanced mix of spices works perfectly with the principal flavors.

— *Scouse onus* —

LIVERPOOL GIN VALENCIAN ORANGE

Halewood International
Liverpool, England
{ halewood-int.com }
GIN, 43%

Created by Liverpool Organic Brewery, the Liverpool Distillery makes 100 per cent organic spirits. Liverpool Gin already enjoys cult status, and in recent years it has diversified into flavored gins. This takes its original gin recipe and adds bold and strong orange flavors. The oranges are from Valencia because that's the home town of the daughter-in-law of the head distiller. Orange dominates here, with crystallized ginger and candied citrus. It's not cloying, though, and the taste is balanced by peppery juniper and herbaceous coriander.

— *Small is beautiful* —

DUNEDIN RUM

Strathearn Distillery
Methven, Scotland
{ strathearndistillery.com }
RUM, 43%

Strathearn may well be Scotland's smallest distillery, and it is one of a number of new draft distilleries. In 2017, it started bottling its single cask, single malt whiskies, with the first bottle fetching £4,150 ($5,820) at auction, and the rest of the cask selling at between £325 ($455) and £525 ($736) a bottle. This rum is one of several spirits that Strathearn has released to fill the gap while waiting for the whisky to mature.

It is a golden rum of the type probably first made in Scotland more than 100 years ago. It has a pleasant wave of spices and toasted oak, as well as the more common vanilla and burned sugar notes.

— *Cream of the crop* —
THE WRECKING COAST
CLOTTED CREAM
The Wrecking Coast
Distillery
Tintagel, England
{ thewreckingcoastdistillery.
com }
GIN, 43.9%

It's normal for gin distillers
to look to the past, and
to make their gins on
traditional alembic stills. The
Wrecking Coast wanted to use
ancient methods to make a
new-fangled gin that
incorporated Cornish clotted
cream, but struggled until they
sought help from a distilling
expert in the Netherlands.
Now their 12-botanical gin
is made on a computer-
controlled still, and the
Cornish cream is cold-distilled
in a vacuum. The result is a
classic: juniper-dominated,
but with lots of creamy notes.

— *Anarchy in the UK* —
STEAMPUNK PIRATE:
RASCAL STRENGTH
Steampunk Ltd
Gateshead, England
{ steampunkgin.com }
GIN, 45%

With its distinctive skull bottle
and irreverent approach to
marketing, SteamPunk has
caused quite a stir. There's
a danger that the gimmicks
will overshadow the spirits,
but that would be a shame,
because this gin is excellent.
Steampunk Pirate: Rascal
Strength is the follow-up gin
to the highly successful Steampunk Gin: Extremely Rare. It's
made in a similar way, but has
a higher alcoholic strength.
Botanicals include juniper,
arris root, licorice, star anise,
lemon, orange and grapefruit
zest. The makers say it's good
enough to sip on its own
or to be the base of quality
cocktails.

— *Heavy hitter* —
ZEPPELIN BEND
New Holland Artisan
Spirits
Holland, MI, USA
{ newhollandbrew.com }
**SINGLE MALT
WHISKEY, 45%**

One of the most exciting
current trends in spirits is
the emergence of American
single malt whiskey. By
using American barley, and
combining traditional double
distillation with distinctly
American new oak barrels,
brands such as this are
offering a totally new taste
in whiskey. Zeppelin Bend
is matured for four years, so
that's a lot of wood and char
influence on the spirit. But it
works brilliantly. The whiskey
is a toasty, nutty, and spicy
malt, but the vanilla and
honeyed notes are there from
the oak. Worth seeking out.

— Making waves —
JEFFERSON'S OCEAN AGED AT SEA
Jefferson's
Crestwood, KY, USA
{ jeffersonsbourbon.com }
BOURBON, 45%

Traditionally, the distilleries of Kentucky have tended to shy away from innovation and imagination, although the current boom in craft distilling has pushed them into some reappraisal, and we are starting to see some excellent new whiskeys. When it comes to innovation, Jefferson's is an exception. Everything it does is driven by the desire to explore new directions, and to twist traditional bourbon-making into new and exciting shapes. The company is based a few minutes from downtown Louisville, but glance at the company website and you can tell immediately that this isn't a conventional distillery. From the motto, 'Alchemy is everything', to the competition to win an encounter with a great white shark, this outfit is different. The distillery was founded by father-and-son team Chet and Trey Zoeller, and it is named after Thomas Jefferson, who was known for his curiosity and innovation. This bourbon is the result of an experiment in conjunction with Ocearch, a company that tracks and monitors sea creatures. Three barrels of bourbon, aged for more than six years, were put on Ocearch's boat to see what happened to the liquor when it repeatedly crossed the Equator and was exposed to extreme conditions, variations in temperature, and the rocking of the vessel. The result is distinctive, with hints of rum-like caramel, and distinctive briny and savory notes that are reminiscent of Islay malt. Very unusual, and an exciting twist in the bourbon story.

— *Bio fuelled* —

BELGROVE RYE

Belgrove Distillery
Kempton, Tasmania,
Australia
{ belgrovedistillery.com.au }
RYE WHISKY, 45%

Belgrove Distillery isn't really
a distillery. It's a handmade
still made by Peter Bignell in a
horse shed on his farmstead.
He makes rye whisky on it
using a 100 per cent recipe and
rye grown on his own land.
And the still, the hot water, his
tractors, trucks, and forklift
are all powered by a biofuel
made from used cooking oil
from a roadhouse nearby. This
is Australia's only rye whisky,
and the whole production
process is done on site. But
it's very small batch, and as a
result little of it makes it out
of the country. Which is a pity,
because it's grown into a spicy
delight, with a fresh peppery
note to it.

— *Proudly Japanese* —

KI NO BI

Kyoto Distillery
Kyoto, Japan
{ kyotodistillery.jp }
GIN, 45.7%

The British owners of this
business say that Kyoto was
the only place they considered
when choosing a site for
their gin distillery. The city is
rich in art and culture, and it
just felt right. And it is close
to Fushimi, where the soft
waters help to produce the
finest sake, and there is an
abundance of raw materials
such as yuzu, sansho, and
the legendary teas of Uji. The
botanicals include each of
these, along with hinoki wood
chips and bamboo leaves.
They are divided into six
groups and distilled
individually. The result is a
delicate, floral, fragrant, and
nuanced gin of the finest
quality.

— *A new dawn* —

WOLFBURN AURORA

Aurora Brewing Ltd
Thurso, Scotland
{ scotchwhisky.com }
**SINGLE MALT
WHISKY, 46%**

Wolfburn Distillery is one
of the new wave of Scottish
micro-distilleries, producing
just 33,000 gallons (125,000
liters) of malt spirit each
year. Now the most northerly
distillery on the Scottish
mainland, it is built on a site
close to the original Wolfburn
Distillery, which seems to have
closed down in the middle of
the 19th century. What sets
this whisky apart is its
maturation. Forty per cent
of the spirit is matured in
second-fill quarter casks,
40 per cent in first-fill bourbon
casks, and 20 per cent in first-
fill oloroso sherry. The malt is
young and vibrant, with some
red berry and raisin notes.

— Mind the gap —

GLENDALOUGH 13 YO OLD IRISH
Glendalough Distillery
Glendalough, Ireland
{ glendaloughdistillery.
com }
SINGLE MALT
WHISKEY, 46%

Until a few years ago, Irish whiskey was on its knees, with only Irish Distillers and latterly Cooley keeping it in the game. But now Ireland has joined the world craft distilling revolution with a passion. Glendalough is the creation of a group of friends from Dublin and Wicklow who want to revive Irish distilling. The distillery's first release was poitín, and it is now making whiskey. This one was sourced elsewhere, probably from Cooley, but it is an exciting addition to Ireland's range. It is rich and sweet, with citrus, spice, and oak notes.

— Smoky in Seattle —

WESTLAND PEATED
Westland Distillery
Seattle, WA, USA
{ westlanddistillery.com }
SINGLE MALT
WHISKEY, 46%

No country in the world has embraced craft distilling with greater enthusiasm than the United States. The American Distillers' Institute currently has 1,300 members, and the best small, independent distilleries are being eyed up by international companies. The Westland Distillery makes imaginative American single malts, and this is the best of them — a heavily peated whisky with a distinctive American taste, created by the use of first-fill bourbon and new American oak casks. The balance between smoke and fruit is a true taste sensation, and it's set off by a nuttiness and some savory iodine notes.

— Best of the Breast —

REDBREAST LUSTAU
Irish Distillers
Midleton, Ireland
{irishdistillers.ie }
IRISH POT STILL
WHISKEY, 46%

It would not be too great a stretch to conclude that pot still whiskey — a unique style of whiskey made with a mix of malted barley and another, unmalted grain — kick-started a resurgence in Irish whiskey. Irish Distillers responded to innovation from upstarts Cooley with a string of wonderful pot still whiskeys, of which this is among the very best. Lustau is matured for nine to 12 years in a mix of American and European oak before being transferred to an oloroso sherry cask for a further year. It has plum and raisin notes, along with milk chocolate and honeycomb, and a pot-still oiliness.

— Dragon force —
**PENDERYN MADEIRA
FINISH**
Penderyn Distillery
Penderyn, Wales
{ penderyn.wales }
**SINGLE MALT
WHISKY, 46%**

If this whisky doesn't taste
much like Scottish single
malt, that's because it's not
meant to. When Penderyn was
devised, its producers set out
to make a whisky that was
different. The Madeira cask is
part of that, giving the spirit
a floral, sweet, and perfumey
quality. But the owners also
employed David Faraday — a
descendant of the great
scientist Michael — to design
a unique still to produce a
different spirit. This whisky is
matured not only in Madeira
casks, but also partially in
ex-bourbon casks and casks
previously used to make
Scotch whisky.

— Monster flavors —
PEAT MONSTER
Compass Box
London, England
{ compassboxwhisky.com }
**BLENDED MALT
WHISKY, 46%**

We have put London as the
address of Compass Box,
but that is only partially true
these days. This whisky is
made with Scottish malts from
various distilleries, and these
ingredients have been brought
together by alchemist John
Glaser in London. But Scotch
whisky rules demand that
bottling should take place in
Scotland. So the core whiskies
are made and bottled north
of the border. The genius bit,
though, is done in London.
The coastal, medicinal, and
barbecue notes are all there.
It's just that they're offset by
some delicious fresh fruit and
malt. Excellent whisky.

— Port in a stormer —
**BENRIACH 21 YEAR OLD
TAWNY PORT FINISH**
BenRiach Distilling Co
Longmorn, Scotland
{ benriachdistillery.co.uk }
**SINGLE MALT
WHISKY, 46%**

The sale in 2016 of BenRiach
to American drinks producers
Brown Forman, owners of
Jack Daniel's, marked the
end of a remarkable era for
the three-person team that
reopened the distillery in
2004. In the intervening 12
years there were scores of
BenRiach expressions, but this
is one of the most exciting —
classic Speyside whisky aged
for 21 years and finished in a
tawny port cask. The result
is a sumptuous mix of rich
summer fruits, orange peel,
tannin from the oak and
spiciness with a delicious
raspberry tartness.

— All things nice —
THE SPICE TREE
Compass Box
London, England
{ compassboxwhisky.com }
BLENDED MALT WHISKY, 46%

Compass Box is an innovative set-up that was once out on its own when it came to exciting new whisky ideas. But innovation can be controversial, even (or perhaps especially) when it's effective, and Compass Box has sometimes upset the more traditional elements of the whisky industry. The company takes a range of high-quality Scottish single malts, mainly from Diageo, and brings them together to make a new whisky. A mixture of malt whiskies with no grain whisky is known as a blended malt whisky. This one was, once upon a time, among the most controversial. It's a mixture of Highland malts, so it's a full-bodied and robust mix. The whisky attains its spiciness from maturation in a cask that contained virgin oak staves, but this was deemed to be outside the rules governing Scotch whisky production. So Compass Box worked with coopers in Scotland and France to produce a hybrid cask that is made mainly of traditional American oak, but with heads made of French oak. It is the latter that provide the spiciness, but not so much that it overwhelms the spirit. The company describes this product as 'a rich, intense malt whisky redolent of baking spices and layered with toasty oak accents'. Those spices are a mixture of sweet and savory, with ginger, cardamom, and chili all making a play.
But that's not the whole story — there are bourbon notes here, too, with vanilla, honey, and toffee offsetting the spiciness. A total treat from start to finish.

154

— *Rule Bretagne* —
ARMORIK MAÎTRE DE CHAI
Distillerie Warenghem
Boutill, France
{ distillerie-warenghem.com }
SINGLE MALT WHISKY, 46%

France may have built a reputation for quality wine, but when it comes to beer and apple-based alcohol, it is not too shabby either. Its whiskies can be excellent, too. Distillerie Warenghem is run by David Roussier, who brought in the late Jim Swan to 'tweak' the production process. The whiskies from the distillery have improved significantly, putting them among the finest, not only from France, but also from the whole of mainland Europe. Maître de Chai, which means 'cellar master', is matured in oloroso casks for several years. Macadamia nuts, overripe plums, aniseed, and some pepper run through the heart of this malt, which has a pleasant dryness to it, too.

— *Yellow and brave* —
CHASE ISLAY WHISKY CASK VODKA
Williams Chase
Hereford, England
{ chasedistillery.co.uk }
VODKA, 46%

How about orange marmalade vodka, or oak-smoked vodka? Need some convincing? William Chase and his team aren't afraid of a challenge, or of taking their spirits in new and exciting directions. This is one of their less unconventional creations, but there's nothing humdrum about a vodka that tastes like whisky. The effect is achieved by maturing the base potato-derived spirit for several months in a cask that previously contained Laphroaig Islay single malt. It is then bottled without chill filtration. The product has a slightly yellowish hue, and a smokiness that extends from nose to aftertaste. There are also strong hints of peaty pine, vanilla, and licorice.

— *Signet sings* —
GLENMORANGIE SIGNET
Glenmorangie
Tain, Scotland
{ glenmorangie.com }
SINGLE MALT WHISKY, 46%

If you're looking for a lush, rich, luxury malt
with oodles of style and more depth than your
local reservoir, then this one is for you. It drives
a coach and horses through the argument that
whiskies without an age statement are in some
way inferior to aged whiskies. Signet is one of
a number of bottlings put together by Dr Bill
Lumsden, who has experimented with historic
whisky recipes, unusual casks, and grains from
specific fields or regions of Scotland. Some of
his whiskies have been earthy and traditional,
but from the beautiful packaging to the
exquisite taste, Signet is a dark and sensual
slice of sleek luxury — and a venture into the
unknown. It is also one of the best Scotch
whiskies you will ever taste. Don't take our
word for it — there are 50 five-star reviews
on the website of online retailer The Whisky
Exchange. A range of malts were used in its
production, including heavily toasted chocolate
malt, and the spirit has been matured in a
number of different casks. The resulting malt
whisky is very complex, but it is a little like a
box of hand-crafted Belgian chocolates: dark
and super-smooth, with a twist of coffee, nut,
orange peel, and cherry. It melts in the mouth,
and the finish is long, refreshing, and citrusy.
It's not the cheapest, but if you're looking to up
your game for a special occasion, or you come
in to some cash, you really cannot do better
than this.

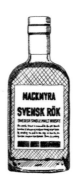

— *Winter wonderland* —

MACKMYRA VINTERDRÖM

Mackmyra Whisky
Gävle, Sweden
{ mackmyra.com }
SINGLE MALT
WHISKY, 46.1%

When a group of Swedes
went skiing in the north of
their country, and each of
them took a different bottle
of Scottish malt for the host,
it got them thinking about
making whisky themselves.
The result was an adventure
into the unknown that would
take them from a small
distillery in an old stables to a
futuristic gravity distillery and
bars all over the world. Their
seasonal whiskies are well
worth seeking out. This one
is matured in rum casks, so it
has a delightful tropical fruit
angle, as well as spices from
the oak.

— *Up in smoke* —

SVENSK RÖK

Mackmyra Whisky
Gävle, Sweden
{ mackmyra.com }
SINGLE MALT
WHISKY, 46.1%

An increasing number of
countries are distilling whisky.
Some of the products are
excellent. But how much
regional character do they
really have? Peat is flora and
fauna crushed over centuries,
so different areas will create
different peats, from savory
smoke to sweet peat from
treeless Scottish islands.
Rök means 'smoke', and in
Sweden that promises a salty,
tangy taste, because much
of the nation's peat was once
under the Baltic Sea. There is
juniper here, too, from drying
the barley in the traditional
Swedish way. An intriguing
take on smoky whisky.

— *Highway to Hellyers* —

**HELLYERS ROAD PINOT
NOIR FINISH**

Hellyers Road
Tasmania, Australia
{ hellyersroad.com.au }
SINGLE MALT
WHISKY, 46.1%

Much has been made of
the fact that the distillers
of Tasmania have worked
together to create a forceful
unit. But Hellyers Road is
different. It's a dairy that
makes whiskies because it
was worried about being
driven out of the milk trade
by a mainland competitor. It
is on the opposite side of the
island to most Tasmanian
whisky-makers, and its whisky
is lighter than that of many
heavy hitters in the southeast.
This product has oranges and
lemons on the nose, a spicy
heart, and then some plummy,
berry-like notes from the wine
influence.

— *Drinky spice* —
RUMBULLION XO 15 YEAR OLD
Ableforth's
Tunbridge Wells,
England
{ ableforths.com }
SPICED RUM, 46.2%

Ableforth's is the name given to a range of spirits from online retailer Master of Malt. This is a spiced rum, but describing it as such is a little like describing the Harlem Globetrotters as a basketball team. There's a strong naval theme here, but one that is based on the Captain's bottle of Special Reserve, rather than the grog distributed to the crew. It blends top-quality Caribbean rum with vanilla, orange peel, and spices. There is distinct rum-and-raisin dark chocolate, and a spiciness from a recipe that the makers are keeping secret. It's topped off with some oaky notes.

— *Great Dane* —
STAUNING KAOS
Stauning
Skjern, Denmark
{ stauningwhisky.com }
SINGLE MALT WHISKY, 46.5%

In the 1920s, when Thorvald Stauning stood for election in Denmark, his campaign slogan was: 'If you don't vote for Stauning, you'll get chaos'. So the owners of this distillery launched a whisky that provides both in a single bottle. Danish whisky isn't always the most approachable of styles, and this is an assault on the senses. It's made up of the distillery's traditional whisky, a young rye, and peated whisky. So it's smoky, oily, and spicy all at once. And not just one spice — lots of different ones, battling each other for dominance. A glass of this is quite an experience.

— *Takes no prisoners* —
BOURBON BARREL BIG GIN
Captive Spirits
Distilling
Seattle, WA, USA
{ captivespiritsdistilling.com }
GIN, 47%

Life is treating Captive Spirits well. The distillery launched in 2012, and its first gin was an immediate award winner. In late 2017, the company moved in to new harborside premises in Seattle, and having conquered gin, set about making imaginative aged bourbons. This is the company's bourbon barrel gin, and the distillery also makes a peated barrel gin. It also refers to them as 'big gins', and that's spot-on. This one spent six months in once-used bourbon barrels from Heaven Hill Distilleries. The result is a gin with strong juniper notes accompanied by warm, woody spices.

158

— World beater —
SULLIVAN'S COVE FRENCH OAK
Sullivan's Cove
Tasmania, Australia
{ sullivanscove.com }
SINGLE MALT WHISKY, 47.5%

What a difference a decade makes. In the early
part of the new millennium, Sullivan's Cove
was not great. The early casks left a lot to be
desired, and in the end the owners gave up.
Under the new management of Patrick Maguire,
though, the whisky has gone from strength
to strength, and in 2014 it scooped the title
of world's best whisky in the World Whisky
Awards. French Oak is a single barrel whisky,
and consequently every barrel will be different.
But all the whisky is aged in 66-gallon (300-liter)
French oak ex-tawny barrels. The resulting
whisky combines jellied fruits, kitchen spices,
and chocolate.

— Highland warrior —
GLEN GARIOCH VIRGIN OAK
Glen Garioch
Oldmeldrum, Scotland
{ glengarioch.com }
SINGLE MALT WHISKY, 48%

Glen Garioch — pronounced 'geery' — is a true
hidden gem of a distillery, off the beaten track
and often overlooked by whisky enthusiasts
fast-tracking it from Aberdeen airport to
Speyside. The distillery is quaint and beautifully
maintained, with a visitor center and an
excellently organized tour. Production is
traditional and labor-intensive. This particular
expression is one of the more recent bottlings,
and it comes with its own set of challenges.
It's a feisty Highland warrior with a deceptive
vanilla and grain nose, then big toffee, spice,
and chocolate notes on the palate, before a
final wave of oaky tannins. Not subtle, but lots
of fun.

— *Pure luxury* —

CLÉMENT 2016 CANNE BLEUE

Clément

Martinique

{ rhumclementusa.com }

RHUM AGRICOLE, 50%

Rhum agricole is rum made from freshly squeezed sugar cane juice rather than from molasses. It's a Caribbean specialty, and Martinique is one of the main producers. This example is made and bottled at the heart of the island's liquor industry — Habitation Clément. The production process begins with the selection of the finest sugarcane, in this case the Canne Bleue variety. Only its juice is used in this rum. The result is a luxurious, sophisticated mouthful with an almost oily vegetal note that prevents the overall effect from becoming cloying.

— *Rye smiles* —

MILLSTONE 100 RYE

Zuidam

Baarle-Nassau,

Netherlands

{ millstonewhisky.eu }

RYE WHISKY, 50%

Zuidam is a family-owned business making some 600 spirits and liqueur products and using the fresh and finest ingredients to do so. Don't be surprised to see piles of apples and cherries if you visit. The company produces some of the best whisky in Europe, and this is a gem. It is named for its composition — 100 per cent rye, bottled at 50.0% (100 proof) — and it is eight years and four months — 100 months — old. The nose is fragrant and herbal, but the taste is excellent — an intriguing mix of fruits, toffee, red licorice, and firecracker spices, including pepper and cardamom.

— *Bang on* —

JOHNNY DRUM PRIVATE STOCK

Willett Family Estate

Bardstown, KY, USA

{ kentuckybourbonwhiskey. com }

BOURBON, 50.5%

Formerly known as Kentucky Bourbon Distillers, this was an independent bottling company, buying in bourbon and rye, and bottling it under a variety of names. But the company is private and family-owned, and it was always its wish to build and open a distillery of its own, and it's now done so. Johnny Drum isn't the product of the new distillery, but it's a fine bourbon, a meaty classic perfected over five genera-tions and bursting with flavor, complexity, and richness. Cinnamon, clove, and oaky tannins set off the caramel and vanilla notes.

— *Fun rum* —
RUMBULLION NAVY STRENGTH
Ableforth's
Tunbridge Wells,
England
{ ableforths.com }
SPICED RUM, 57%

There's something playful and fun about Rumbullion from Ableforth's. Taste it, and you think of midwinter festivals. It tastes brilliant in a Christmas fruit salad. Steady as you go with this version of it, though, because it packs a punch and will have grandma doing Madonna karaoke if you're not careful with it. The rum comes from the Caribbean, and the extra alcoholic strength brings a whole set of new lights to the party. Expect intense vanilla and orange peel, and blasts of cardamom, cinnamon, and sweet kitchen spices. It tastes great in ginger beer, too.

'CLARET IS THE LIQUOR FOR BOYS; PORT FOR MEN; BUT HE WHO ASPIRES TO BE A HERO MUST DRINK BRANDY.'
SAMUEL JOHNSON

— *Kicks butt* —
KAVALAN SOLIST FINO
Kavalan
Yilan County, Taiwan
{ kavalanwhisky.co.uk }
SINGLE MALT WHISKY, 57%

Kavalan is a Taiwanese whisky distillery founded in 2005, and it hit the ground running. Two trial spirits — one deep chestnut brown from a sherry cask; the other golden yellow from a bourbon cask; both marked 'China' — blazed a trail for a run of outstanding whiskies. The Solist comprises single-cask, cask-strength bottlings, so this is a weighty 57% ABV. Fino is a dry sherry, so the casks impart some astringency to an excellently made malt. But the Fino is not over-assertive either, and it allows the fruitiness of the whisky to shine through. There are also some very smoky wood aromas.

— *Malt sandwich* —

AMRUT INTERMEDIATE SHERRY CASK

Amrut

Bangalore, India

{ amrutwhisky.co.uk }

SINGLE MALT WHISKY, 57.1%

Amrut has a 70-year history, but its main spirits have been sold to the local market, and it was only when the owner's son went to university in England and explored the possibility of selling malt whisky to Scotland as a student project that Amrut single malt was formed. The whiskies are among the most progressive and imaginative in the world. They have been made and matured on two different continents, on German islands, in a range of different casks, and using unpeated grain from India and peaty grain from Scotland. Innovation is a key part of of the Amrut story, and the distillery's Greedy Angels bottling, in which a whopping three-quarters of the barrel was lost to the elements, is one of the world's great whiskies. Intermediate Sherry Cask is a limited edition whisky that was matured in bourbon, moved into a sherry cask, and then returned to a bourbon cask to complete its maturation. As you might expect, then, there are stewed fruits and berries from the sherry, and vanilla and caramel notes from the bourbon wood. But there's something more exciting going on in here, too. Instead of the usual toasted and berry fruit notes, there are hints of cementing fruit, and a deep complexity. The structure is oak-based, but citrus fruits, honeycomb, and licorice are also in the mix. The overall effect is simply incomparable with any other whisky in the world.

162

— *The real deal* —
KAVALAN SOLIST EX-BOURBON
Kavalan
Yilan County, Taiwan
{ kavalanwhisky.com }
SINGLE MALT WHISKY, 57%

The debate rages on: is Kavalan making great whisky, or is it merely imitating Scotch whiskies with malts that have no legs and will not age well? Kavalan Solist Bourbon is a hearty case for the defense. Produced in a sleek modern distillery under the guidance of Dr Jim Swan until his death in 2017, this is a pure joy, and as good an example of a malt matured in a bourbon cask as you will find. It is described as a complex, multi-dimensional whisky, with vanilla, fruit, and coconut highlights, but where it really scores is with its juxtaposition of creamy oak and barley alongside tropical fruits and a delightful whisky rancio note.

— *Full throttle* —
OVEREEM SINGLE SHERRY CASK
Lark
Hobart, Australia
{ overeemwhisky.com }
SINGLE MALT WHISKY, 60%

Overeem is a great example of the special relationship between the distillers of Tasmania. Casey Overeem became interested in distilling when he saw micro-distilleries while visiting relatives in Norway, and he set up his own works with the help of Bill Lark. But having established his two expressions of whisky, he retired and sold the business to Lark, under whose aegis it retains its original identity. Casey's daughter, Jane, has stayed at the company, and is head of marketing there. The Sherry Cask is the less subtle of the two whiskies. It is matured in quarter casks, which create an intense sherried whisky experience. Wood spice and oaky notes play off sherry trifle.

— *Fast and furious* —

OVEREEM SINGLE PORT CASK
Lark

Hobart, Australia

{ overeemwhisky.com }

SINGLE MALT WHISKY, 60%

As the name suggests, this is a single cask bottling, so batches will vary. But every bottle will contain malt aged in ex-port French oak barrels. These hand-selected containers have been cut down to 22-gallon (100-liter; quarter-cask) capacity, and this results in a busy, bustling, rich-flavored, and complex whisky. It's all kicking off here, and among the dark chocolate, praline, spice, and orange fruit bursts, there's an almost smoky earthiness. The high strength allows water to add to the party without reducing the the intensity. It's a Roger Waters gig in a glass.

— *Pär-fection* —

SMÖGEN 4 YEAR OLD FRENCH QUARTER
Pär Caldenby

Hunnebostrand, Sweden

{ smogenwhisky.se }

SINGLE MALT WHISKY,

61.6%

Sweden produces some of the world's most passionate whisky enthusiasts. Prominent among them is Pär Caldenby, a lawyer and author who has turned to whisky with vigor and creativity. The name of this whisky tells you pretty much everything you need to know about it: it's a four-year-old malt matured as a limited edition in four freshly toasted quarter casks made of French oak. But it's also made with peated malt and rarely found optic barley. Peat, oak, spice, and toasted grain: what's not to love?

— *Precocious genius* —

PORTONOVA
Amrut

Bangalore, India

{ amrutwhisky.co.uk }

SINGLE MALT WHISKY,

62.1%

Portonova is possibly the finest example of how the climate in Bangalore affects malt maturation. This is less than six years old, but it has nowhere to go from here, and is at the top of its game, holding up well against whiskies three times its age. Matured in American ex-bourbon casks, and finished in port pipes, it is sublime. What a way to finish the 'imaginative' category of this book! The malt is super-fruity, with banana, tropical fruits, and citrus all vying for attention. Milk chocolate, red berries, and mild spice make up the mix. From another world.

DRINKING SPIRITS WITH FOOD
IS WIDELY ACCEPTED IN MANY
CULTURES. TODAY, MANY
CRAFT DISTILLERIES HAVE
REVIVED THE TAPROOM, AND
SERVE FOOD ALONGSIDE THEIR
SPIRITS, OR USE SPIRITS AS
INGREDIENTS IN FOOD DISHES.

GASTRONOMIC

SPIRITS AND FOOD MATCHING

VODKA

In vodka-producing nations, the spirit is often served with savory foods. Chill your vodka in the freezer; drink it cold, then follow it with some fortifying pickled tomatoes, blini, caviar, or herring and mayonnaise. Vodka goes well with anything salty or vinegar-pickled.

GIN

Think of gin as a seasoning for bland food. Gin is made up of botanicals, with juniper and often citrus and spice flavors to the fore, so matching individual craft gins with food is a case of trial and error. Plain meats or fish could work well, though.

BOURBON

The spirit is matured in charred or toasted oak barrels, and the flavor is dominated by vanilla, honey, spice, and candied fruits, all of which are elements in condiments for the barbecue. Barbecued meats and bourbon are a marriage made in heaven.

PEATY WHISKY

A moderately peaty whisky works surprisingly well with oysters or prawns. But the best whisky and food combination is a heavily peated, fruity whisky with blue cheese. The whole is quite different from — and even greater than — the sum of the parts, so if you're not sure about either component, give them a go together.

HIGHLAND WHISKY

Mixing Highand Whisky with chocolate might seem like an odd combination, but it's no stranger than mixing chilli and chocolate. The right Highland-style whiskies have an earthy, meaty, peat base that works brilliantly with dark chocolate and chocolate orange.

RUM

Rum is rich in caramel and toffee notes, and these features lend themselves well to a wide range of desserts, from ice cream to fruit salads, and from cake-based desserts to trifles. But barbecuing was invented in the West Indies, so try it with grilled meat or fish, or as a drizzle for kebabs.

— In the pink —
CIROC PINK GRAPEFRUIT
Ciroc
Villevert, France
{ ciroc.com }
VODKA, 37.5%

What sets Ciroc apart is the fact that it is a gluten-free vodka made from grapes by an acclaimed wine-maker and distiller in a process that has been perfected over hundreds of years. It is distilled five times in all. The basic wine is distilled four times before a final distillation in a traditional, tailor-made, copper pot still at the historic Distillerie de Chevanceaux in the South of France. Ciroc Pink Grapefruit was launched in 2016, and it balances grape and grapefruit perfectly. Try it with crab, ideally with a white wine sauce, although it's pretty good on its own, too.

— Shine on crazy diamond —
CIROC PEACH
Ciroc
Villevert, France
{ ciroc.com }
VODKA, 37.5%

Now we're motoring, and as it's almost impossible to have too much grape-based vodka, let's tickle our taste buds with a dose of hedonistic delight. Ciroc Peach is a a class vodka and a delight with food. This one works well with crab or lobster but, for a total taste sensation, play the delicate flavors of the fresh peach and tropical fruit essences and the grape core of this vodka off against a salt caramel cheesecake. It makes for a chaotic, exuberant, oral Pink Floyd show.

— Let's cut to it —
CHASE RHUBARB
Williams Chase
Hereford, England
{ chasedistillery.co.uk }
VODKA, 40%

William Chase is a vegetable farmer who diversified into spirit production, so it's perhaps only to be expected that his best drinks lend themselves well to pairing with food. A rhubarb-based vodka might not look promising on paper, but in practice the fruit's tanginess is particularly well suited to a large range of food. It's good alongside mackerel and duck, for instance, and works pretty well with the likes of almonds and coconut. But perhaps the best concomitant of all is pork loin. Just as a tangy apple sauce does, the taste of the rhubarb bounces off the fat-rich meat.

— *Don't be afraid* —
DARK MATTER SPICED
Dark Matter Distillery
Banchory, Scotland
{ darkmatterdistillers.com }
RUM, 40%

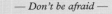

— *Cocktail bound* —
CEYLON ARRACK
Rockland Distilleries
Colombo, Sri Lanka
{ ceylonarrack.com }
ARRACK, 40%

— *East meets West* —
WOODY CREEK POTATO
VODKA
Woody Creek Distillery
Basalt, CO, USA
{ woodycreekdistillers.com }
VODKA, 40%

Rum is the barman's mistress, whispering seductively in his ear that she'll be whatever he wants her to be. It's the cocktail-maker's flexible friend, and proof that it is possible for one spirit in its many guises to be all things to all people. Chefs get on with it too, and it makes a great ingredient for cooking, especially in its spiced form. It can be part of a great glaze for chicken or gammon, for instance. Dark Matter Spiced comes into its own at Yuletide. It peps up Christmas cake recipes, but is at its struttiest best when liberally included in the seasonal fruit salad.

There are various spirits with names similar to this one, but this is the traditional Sri Lanka spirit made from the fermented juice of the coconut palm, extracted by cutting the flowers from the tree and hanging a bucket below the cut to gather the free-flowing sap. It is collected by young 'toddy tappers', who swing by rope from coconut tree to coconut tree. They start early in the morning, and the heat of the day stirs natural yeasts that ferment the sap into palm wine in a few hours. This arrack is refined into a premium spirit. Arrack tastes a little like rum, and goes well with Thai and Malaysian food.

Woody Creek was founded by husband-and-wife team Mary and Pat Scanlon and their friend Mark Kleckner. They make all their spirit on a custom-built still, and grow many of the ingredients, including the potatoes used here. Food-matching with vodka is popular in Northern and Eastern Europe. There are bars that offer three different vodkas with four types of caviar. If that's a bit rich for you, try this vodka frozen with a Swedish meal of pickled herring, gravlax, pickles, cheese, meatballs, venison, stuffed chicken, and potato with anchovies — all served with homemade bread.

— *Honey and heather* —
ABERFELDY 21 YEAR OLD
John Dewar & Sons
Aberfeldy, Scotland
{ dewars.com }
SINGLE MALT WHISKY, 40%

There has been a marked change in attitude at John Dewar & Sons. For many years, the company allowed — indeed, encouraged — the public to visit Dewar's World of Whisky tourist experience at Aberfeldy, but kept its actual distilleries — one on the outskirts of the same town, the others at Aultmore, Craigellachie, Macduff, and Royal Brackla — strictly out of bounds, so that the distillers could get on with their work undisturbed by prying journalists. That has now changed, and all-comers are welcome at the Aberfeldy Distillery, in which a new visitor center offers the chance to taste old and rare whiskies from this location and the company's other establishments. This classic Highland malt has a ruggedness that is offset by a warming, honeyed note. At the age of 21 years, it is mature, verging on venerable, and truly sublime. Although the following assertion might upset single malt whisky aficionados, who struggle to accept food along with whisky at all, let alone with an aged and stately malt such as this, Aberfeldy is well suited to food pairing. You can start with the most basic pairing of all, porridge — the creamy oats work well alongside the barley and honey of the whisky. Aberfeldy is also really nice with a simply grilled piece of sirloin. No onions, no mushrooms, no tomatoes. Simple, and simply wonderful.

— *Witch's brew* —
LIQUORE STREGA
Strega Alberti
Benevento
Benevento, Italy
{ strega.it }
HERBAL LIQUEUR, 40%

Strega means 'witch' in Italian. Liquore Strega is a herbal liqueur served as a digestif and with a history stretching back to 1860, when it was invented by an entrepreneur in Benevento. The recipe for the drink, which includes 70 herbs and spices, is secret, but the yellow color is due to the presence of saffron. Its other ingredients include cinnamon, iris, juniper, mint, and fennel. It's not easy to get this to work well with food, but it's not impossible: mix it with a fragrant gin, and serve it alongside Indian mango curry or something tangy and fruity from Morocco.

— *Spanish fame* —
LARIOS 12
Destileries y Crianza
Segovia, Spain
{ beamsuntory.com }
GIN, 40%

Spain's best-selling gin, Larios is distilled and matured in Segovia at Destilerias y Crianza, an impressive, all-purpose distillery that makes whisky as well as gin, and has kept its old-world Spanish charm even though it's now part of Beam Suntory. Larios contains 12 botanicals which ensure that it can hold its own with the very best gins on the market. It is a citrus-dominated gin, and it's vibrant and zesty. That means it works nicely with crispy duck, and is delicious with prawns and other seafood, but it may be best of all with a fruity cheese — manchego, or a rich Cheddar.

— *Fragrant and aromatic* —
OPIHR ORIENTAL SPICED
Quintessential Brands
Warrington, England
{ quintessentialbrands.com }
GIN, 40%

Opihr Oriental Spiced Gin is a unique style of London Dry Gin created by the world's first female master gin distiller, Joanne Moore, using exotic botanicals, herbs, and spices. Opihr's hand-picked botanicals epitomize the exotic intensity of the Orient, with spicy cubeb berries from Indonesia, and black pepper and cardamom from India; the accompanying coriander is from Morocco. The spices, particularly the coriander, are to the fore here. This is delicious with lamb, particualrly lamb that has been slow-roasted with added cinnamon, cloves, ginger, garlic, and pepper.

— *A piece of cake* —
IRIDIUM
Mt Uncle Distillery
Walkamin, Australia
{ mtuncle.com }
DARK RUM, 40%

— *C'est formidable* —
WHISKY DE TABLE
Compass Box
London, England
{ compassboxwhisky }
SINGLE MALT WHISKY, 40%

— *Sugar and spice* —
BOMBO CARAMEL & COCONUT
The Real Rum
Company
Newquay, England
{ bomborum.com }
RUM, 40%

Founded in 2002 by Mark Watkins and his family, Mt Uncle Distillery produces a range of different spirits. A clutch of awards has ensured that the distillery has found itself at the forefront of the craft distilling phenomenon. Iridium is a naturally golden rum, aged for four years, and it has a delightful vanilla, caramel, and oak taste. Iridium simply screams 'Let them eat cake!' — a bluesy and boozy cake at that. You can use this to provide a drizzle on pretty much any cake, but, better still, set yourself a weekend afternoon aside, pour yourself a glass, look up a rum cake recipe, and get baking.

It started as a bit of harmless fun between John Glaser of Compass Box and Thierry Benitah of La Maison du Whisky in Paris. Thierry wanted to do an exclusive bottling for his store. John let Thierry taste some of his young 'works in progress', and Thierry was so impressed with the spirited, oak-free malt that, before you could say, 'Ooh la la', a new concept was born. This looks like a white wine, is bottled in a wine bottle, and is probably as close to being a table spirit as a malt whisky will ever get. Serve it with whatever you'd serve a chardonnay with.

Bombo, say its makers, is the rum of pirates, and Cornwall, pirates, and rum are the perfect combination. Not sure about that, but let's go with it. Bombo Caramel & Coconut comes in two strengths, but opt for the higher one at 40% because in this one all the flavors are in clear focus. Rum suits most desserts, but the coconut component in this one makes it particularly good with chocolate dishes. If you're feeling adventurous, rum and West Indian jerk chicken is a perfect combination.

— *Go Mexico* —

MCQUEEN SMOKY CHILI

McQueen

Callander, Scotland

{ mcqueengin.co.uk }

GIN, 42%

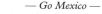

Vicky and Dale McQueen launched their company in 2016. Vicky's background as a chef has meant that the couple's spirits have a huge gastronomic side to them. Their gins include white chocolate, Scottish raspberries, and chocolate orange. This Smoky Chili gin has been described as a liquid Mexican meal. It makes a great accompaniment to Mexican food, but if you want a slight variation on the theme, try it with dark chocolate with a high cocoa content. Chili and chocolate are the ultimate good cop/bad cop combination. McQueen is a company to watch out for.

— *Pomme de flair* —

CHRISTIAN DROUIN 1997 VINTAGE CALVADOS

Domaine Coeur de Lion

Pont-l'Évêque, France

{ calvados-drouin.com }

CALVADOS, 42%

A specialty of Normandy in northern France, Calvados is made from the cider of apples and pears. There are about 200 varieties of fruit that may be used, divided into four categories: sweet, bittersweet, bitter, and sour. The quality of the Calvados depends on where the fruit comes from, how it is pressed, and how long the spirit is aged for. The 1997 vintage is double-distilled, and aged in old Calvados casks and casks that held Pommeau de Normandie. It is delicate, with some menthol rancio notes. Use it to make a crêpe or an omelette, and serve with crème fraîche or vanilla ice cream.

— *Taking the biscuit* —

ZWETSCHGENWASSER PLUM SCHNAPPS

Schladerer

Staufen, Germany

{ schladerer.de }

SCHNAPPS, 42%

Germany makes some great schnapps drinks, and this one comes from a small, family-run distillery founded in 1844. Zwetschgenwasser is the distillery's plum brandy. Rich and fresh-tasting, it is made using late-ripening zwetschgen plums from Baden. The schnapps is a clear drink that has aged for some years in tanks to take some of the sharpness off it. Normally drunk neat from a small shooter glass, it goes well with cake or sweet German biscuits, and it is a decadent treat when served alongside gammon or unsmoked streaky bacon.

— *Darkest pleasure* —

BOWMORE 15 YEAR OLD DARKEST
Bowmore
Isle of Islay, Scotland
{ bowmore.com }
SINGLE MALT WHISKY, 43%

One of the hardest tricks to pull off in single malt whisky production is combining peated whisky with first-fill sherry casks. The rich and ripe berry notes and rumbling smoke are not necessarily natural partners, and when they clash, it may make for a train wreck of a whisky. Get it right, though, and you have the whisky equivalent of the Cirque du Soleil — a complex work of beauty in which every part of the experience is perfectly balanced and impressive. This triumphant product is matured for 12 years in an ex-bourbon cask, and then spends another three years in an oloroso sherry cask. Bowmore is one of the distilleries on the Scottish island of Islay, which is renowned for its peaty whisky. But while Bowmore is peated, most of its core brands are not as smoky as some of the heavyweight distillers elsewhere on the same island, and that's ideal in this malt. Some oaky tannins increase the complexity here, and burned raisins, licorice, and spiced fruits all play off the peat smoke to provide an earthy backdrop to the overall experience. The end result is a hefty, substantial, big-flavored whisky which is perfect on a cold winter's day. Why not serve it alongside pheasant or game? It's also great with a warming winter casserole and baked potatoes.

SEVEN MOODS OF CRAFT SPIRIT   GASTRONOMIC

— Flexible friend —

HAKUSHU 12 YEAR OLD

Beam Suntory

Chita, Japan

{ suntory.com }

SINGLE MALT WHISKY, 43%

Although there have been attempts to change the West's attitude to drinking whisky alongside food, it's still not a common practice. It's a different matter in the Orient, however, especially when the whisky is diluted or served with ice in a Highball. Hakushu 12 year old is well suited for food matching. It has an aroma of pears, and a hint of citrus. On the palate, there is subtle smokiness and poached pears, and the whisky has a drying but very clean finish. It works really well with sushi or sashimi, most seafoods, and anything involving soy sauce. Try it with crispy duck with spring onion, cucumber, and soy sauce.

— Black magic —

PURE MALT BLACK

Nikka

Yoichi-Cho, Japan

{ nikka.com }

BLENDED MALT WHISKY, 43%

Nikka Pure Malt Black is part of a three-whisky series. It is a blended malt, which means that it contains only malt whisky, but malt whisky from more than one distillery (in this case, two: Yoichi and Miyagikyo). This is something of a bruiser of a whisky, with a savory nose, reminiscent of damp autumnal forest, and a taste that mixes orange fruit, cherry throat lozenges, and earthy peatiness. Bizarrely, this works best with savory Scandinavian foods — rollmop herrings, anything preserved in salt, and big, smoky cheeses all work equally well.

— A French connection —

FUJIKAI 10 YEAR OLD

Monde Shuzo

Isawa, Japan

SINGLE MALT WHISKY, 43%

This whisky is so named because Monde Shuzo, which is primarily a wine producer, has its headquarters at the foot of Mount Fuji. The company dabbles in whisky, and has a blended whisky named Isawa. This 10-year-old was released in association with Whiskies du Monde, and may well have been bottled in France. It is limited to 8,808 bottles. Tastewise, the whisky is quite polite. There are traces of nuts and coal smoke in the mix here, but the main flavors are of apples and herbs, so it works admirably with roast pork and crackling. It's good with mild and medium cheeses, too.

— *Leaping Tom* —

HERNO OLD TOM

Herno
Härnösand, Sweden
{ hernogin.com }
GIN, 43%

Herno is a serious gin lover's gin, having won more awards than any other spirit of its type in each of the years 2014 to 2017. The distillery was founded in 2011 by gin enthusiast and former bartender Jon Hillgren, and here he's created a product with some citrus and honey notes alongside classic juniper. Imagine, if you will, a cattle farm in Southwest England in the late fall, with apple juice fermenting in a vat near your chair. You have Cathedral City cheese in one hand, a glass of Herno Old Tom in the other. Taste the gin. Eat the cheese. Admire the view. Pure heaven.

— *Anno mirabilis* —

ANNO KENT

Anno Distillers
Marden, England
{ annodistillers.co.uk }
GIN, 43%

Marden is in Kent, which is known as the Garden of England. It's a region famed above all for its hops and fruit. The first new distillery in the county for more than 200 years, Anno was founded by two scientists who have combined their technical knowledge with their passion for distilling. The small team at the distillery wanted to capture some of the character of Kent in its gin, so here the botanicals include hops, lavender, rose hip, samphire, and local florals. Anno Kent is a crisp, clean, citrusy gin with spice from the hops. It works with pork pies or pork sausages.

— *Malty perfection* —

**BALVENIE DOUBLEWOOD
17 YEAR OLD**

Balvenie Distillery
Dufftown, Scotland
{ williamgrant.com }
SINGLE MALT WHISKY, 43%

William Grant & Sons remains a family-run business, but it punches above its weight. It owns the hugely successful Glenfiddich Distillery, makes Monkey Shoulder blended malt whisky and premium gin Hendricks, and has distilleries in America and Ireland. Its best whiskies, however, come from Balvenie, an artisanal distillery on the Glenfiddich site but with an emphasis on traditional production methods. Doublewood 17 Year Old is a heady mix of honey, vanilla, and green fruits with some gentle spice. In summer, pair it with peaches or pears. In winter, drink it with a hearty lamb casserole or Irish stew.

— *Breakfast treat* —
CLÉMENT RHUM XO
Clément
Martinique
{ rhum-clement.com }
RUM, 44%

Clément was originally established in the early part of the 20th century by Homère Clément. It pioneered rhum agricole, a style of pure rum. This XO is released every year, and features carefully selected rhum agricole aged for a minimum of six years in a combination of virgin and re-charred oak barrels. It is accentuated by the intense charred wood flavors balanced by the natural sweetness of the sugarcane distillate, and it also has floral notes. Clément XO works well with banana bread, and may be equally suited to an indulgent late breakfast of toast with orange marmalade.

— *Cracking crackling* —
LAIRD'S APPLE BRANDY 12 YEAR OLD
Laird & Company
Scobeyville, NJ, USA
{ lairdandcompany.com }
APPLE BRANDY, 44%

There is a view that apple brandy is set to spend time in the fashion spotlight, and if it does, this expression from Laird & Co is likely to prove popular. You tend to associate apple brandy with the Calvados region of France, but an increasing number of craft distillers are making it, and some of the best of them are American. Laird's claims this one to be among the very best. It is a straight apple brandy, unblended with any other products. After charcoal filtering, it is reduced to 44% ABV and bottled by hand. It may be an obvious choice, but this is perfectly suited to roasted suckling pig.

— *Coming up Roses* —
FOUR ROSES SMALL BATCH
Four Roses Distillery
Lawrenceburg, KY, USA
{ fourrosesbourbon.com }
BOURBON, 45%

Four Roses makes 10 separate bourbons using two mash recipes and five strains of yeast. In addition to the distillery's standard Yellow Label product, which is a combination of all 10 expressions, there are also several other combinations of two or more of the original batches. The best four go into this lively and highly potable small batch bourbon. The apple and pear notes work well with grilled scallops with a honey glaze, while the Four Roses website suggests mixing Small Batch Four Roses with hard cider, and serving it alongside fried green tomatoes.

— *Tree-mendous* —
BUFFALO TRACE SINGLE OAK
Buffalo Trace
Frankfort, KY, USA
{ singleoakproject.com }
BOURBON, 45%

Buffalo Trace's Single Oak Project has taken 25 years and is the most ambitious cask project ever undertaken. Ninety-six oak trees were selected, all of different ages and from different locations. Each was cut in half, and each top and bottom section was made into a single barrel — a total of 192 separate barrels. Prior to construction, the staves were seasoned for varying periods. The 192 barrels were then charred differently. These single oak barrels were then filled with different recipe whiskeys, at various entry proofs, and then aged in a variety of different warehouse types. The result is that each of the 192 bottles is different, and from the differences Buffalo Trace have acquired a greater understanding of how oak affects bourbon production. The weighty 45% ABV makes for a full and rich bourbon. If you can pinpoint an expression that has been filled into a heavily charred cask so that the woody tannins and char burn are present in the whisky, then that goes very well with barbecued food. Try it also with this lamb ball recipe: mix lamb mince with fresh mint; take a square of medium Cheddar cheese and form a ball of lamb and mint around it. Then barbecue. When melted cheese starts appearing through the cooked lamb, serve with your woody Buffalo Trace. It's not a conventional pairing, but it takes some beating.

— Spice exploration —
JEFFERSON'S RESERVE
McLain & Kyne
Crestwood, KY, USA
{ jeffersonsbourbon.com }
BOURBON, 45.1%

Jefferson's is produced at the Kentucky Artisan Distillery near Louisville in very small batches indeed. The company was set up by a father-and-son team that specializes in experimentation, constantly questioning what and why bourbon is. Founder and master blender Trey Zoeller teamed up with Korean-American chef Edward Lee to produce a bourbon especially suited to spicy Southern Asian cuisine. It was made up of five- and eight-year-old bourbon and some 14-year-old, rye-dominated bourbon. If that sounds like too much effort, this Jefferson 's Reserve is pretty good with all sorts of sweet spiced Asian dishes.

— Taken for Granted —
GLENFARCLAS 15 YEAR OLD
J & G Grant
Ballindalloch, Scotland
{ glenfarclas.com }
SINGLE MALT WHISKY, 46%

Glenfarclas is something of a rarity — an independent distillery that has been in the same family for generations. When Seagram's Sam Bronfman wanted to buy it, and asked John Grant to name his price, Grant wasn't interested. 'What else would I do without it?', he is alleged to have said. Glenfarclas is a no-frills distillery, maturing its whiskies in quality ex-sherry casks. Fifteen years in the cask means that there are some oaky tannins here, and some spiciness, as well as classic sherried notes. This makes it ideal to have with spicy meat such as chorizo, with olives, and with sardines.

— No grain, no gain —
TEELING SINGLE GRAIN WHISKEY
Teeling
Dublin, Ireland
{ teeling.com }
SINGLE GRAIN WHISKEY, 46%

One of the traditional ways of cooking in Maori and Polynesian culture is to heat stones until they are white hot, and then put them into the ground. Meat is placed on top, potatoes and vegetables on top of the meat, and dessert on a third layer. The food is covered by flax matting or leaves, and the hole filled in with earth. The food must be cooked for at least three hours, and once it is ready it doesn't look much, but it tastes amazing. While you're waiting for the food, crack open a bottle of this sweet whiskey and continue to enjoy it with your food.

180

— *Aussie rules* —

LARK HEAVILY PEATED BOURBON CASK

Lark Distillery
Hobart, Australia
{ larkdistillery.com }
SINGLE MALT WHISKY, 46%

Bill Lark has played a massive role in the development of Tasmanian whisky: he not only reintroduced distilling to the island, but also lent his support to the other distillers who now produce whisky there. Lark's whiskies are full and fruity, and may be made with Tasmanian peat, which tends to be sweet and aromatic. So how about this for a bucket-list item: climb up to the Lakes in Tassie, and catch yourself a trout. Then cook it over a Tasmanian peat fire until it's nicely smoked, drizzle some Lark on your fish, and eat it with a glass of this wonderful whisky. That's better, isn't it?

— *All Greek to us* —

BARBAYANNI BLUE LABEL

Barbayannis Liquor
Distilleries
Plomari, Greece
{ barbayanni-ouzo.com }
OUZO, 46%

Are you one of the people who has a barely touched the bottle of ouzo lurking at the back of the drinks cupboard because you found it didn't taste anywhere near as good as it did while watching the sunset on a balmy evening in the Aegean? Perhaps you need to get out the olives, salted nuts, stuffed peppers, and cold meats, and try drinking ouzo with your Mediterranean picnic. This brand of ouzo has been made by the Barbayannis family since 1860 using traditional methods. There are various versions, but the Blue Label has some delicate herbal notes that suit all the above foods.

— *Blue peater* —

BIG PEAT

Douglas Laing & Co
Glasgow, Scotland
{ douglaslaing.com }
BLENDED MALT WHISKY,
46%

Big Peat is a mix of malt whiskies from the Scottish West Coast island of Islay, put together by independent bottler Douglas Laing. The label states that it combines whisky from Ardbeg, Caol Ila, Bowmore, and, amazingly, Port Ellen (amazingly because Port Ellen whisky is so rare and expensive). That's not in itself a compelling reason to head for this whisky, though, because this is a peaty team effort, a blended malt of real class. It takes some standing up to, but a strong-flavored blue cheese will do the trick. Try it with Roquefort for an after-dinner or Christmas treat.

— Right on Kew —

KEW ORGANIC GIN

London Distillery
Company
London, England
{ londondistillery.com }
GIN, 46%

The London Distillery
Company is the business
set up by Darren Rook, who
makes the award-winning
Dodd's Gin. Kew here refers
to Kew Gardens in London,
and this gin was created in
partnership with the Royal
Botanical Gardens. It is
deliberately floral, and
includes 42 botanicals. There
are big dashes of citrus from
lemon, lime, and grapefruit
peel; spice from cassia,
nutmeg, and licorice; and
savory notes from eucalyptus,
lemon grass, and rosemary.
Kew Organic Gin goes well
with fish and chips, and, since
junipers are often used to
season pâté, that works, too.

— Going for Bold —

PAUL JOHN BOLD

John Distilleries
Bangalore, India
{ jdl.in }
SINGLE MALT WHISKY, 46%

John Distilleries was only the
second Indian company to
launch single malt whiskies
onto the international market,
and the company has now
established itself in the
vanguard of the New World
whisky movement. Bold is
one of the distillery's core
releases. It's peaty, but not
aggressively so, and there are
some pleasant candied fruit
notes, with orange and stewed
apples in the mix. John
recommends lamb shish
kebabs rich in chili because
they work well with the
sweetness and spiciness of the
whisky, and the whisky cuts
through the fatty lamb. It is,
says the chef on the video, a
marriage made in heaven.

— A Welsh wizard —

PENDERYN PORTWOOD
FINISH

Penderyn Distillery
Penderyn, Wales
{ penderyn.wales }
SINGLE MALT WHISKY, 46%

When Penderyn was launched,
the team behind it was
determined to make a whisky
that had as little as possible
in common with the malt
whiskies of Scotland. A special
hybrid still was created for
this distillery, and its spirit is
matured in a mix of barrels
to give it a distinctive light
and floral taste. This port
wood finish is even more
fruity, sweet, and floral, and is
arguably the distillery's best
whisky. The port notes are well
suited to a range of cheeses,
particularly Red Leicester and
mild Cheddar. Alternatively,
try it with melted cheese on
toast or a cheesy fondue.

182

— *Fine and winey* —
MACKMYRA SKÖRDETID
Mackmyra
Gävle, Sweden
{ mackmyra.com }
SINGLE MALT WHISKY,
46.1%

Special releases from Swedish whisky-maker Mackmyra can go in one of two directions: they are either growly, industrial, peat-loaded, smoky monsters, or they are sweet, easy-drinking, delicate, and elegant. This whisky is firmly in the latter category. It spent its final six months in Masi Costasera Amarone casks, which gives it sweet, vinous notes of grapes and raisins, and a herbal spiciness. There are flavors of dried pears, as well as ginger and vanilla. Skördetid is ideal to accompany chocolate cake or an elegant dark chocolate dessert, and chocolate or caramel mousse.

— *Early days* —
**JAMES E PEPPER 1776
STRAIGHT BOURBON**
Georgetown Trading
Company
Lexington, KY, USA
{ jamesepepper.com }
BOURBON, 50%

Like classic Irish whiskey, bourbon and rye are on the move upward. James Pepper is a name that goes back to the very earliest days of Kentucky and the production of whiskey — 1776, in fact — and the owners of this brand are in the process of opening a micro-distillery and museum within the ruins of the original James E Pepper Distillery. It's not clear where the bourbon has been coming from up to now, though. This one has some orange and honey notes, and goes splendidly with glazed chicken wings, sweet-and-sour spare ribs or ribs with orange-and-soy sauce.

— *A slice of Evan* —
**EVAN WILLIAMS WHITE
LABEL**
Heaven Hill
Louisville, KY, USA
{ evanwilliams.com }
BOURBON, 50%

Evan Williams White Label is one of Heaven Hill's core bourbons, and the White Label Bottled In Bond is a good-value-for-money, no-nonsense, straight bourbon aged for around four years. It's 100 proof, so it's a powerful, meaty, cocktail-friendly bourbon. There are no fancy tricks, so you get typical vanilla, candied fruits, leather saddle, spice, and oak. It goes very well with a range of desserts, particularly with pecan pie or peach crumble. You can add it to ice cream, too. And for something more savory, try it with spicy meatballs.

— *Mixing it up* —
KADHAMBAM
Amrut
Bangalore, India
{ amrutdistilleries.com }
SINGLE MALT WHISKY, 50%

What makes Amrut so special is not that it has brought top-quality Indian whisky to the attention of the world — which it has — but that it has been an exemplar of a refreshing and innovative approach to whisky-making, playing with different grains, different cask woods, and different locations to mature its spirit. The company makes a whole range of spirits, including mainstream whisky brands for the Indian domestic market. But its single malt operation is a labor of love for the distiller, and unique climactic conditions give Amrut a strong advantage. Its core range consists of peated and unpeated whisky at 46% ABV and at cask strength. But the special bottlings have been a total revelation. Here's a case in point. *Kadhambam* means 'mixture' or 'combination', and that's a big clue to what's happening with this. It's a mix of normal and peated Amrut that started life in ex-oloroso casks before being transferred, first into brandy casks, and then into rum casks. Who even thought of doing that, and how many other combinations were tried and failed? When it comes to taste, it's all over the place, but not in a bad way. Indeed, it's a bewitching whisky, with a rich tropical fruit, fresh, and floral nose, and a Starburst-like palate, with hints of peat and spice. It works particularly well with fruity curries, such as chicken Ceylon or korma, and with anything tangy and tomatoey, such as jalfrezi.

— *Hard to refuse* —
FUSION
Amrut
Bangalore, India
{ amrutdistilleries.com }
SINGLE MALT WHISKY, 50%

This whisky is called Fusion because it's made of barley from Scotland and India. It is matured in ex-bourbon casks, and vanilla is present. But so, too, are fruity sherry notes, smoke, peat, and dairy chocolate. It's a complex and beguiling mix, a feisty malt that can hold its own with big flavors. It is hard to think of a menu that would overwhelm it, and rather easier to identify foods that would trade blows with it on level terms. Among the dishes it would most comfortably supplement are chili con carne and lamb bhuna. It's not a drink for the faint-hearted, though.

— *An Italian job* —
GRAPPA RISERVA
Bortolo Nardini
Bassano, Italy
{ nardini.it }
GRAPPA, 50%

Traditionally made from the pulp of grapes, and therefore closely related to brandy, grappa is an Italian drink that has started winning admirers in other countries, and which is now being produced by some of the new craft distillers. It is often consumed while very young, often after only six months stored in glass bottles. Grappa Riserva is at the premium end of the market, therefore, having been matured for at least three years in Slavonian oak barrels. The fresh grape pomace comes from the Veneto foothills and Friuli. It is recommended as an after-dinner drink and pairs well with dark chocolate or a cigar.

— *No flies on this* —
WASHINGTON BOURBON 101
Dry Fly
Spokane, WA, USA
{ dryflydistilling.com }
BOURBON, 50%

Dry Fly was set up in 2007 by anglers Don Poffenroth and Kent Fleischmann, who came up with the idea for a micro-distillery while up to their thighs in water. It was the first new distillery in Washington State since Prohibition. It makes a range of spirits, including wheat whiskey, and the distillers pride themselves on using local products. Bourbon 101 is made up of 60 per cent corn, 20 per cent wheat, and 20 per cent barley. It is very much a corn-forward beverage, but there are some cinnamon and pepper notes. Try it with spicy chicken or pepperoni pizza.

— Best of blends —

NIKKA WHISKY FROM THE BARREL
Nikka
Yoichi-Cho, Japan
{ nikka.com }
BLENDED WHISKY, 51.4%

Absolute proof, were any needed, that blended whisky can be absolutely fab. This mix of malts and grain whiskies is malt-heavy and delivered at a weighty 51.4%. It just bursts with flavor, and is exquisitely balanced. It has been described as one of the best-value-for-money whiskies in the market, and it's hard to disagree. It has a bit of everything, with spice, vanilla, and summer fruits competing for prominence. It packs a punch, so if you're going to have food with it, go for something bold. Red Thai curry works very well, and spicy Moroccan dishes are good with it, too.

— Deliciously fragrant —

SÄNTIS EDITION DREIFALTIGKEIT
Locher
Appenzell, Switzerland
{ saentismalt.com }
SINGLE MALT WHISKY, 52%

Switzerland, Germany, and Austria have centuries of distilling experience, but when it comes to making whiskies, there has always been a high level of inconsistency in their output, mainly because what works for brandy or genever is not always well suited to whisky. They're raising their game now, though, and it's only a matter of time before Alpine malts are competing with the best of world whisky. Säntis is setting the pace, and has been for some years. The brewery has used ex-beer barrels for maturation, along with a unique peat to create this, a fragrant, floral, and almost incense-like malt. The whisky goes nicely with beef fondue or a simple pâté.

'IT WAS MY UNCLE GEORGE WHO
DISCOVERED ALCOHOL WAS
A FOOD WELL IN ADVANCE OF
MODERN MEDICAL THOUGHT.'
P G WODEHOUSE

GASTRONOMIC

SEVEN MOODS OF CRAFT SPIRIT

— The Devil's spirit —

BRIMSTONE
Balcones
Waco, TX, USA
{ balconesdistilling.com }
CORN WHISKEY, 53%

You could describe this as a smoky whiskey, but it's more a case of it being smoked. American craft distiller Balcones is at the forefront of the micro-distilling phenomenon, and is doing some wonderful things with American single malt. Here, though, it has taken one of its blue corn recipe whiskeys and smoked it over Texan scrub oak. The result is a barbecue-smoked spirit that tastes like hot charcoals crushed into bourbon. It's a unique, sweet-and-sour drinking experience that probably works very well with roast pork. But actually it's the ultimate barbecue whisky. Unforgettable.

— The Belle chimes —

BELLE MEADE BOURBON 11 YEARS OLD
Nelson's Greenbrier Distillery
Nashville, TN, USA
{ greenbrierdistillery.com }
BOURBON, 55%

The original Nelson's Greenbrier Distillery was set up in Nashville by Charles Nelson, who had arrived penniless in America with his family from Germany. He had run a store specialising in meat, whiskey, and coffee but focused on whiskey and at one point was selling two million bottles a year. Prohibition finished the distillery off, but in 2006 brothers Charlie and Andy Nelson resurrected the family business, created by their great great great grandfather. This is a sweet bourbon, but has a high rye content so there's a delightful spiciness to it. Water opens it up and gives it a velvety and smooth mouth feel and fruity taste. Varies from batch to batch as only four barrels are used in each run.

— Finely crafted —

GLENGOYNE CASK STRENGTH

Glengoyne Distillery
Drumgoyne, Scotland
{ glengoyne.com }
SINGLE MALT WHISKY,
58.7%

Glengoyne Distillery is located a few miles north of Glasgow, and is distinguished by the fact that the distillery is in the Highlands region of Scotland but its warehouses across the road are in the Lowlands. It is a pretty and compact distillery, justly proud of its clean, peat-free whisky. This is a fruit bowl of a malt, with overripe bananas, some tropical fruits, and hints of summer berries, all delivered with a punch. There's a lot going on here, so any food should be simple and straight down the line. How about gammon, or even roast beef?

— Very sherried —

GLENFARCLAS 105

Glenfarclas
Ballindalloch, Scotland
{ glenfarclas.com }
SINGLE MALT WHISKY, 60%

There are few bigger whiskies than this classic single malt from Glenfarclas. 105 is the British measure of proof for 60% ABV — a different measure from American Proof, which in this case would be 120. British proof 100 equates to 57.15% ABV, and is the strength when alcohol-soaked gunpowder can be set on fire by a match. It's complicated but, basically, this is a very strong whisky, and it's loaded with sherry notes, so you can make very boozy trifles with it. Add a considerable amount of water, and it goes well with liver or kidney, and it's not bad with spicy sausages.

—Vanilla slice —

GLENLIVET NADURRA FIRST FILL

Ballindalloch
Ballindalloch, Scotland
{ ballindallochdistillery.com }
SINGLE MALT WHISKY,
ABOUT 60.0%

There are two versions of this whisky, one at a much lower strength, but this is the one you need to get because it's an absolute beauty. With some water it bursts into vibrant and colorful life, with lots of vanilla and tropical fruits such as pineapple and mango to the fore. This makes it ideal for any number of desserts, as well as fruity cheese, but the best combination may well be with pork steaks with onions and cooking apples, baked in cider and cream. If anyone ever tells you that they just don't like whisky, sit them down with this food and drink combo and put them right.

THESE ARE QUALITY SPIRITS
TO SIP AND SAVOR THAT
PROVIDE A PLATFORM TO
PONDER ON WHAT LIFE
THROWS AT US.

CONTEMPLATIVE

WHISKY AND SPIRITS BOOKS

CONTEMPLATIVE

SEVEN MOODS OF CRAFT SPIRIT

THE MALT YEAR BOOK
Ingvar Ronde
(Annually)

The Malt Year Book is published annually. It includes series of articles by leading whisky writers, as well as in-depth coverage of all of Scotland's malt distilleries and an ever-growing summary of the burgeoning world whisky market. Packed with up-to-date statistics and information on small distilleries.

DISTILLED
Joel Harrison and Neil Ridley
(2015)

An excellent guide to the world's best spirits, including plenty of lesser known and obscure ones. The authors take you on a journey, and spirit by spirit tell you all you need to know to enjoy each one, giving examples of the best in class for each spirit.

WHISKY: THE DEFINITIVE WORLD GUIDE
Michael Jackson
(2017)

The original great world whisky book by the late beer and whisky legend Michael Jackson was written in 2005 but has since been completely updated. The new version is vastly different from the original book, and has been brilliantly redesigned, reflecting the huge changes in the world of whisky in recent years.

RUM
Dave Broom
(2003)

Dave Broom has written a number of books on rum, but this one, illustrated by Jason Lowe, is the best. It is a great book to flick through for the photos, and it is written with authority. A comprehensive journey around the world's rum-making nations.

THE BOOK OF GIN
Richard Barnett
(2012)

Subtitled 'A Spirited World History from Alchemists' Stills and Colonial Outposts to Gin Palaces, Bathtub Gin, and Artisanal Cocktails', this is a thorough examination of what gin is, where it comes from, and who has drunk it. Packed with illuminating anecdotes and solid information, it's the perfect accompaniment to a craft G & T.

THE DRINKABLE GLOBE
Jeff Cioletti
(2017)

The title says it all, really. This is a journey around the world, from Australia to Kentucky, looking at the tradition, consumption, and production of alcohol on every continent. The book also looks at some weird and wonderful concoctions, including onion-infused vodka.

— *Fine 'n' brandy* —
URAIT
Asbach
Rüdesheim-am-Rhein,
Germany
{ asbach.de }
BRANDY, 38%

Urait is a highly popular German brandy made by Rheinland company Urait, which also makes chocolate. The brandy is blended from 25 wine distillates before being matured for up to three years in Limousin oak casks. It enjoys some loyalty among British ex-servicemen who served in Germany. It has a long pedigree, having been created originally by Hugo Asbach in 1892. The flavor is fruitier than most Cognac, with a clean, crisp taste, and some astringency late on. It's a sipping brandy, ideal for evenings with a good book. A sibling three-year-old version is also worth seeking out.

— *Grape expectations* —
**ETICHETTA NERA BLACK
LABEL**
Vecchia Romagna
Bologna, Italy
{ vecchiaromagna.com }
BRANDY, 38%

Vecchia Romagna is a classic brandy from Italy, but it has its roots in France. It was created by Jean Bouton, who came from a long line of distillers, and who built a sizeable business in the southwest of France before spotting an opportunity to move to the other side of the Alps. That was 200 years ago, but he found that the soil in the region was ideal for growing Trebianno Bianco grapes, from which this is made. The brandy is matured in small oak casks and aged for three years. Expect a smooth, strong, and dry brandy, with an aromatic, complex fragrance and a warm, intense color.

— *Gin genius* —
XORIGUER
The Pons Family
Mahon, Menorca, Spain
{ zoriguer.co.uk }
GIN, 38%

They have been making gin on Menorca ever since it became a British colony in the 1700s, and some local craftsmen started importing juniper berries to make gin for British residents. Xoriguer — pronounced 'sho-ri-gair' — came into existence about 100 years ago, produced by Miguel Pons Justo, the head of one of the first Menorcan families to produce gin. It remains in family hands today. It currently enjoys cult status, and is one of the few gins to have a geographical indication recognized by the European Union. It is highly aromatic and flavorsome due to a recipe of herbs that is a strictly guarded family secret.

— Stock of ages —
TORRES 30 JAIME 1
Torres
Barcelona, Spain
{ torres.es }
BRANDY, 38%

— Bewitching —
LA HECHICERA FINE AGED
Riascos Family
Barranquilla, Colombia
{ lahechicera.co }
AGED RUM, 40%

—With love… —
ZYR
Zyr Vodka Company
Russia
{ zyrvodka.com }
VODKA, 40%

The Torres family bought its first vineyard in the Penedès region of Spain in the 18th century. They have been producing wine ever since. The Torres company was founded in 1870, and expanded into spirits production. Named after founder Jaime Torres Vendrell, this is a 30-year-old blend of brandies from the distillery's oldest soleras, including Parellada wines originally destined for the Torres 10, and a small amount of rare 1972 Folle Blanche eaux-de-vie. On the nose there are aromas of dried fruit and toasted hazelnut, with hints of vanilla and toffee. The taste is balanced and smooth, fruity, oaky, and complex.

The Riascos have built a reputation for creating fine rums in Colombia over two decades. They did it by traveling around the Caribbean to source the finest raw spirits, find the richest casks, and attract the most talented master blenders. The family owns an unassuming little bodega in the center of Barranquilla, nestled between the Magdalena River and the Caribbean Sea. Fine Aged is a rum created using the solera method. The spirit is aged for between 12 and 21 years in ex-bourbon barrels. You can taste the quality immediately — plummy jam, dark coffee, a touch of pepper spice, and a pleasant oakiness.

Pronounced 'zeer', ZYR is competing in a highly competitive field, but it is a grain-based premium vodka, and it has been described by one expert as the smoothest, most finely crafted he has ever sampled. This may well be down to its unique 9-5-3 manufacturing process: the water from the northwest of Russia is filtered five times before distillation, and the distilled spirit is then filtered another four times — a total of nine. The wheat- and rye-based mix is then distilled five times. Finally, there are three tastings — one of the water, one of the grain alcohol blend, and one of the finished spirit.

— The real deal —

THE REAL McCOY
12 YEAR OLD
Four Square Distillery
Barbados
{ foursquare.com }
RUM, 40%

———— ❧ ————

The Real McCoy is named
after Bill McCoy, a renowned
spirits smuggler who sold his
wares offshore in the United
States during Prohibition. His
customers included speakeasy
owners. He was different
from many suppliers of the
period, in that he didn't water
the spirits down to make a
fast buck, so he earned a
reputation for quality. Visitors
to speakeasies would seek
his spirits out, asking for 'the
Real McCoy', a phrase that has
entered the English language.
This rum has no added sugars,
perfumes or flavorings. It is
made with pure spring water,
and matured for 12 years in
heavily charred ex-bourbon
barrels. The result is a rum rich
in vanilla, caramel, spice, dried
raisins, and oaky tannins.

194

— From darkest Peru —

RON CARTAVIO XO 18
YEARS OLD
Ron Cartavio Distillery
Cartavio, Peru
{ facebook.com/ron.cartavio }
RUM, 40%

———— ❧ ————

Peru isn't the first place you'd
think of when looking at rum
production, but Ron Cartavio
is both distinctive and very
good. The distillery lies in
the fertile Chicamo valley in
northern Peru, and the special
character of this XO may be
attributable to the climate
and humidity of the terrain in
which its component rums are
laid to mature. The distillery
has been making rum since
the early 20th century, and it is
matured in American, French
Limousin, and Slovenian casks
in a solera system. The rum
that is produced this way is
sweet, with buttery and spicy
flavors. This is the oldest rum
the distillery produces.

'I FEEL SORRY FOR PEOPLE WHO
DON'T DRINK. WHEN THEY WAKE
UP IN THE MORNING, THAT'S AS
GOOD AS THEY'RE GOING TO
FEEL ALL DAY.'
JACK LEMMON

— The critics' choice —

RON ZACAPA CENTENARIO

Rum Creation and Products

Guatemala

{ zacaparum.com }

RUM, 40%

Ron Zacapa is made by Rum Creation and Products, a subsidiary of Guatemala's biggest distillery, Industrias Licoreras, which produces a wide range of spirits. The company was created at the beginning of the 20th century by two distillers who immigrated from Spain. Ron Zacapa Centenario was introduced in 1976 to mark the 100th anniversary of the founding of the eastern Guatemalan town of Zacapa, and it is widely regarded as one of the best rums on the market anywhere. It is made by blending a range of rums created using a solera system, which means that, as rum is taken from the bottom of the cask, more rum is added at the top, ensuring an evolving spirit. It is matured in a mix of ex-sherry and ex-bourbon casks for a period of between six and 23 years. The results are highly impressive. Ron Zacapa Centenario has won a large number of awards, including a platinum medal and first place in the highly prestigious awards organized by the Beverage Testing Institute in Chicago, Illinois. The owners describe the rum as having a complex nose with caramel, cacao, vanilla, and butterscotch; a diverse palate that includes raisins, fruit, and apricot jam; an intense heart of savory oak, nutmeg, leather and tobacco, vanilla, and fruit; and a finish that is astringent and very long.

— *East meets South* —

FOUR PILLARS RARE GIN

Four Pillars Distillery
Healesville, Australia
{ fourpillarsgin.com.au }
GIN, 41.8%

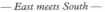

A craft distillery founded in
2013, Four Pillars has fully
embraced the concept of
fusion. It has thought carefully
about how to combine the
best Australian and Asian
ingredients, and worked
with Melbourne Japanese
restaurant Kisumé to produce
a sophisticated Japanese-
style gin. The Four Pillars here
are the stills, the water, the
botanicals, and love. Rare
Gin is made using whole
Australian oranges, which
are highly aromatic, and
spices including cardamom,
cinnamon, and star anise.
Tasmanian pepper adds
warmth, and lemon myrtle
is an attractive alternative to
lemon peel.

— *Holy moly* —

ST JAMES 15 YEAR OLD

St James Distillery
Saint Pierre,
Martinique
{ saintjames-rum.com }
RHUM AGRICOLE, 42%

This rum has its roots in a
business set up by Father
Edmund Lefebure in 1765. He
was the superior of a convent
on the island, but he was also
a skilled businessman who
sold his rum to British colonies
in North America. It was
originally called Jacques, but
the name was changed to
make it more British-sounding
(and less French). This is aged
for a minimum of 15 years
in small oak casks in the
tropical aging conditions on
Martinique to create a
high-end tasting experience
— an oaky, tannin-fueled,
slow-sipping rum, perfect to
drink while reflecting back on
a busy day.

— *Good habits* —

OLD MONK SUPREME XXX

Mohan Meakin
Mohan Nagar, India
{ mohanmeakin.com }
RUM, 42.8%

Old Monk rum is the collective
name for a group of rums
owned by Mohan Meakin, an
Indian business that grew out
of two separate beer brewery
operations. These days, the
company makes and owns
a wide range of products,
including spirits, fruit juices,
and breakfast cereals. It
owns three distilleries in all.
Supreme XXX is a blend of
old rum presented in a quirky
monk-shaped bottle, so it
makes a good present. The
rum is quirky, too. It is
effectively an upmarket
version of the brewery's
seven-year-old rum, and is
dark, sweet, and full-bodied,
with notes of caramel, sweet
spices, and butterscotch.

— *Last man standing* —
1931 4TH EDITION
St Lucia Group
Roseau, St Lucia
{ saintluciarums.com }
RUM, 43%

— *Pure poetry* —
ISLE OF ARRAN ROBERT BURNS
Isle of Arran Distillery
Arran, Scotland
{ arranwhisky.com }
SINGLE MALT WHISKY, 43%

— *All Barrels firing* —
MOUNT GAY BLACK BARREL
Mount Gay Distilleries
Bridgetown, Barbados
{ mountgayrum.com }
RUM, 43%

The St Lucia Group of Companies came into being in 1972. The island once had numerous rum distilleries, but they gradually closed until just two remained, and then the last pair merged. Today, there is just one small distillery site, but it is proud of the rums it makes and the emphasis it places on innovation and quality. This fourth edition 1931 rum was released to mark the 83rd anniversary of rum production on St Lucia. It is a blend of six- and 12-year-olds that includes rums distilled in pot stills and Coffey stills. It is an exquisite rum, with tropical fruit, some orange, and lots of spice.

This distillery describes itself as 'independently owned and independently minded', and that well sums up this dinky operation. It was founded in 1995, and its earliest releases were too young. But by 2005 it had hit its stride, and it now makes quality malts in a range of styles. Robert Burns was released in 2009 to mark the 250th anniversary of the birth of Scotland's greatest poet. It was a limited edition release initially, but seems to be a permanent fixture now. It starts off sweet, with heather, floral notes, and fruitiness, and then has a pepper twist in its finale.

Mount Gay is named after Sir John Gay Alleyne, an 18th-century English aristocrat who ran the business this rum came from with such success that he became known internationally. He served as a politician in Barbados for 40 years, and campaigned against slavery. Today, the principal shareholder in the business is Rémy Cointreau. Black Barrel is a small-batch, hand-crafted blend of matured double pot distillates and aged column distillates. It is finished in heavily charred ex-bourbon barrels to give it toasty vanilla notes. There's also a nice sugar and spice thing going on in the finish.

— *Speyside wonder* —
GLENROTHES 1995
Berry Bros & Rudd
Glenrothes, Scotland
{ theglenrothes.com }
SINGLE MALT WHISKY, 43%

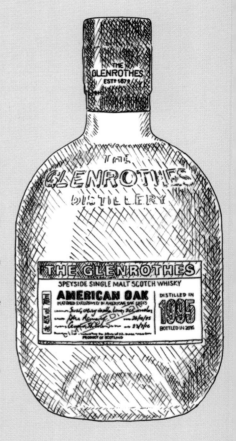

Glenrothes the brand is owned by one of London's oldest and most respected wine merchants, but the distillery itself belongs to major whisky producer Edrington, which owns an array of distilleries, as well as The Famous Grouse and Cutty Sark blended whiskies. Glenrothes is a core malt in the latter. It's a strange relationship, but one which has allowed Glenrothes single malt to flourish through the love and attention of a small but respected retailer. The distillery lies at one end of the main thoroughfare in the town of Rothes in Speyside, and it as sedate a place as you could ever imagine or wish for. The whisky, in its distinctive bottle with its much-copied labeling, epitomizes sophistication and class. Glenrothes is one of the few malt whiskies to carry a vintage rather than an age statement, and did so long before the current trend for whiskies without an age statement had taken hold. There are very few poor expressions of it, but even by its own high standards, the 1995 vintage is extraordinarily good. It was bottled in 2014, so the malt is 19 years old, and it was the first Glenrothes expression matured for a specific taste profile. It is arguably an after-dinner malt, and has a delicious spicy nose, lots of soft butterscotch notes on the palate, and a full-on fruity and spicy finish. This is beyond doubt whisky-making at its finest.

— *Herbaceous delight* —

HAKUSHU DISTILLER'S RESERVE SINGLE MALT
Beam Suntory
Hokuto, Japan
{ suntory.com }
SINGLE MALT WHISKY, 43%

Demand for Japanese whisky so far outstrips supply that, although most people seem to know that it's a good spirit, few of them have had the pleasure of drinking it. Suntory dominates the Japanese market, and Hakushu is the lesser known of its two distilleries (the other is Yamazaki). This Distiller's Reserve carries no age statement, but there has been no compromise on quality. The distillery's characteristics can be summed up by the words 'smoky' and 'herbaceous', and both are on display here, though subtly. Pine, mint, and citrus are in the mix, too.

— *A full English* —

THE ENGLISH SMOKEY
The English Whisky
Company
East Harling, England
{ englishwhisky.co.uk }
SINGLE MALT WHISKY, 43%

It seems a long, long time since the world of whisky laughed or sneered at the idea of an English distillery producing quality single malt. The English Whisky Company has been in the vanguard of a revolution. It has stayed true to its original Scottish blueprint, but has experimented with a range of maturation methods and grain usage. The English Smokey is the new-look version of its original Chapter 9 peated whisky. You'd expect smoke to be to the fore, and it is, but there are elements of buttered toast here, too, together with some light ginger and vanilla notes.

— *Fave to the grind* —

MILLSTONE 10 YEAR OLD AMERICAN OAK
Zuidam
Baarle-Nassau,
Netherlands
{ millstonewhisky.eu }
SINGLE MALT WHISKY, 43%

In true Dutch fashion, family liqueur- and spirit-makers Zuidam use the power of a windmill to grind their grain, and all available Dutch know-how to mature quality malt whisky. It's not the company's core business, but it does make very fine whisky. Various cask-influenced malts have been released by the distillery over the years, and this one is a real beauty. Curiously, some bottlings seem to contain much older malt — up to 14 years of age. There's a creaminess to this, with honey, vanilla, oak, and gentle spice, and a lot else, too: it's a world-class malt.

— *They'll be Boks* —
BAIN'S CAPE MOUNTAIN
Distell
Western Cape,
South Africa
{ bainswhisky.com }
GRAIN WHISKY, 43%

South African company
Distell, which owns Bain's
Cape Mountain grain whisky,
is becoming one of the great
success stories of the 21st
century. Its whisky products
in particular have come on
in leaps and bounds; the
company has developed its
export markets, and in recent
years it has bought up a
handful of Scottish distilleries.
Bain's has long been well
regarded, and it has won
awards for the world's best
grain whisky on more than one
occasion. Its Cape Mountain is
a smooth, sweet, relaxing and
easy-going whisky, with vanilla
and honey and a full taste. A
gentle, sweet finish, too.

— *A divine gin* —
DAFFY'S SMALL BATCH
Daffy's Gin Company
Strathmashie, Scotland
{ daffysgin.com }
GIN, 43.4%

Gin has become such a
crowded market that it takes
something pretty special to
stand out. Daffy's manages it.
This is the ultimate thinking
person's gin. Named after the
goddess of gin, Daffy's Gin
Company is a craft distillery
operating in the heart of the
Scottish Highlands, close to
the ski resort of Aviemore.
This small batch gin is made
using a quality base French
grain spirit, distilled on an old
copper still, and the botanicals
include Lebanese mint and
rare varieties of lemon. The
strength is perfect, says the
distillery, because anything
more gives it a burn 'that
breaks the concentration'.

— *Hebridean princess* —
WILD ISLAND
Langley Distillery
Colonsay, Scotland
{ wildislandgin.com }
GIN, 43.7%

If you want a remote island,
Colonsay fits the bill: it's about
three and a half hours by boat
from mainland Scotland. Only
130 people live there, and it is
wild because it's at the mercy
of the Atlantic Ocean and
extreme weather conditions.
There is not much there,
and yet the community has
still managed to produce a
beautifully packaged premium
gin using foraged island
botanicals. Six native plants
are included in the mix. This
is classic quality gin — with
juniper and citrus leading the
way, but with some floral,
herbal mint tea notes. Perfect
for sipping while enjoying
some relaxing downtime.

— *Blending at its best* —
TOGOUCHI 15 YEAR OLD
Chugoku Jozo
Hatsukaichi City, Japan
{ chugoku-jozo.co.jp }
BLENDED WHISKY, 43.8%

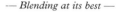

Japanese whisky is dominated
by two companies, Suntory
and Nikka, and whisky from
other sources is extremely
rare. What's more, this isn't
Japanese — the core whiskies
are sourced from Scotland and
Canada, blended, and then
matured in a railroad tunnel.
Don't be put off by that, or by
the fact that this is blended
whisky. Blended whiskies get
a bad press because when
they're bad they can be very,
very bad. Premium blends like
these, though, are works of
art. Beautifully presented, this
is a study in sophistication and
subtlety. It has spice, vanilla,
and chocolate notes on the
palate, and wispy smoke and
pepper in the finish.

— *Pinky and perky* —
PINK GRAPEFRUIT
Sacred
London, England
{ sacredspiritscompany.com }
GIN, 43.8%

The debate rages on as to
what is and isn't deemed to
be craft or micro-distilling.
Nobody would dispute that
Sacred most definitely is. It is
the brainchild of Ian Hart, who
started making gin in 2008 in
the kitchen of his Highgate
home, and who still produces
quality gin in his own kitchen.
Sacred was ahead of the
current fashion wave of
gins, and has succeeded in
preserving its reputation as
one of the best proponents
of the distilling art. Pink
Grapefruit Gin is organic,
and made using whole pink
grapefruits, including pips and
peel. It's a highly refreshing,
zesty and (no surprise coming
up here) very grapefruity.

— *Très magnifique* —
CLÉMENT RHUM XO
Clément
Martinique
{ rhum-clement.com }
RUM, 44%

Clément Rhum comes from
Habitation Clément, which
claims to be the birthplace
of rhum agricole. Thousands
of tourists travel here each
year to immerse themselves
in traditional Creole lifestyle,
and discover the history of a
people whose Afro-European
ancestry has forged a culture
of its own. Each year, some of
the finest aged rum casks are
selected to produce an XO.
Some of it is very old indeed.
Each one combines the
sweetness of sugarcane with
the smokiness of re-charred
oak casks. Spiciness comes
from some rum matured in
virgin oak. This is exceptional
contemplative sipping whisky.

— Dotty P's G&T —
DOROTHY PARKER
New York Distilling Company
New York, NY, USA
{ nydistilling.com }
GIN, 44%

The New York Distilling Company is based in
Brooklyn. It is one of only a handful of
distilleries in the Big Apple, which is surprising
when you consider that the city has a distilling
history going back to the 1700s, and had an
estimated 50,000 illicit stills during Prohibition.
This gin is named after screenwriter, poet and
critic Dorothy Parker, New Jersey-born but
a New Yorker at heart. 'In an age of restless
brilliance, Dorothy Parker was a singular
sensation', say the distillers. 'Her national
celebrity sprang from her sharp, biting humor
and widely quoted quips. Regularly seated
at the famed Algonquin Round Table, she
occupied the city's cultural and intellectual
center stage. An iconic enthusiast of gin, and
an unconventional woman, no one could have
been a more interesting drinking companion'.
Her most famous verse referencing gin is this:
'I like to have a Martini, two at most.
Three, I'm under the table, four I'm under
my host!"
This gin takes a classic recipe and gives it a
twist. Botanicals include juniper, elderberries,
citrus, cinnamon, and hibiscus. The nose is very
proper, with juniper to the fore. On the palate,
the hibiscus makes its presence felt, but not
at the expense of the juniper. Berry fruit and a
spicy twist are in evidence, too.

— Aged to perfection —

ISLE OF JURA 21 YEAR OLD
Whyte & Mackay
Isle of Jura, Scotland
{ jurawhisky.com }
SINGLE MALT WHISKY, 44%

Isle of Jura Distillery stands as a reproach to anyone closing a brewery or distillery on economic grounds. To reach it from any center of population, you must make a lengthy road journey or take an expensive flight over to Islay, cross that island, and then take a ferry across a very lively stretch of water. Back on land, you may well have to maneuver around feisty cattle blocking the narrow road to your final destination. That's fine if you have a car, but countless lorries have to make the trip to bring grain to the distillery, and to take whisky spirit and effluent away from it. Waste products have to be removed to comply with environmental standards. Making whisky on Jura is a serious thing, and the distillery owners, and those of distilleries on Skye, Islay, Arran, Orkney, and Mull should be praised for their dedication to providing unique malts from the farthest reaches of Scotland. The standard expressions of Jura are well known to whisky drinkers, and can be found on supermarket and drinks shop shelves across the world. They have been stylishly repackaged, and the malt in the bottle has improved. A greater diversity of flavors is also on offer. But this particular expression is exceptional, and one of Scotland's finest whiskies, period. The malt is matured in vintage 1963 oloroso casks (1963 was the year the distillery was rebuilt and reopened). Oaky tannins wrap zingy orange, overripe pear, and soft licorice. The medium-length finish is pleasantly dry.

— *Trans-Tasman alliance* —
DIGGERS & DITCH
New Zealand Whisky
Company
Oamaru, New Zealand
{ thenzwhisky.com }
BLENDED MALT WHISKY,
45%

Kiwi whisky alchemists have
been recasking old
Willowbank Distillery whisky
and putting it in top-quality
casks in an effort to breathe
new life into old stocks.
Diggers & Ditch is a blended
malt — it is made only with
malt whisky, but malt whisky
from more than one distillery:
in this case, the Dunedin
Distillery and an undisclosed
distillery in Tasmania. It's
bottled to honor the courage
and sacrifice of the thousands
who served Australia and New
Zealand in wartime. Expect
mixed, dried berry fruits,
raisins, grapes, maraschino
cherries, and complex spices.

— *Dark Crusader* —
ALBERTA RYE DARK BATCH
Alberta Distillers
Calgary, Canada
{ albertarye.com }
RYE WHISKY, 45%

Alberta Distillers is the oldest
distillery in Western Canada,
and it has been producing
distilled beverages for more
than 70 years. The company
makes five different whiskies
and two vodkas, and as well
as supplying whisky across
Canada, it now exports to 30
countries. The rules governing
Canadian whisky production
allow for a small amount of
non-Canadian whisky in the
mix, so this is made up of 91
per cent rye whisky, eight per
cent American bourbon, and
one per cent sherry. It is aged
in American oak, and there are
notes of dried fruit, pepper,
and vanilla, along with traces
of smoke. There is also some
trademark rye spice.

— *It's rye by George* —
ST GEORGE DRY RYE
St George Spirits
Alameda, CA, USA
{ stgeorgespirits.com }
GIN, 45%

'We're proudly independent.
Passionate about innovation.
Committed to craft', say St
George Spirits. And the claim
is justified. The distillery was
founded in 1982, and has
grown organically ever since,
making whiskies, absinthe,
and gins, as well as some
inventive hybrid spirits.
The whiskies are genuinely
different, and worth exploring.
This gin — or, more accurately,
this gin–whisky hybrid — is
made with 100 per cent rye
spirit. It has malty and spicy
rye notes, but juniper, citrus,
and coriander are also in the
mix. Another version of the
same product is matured
in French and American oak
wine casks.

— *Appetite for construction* —
BOTANIVORE
St George Spirits
Alameda, CA, USA
{ stgeorgespirits.com }
GIN, 45%

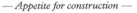

St George Distillery could have had half a dozen entries in this book, what with its wacky absinthe, chile- (*sic*) flavored vodka, all manner of 'hybrid' concoctions, and some delicious whiskies, including Baller, a floral number matured in American and French oak before being finished in casks that previously contained umeshu plum brandy. For Botanivore, juniper berries, bay laurel, and fresh cilantro are laid in the botanical basket. The other 16 botanicals are steeped overnight in a pot still. The following day, steam is applied to coax out flavors and aromas. The process yields 800 bottles.

— *A Miller's tale* —
MARTIN MILLER'S WESTBOURNE STRENGTH
Martin Miller
London, England
{ martinmillersgin.com }
GIN, 45.2%

It says above that Westbourne Strength is from London, England, but that's not the whole story. Iceland has got a lot to do with it, too. Martin Miller is a restless soul. He is described on his own website as 'a bon viveur and connoisseur in the finer things of life — a maverick, iconoclast and an entrepreneur', and he looks like Bob Geldof at a Rick Wakeman convention. He also invented this gin, which pre-dates the current gin resurgence. It is made in London, but then transported to Iceland, where it is blended with pure spring water. The result has won the title of best gin the world.

— *Beggars belief* —
JACK RYAN BEGGARS BUSH 12 YEAR OLD
Ryan's Beggars Bush
Dublin, Ireland
{ beggarsbush.com }
IRISH SINGLE MALT WHISKEY, 46%

The people behind this are not distillers, and it's not clear who made the whiskey. Ryan's Beggars Bush is a pub in Dublin, and this 12-year-old was selected to mark its 200th anniversary in 2013. The Ryan family has a long association with whiskey, and used to have its own bottling made for it by the long-gone Dublin Whiskey Distillery. Perhaps pub bottlings will return to the city now that craft whiskey is booming and several distilleries are producing spirit in the city once more. This is classic Irish whiskey, with sweet, fruity notes and lots of woody spice.

— Peerless in Seattle —
WESTLAND AMERICAN OAK
Westland Distillery
Seattle, WA, USA
{ westlanddistillery.com }
SINGLE MALT WHISKEY, 46%

It's not every day you witness the birth of a
drinks category, but that's what's happening
here. Westland wasn't the first American
distillery to make single malt whisky — the likes
of St George have been doing so for years. Of
the dozens of distilleries that have created the
current American craft phenomenon, distilleries
such as Balcones and Corsair were way ahead
of the curve. But Westland's emergence as a
major player, and its elevation onto the world
stage thanks to funding from 'hands-off' new
owner Rémy Cointreau, have well and truly
opened the door for American single malt
whiskey, and already we are witnessing the
emergence of multiple quality brands. So what
makes American single malt different? It's that
the new distillers are using bourbon-making
processes in the creation of single malt whiskey.
Most notably, that means using virgin white oak
American casks. The Americans are not bound
by rules on minimum maturation times, so they
can take big hits from the wood in relatively
short periods before taking the spirit out. The
result is malt whiskey with sweet vanilla and
spice notes. Westland has three principal malt
whiskey releases, all of which are excellent. The
distillery is also taking great strides with peated
whiskey. This, though, is all about vanilla,
toffee, and tobacco traces with a malty heart.

— *Rock solid* —

ROCK TOWN ARKANSAS BOURBON

Rock Town Distillery
Little Rock, AR, USA
{ rocktowndistillery.com }
BOURBON, 46%

If Westland represents one extreme of American craft distilling, Rock Town Distillery represents the other. Husband-and-wife team Phil and Diana Brandon and distilling friend Andy Lewis epitomize the sort of home-grown operation that is pumping new life into the world of whiskey. Founded in 2010, the distillery took three months to build, and includes a 220-gallon (1,000-liter) custom-made still. This is the grown-up version of Rock Town's award-winning baby bourbon. Matured in small, new charred oak barrels, it bounces sweetcorn off raisin notes, and has traces of oak.

— *No trifle* —

MILLSTONE SHERRY CASK 12 YEAR OLD

Zuidam
Baarle-Nassau,
Netherlands
{ millstonewhisky.eu }
SINGLE MALT WHISKY, 46%

There is an argument that this single malt whisky was the one that proved that whisky from unexpected territories could be every bit as good as whisky from Scotland. There were plenty of other great world whiskies before this one, but they all made a virtue of the fact that they were different from Scotch. Nothing wrong with that. But this went head-to-head with the top sherried Speysiders with all guns firing, maxing on both age and experience, and holding its own with aplomb. This is a big whisky, with heavy sherry notes, lots of orange and plums, and lots of cocoa.

— *Tain-ted love* —

BALBLAIR 1983
Balblair
Tain, Scotland
{ balblair.com }
SINGLE MALT WHISKY, 46%

Balblair isn't the malt whisky that immediately springs to mind when you consider the whiskies of Scotland, and the distillery is way up in the northeast of the country, on what has been dubbed the forgotten coastline between Inverness and Wick. But the whiskies from here are a delight, a mix of Starburst fruity flavors and Highland maltiness and earthiness.

Balblair is one of the distilleries that use vintages rather than age. The 1989 is the ideal bird-watcher's or fisherman's malt, best enjoyed in silence. The tangy citrus and tropical fruits here are joined by butterscotch, some spice, and traces of oak.

— *Jim's swan song* —

KAVALAN SHERRY OAK

Kavalan
Taiwan
{ kavalanwhisky.com }
SINGLE MALT WHISKY, 46%

Kavalan Distillery's parent company is the King
Car Group, a conglomerate that owns various
subsidiaries in food, beverages, bottled water,
and cleaning products. As a result, there is an
argument that Kavalan cannot be considered
a craft distillery. But making malt whisky in
Taiwan is not easy, and it took a great deal
of dedication, expertise, and innovation to
overcome some serious obstacles, not least the
problem of heat.

Taiwan has the same sort of high humidity as
Scotland. The difference is that the average
temperature in the former is more than 15
degrees higher than in the latter. While much
is made of the purity of the source of water
needed for whisky-making, it is even more
important that the water supply should be
plentiful and sufficiently cool to re-condense
the malt spirit after it has been distilled.

To overcome this barrier, Kavalan brought in
international whisky troubleshooter Dr Jim
Swan, who worked with head distiller Ian Chang
to produce a cooling system for the distillery.

The upside of the climate issue is that
maturation is rapid, and Kavalan is now
shooting above its weight with relatively
young whiskies.

Jim Swan is no longer with us, and is sadly
missed. But whiskies such as this one are a
strong testament to him. It is full-bodied and
rich in sherry berry notes, delicious spices,
and juicy plums.

— *Maverick malt* —

CRAIGELLACHIE 23 YEAR OLD

John Dewar & Sons
Craigellachie, Scotland
{ craigellachie.com }
SINGLE MALT WHISKY, 46%

You'll find the Craigellachie Distillery in the village of the same name, right in the heart of Speyside. It's an ordinary-looking place, but the malt whisky it makes is in stark contrast to the sweet, clean, and fruity whiskies the region is known for. Craigellachie makes a virtue of a meaty, sulfur-driven spirit. It even dries some barley over sulfur fires. Each of the distillery's whiskies is bottled at an age that is a prime number. The 23-year-old is an enigma in which the earthy notes are offset by some delicious fruit notes, and some distinctly herbal ones. Refreshingly different and unforgettable.

— *Not corny at all* —

CORSAIR QUINOA

Corsair Distillery
Bowling Green, KY, USA
{ corsairdistillery.com }
SINGLE GRAIN WHISKEY, 46%

Corsair is the brainchild of Darek Bell and Andrew Webber, who started brewing beer and making wine, and then turned their attention to distilling. With a touch of irreverence, a large dollop of stylish imagery, and an open approach to all styles of whiskey, Corsair has grown into a thriving business with critical acclaim. Quinoa is a supergrain that has become the darling of the health-conscious, but very few distillers are making whisky with it. Corsair Quinoa is made from red and white quinoa grains and malted barley. It's a clean, no-frills drink, with some nutty and earthy notes.

— *Real wild style* —

COLONSAY GIN

Wild Thyme Spirits
Colonsay, Scotland
{ wildthymespirits.com }
GIN, 47%

The island of Colonsay in the Inner Hebrides is small — 8 miles (13 km) long and 3 miles (5 km) wide — remote — it's three and a half hours by ferry from the mainland port of Oban — and sparsely populated — at the last count, it had only a little more than 100 inhabitants. And yet it supports two gin-making companies. This one belongs to Finlay and Eileen Geekie, who moved here in 2016 after 30 years in Oxfordshire. Their Colonsay Gin has classic juniper notes up front, then a wave of earthy, herbaceous notes, all delivered with a robust citrus base. It's perfectly suited to whiling away long days in solitude.

— *Easy Tiger* —

GARDEN TIGER

Capreolus Distillery

Cirencester, England

{ capreolusdistillery.co.uk }

GIN, 47%

Capreolus Distillery lies in the
heart of England's picturesque
Cotswolds region. It is the
creation of photographer
Barney Wilczak, who in his
former career focused on
conservation stories. He has
long experimented with fruit
liqueurs, so perhaps inevitably
he was drawn to the idea of
making a gin. Garden Tiger
is named after a species of
moth. Made with 34 botanicals
in very small batches, it won
The Whisky Exchange's Spirit
of The Year for 2017, and
is described as zesty, with
juniper and orange to the
fore, but with exceptional
complexity and depth.

— *A high flyer* —

BRABAZON SERIES 1

Teeling

Dublin, Ireland

{ teelingwhiskey.com }

IRISH SINGLE MALT

WHISKEY, 49.5%

Teeling is run by brothers
Stephen and Jack Teeling,
whose father, John, set
the modern era of Irish
whiskey-making on fire when
he created Cooley in the
late 1980s. Aided by skilled
whiskey-maker Alex Chasko,
the brothers have further
revitalized Irish whiskey, and
brought distilling back to
Dublin. The Brabazon Series
is a limited edition of unique
single malts. Series 1 focuses
on whiskeys from sherry casks.
This is a stylish combination of
sweet green fruits, red berries,
licorice, almonds, and toffee,
with a delicious spicy twist
in the tail. Irish whiskey is so
exciting right now.

— *Dodd's on favorite* —

DODD'S

The London Distillery

Company

London, England

{ londondistillery.com }

GIN, 49.9%

The London Distillery
Company was launched by
Darren Rook, who brought
distilling back to the capital
for the first time in more
than 100 years. His aim was
to make an English whisky,
but he launched this gin just
before the current wave of
interest in the spirit took
off, and was soon picking
up awards for his efforts.
Dodd's is made with organic
botanicals, including juniper,
angelica, fresh lime peel,
cardamom, red raspberry leaf,
bay laurel, and honey. It is a
sprightly juniper-and-lime-
fueled gin, with some pleasant
sweet notes on the palate.

— *Philadelphia freedom* —
RITTENHOUSE STRAIGHT RYE
Heaven Hill
Bardstown, KY, USA
{ heavenhill.com }
RYE WHISKEY, 50%

Pennsylvania rye was once the most widely favored style of whiskey in America, and this weighty version of it has earned a reputation for top quality. It's an ideal mixing whiskey for a range of classic cocktails, but it is best served straight over ice and sipped while reflecting on how to put the world to rights. As you'd expect from a quality rye, spice is to the fore, but there are also notes of tobacco, oak, toffee, honey, and oranges. It is a rounded and smooth whiskey, with an outstanding citrusy rye aftertaste that leaves a pleasantly lingering coating in the mouth.

— *Taylor made* —
COLONEL E H TAYLOR SINGLE BARREL
Buffalo Trace
Frankfort, KY, USA
{ buffalotracedistillery.com }
BOURBON, 50%

Colonel Edmund Haynes Taylor is one of the founding fathers of the bourbon industry, buying the OFC Distillery after the American Civil War and using it as a base to introduce innovations that are still employed today. One of these was climate-controlled warehouses, and today those warehouses still stand at this distillery. The bourbon for this single barrel bottling is always drawn from Warehouse C, which Haynes built in 1881. The quality varies from batch to batch, but expect a warming, rich bourbon, with figs, plums, hints of orange, and possibly traces of tobacco smoke.

— *Without equal?* —
PEERLESS STRAIGHT RYE
Kentucky Peerless
Distilling Company
Louisville, KY, USA
{ kentuckypeerless.com }
RYE WHISKEY, 53.5%

Kentucky Peerless has certainly got American whiskey aficionados thinking about what should and shouldn't be done when making whiskey. The process here for both bourbon and rye has dispensed with the sour mash process altogether, and the spirit is put into the barrel at unconventional strength. We'll have to wait for the bourbon but, if the rye is anything to go by, it'll be great.
This is a sweet mash barrel proof rye with no added water, and it has a lovely maple and citrus palate, with the gentlest hints of oak. It made American magazine *Whisky Advocate*'s top 20 whiskies for 2017.

— Cnoc on good —

ANCNOC BLAS
Inverhouse Distillers
Knock by Huntly,
Scotland
{ ancnoc.com }
SINGLE MALT WHISKY, 54%

AnCnoc — pronounced 'a-nock' — is malt whisky made by Highland Distillery Knockdhu, so named to avoid confusion with the Strathspey distillery Knockando. Knockdhu malts are consistently excellent, with a balance of fresh fruits and just enough Highland earthiness. Blas (meaning 'taste') is a special release, created in partnership with fashion designer Patrick Grant. On the nose, it presents boiled lemon and honey cough sweets. The palate is plum and peach, with some floral summer meadow notes. The finish is more fruit, orange peel, and dark chocolate.

— Down the hatch —

**BATHTUB GIN NAVY
STRENGTH**
Ableforth's
Tunbridge Wells,
England
{ ableforths.com }
GIN, 57%

The name refers to the fact that in the 1920s, when gin became popular if Prohibition-era America, alcohol was of a very poor quality. So producers put it in to a bath tub and added botanicals, leaving them to seep for several days to improve the flavor. This is the cask strength version of the iconic Ableforth's Bath Tub gin, but it is not just a stronger spirit. The botanicals have been given extra treatment to extract even more flavors. This is a rich, oily, and very spicy gin that coats the mouth and leaves lingering flavors long after you've wiped it.

— Cornish cream —

**HICKS & HEALEY
CORNISH WHISKEY**
Hicks & Healey
St Austell, England
{ staustellbreweryshop.
co.uk }
**SINGLE MALT WHISKEY,
57.1%**

Healey Cyder Farm and the St Austell Brewery (founded in 1851 by Walter Hicks) have joined forces to make whiskey — note the spelling — from brewery wash on apple brandy stills. The company could have bottled the first English whisky for more than 100 years, but chose to wait until this one was 10 years old, then launched the first Cornish whiskey for more than 300 years. This whiskey is rare, but worth seeking out. It is a clean, youthful malt with some pleasant spiciness and creamy apple notes, honey, vanilla, and cocoa.

— *Spot on!* —

INNER CIRCLE GREEN DOT
Vok Beverages
Salisbury South, SA,
Australia
{ vok.com.au }
RUM, 57.2%

This rum is named Inner Circle
because originally it was given
only to the directors of
Australia's Colonial Sugar
Refining Company and a
handful of its prized clients.
But its reputation for
outstanding flavor spread. The
brand was later purchased
by Vok, one of Australia's
fastest-growing beverage
companies. Inner Circle is now
totally Australian-owned and
operated. Green Dot is made
with Fijian sugarcane grown
using traditional harvesting
techniques. Despite the rum's
high strength, its flavors hold
up well, and it is surprisingly
rounded and smooth.

— *A mighty mouthful* —

**1792 FULL PROOF
KENTUCKY BOURBON**
Barton 1792 Distillery
Bardstown, KY, USA
{ 1792bourbon.com }
BOURBON, 62.5%

The date refers to the year that
Kentucky was founded, and
this is a great example of a
bourbon at its robust, colorful,
and impressive best. It's made
at Kentucky's oldest distillery.
The spirit under consideration
here is a brute in the best
possible sense of the term,
with black cherry, menthol,
licorice, and hefty dollops of
tannin and spice. As you would
probably expect, it opens up
into a fruity, spicy bourbon,
but you owe it to yourself to
take a sip of the full-strength
liquid and hold it in your
mouth for as long as it takes
to get the full effect, which is
truly amazing.

'A PERFCT MARTINI SHOULD BE
MADE BY FILLING A GLASS WITH
GIN AND THEN WAVING IT IN THE
GENERAL DIRECTION OF ITALY.'
NOËL COWARD

— Not in a rut —
GEORGE T STAGG
Buffalo Trace
Frankfort, KY, USA
{ elijahcraig.com }
BOURBON, 68%–72%

George T Stagg is an iconic character in the history of bourbon-making. Born in 1835, he worked first as a whiskey salesman until he met E H Taylor, Jr, and the two of them went on to build the most dominant distillery of the 19th century. In 1904, the distillery was named after him, and remained so for nearly 100 years. It is now known as Buffalo Trace. Stagg whiskey is released in limited batches of rare and aged whiskeys, such as Eagle Rare and Sazerac. It is unlikely that you will be able to get hold of any of them because demand is huge, and they tend to be reserved on allocation. The jewel in the crown each year is George T Stagg, which is widely regarded as the best bourbon in the world — bourbon with bells on, and lots of licorice, dark chocolate, and cherry.

— Take the Strane —
STRANE UNCUT STRENGTH
Smögen Distillery
Hunnebostrand, Sweden
{ strane.se }
GIN, 76%

Strane is a range of gins made by the Smögen Distillery, which was set up in 2009 by former lawyer Pär Caldenby. It released its first single malt in 2017, and produced this gin while waiting for the whisky to mature. The distillery is in the west of Sweden, some 80 miles (130 km) north of Gothenburg, not far from the Norwegian frontier. The gins come in three strengths, with this Uncut being the strongest. Caldenby describes it as 'the Odin of gins', and insists that it has to be tasted to be believed. Made in very small batches in a 22-gallon (100-liter) pot still, its botanicals include lemon flesh, lime rind, garden mint, and basil. It's a classic London gin, though, so juniper is dominant.